THE COMMERC.
OF ENGLISH ᴜᴜᴜᴜᴌᴌᴀ ᴀ
1000–1500

The commercialisation of English society was welcomed on its first publication as an up-to-date presentation of English medieval social history in which the developing role of money and commerce over five centuries is put into perspective alongside other features of change. It supplies evidence that the emerging commercial institutions and practices in medieval England had important long-term implications for economic development and welfare, and examines ways in which these affected the exercise of power by kings and lords. This is one of the most active areas of current medieval research, partly because such re-evaluation of the role of commercial development in the Middle Ages is substantially modifying earlier interpretations of the period. The book serves as a valuable introduction to a wide area of current research and debate.

The second edition takes the opportunity to clarify some of the issues raised in recent discussion and to update the bibliography to include books and articles published since 1992. The book will be valuable to any student whose course includes a component of medieval social history, to professional historians working on medieval topics, to historical sociologists, and to general readers of history who enjoy seeing a broad sweep of social change carefully discussed and evaluated.

Richard H. Britnell is Reader in History at the University of Durham.

Manchester Medieval Studies

SERIES EDITOR Dr S. H. Rigby

SERIES ADVISORS Professor J. H. Denton
Professor R. B. Dobson Professor L. K. Little

The study of medieval Europe is being transformed as old orthodoxies are challenged, new methods embraced and fresh fields of inquiry opened up. The adoption if inter-disciplinary perspectives and the challenge of economic, social and cultural theory are forcing medievalists to ask new questions and to see familiar topics in a fresh light.

The aim of this series is to combine the scholarship traditionally associated with medieval studies with an awareness of more recent issues and approaches in a form accessible to the non-specialist reader.

MANCHESTER MEDIEVAL STUDIES

THE COMMERCIALISATION OF ENGLISH SOCIETY, 1000–1500

Second edition

Richard H. Britnell

Manchester University Press
Manchester and New York

distributed exclusively in the USA by St Martin's Press

Second edition copyright © R. H. Britnell 1996

First edition copyright © Cambridge University Press 1993

Published by Manchester University Press
Oxford Road, Manchester M13 9NR, UK
and Room 400, 175 Fifth Avenue, New York, NY 10010, USA

Distributed exclusively in the USA
by St Martin's Press, Inc., 175 Fifth Avenue, New York, NY 10010, USA

British Library Cataloguing-in-Publication Data

A catalogue record for this book is available from the British Library

Library of Congress Cataloging-in-Publication Data applied for

ISBN 0 7190 5042 1 *hardback*
　　　0 7190 5041 3 *paperback*

First published 1996

00 99 98 97 96　　10 9 8 7 6 5 4 3 2 1

Printed in Great Britain
by Bell & Bain Ltd, Glasgow

Contents

For
Edith Britnell
and in loving memory of
Ronald Frank Britnell

Figures

Tables

Acknowledgements

I am particularly grateful to Jennifer Britnell, Bruce Campbell, Paul Harvey, Michael Prestwich and Linda Randall, whose comments improved the accuracy and intelligibility of the following pages.

Chapters 1–9 of this second edition follow the first edition except for a handful of minor corrections. Table 5 is modified in the light of recent work by Nicholas Mayhew.

The biggest differences from the first edition are in the Introduction and the Conclusions, which have been rewritten to take account of comments by reviewers, to incorporate some of my later reflections on the subject and to note some work published since 1992. A number of recent studies would have received more attention in the main text had they been available at the time it was written, but I have taken this opportunity at least to acknowledge their importance and to add them to the bibliography. Since many historians of the medieval economy have for some time been thinking along the same lines as I have, most recent work has been complementary to my views and substantial rewriting has not been necessary.

R. H. B.

Abbreviations

AHEW	*The Agrarian History of England and Wales*, vol. II, ed. H. E. Hallam (Cambridge, 1988), vol. III, ed. E. Miller (Cambridge, 1991), and vol. IV, ed. J. Thirsk (Cambridge, 1967)
AHR	*Agricultural History Review*
Arch., Archl.	Archaeology, Archaeological
BAR	British Archaeological Reports
BARSEH	British Academy, Records of Social and Economic History
BBC	*British Borough Charters, 1042–1216*, ed. A. Ballard (Cambridge, 1913); *British Borough Charters, 1216–1307*, ed. A. Ballard and J. Tait (Cambridge, 1923)
BIHR	*Bulletin of the Institute of Historical Research*
BL	British Library
CChR	*Calendar of Charter Rolls*, HMSO, 6 vols. (London, 1903–27)
CCR	*Calendar of Close Rolls*, HMSO, 46 vols. (London, 1892–1963)
CPR	*Calendar of Patent Rolls*, HMSO, 54 vols. (London, 1891–1916)
CR Henry III	*Close Rolls of the Reign of Henry III*, HMSO, 14 vols. (London, 1902–38)
CUL	Cambridge University Library
DB	*Domesday Book*, ed. A. Farley, RC, 2 vols. (London, 1783)
EcHR	*Economic History Review*
EHR	*English Historical Review*
EPNS	English Place-Name Society
E.R.	East Riding (of Yorkshire)
EYC	*Early Yorkshire Charters*, ed. W. Farrer and C. T. Clay, Yorks. Archl. Soc. Rec. Ser., extra series, 12 vols. (Edinburgh, 1913–65)

Geog.	Geography
Hist., Histl.	History, Historical
HMC	Historical Manuscripts Commission
J.	*Journal*
Med.	*Medieval*
MH	*Midland History*
NH	*Northern History*
N.R.	North Riding (of Yorkshire)
OMT	Oxford Medieval Texts
PIMSST	Pontifical Institute of Medieval Studies, Studies and Texts
PP	*Past and Present*
PR	Pipe Roll: *The Great Rolls of the Pipe*, 5 Henry II to 5 Henry III, various editors, Pipe Roll Soc., 58 vols. (London, 1884–1900)
PRO	Public Record Office
R.	*Review*
RC	Record Commission
Rec.	Record
RH	*Rotuli Hundredorum*, ed. W. Illingworth, RC, 2 vols. (London, 1812–18)
RLC	*Rotuli Litterarum Clausarum*, ed. T. D. Hardy, RC, 2 vols (London, 1833–4)
RO	Record Office
RRAN	*Regesta Regum Anglo-Normannorum*, ed. H. W. C. Davis, C. Johnson, H. A. Cronne and R. H. C. Davis, 4 vols. (Oxford, 1913–69)
RRS	*Regesta Regum Scottorum*, ed. G. W. S. Barrow and B. Webster, 3 vols. (Edinburg, 1960–82)
RS	Rolls Series
Ser.	Series
SH	*Southern History*
SR	*Statutes of the Realm (1101–1713)*, ed. A. Luders, T.E. Tomlins, J. France, W. E. Taunton and J. Raithby, RC, 11 vols. (London, 1808–28)
Stud.	*Studies*
Trans.	*Transactions*
TRHS	*Transactions of the Royal Historical Society*
VCH	*The Victoria History of the Counties of England*
W.R.	West Riding (of Yorkshire)

Introduction

Commercialisation, a pervasive topic in economic and social history, may be given a weaker definition or a stronger one. The weaker definition signifies simply growth in the total amount of commercial activity over a period of time. Indications of commercialisation of this sort would include the multiplication of trading institutions, the growth of towns and growth in the quantity of money in circulation. Nobody doubts that in this sense the medieval economy became more commercialised between 1000 and 1300, even if not between 1300 and 1500. Yet commercialisation of this sort was not necessarily associated with changes in social institutions. We know, for example, that population was also growing between 1000 and 1300, so that without further enquiry it would be impossible to say whether trade was becoming more important for the conduct of daily life.

The stronger definition of commercialisation signifies that commercial activity was growing faster than population. This would suggest that commerce grew faster than the total output of goods and services, that an increasing proportion of goods and services produced each year was traded and that people were increasingly dependent upon buying and selling for their livelihood. So defined, commercialisation is an aspect of profound social change. The relevance of commercialisation in this second sense to the medieval economy is more difficult to demonstrate, since we have no reliable measures either of commercial activity or of population. However, a good case can be made for supposing that the social changes of this period were associated with greater dependence upon money and trade.[1] There is a strong probability that the proportion of the English population living in towns increased;[2] there is good evidence that the amount of money in

[1] Below, pp. 102–27; R. H. Britnell, 'Commercialisation and Economic Development in England, 1000–1300', in R. H. Britnell and B. M. S. Campbell, eds., *A Commercialising Economy: England 1086 to c. 1300* (Manchester, 1995), pp. 7–26.

[2] See, in particular, B. M. S. Campbell, J. A. Galloway, D. Keene and M. Murphy, *A Medieval Capital and its Grain Supply: Agrarian Production and Distribution in the London Region c. 1300*, Histl. Geog. Research Ser., 30 (London, 1993), pp. 8–12. This important study relates closely to the discussion in chapters 4 and 5 below.

circulation grew many times faster than population;[3] there is also reason to suppose that occupational and regional economic specialisation became more advanced.[4] Recent studies have supplied impressive quantitative evidence relating to the extent of commercialisation in various branches of agrarian activity around 1300.[5]

This line of enquiry is not only interesting for its own sake. It helps to resolve some of the difficulties confronted by historians in their interpretation of economic change. Increasing commercialisation created opportunities for specialisation and productivity growth and so helps to explain how population growth was possible.[6] This does not necessarily imply an optimistic assessment of economic development during the period when population was growing, since the evidence strongly suggests that the benefits of increases in productivity went chiefly into sustaining a larger population, and that only a small proportion of the population obtained significant improvements in material welfare.[7]

Commercialisation helps to explain why English society in the fifteenth century was more urbanised and wealthy than in the eleventh century, even though the level of population was much the same in the two periods.[8] In addition, the study of commercialisation interlocks with the debate about the transition from feudalism to capitalism, which has been a large and problematic item on the agenda of Marxist historians. If the medieval period saw a significant increase in the importance of trade between town and country, in the production of goods for sale and in the employment of wage labour, this strengthens the case for interpreting the development of capitalism as a long and slow one, and gives greater importance in this transition to the period 1000–1300 than it has usually received.[9]

---

[3] N. J. Mayhew, 'Modelling Medieval Monetisation', in Britnell and Campbell, eds., *Commercialising Economy*, pp. 55–77 and *idem*, 'Population, Money Supply and the Velocity of Circulation in England, 1300–1700', *EcHR*, 48 (1995), pp. 238–57.

[4] Campbell, Galloway, Keene and Murphy, *Medieval Capital*, pp. 111-44; M. Kowaleski, *Local Markets and Regional Trade in Medieval Exeter* (Cambridge, 1995), pp. 41–9.

[5] Notably Campbell, Galloway, Keene and Murphy, *Medieval Capital*, and B. M. S. Campbell, 'Measuring the Commercialisation of Seigneurial Agriculture c. 1300', in Britnell and Campbell, eds., *Commercialising Economy*, pp. 132–93; *idem*, 'Ecology Versus Economics in Late Thirteenth- and Early Fourteenth-Century English Agriculture', in D. Sweeney, ed., *Agriculture in the Middle Age: Technology, Practice, and Representation* (Philadelphia, 1995), pp. 76–108. For a study that both explores the way in which commercialisation may be assessed from manorial records and examines development over a long period of time, see D. L. Farmer, 'Woodland and Pasture Sales on the Winchester Manors in the Thirteenth Century: Disposing of a Surplus or Producing for the Market?', in Britnell and Campbell, eds., *Commercialising Economy*, pp. 102–31.

[6] Below, pp. 103–4, 123–5.

[7] Below, pp. 125–7.

[8] Below, pp. 166–8.

[9] R. H. Britnell, 'Commerce and Capitalism in Late Medieval England: Problems of Description and Theory', *J. Histl. Sociology*, 6 (1993), pp. 359–76.

Some historians have latched on to particular developments as prime movers of economic change in the Middle Ages, the chief favourites for this role being population change, variations in the money supply and changes in the level of class conflict. The possibility of identifying such a prime mover, in order to give a central meaning to five centuries of history, is rejected in this study. Theoretical models of any practical use discuss the relationship between only a small number of variables, usually with a restrictive range of assumptions. No single model can be expected to generate more than a caricature when employed to explain social change over a long period, since the variables necessary to explain social change are more numerous than any single model can accommodate. [10]

The growth of trade ought not to be singled out as a prime mover of medieval economic and social development any more than population, money or class conflict, since commerce had no more historical autonomy than they did. Indeed, any explanation of the growth of commerce needs to take into account changes in population size, changes in the monetary medium and changing relations between lords and tenants, using appropriate purpose-built models to do so. The theoretical underpinnings needed to analyse the commercialisation of medieval society are necessarily eclectic.

Commercialisation is presented in what follows not as a unitary process but as the complex outcome of decisions taken by governments, landlords, merchants, peasants, artisans and labourers. Their decisions were often motivated by acquisitiveness, though much of the impetus to occupational specialisation and productivity growth came from unemployment and dearth amongst the kingdom's poorer families. This emphasis on large numbers of decisions, in different contexts, retains a lively sense of the importance of men and women as the makers of history. It is not 'natural' that a society should depend upon market mechanisms for important aspects of its maintenance and continuity, and no simple principle of human behaviour can explain it. Even those theoreticians most committed to the market as an allocative system cannot doubt that the device is a ramshackle social construct, built over the centuries partly through the activities of private individuals and partly through government intervention. The market order has a history relevant to the growth of society as we know it, to which many different considerations of culture and utility have contributed. An important part of that history is medieval. The abstract idea of a market order in society is nevertheless a modern one which had no parallel in the Middle Ages. Many of the principles to which medieval lords and townsmen were committed were antagonistic to the idea of freedom of contract.

---

[10] S. H. Rigby, *English Society in the Later Middle Ages: Class, Status and Gender* (London, 1995), pp. 141–3.

The following study aims to be coherent rather than exhaustive. It describes the development of market relationships in the later Middle Ages, chiefly with respect to inland trade, since it is very difficult to integrate what little is known of England's overseas trade before 1250 into a study of social change.[11] The discussion of commercial development is further related to some aspects of the history of lordship and law in order to assess the impact of money and trade on some of the traditional bonds of subordination in society.

The dates 1000 and 1500 do not mark the beginning and end of a distinct episode in the history of commerce and they have been chosen solely for convenience. English experience during these centuries was not that of a transition from 'natural economy' to 'market economy' since there was a market sector throughout the period. The 'commercialisation' of the book's title relates, in the stronger sense of that word discussed above, to the slowly growing relevance of that sector to everyday life, rather than to any particular beginning or ending.

The period 1000–1500 is divided, for ease of exposition, into three approximately equal parts, from 1000 to 1180, from 1180 to 1330 and from 1330 to 1500. It is tempting, when working with a chronological structure of this kind, to shape the evidence so that each period looks different from the previous one, and thereby to create definite stages of development. I have tried to counter this by stressing continuities between one period and the next. In general, in order to be able to make comparisons over time, I have written only about topics that can be discussed for all three periods. Many interesting aspects of the subject have been ignored for this reason.

---

[11] But see E. Miller and J. Hatcher, *Medieval England: Towns, Commerce and Crafts, 1086–1348* (London, 1995), pp. 182–254.

THE COMMERCIALISATION
OF ENGLISH SOCIETY

Part 1

1000–1180

1   Markets and rules

I

Even in its central and southern parts, rural England in the eleventh century was an unlikely setting for an advanced division of labour governed by market demand. There were perhaps fewer than 3m people living in the 13,278 places recorded in Domesday Book.[1] In fact population was even more dispersed than this ratio suggests, since many Domesday place-names corresponded to more than one settlement. 'Lauuendene' (Bucks.), with seven manors and three other estates, included not only the modern villages of Lavendon, Cold Brayfield and Newton Blossomville, but also a hamlet called Abingdon that was deserted in the later Middle Ages.[2] Comparison of Domesday Book with later records reveals many such examples.[3] Population growth had probably increased the number of nucleated villages in the course of the previous century or two.[4] Even so, archaeological evidence from the post-Conquest period encourages historians to stress the smallness of human communities.[5]

It was common, even in the larger villages, for individuals to be known by one name, implying that such communities were sufficiently small for there to be no confusion. On the abbot of Burton's manor of Leigh (Staffs.) in 1114–15 the twelve villains were recorded as Soen, Rainald, Ailwin, another Ailwin, Lemar, Godwin, Ordric, Alric, Saroi,

---

[1] H. C. Darby, *Domesday England* (Cambridge, 1977), p. 15; E. Miller and J. Hatcher, *Medieval England: Rural Society and Economic Change, 1086–1348* (London, 1978), p. 5.

[2] *DB*, II, fos. 145c, 146d, 148a, 152d, 153b; R. H. Britnell, 'Abingdon: A Lost Buckinghamshire Hamlet', *Recs. of Bucks.*, 22 (1980), pp. 48–51.

[3] F. W. Maitland, *Domesday Book and Beyond: Three Essays in the Early History of England* (Cambridge, 1897), p. 14.

[4] P. J. Fowler, 'Agriculture and Rural Settlement', in D. M. Wilson, ed., *The Archaeology of Anglo-Saxon England* (Cambridge, 1976), pp. 42–4.

[5] T. H. Aston, 'The Origins of the Manor in England' with 'A Postscript', in T. H. Aston, P. R. Coss, C. Dyer and J. Thirsk, eds., *Social Relations and Ideas: Essays in Honour of R. H. Hilton* (Cambridge, 1983), pp. 34–5; C. Taylor, *Village and Farmstead: A History of Rural Settlement in England* (London, 1983), pp. 122–4.

Ulviet, Ulfac and Richard. The eight tenants whose rents were paid in money were Aviet, Levegrin, Osbern, Richard, Award, Gosfrid, Alwin and Aileva. The miller was Edric and the manor was leased by Orm.[6] As the two Ailwins imply, there was no systematic way of distinguishing between two people with the same name. Second names became more common in the course of the twelfth century, but even in larger villages many people were known without one. In Witham and Cressing (Essex) the Templars had 108 tenants in 1185 of whom fourteen are recorded with single names.[7] The other ninety-four were distinguished by a patronymic, by occupation or by place of origin. Such additions were not hereditary in the majority of instances.

In small settlements families must have complemented each other's strengths and weaknesses. This feature of village life was the foundation of policing. The frankpledge system, by which men were compulsorily organised into groups of neighbours to provide each other with mutual suretyship, was already known by 1115. It was widespread in the thirteenth century, except in northern England and the counties bordering Wales. In the event of a breach of the peace by one member of the group the others were to produce him in court to answer for it.[8] Each hundred court was made responsible for ensuring that men were sworn into these tithing groups.

Within village communities there was scope for exchanges of goods and services between households. Of the recorded population of the kingdom in 1086, a third were cottagers, and most of these were probably labourers, craftsmen or traders since it is difficult to see how they could have made a living otherwise. Many must have depended for employment upon the larger agrarian units, including manorial demesnes.[9] Calculations from Domesday Book underestimate the proportion of families with slight independent resources. Subtenants are not recorded, and the count of small tenants is probably less complete than that of large ones.[10] It is more likely that the commissioners should have ignored landless families and subtenants – the wage-earners and food-buyers of the countryside – than that they should have omitted to

[6] 'The Burton Abbey Twelfth-Century Surveys', ed. C. G. O. Bridgeman, *Collections for a History of Staffordshire*, William Salt Archl. Soc., vol. for 1916 (1918), pp. 225–7.

[7] *Records of the Templars in England in the Twelfth Century: The Inquest of 1185 and Illustrative Charters and Documents*, ed. B. A. Lees, BARSEH, 1st ser., IX (Oxford, 1935), pp. 1–8.

[8] W. A. Morris, *The Frankpledge System* (New York, 1910), pp. 29–41, 90–1.

[9] Darby, *Domesday England*, pp. 63, 337–9; R. Lennard, *Rural England, 1086–1135: A Study of Social and Agrarian Conditions*, 2nd edn (Oxford, 1966), pp. 342–7; Maitland, *Domesday Book*, p. 41.

[10] S. P. J. Harvey, 'Domesday England', in *AHEW*, II, p. 49.

record more substantial tenants whose rents were a source of income for some manorial lord and whose taxes were of interest to the king.

Complex personal ties and responsibilities between members of a small group are discouraging to the development of regular exchanges founded on the idea of money values. Market relationships depend upon a degree of impersonality more easily maintained between strangers than between neighbours and relatives. The very complexity of interaction between village households meant that transactions were of many different kinds. It was not simply that some were commercial and some not. The distinction between commercial exchange and reciprocal gift-giving might be impossible to make. Relations between landlords and craftsmen were often tenurial rather than commercial; the village smith often held land on condition that he should maintain the demesne ploughs.[11] The frequent necessity for barter inhibited dependence on market prices. In these circumstances there could be economic inter-dependence between families without any need for regular markets. Contacts between villagers and rural craftsmen (such as blacksmiths) or specialists from elsewhere (such as traders bringing salt, textiles or fish) were no doubt more obviously commercial in character, though in a small settlement they required little in the way of institutional marketing arrangements. Villagers often had to travel for such things, and some had to fetch them on their lord's behalf as well.[12] The absence of an institutional structure was particularly evident in northern England, where there was little formal organisation of trade outside York in the early eleventh century. At Durham, one of the only two northern mints, the earliest evidence of urban development is the record of a market place in 1040.[13]

Nevertheless, even villagers whose transactions were predominantly of a mixed character needed both coinage and some goods their neighbours could not produce. By 1086 there were many contexts in which goods changed hands not according to traditions of kinship, neighbourhood or community but according to rules of the market. This formality was encouraged, above all, by the activities of specialised craftsmen and traders. A settlement in which many families were dependent for their income upon being able to supply a small range of goods to a large number of customers was more likely to isolate trade as

[11] P. D. A. Harvey, 'Non-Agrarian Activities in Twelfth-Century English Estate Surveys', in D. Williams, ed., *England in the Twelfth Century* (Woodbridge, 1990), pp. 108, 111.

[12] E.g. 'Burton Abbey Surveys', ed. Bridgeman, pp. 222, 229, 238, 239, 246.

[13] M. Beresford, *New Towns of the Middle Ages: Town Plantation in England, Wales and Gascony* (London, 1967), pp. 432–3; M. Bonney, *Lordship and the Urban Community: Durham and its Overlords, 1250–1540* (Cambridge, 1990), pp. 12–14, 26.

an activity, and to create impersonal rules of trading, than one where market dependence was lower.

The most unambiguous instances of market-orientated society were the towns. In the eleventh and twelfth centuries London was already England's principal centre of local and long-distance trade. It probably had 10,000 inhabitants and may have had twice as many. There were numerous sorts of craftsmen to be found, some of them catering for expensive tastes. Norman London was outstanding for both the variety and the number of craftsmen and tradesmen who depended on being able to buy food or raw materials and to sell their wares.[14] The city had a dispersed pattern of markets, some of them specialised in particular commodities. The Pantry was the centre of the bakers' craft by 1140. The shambles inside Newgate were the centre of the retail meat trade, and the fish market was nearby to the east. Cheapside was a major market for the London crafts, though some had their separate centres elsewhere.[15]

Outside London, there were smaller urban communities requiring traded foodstuffs for their basic supplies. Towns developed rapidly in the late tenth and eleventh centuries, particularly in southern England, partly as a result of growing trade with the continent.[16] By 1086 the bigger provincial towns were Norwich, York, Winchester and Lincoln, all of which are likely to have had over 5,000 inhabitants. Most people in populations of this size must have been employed outside agriculture. Market-orientated conduct prevailed in smaller towns as well. Amongst the burgesses of Colchester (Essex) or Bury St Edmunds (Suff.) in 1086 the average tenement was too small to feed a family.[17] Altogether Domesday Book records about 112 boroughs, and a further 39 places had markets.[18] Some Domesday market centres were like small boroughs in having communities of non-agrarian residents. The growth of Abingdon (Berks.) was encouraged by the refounding of the abbey in the 950s. In 1086 ten 'merchants' lived there in front of the church door.[19] In many of these places urban characteristics were outweighed by rural ones, but they all acted as centres of demand where countrymen sold their produce.

There was, then, a recognisably urban sector to the economy. But it is

---

[14] F. M. Stenton, *Preparatory to Anglo-Saxon England*, ed. D. M. Stenton (Oxford, 1970), pp. 41–5.

[15] C. Brooke, *London, 800–1216: The Shaping of a City* (London, 1975), pp. 276–8.

[16] G. G. Astill, 'Towns and Town Hierarchies in Saxon England', *Oxford J. of Arch.*, 10 (1991), pp. 112–13.

[17] M. D. Lobel, *The Borough of Bury St. Edmund's: A Study in the Government and Development of a Monastic Town* (Oxford, 1935), p. 11; J. Tait, *The Medieval English Borough: Studies on its Origins and Constitutional History* (Manchester, 1936), pp. 73–6.

[18] Darby, *Domesday England*, pp. 290, 364–70 (excluding St Germans and Hoxne).

[19] G. G. Astill, 'The Towns of Berkshire', in J. Haslam, ed., *Anglo-Saxon Towns in Southern England* (Chichester, 1984), p. 65.

Table 1 *Domesday boroughs and markets related to recorded rural population*

	Recorded rural population	Recorded boroughs	Recorded markets (excluding boroughs)	Total
Eastern counties	80,845	16	13	29
Western counties	77,975	46	9	55
Southern counties	41,377	23	8	31
Central counties	49,871	15	9	24

Source: H. C. Darby, *Domesday England* (Cambridge, 1977), pp. 336, 364–70.

a curious feature of Domesday Book's testimony to trading life that the boroughs and markets are distributed very differently from recorded population. We can see this by comparing some Domesday statistics of the eastern counties (Essex, Suffolk, Norfolk and Lincolnshire) with those of the western counties (Cornwall, Devon, Somerset, Dorset, Wiltshire, Gloucestershire, Worcestershire, Herefordshire, Staffordshire and Shropshire), the southern counties (Hampshire, Surrey, Sussex, Berkshire, Kent) and the central counties (Oxfordshire, Buckinghamshire, Middlesex, Hertfordshire, Cambridgeshire, Huntingdonshire, Bedfordshire, Northamptonshire, Leicestershire and Warwickshire). This is shown in Table 1. The oddity here lies in the apparent weakness of urban institutions in the more populous and less manorialised counties of the east in comparison with the rest of the country. The contrast between the eastern and western counties is particularly marked. These figures say something about the inconsistencies of the Domesday commissioners, something about different traditions of borough making in different parts of England and something about the imprecision with which the words 'market' and 'borough' were used in the eleventh century.[20] They can hardly be telling us anything about regional volumes of local trade. Eastern England was the freest as well as the most heavily settled part of England, and its North Sea ports permitted regular trading links with Europe. It is unbelievable that there was less trade there than in the west country – less trade in Essex than in Staffordshire. We must suppose that there were trading institutions in eastern England that do not meet the eye.

Our early documented evidence of markets and boroughs does not, in

[20] S. Reynolds, 'Towns in Domesday Book', in J. C. Holt, ed., *Domesday Studies* (Woodbridge, 1987), pp. 296–300.

fact, identify the origins of regular local trade. Marketing patterns were developing long before landlords took any interest in the matter, and continued to evolve informally alongside the recorded institutional developments. Specialist and semi-specialist craftsmen did not necessarily need publicly regulated markets, especially when there was little competition between them. The interests of such groups could be met by intermediate trading arrangements that were not legally defined. Such were the assemblies around churches, which have analogies in Scandinavia.[21] Such too were other informal gatherings whose legal status became more problematic as the law relating to markets was formulated in new definitions and new principles.[22] Chopwell (co. Dur.) is likely, from its name and its location, to have been the site of some sort of informal horse fair.[23] The number of such events may have increased more rapidly than that of formal markets during the eleventh and twelfth centuries. This would help explain the surprising rarity of market charters from the reign of Henry II.

We find adequate evidence of early trading institutions only at the points where the interests of landlords became actively involved. The market order which figures so large in modern society has, from one point of view, been created piecemeal over many centuries by buyers and sellers seeking to reduce the costs of trading. Yet events have been shaped at innumerable points by governments and property owners stepping in to provide and control trading facilities for the private advantages to be gained by doing so. It was this that created legally defined markets and fairs. The historical record does not allow us to see the growth of trade except as the product of such seigniorial intervention, and this explains the distortion in the evidence which we have observed. The development of formal markets in medieval England, as in the rest of western Europe, was inseparable from the exercise of power and the creation of law.

II

Markets and fairs were a potential source of income. To manage them had certain costs, but given a sufficiently large number of transactions,

---

[21] P. Sawyer, 'Early Fairs and Markets in England and Scandinavia', in B. L. Anderson and A. J. H. Latham, eds., *The Market in History* (London, 1986), pp. 64–71; P. H. Sawyer, 'Fairs and Markets in Early Medieval England', in N. Skyum-Nielsen and N. Lund, eds., *Danish Medieval History: New Currents* (Copenhagen, 1981), pp. 160–1.

[22] L. F. Salzman, 'The Legal Status of Markets', *Cambridge Histl. J.*, 2 (1928), pp. 205–12.

[23] J. R. Ellis, 'Chopwell: A Problematical Durham Place-Name', *Nomina*, 22 (1988–9), pp. 68–72.

and a sufficient income from tolls, a landlord could make money from other people's trading. Such a concern with profitability is clearly stated in Domesday Book's account of the predicament of Hoxne market (Suff.), whose value had recently declined.[24] A major difference between the period 1000–1180 and later ones was that legal concepts relating to markets and fairs had yet to be clarified. Our observation of England before 1180 is obscured not only by poor surviving evidence, but also by the unformed state of concepts and terminology at the time.

The law relating to markets and fairs was defined only gradually to the point where, in the thirteenth century, kings claimed the right to suppress those that operated without licence, and landlords took their neighbours to court to suppress rival concerns. For such powers to operate, a succession of practical and conceptual developments must already have occurred. The most basic requirement for formal trade was a known meeting place. Then, in order to be effective in reducing costs for buyers and sellers, there had to be agreement about the days and times when trade would take place. A trading assembly upon which numbers of people depended implied a set of rules of fairness, however simple. Further, to have any legal status the market had to belong to somebody. Markets and fairs would hardly need to be recorded till they reached at least this stage of sophistication. Beyond that, it required a successful royal initiative to get markets and fairs recognised as franchises specific to particular times and places. There would be no reason for lords to single out markets or fairs for mention in their charters unless they were distinguished in law from simple appurtenances of the manor like mills and ovens. For the crown to have the right to order the suppression of illegal markets and fairs the criteria of legality had to be explicit and generally understood. So the legal concept of a market or a fair, as it existed by the early thirteenth century, was built upon a variety of notions of public and private rights and duties. It was the product of a long historical development.

In the earlier eleventh century the English language had no word in regular use for a market organised as a weekly event. This may be because in many town centres trading took place daily and more or less continuously during daylight hours, but the main reason was that a market had as yet no defined status as a seigniorial franchise.

The word market occurs in the compound form *gearmarket* (i.e. 'year-market', the modern German *Jahrmarkt*) in a document composed shortly before the Norman Conquest concerning St Mary at Stow

[24] *DB*, II, fo. 379a.

(Lincs.).[25] This particular expression – equivalent to the later notion of an annual fair – has analogies in Old High German, Old Saxon and Middle Dutch, and was perhaps the form in which the term market was introduced to England. Although 'market' derives ultimately from the Latin *mercatum*, the standard English form did not come from France. French would have given a word such as 'merchet', with a softened central consonant, as in the words merchant and merchandise. The English Normans did, in fact, have the word *merchet*, but it meant something quite different – a fine paid by a personally dependent tenant when his daughter got married.[26] The origins of 'market' with a 'k' were Germanic.[27] By implication, the English word was established before the influence of Norman French had come to dominate technical vocabulary of this type. Perhaps it was originally borrowed to describe some type of meeting with merchants from Scandinavia or the Low Countries. But we are speaking of a very rare expression. In its simple, uncompounded form 'market' does not occur in English before the twelfth century,[28] and by implication it was a word little used in any technical sense before the Norman Conquest.

The word *port*, derived from the Latin *portus* meaning a harbour, was commonly used, but it designated an urban centre of trade, whether on the coast or inland, rather than a market in any more narrow sense.[29] Like the word *burh*, with which it had become almost equivalent by the middle of the eleventh century, it resists any attempt to give it an exact legal or geographical meaning. Ports were the sort of town that had a mint. The term could be used to refer to a whole urban community, such as Northampton or Worcester.[30] At other times we find *port* used for a suburb, as in Newport on the northern side of Lincoln, which had its own market.[31] No doubt trading towns had market places of some sort, but the term *port* was not used specifically to refer to them in either a physical or institutional sense. The inhabitants of Canterbury might be

[25] *Anglo-Saxon Charters*, ed. A. J. Robertson, 2nd edn (Cambridge, 1956), no. 115, p. 216; F. E. Harmer, '*Chipping* and *Market*: A Lexicographical Investigation', in C. Fox and B. Dickens, eds., *The Early Cultures of North-West Europe* (Cambridge, 1950), pp. 350–1.

[26] P. Vinogradofff, *Villainage in England* (Oxford, 1892), p. 153. For early examples, see J. Scammell, 'Freedom and Marriage in Medieval England', *EcHR*, 2nd ser., 27 (1974), p. 531.

[27] N. Davis, 'The Proximate Etymology of "Market"', *The Modern Language R.*, 47 (1952), pp. 152–5.

[28] Harmer, '*Chipping* and *Market*', p. 360.

[29] Sawyer, 'Fairs and Markets', pp. 158–9; Tait, *Medieval English Borough*, pp. 9–10, 13, 22.

[30] Tait, *Medieval English Borough*, pp. 25, 27.

[31] F. Hill, *Medieval Lincoln* (Cambridge, 1965), pp. 35, 170.

termed *portware*, but this meant that they lived in a trading town, not that they all lived in the market place.[32]

In Middle English *ceaping* was used for a market, and this gave the first place-name element to Chipping Barnet (Mdx.), Chipping Campden (Oxon.), Chipping Norton (Oxon.), Chipping Ongar (Ess.), Chipping Sodbury (Glos.) and Chipping Warden (Northants.).[33] The site of the earliest market in Witham (Essex) retained the name Chipping Hill.[34] Some other place-names of this type, such as Chipping Faringdon (Berks., now Great Faringdon), Chipping Lambourn (Berks., now just Lambourn), Chipping Marlow (Bucks., now Great Marlow) or Chipping Walden (Essex, now Saffron Walden) have been changed since the Middle Ages. Other market towns retain the same element in their street names. Wotton under Edge (Glos.) and Tetbury (Glos.) both have streets called The Chipping, and there used to be a Chipping Street in Cirencester (Glos.).[35] This word was certainly current in English before 1066. By a charter possibly of 904 King Edward the Elder granted the bishopric of Winchester rights in the *cyping* of Taunton (Som.).[36] But *cyping* was here a translation of the Latin *mercimonium*, a word whose significance in this context is uncertain.[37] Another early example is the place-name Chipping in Amounderness (Lancs.), which had given its name to 'Chipinden', the modern Chippingdale, by 1086.[38] Sometimes the term *cyping* was used simply to mean trading, as in the phrase *Sunnandaeges cyping* ('Sunday trading').[39] There seems to be no unambiguous example of the word *ceaping* being used to mean a market in a pre-Conquest text.

A term used more in south-east England was *ceapstede*, as in the place-names Chipstead (one in Surrey and one in Kent) and the lost Chepsted in Kingsdown (Kent).[40] The terms *ceapstow* (as in Chepstow, Monms.) and *ceap straet* (as in Winchester by about 900)[41] are closely compar-

---

[32] F. M. Stenton, *Anglo-Saxon England*, 2nd edn (Oxford, 1947), p. 519.
[33] Harmer, '*Chipping* and *Market*', p. 335.
[34] R. H. Britnell, 'The Making of Witham', *Hist. Stud.*, 1 (1968), p. 13.
[35] A. H. Smith, *The Place-Names of Gloucestershire*, EPNS, 4 vols., XXXVIII–XLI (Cambridge, 1964–5), I, pp. 62, 110, II, p. 256.
[36] Harmer, '*Chipping* and *Market*', pp. 342–3.
[37] Cf. 'illud mercimonium quod dicitur Hamwih' from which St Willibald sailed in *c.* 721: M. Biddle, 'Towns', in Wilson, ed., *Archaeology of Anglo-Saxon England*, p. 112.
[38] E. Ekwall, *The Place Names of Lancashire* (Manchester, 1922), p. 143.
[39] VI Aethelstan, 10: *Die Gesetze der Angelsachsen*, ed. F. Liebermann, 3 vols. (Halle, 1903–16), I, p. 182.
[40] J. E. B. Gover, A. Mawer and F. M. Stenton, *The Place-Names of Surrey*, EPNS, XI (Cambridge, 1934), p. 290; J. K. Wallenberg, *The Place-Names of Kent* (Uppsala, 1934), pp. 44, 54.
[41] Biddle, 'Towns', p. 119.

able. These names indicate a set place for trading in. They correspond to the Latin *forum* (in later texts normally meaning a market place) rather than to the more abstract *mercatum* (normally referring to the market as an event or legal right). In some places, if not everywhere, market places were indeed associated with recognised seigniorial rights. In the late ninth century the bishop of Worcester had rights in the *ceapstow* of Worcester. However, such rights were not dependent upon the existence of markets as a distinct franchise. Tait considered the market at Worcester to be an incidental result of the fortifications there.[42]

Even the Latin terms *mercatum* and *forum* are uncommon in pre-Conquest texts. In all the 1,875 know Anglo-Saxon charters, genuine and spurious, *mercatum* occurs only in some twelfth-century fabrications from Peterborough (Northants.).[43] From later evidence we know that recognisable markets existed on the eve of the Norman Conquest. Markets at Great Dunham (Norf.), Hoxne and Clare (Suff.) were described as having been there in 1066 as well as in 1086.[44] But there is no known example before the Conquest of a market outside the royal demesne having been created by royal licence. This, even more than the rarity of English equivalents, implies that at the time of the Norman Conquest a market was not thought of as a distinct franchise, or at least that such a concept was very recent. Where market places existed they were understood as part of some more complex institution of lordship. 'Market place' is, on the face of it, a descriptive term and not a legal one, and it is unnecessary to assume that it implies any definite notion of what rights it entailed.

The fair was equally foreign to the legal vocabulary of the Old English kingdom, and the relevant terminology had to be imported from France. Both the words later used for this institution, *nundina* and *feria*, originally signified a festival day, though the former had had associations with trading activity since Roman times. In its classical origins the *nundina* was a market day every ninth day, the Roman equivalent of the medieval weekly market, but in France the word was already used to mean an annual fair by the middle of the ninth century and was widespread in this sense by the eleventh. The word *feria*, though less long-established, was being used more frequently for a fair in the later eleventh century, especially in Normandy and Anjou.[45] *Feria* became the commonest Latin word for a fair in Anglo-Norman and Angevin England.

---

[42] Tait, *Medieval English Borough*, p. 22.
[43] Harmer, '*Chipping* and *Market*', pp. 348–9.   [44] *DB*, II, fos. 137a, 379a, 389b.
[45] T. Endemann, *Markturkunde und Markt in Frankreich und Burgund vom 9 bis 11 Jahrhundert* (Konstanz and Stuttgart, 1964), pp. 207–8.

In medieval Europe the annual festivities that brought people together were those of the liturgical calendar, but different places celebrated different saints as well as the main feasts of the Christian year. Predictable crowds meant a certain amount of predictable trade. Festivals and trade must have gone together to some extent in England, both before the Norman Conquest and after, even without any formal recognition of the fact. The day before a feast was technically known as the vigil or wake, and it was on the wake of a big annual celebration, rather than on the day itself, that people assembled for trade and conviviality. The abbot of Abingdon protested in 1212 that he did not hold a fair at Sallingford (Berks.) but only a wake (Latin *vigilia*). Bolton Priory was similarly to claim in 1279–80 that an assembly at Embsay (W.R. Yorks.) was not a fair but 'a certain gathering of men which is called a wake *(wach)*'. The abbot's comment implies that he expected people to assemble on the eve of their patronal festival rather than on the day itself, and he expected a certain amount of trade. But the wake had no legal significance in this sense. In saying that the people of Sallingford had no more than a wake, the abbot of Abingdon implied that he needed no special permission for the event. Probably he received no profit from it; sixty years later the fair at Sallingford was described as free of tolls. Other informal occasions of this sort were tolerated well into the thirteenth century, and perhaps beyond, half for business and half for pleasure. There was a comparable wake at 'Wyleham' (unidentified, Berks.) in 1246.[46]

Domesday Book records that in 1086 a third part of a fair belonged to a small estate in Aspall (Suff.). By implication this fair was subject to lordship though, in view of its partition, it is unlikely to have been a very recent foundation. Its legal status is unknown.[47] By this time, however, the fair as a franchise, dependent on royal grant, had entered English law from Normandy. William I licensed fairs at Battle (Suss.) in 1070–1 and at Malmesbury (Wilts.).[48] From the following couple of decades there are examples of fairs authorised by the crown at Winchester (Hants.) in 1096, Bath (Som.) in 1102, Canterbury (Kent) in 1103, St Albans (Herts.) in 1105, Romsey (Hants.) in 1100–6, Hoxne (Suff.) and Lynn (Norf.) in 1106, and Rochester (Kent) in 1100–7.[49] Licensed annual fairs, follow-

---

[46] *CR Henry III, 1242–7*, p. 400; I. Kershaw, *Bolton Priory: The Economy of a Northern Monastery, 1286–1325* (Oxford, 1973), p. 29.

[47] *DB*, II, fo. 418a.

[48] *RRAN*, I, nos. 61, 247, pp. 16, 65.

[49] *RRAN*, I, no. 377, p. 96 (Winchester); *RRAN*, II, no. 573, p. 19 (Bath); *RRAN*, II, no. 652, p. 33 (Canterbury); *RRAN*, II, nos. 689, 690, pp. 41, 42 (St Albans); *RRAN*, II, no. 802, p. 63 (Romsey); *RRAN*, II, no. 762, p. 55 (Hoxne and Lynn); *RRAN*, II, no. 868, p. 77 (Rochester).

ing the tradition of informal wakes, usually started the day before a named saint's festival but they continued for at least a day or two longer.

The absence of anything in Anglo-Saxon law corresponding to the Anglo-Norman market or fair may seem a small point. There were, after all, urban market places, however weakly conceptualised their legal status may have been. There were probably hundreds of informally institutionalised trading places that we know nothing about. The interesting inferences are that such trading places as existed were rarely lucrative enough to be worth much thought, and that they were rarely subject to seigniorial rights.

The idea of a market is more in evidence soon after 1066. In Normandy the term market had already come to be used to describe a weekly event by 1025, so perhaps in this instance Norman rule helped to clarify ideas in England.[50] So little is known about the earliest recorded markets that we cannot tell what the word normally meant. It is impossible to be sure that all those recorded in Domesday Book were described as such by standard criteria. But in a number of cases, at least, the word signified a weekly event, as at Hoxne, where the market was held on Saturdays in the reign of Edward the Confessor. When William Malet founded his new Saturday market at Eye the market at Hoxne was shifted to a Friday.[51] At Wallingford (Berks.) in 1086 the market was held on a Saturday,[52] and at Otterton (Devon) it was on a Sunday.[53] We are also sometimes told that a market had a definite market place. At Launceston (Cornw.) in 1086 the canons of St Stephen's complained that the count of Mortain had removed a market which had once been held on their manor and that he had put it in his castle.[54] There were seventeen men living in the market (*forum*) at Berkeley (Glos.),[55] and there were twenty-five burgesses living in the market (*mercatum*) at Eye (Suff.).[56] At Worcester Urso held from the bishop twenty-five houses in the market (*forum*).[57] In these cases, at least, the Domesday commissioners were talking about markets essentially the same as those so called in later centuries.

A more formal conceptualisation of market and fair was implied when kings asserted their right to license new foundations. Domesday Book records that Roger Bigod held a market by royal grant at *Caramhalla* (Suff., perhaps Kelsale), and that Robert Malet held another market by

[50] Endemann, *Markturkunde*, p. 79n.   [51] *DB*, II, fo. 379a.   [52] *DB*, I, fo. 56c.
[53] *Libri Censualis Vocati Domesday Book Additamenta*, ed. H. Ellis, RC (London, 1816), p. 177.
[54] *DB*, I, fo. 120d; *Libri Censualis Additamenta*, ed. Ellis, p. 188.
[55] *DB*, I, fo. 163a.   [56] *DB*, II, fo. 319b.   [57] *DB*, I, fo. 173c.

royal grant at Eye.[58] No authentic market charters date from as early as this, though Battle Abbey purported to have a charter from the Conqueror to license its market in Battle (Suss.) on a Sunday.[59] This implies that a market was understood as a franchise restricted to a particular time and place, though not necessarily a time and place chosen by the king. Henry II allowed Robert de Berkeley to have a market on any day of the week he chose.[60] The establishing of new fairs came to be similarly controlled. It became standard practice to specify the dates on which the fair was to be held. In 1110, for example, Ramsey Abbey was granted a fair at St Ives (Hunts.) 'from the Wednesday in Easter until the eighth day'.[61] Alterations in these terms required royal authorisation and a new charter. Already in William II's reign, when the abbot of Malmesbury wanted to extend his fair from three days to five, he obtained a new charter from the king.[62] In 1136 the bishop of Winchester obtained a new charter from his royal brother because he wished to extend the St Giles fair by six days.[63]

The royal right to authorise new markets and fairs is unlikely to have been generally recognised, or even understood, for at least a century after the Norman Conquest. One sign of this is the paucity of twelfth-century market charters, contrasting oddly with what is known of the development of trade. The rarity of such charters from northern England is particularly hard to explain if markets were accepted as a regalian right, since many new foundations in this region must have forced themselves upon the attention of neighbouring lords from the start. The north has one early example. About 1109 the bishop of Durham secured a market charter for his market at Norton (co. Dur.). But the bishop in question was Ranulph Flambard, William II's former chief minister, who knew the legal doctrine in question at exceptionally close quarters.[64] Elsewhere in the north such licences were not sought. The pipe rolls record the licensing of markets at Chesterfield (Derb.) in 1164–5, Trentham (Staffs.) in 1172–3, and at Wolverhampton (Staffs.) in 1179–80.[65] Farther north than this the pipe rolls say nothing of royal licences before the reign of King John.

In Yorkshire numerous borough markets were recorded before 1200

---

[58] *DB*, II, fos. 330b, 379a.

[59] *The Chronicle of Battle Abbey*, ed. and trans. E. Searle, OMT (Oxford, 1980), pp. 84–5.

[60] *The Berkeley Manuscripts*, ed. J. Maclean, 3 vols. (Gloucester, 1883–5), III, p. 82.

[61] *Cartularium Monasterii de Rameseia*, ed. W. H. Hart and P. A. Lyons, RS, 3 vols. (London, 1884–93), I, p. 240.

[62] *Registrum Malmesburiense*, ed. J. S. Brewer and C. T. Martin, RS, 2 vols. (London, 1879–80), I, p. 333.

[63] *RRAN*, III, no. 952, pp. 352–3.   [64] *RRAN*, II, no. 925, p. 89.

[65] *PR, 11 Henry II*, p. 87; *PR, 19 Henry II*, p. 59; *PR, 26 Henry II*, p. 13.

– at Boroughbridge, Doncaster, Helmsley, Knaresborough, Pontefract, Richmond, Skipsea, South Cave, Tickhill, Wakefield, Whitby and perhaps Skipton.[66] In view of the destruction in Yorkshire under William I and the subsequent reconstruction of the rural economy it is unlikely that all or even most of these markets had survived unchanged from before the Conquest. And yet not one of them has a twelfth-century royal market charter or any other indication of having been licensed by the crown. In some cases authorisation was obtained from mesne lords. A market at Alnmouth (Northumb.) was granted to William de Vesci about 1152–5 by the earl of Northumberland.[67]

Even from southern England there are private charters which show that the standing of markets did not depend on settled legal principles. Sometime before 1107 Robert Fitz Hamon gave a charter of liberties to his men of Burford (Oxon.) stipulating that anyone was free to come and buy what he wanted in the market there, except that wool and hides were reserved for Burford men.[68] The charter implies that the lords of markets were able to impose qualifications upon the sort of activity that took place. In other circumstances the consent of landlords other than the king was a desirable additional security. For its market of Yaxley (Hunts.) Thorney Abbey secured licences from Henry of Scotland, earl of Huntingdon, as well as grants or alleged grants from the English crown.[69]

Ambiguities concerning the legal status of markets were resolved only gradually. In the twelfth century the king's clerks and justices employed *mercatum* and *feria* as standard technical terms for the franchise of market and fair, but there is no formal definition of these words from that period. As in other areas of medieval law, technical clarity was hampered by the number and variety of existing institutions. Licences to build castles offer a close parallel.[70] Some historians have supposed that a market came to be regarded as a franchise because of its incidental

---

[66] *PR, 15 Henry II*, p. 37 (Boroughbridge); *EYC*, II, no. 1004, pp. 332–3 (Doncaster); *EYC*, X, no. 95, p. 148 (Helmsley); *PR, 15 Henry II*, p. 37 (Knaresborough); *EYC*, III, no. 1499, p. 191 (Pontefract); *EYC*, IV, nos. 20, 21, pp. 22–3 (Richmond); *EYC*, III, no. 1356, p. 72 (Skipsea); *Charters of the Honour of Mowbray, 1107–1191*, ed. D. E. Greenway, BARSEH, new ser., I (Oxford, 1972), no. 360, p. 231 (South Cave); *DB*, I, fo. 319a (Tickhill); M. Beresford and H. P. R. Finberg, *English Medieval Boroughs: A Handlist* (Newton Abbot, 1973), p. 192 (Wakefield); *EYC*, II, no. 886, pp. 231–2 (Whitby); *EYC*, VII, no. 21, p. 69 (Skipton).

[67] *RRS*, II, no. 3, pp. 124–5.

[68] *Earldom of Gloucester Charters to A.D. 1217*, ed. R. B. Patterson (Oxford, 1973), no. 43, p. 58.

[69] *RRS*, I, nos. 16, 17, pp. 141–2; *RRAN*, I, no. 477, p. 115; *RRAN*, III, nos. 881–4, pp. 322–3; *PR, 31 Henry I*, p. 49.

[70] F. M. Stenton, *The First Century of English Feudalism, 1066–1166*, 2nd edn (Oxford, 1961), pp. 196–206.

features – the right to collect tolls, or the right to exercise certain forms of jurisdiction – but the tenor of all the evidence is rather that a market was regarded as a franchise in itself. We have no reason to suppose that twelfth-century market charters carried with them any rights of jurisdiction. The essential features of a market were probably, in the first place, a fixed time and place for trading, and, secondly, the existence of a seigniorial or community interest, whether this was the collection of tolls, charges for stalls or charges for the use of weights and measures.

Maitland wrote that 'the establishment of a market is not one of those indefinite phenomena which the historian of law must make over to the historian of economic processes. It is', he argued, 'a definite and legal act. The market is established by law.'[71] Should we be so confident? Sadly, no. Maitland's statement is fair comment for the thirteenth century, and to a lesser extent for the twelfth, but its truth for that period depends upon the recent development of the market as a legal concept and the growth of the king's power to enforce it. The creation of a market was indeed a definite and legal act when it was the seigniorial realisation of a legally defined institution. But it was either a less definite or a less legal act if a lord acquired a licence for a market place already in existence, or if he set up a new market place in a region where the king's right to license markets was unrecognised, or if he took over and remodelled a pre-existing assembly and placed his trust in its prescriptive status. There is no evidence of a legal concept of a market in England from before 1066, and without that the origin of trading institutions must largely fall outside the province of the history of law altogether. And because markets did not exist as legal entities whose existence needed recording, the early history of trading institutions is largely inaccessible to economic and social historians as well.

III

Ambiguities of legal status account for much of the awkwardness of the evidence concerning early centres of local trade. In particular, they mean that the earliest appearance of a market in surviving documents is usually of no significance for the origin of institutionalised trade there. About 1153, for example, King Stephen confirmed that the Templars should hold their market in Witham (Essex) as fully as it had been held in the time of Henry I.[72] But this detail does not establish the origins of Witham as a trading centre. The village was the site of a burh of Edward

---

[71] Maitland, *Domesday Book*, p. 193.   [72] *Records of the Templars*, ed. Lees, p. 152.

the Elder and up to Stephen's reign a royal manor, and it was perhaps already a centre of local trade before the Norman Conquest. Witham is representative of a lot of well-established markets which appear in records of the twelfth, thirteenth and fourteenth centuries without any known date of origin. We cannot tell in such cases just how the institution came into being.

By examining the earliest surviving market charters, and by looking carefully at markets whose origins are misty, we can reach some conclusions about the sort of locations where organised trade was developing and where seigniorial interests were becoming involved. Places where people congregated regularly were particularly favourable for such initiatives. Many markets were attached to manors of exceptional importance in local government. These manors, nearly all large ones, were those to which jurisdiction over a neighbouring hundred was attached.[73] The manor of Witham, which gave its name to Witham Hundred, is a good example of this type. Historians have occasionally speculated that in the eleventh century there was a regular association between markets and hundredal organisation. It is unlikely, though, that every post-Conquest hundred had a formal market – that is, a weekly event at which a manorial lord provided marketing facilities and charged tolls.[74] Other early markets were located at important pre-Conquest churches, where trade was facilitated by the number of worshippers congregating at predictable times.[75] Hordon on the Hill (Essex), seemingly an important local market, since coins were minted there in the reign of Edward the Confessor and a market was later held there by prescription, was not a hundred manor but had an early minster.[76]

Many centres were simultaneously important for secular administration and for ecclesiastical centrality. Of thirty-two medieval markets in Norfolk with no recorded royal authorisation, ten were hundredal (Aylsham, Diss, Downham, Foulsham, Harleston, Higham, Holt, Kenninghall, Great Yarmouth, Wighton), two were at early ecclesiasti-

[73] R. H. Britnell, 'English Markets and Royal Administration before 1200', *EcHR*, 2nd ser., 31 (1978), pp. 183–6.

[74] *Ibid.*, pp. 188–9; J. Campbell, 'Was it Infancy in England? Some Questions of Comparison', in M. Jones and M. Vale, eds., *England and her Neighbours, 1066–1453: Essays in Honour of Pierre Chaplais* (London, 1989), p. 14; C. Johnson, 'Domesday Survey', *VCH Norf.*, II, pp. 26–7.

[75] Sawyer, 'Early Fairs and Markets', pp. 65–6.

[76] G. C. Brooke, *English Coins from the Seventh Century to the Present Day*, 3rd edn (London, 1950), p. 72; D. Hill, *An Atlas of Anglo-Saxon England* (Oxford, 1981), p. 159; P. Morant, *The History and Antiquities of the County of Essex*, 2 vols. (London, 1768), I, pp. 216, 218.

cal sites (Burham, North Walsham) and two could be classified either way (Great Dunham, Norwich). Of twenty-two equivalent markets in Essex, five were hundredal (Chipping Ongar, Hatfield Broad Oak, Rayleigh, Witham, Writtle), two were ecclesiastical (Horndon on the Hill, Southminster) and three were both (Barking, Colchester, Waltham Holy Cross). Of the twelve comparable markets in Gloucestershire, one was hundredal (Thornbury) and five belonged to both categories (Berkeley, Cheltenham, Cirencester, Gloucester, Winchcombe).[77] We have a clue here to the conditions where regular marketing became established in the period before seigniorial interest in a market was defined as a regalian right.

Amongst the earliest known markets and fairs there is another group whose location is apparently explained by the feudal and monastic geography of the Anglo-Norman period. Some markets whose date of foundation is known to belong to this period were associated with castles, as at Eye (Suff.), Launceston (Cornw.), Trematon (Cornw.), Saffron Walden (Essex), Beaudesert (Warws.) and Birmingham (Warws.).[78] Early markets without known charters are similarly to be found by baronial castles, as in the Yorkshire examples of Helmsley,[79] Knaresborough,[80] Pontefract,[81] Thirsk[82] and Tickhill.[83] The circumstances would suggest that these are Anglo-Norman foundations whose location reflects a new pattern of feudal geography. Other early chartered markets were founded in close proximity to newly founded monasteries, both large and small, as at Battle (Suss.), Tavistock (Devon), Romsey (Hants.), Binham (Norf.), Great Bricett (Suff.) and Eynsham (Oxon.),[84] and there were other markets with no known

[77] Britnell, 'English Markets', pp. 183–6; R. H. Britnell, 'Essex Markets before 1350', *Essex Arch. and Hist.*, 13 (1981), pp. 15–16; Hill, *Atlas*, pp. 157–62.
[78] *DB*, I, fo. 122a; *DB*, II, fo. 379a; *Libri Censualis Additamenta*, ed. Ellis, pp. 182, 188, 235; *RRAN*, III, nos. 274, 597, pp. 99, 220; *Cartae Antiquae*, ed. L. Landon and J. C. Davies, Pipe Roll Soc., 2 vols., new ser., XVII, XXXIII (London, 1939, 1960), II, no. 613, p. 190.
[79] *EYC*, X, no. 95, p. 148; Beresford and Finberg, *English Medieval Boroughs*, p. 187; I. J. Sanders, *English Baronies: A Study of their Origin and Descent, 1086–1327* (Oxford, 1960), p. 52.
[80] *PR, 15 Henry II*, p. 37; Beresford and Finberg, *English Medieval Boroughs*, p. 190; Sanders, *English Baronies*, p. 59.
[81] *EYC*, III, no. 1499, p. 191; Beresford and Finberg, *English Medieval Boroughs*, p. 191; Sanders, *English Baronies*, p. 138.
[82] *Charters of the Honour of Mowbray*, ed. Greenway, pp. xxiv, liii–iv; Sanders, *English Baronies*, p. 146.
[83] Beresford and Finberg, *English Medieval Boroughs*, p. 192; Sanders, *English Baronies*, p. 147.
[84] *RRAN*, I, no. 61, p. 16 (Battle); *RRAN*, II, nos. 773, 802, pp. 57, 63, 69 (Tavistock, Romsey, Binham); *RRAN*, III, nos. 118, 293, pp. 44, 111 (Great Bricett, Eynsham).

charters which had the same characteristic, such as Whitby (N.R. Yorks.) and St Osyth (Essex).[85] In a few cases this observation supplies an alternative explanation for markets that might otherwise be identified as hundredal, but of those noted above Chipping Ongar and Rayleigh seem to be the only instances. At both these places an Anglo-Norman lord established his barony at a manor that had, or came to have, a hundred attached to it. Our ignorance of the early history of these markets precludes our saying whether they were already in existence or what the decisive circumstances of their foundation were.

Such indeterminacy in our evidence does not obscure the picture very significantly. We may safely conclude that many markets and fairs were at places important for other reasons, notably as centres to which the institutions of law and religion regularly attracted large numbers of people. It was for this reason that earlier markets and fairs were often poorly situated with respect to roads or rivers.[86] This feature of the late eleventh and twelfth centuries became less prominent thereafter. There were no doubt advantages for a market's users in having it fixed at a central point to which they were likely to be going for other reasons. But there were also advantages for lords. An accessible market helped large households or large manors to dispose of surplus goods at a time when much of their receipts were in agricultural produce. Perhaps, too, the provision of such a facility made it easier for large estates to manage their tenants.

IV

As markets and fairs were drawn within the scope of seigniorial control, landlords became guarded about how many the countryside could profitably contain, and their own interests induced them to limit the number of formal trading places where they could. They were presumably afraid that the multiplication of marketing institutions would reduce the value of existing ones. In the palatinate of Durham the bishop exercised his powers to prevent any competition with his own markets, and in the late 1220s it was agreed by several witnesses that no one but the bishop held a market or fair in the Haliwarefolc between the Tyne and the Tees.[87] The abbot of Ramsey claimed that no one had a

---

[85] *EYC*, II, no. 886, pp. 231–2 (Whitby); *Cartae Antiquae*, ed. Landon and Davies, I, no. 172, p. 86 (St Osyth).

[86] Britnell, 'Essex Markets before 1350', pp. 18–19.

[87] *Feodarium Prioratus Dunelmensis*, ed. W. Greenwell, Surtees Soc., LVIII (Durham, 1872), pp. 230, 235, 238, 240.

right to erect a new market in his hundred of Clacklose.[88] A Norman landlord who wanted to set up a new market under the protection of his castle might shift an existing one some distance in order to do so. So by 1086 the Count of Mortain had moved one market from St Stephens to Launceston (Cornw.) and another from St Germans to Trematon (Cornw.). When Geoffrey de Mandeville established a market at Saffron Walden (Essex) he did so by gaining permission to shift the market from Newport, three miles away.[89]

In the course of the period 1050–1180 the number of markets and fairs was nevertheless slowly increasing to accommodate a growing volume of local transactions. Some of the evidence goes back to the eleventh century; eight of the Domesday markets are described as new or recently founded.[90] From that time onwards the creation of new markets is attested by surviving charters and ultimately, from the 1160s, by the record of fees accounted for in the exchequer and recorded in the pipe rolls. There are also various miscellaneous sources of later date which contain retrospective information. A number of these new markets and fairs were associated with older centres of trade. Henry I's prolongation of Norwich fair in c. 1106 is a good example.[91]

The number of new markets supplied the needs of a growing number of specialist craftsmen and traders in the countryside, and this can be best seen through topographical study. Increasing division of labour was characteristic of many village communities, if only because of a multiplication of families with little or no land. But the most perceptible consequence of specialisation was its effect upon the number and size of market-centred settlements. Families whose income depended upon services and manufacturing, because they had neither land nor agricultural skills adequate to ensure their livelihood in agricultural employment, were often constrained to live where they found the institutional provision to support them, so that some places stand out in twelfth-century estate surveys for the number of craftsmen who lived there.[92] The growth of commercial settlements has been a normal response to population growth in history since prehistoric periods. But in the context of a land shared out between the crown, nobles, knights, monks

---

[88] *Cartularium Monasterii de Rameseia*, ed. Hart and Lyons, II, p. 156.
[89] *Libri Censualis Additamenta*, ed. Ellis, pp. 182, 188, 235; *RRAN*, III, no. 274, p. 99.
[90] I.e. those of Cookham (Berks.), Trematon and Launceston (Cornw.), Cirencester and Tewkesbury (Glos.), Bolingbroke (Lincs.), 'Caramhalla' and Eye (Suff.). St Germans and St Stephens (Cornw.) are described as discontinued: Darby, *Domesday England*, pp. 369–70.
[91] *RRAN*, II, no. 762, p. 55.
[92] Harvey, 'Non-Agrarian Activities in Twelfth-Century English Estate Surveys', pp. 103–4.

and clergy, it was inevitable that landlords should be involved in the procedures that made urbanisation possible.

When new markets were founded landlords often laid out the market place with accommodation for potential tradesmen. Such market communities might become new towns, though often they never grew big enough to be considered urban. At Eye (Suff.) Domesday Book records the presence of twenty-five burgesses associated with the new market. Launceston is described in the survey as a new town associated with the resited market, and the town of Trematon (Cornw.) too is dated by Professor Beresford to the foundation of the market there between 1066 and 1086.[93] At Battle (Suss.), another of the earliest markets founded after the Conquest, a new settlement of this kind was constructed while the abbey church was still being built. The late twelfth-century chronicler of the abbey tells how 'the brethren in charge of the building began to apportion to individuals house-sites of definite dimensions near the boundary of its site'. There were in all 115 plots, whose tenants were designated burgesses 'on account of the outstanding dignity of this preeminent place'.[94] These examples illustrate the relationship between the founding of markets and the growth of market communities, a relationship which was particularly strong in Anglo-Norman foundations. It was so strong, indeed, that we may infer that the multiplication and development of formal markets in the period 1066–1180 was encouraged by developments in the specialisation of labour, the consequent need for more marketing facilities and the interest of landlords in supplying them.

V

Centrally defined regulations controlling trade in pre-Conquest England were few. Crime prevention required trade involving cattle to be witnessed by a trustworthy man.[95] But normally no attempt was made to restrict such transactions to any particular sort of location. At one stage, about 935, Aethelstan and his advisers had ruled 'that no one shall buy goods worth more than 20d outside a town (*port*), but he shall buy within the town in the presence of the port-reeve or some other truthworthy man, or again, in the presence of the reeves at a public meeting'.[96] That was designed to reinforce the rules relating to the

[93] *DB*, II, fo. 319b; Beresford, *New Towns*, pp. 405, 411–12.
[94] *Chronicle of Battle Abbey*, ed. Searle, pp. 50–9, 76.
[95] E.g. II Aethelstan, 10: *Gesetze*, ed. Liebermann, I, pp. 156–7.
[96] II Aethelstan, 12: *Gesetze*, ed. Liebermann, I, pp. 156–7.

cattle trade rather than to regulate expenditure for household consumption; 20d was approximately the value of a cow or of two pigs.[97] Even so it soon proved impossible to keep the law in force, and it was abandoned.[98] The same preoccupation with theft explains why under King Edgar's laws officers for attesting sales of cattle were to be appointed in boroughs and 'in each hundred'.[99] A hundred court was the only public meeting most rural freeholders would be likely to attend. But these rules could be compatible with much local variation. Though they confirm that there were recognised foci of public trade with officers responsible for maintaining the king's peace, they do not indicate any more than this about the degree of regulation involved. The stress is all on the men who were to be present at a sale, rather than upon the place or time where it was to be made, and this is so out of line with later market regulations as to defy all search for continuity. Evidence that trading in churchyards was common even in towns of the twelfth century suggests that the official regulation of trade had not progressed very far up to that time.

The only other royal legislation concerning urban trade in this period is that governing weights, measures and the coinage. It was expected in the ninth century that officials at the main markets, at least, should keep standard weights and measures.[100] King Edgar's laws later required the measures and weights of London and Winchester to be observed throughout his kingdom, and the same principle was maintained in the legislation of Aethelred and Cnut.[101] The principle of a national standard was kept alive through the eleventh and twelfth centuries, but it was not in practice maintained. Individual trading towns enforced internal uniformity, and this may explain the 'Officers of Measures' at York in 1175.[102] Even so, different towns had different standards, so that the kingdom was divided up into different mensural zones. In 1174 the king's own officers recorded purchases of large quantities of wheat 'by Norwich measure' and 'by Abingdon measure'.[103]

Regulation of the principal food trades in this period was a matter only of local or private concern. Individual towns exercised some control over brewing and baking. At Chester in 1086 anyone brewing bad ale was

[97] VI Aethelstan, 6.2: *Gesetze*, ed. Liebermann, I, pp. 176.
[98] VI Aethelstan, 10: *Gesetze*, ed. Liebermann, I, pp. 181–2.
[99] Maitland, *Domesday Book*, p. 194.   [100] Tait, *Medieval English Borough*, p. 10.
[101] III Edgar, 8.1; VI Aethelred, 32.2; II Cnut, 9: *The Laws of the Kings of England from Edmund to Henry I*, ed. A. J. Robertson (Cambridge, 1926), pp. 28–9, 100–1, 178–9.
[102] *PR, 21 Henry II*, p. 180.   [103] *PR, 20 Henry II*, pp. 37, 112.

either put in an unpleasant apparatus described as the 'dung seat' or made to pay a fine of 4d.[104] The borough of Newcastle upon Tyne (Northumb.) had regulations about baking and brewing in Henry I's reign with a gradation of penalties up to a third offence. A charter granted to Tewkesbury (Glos.) between 1147 and 1183 speaks of an assize of bread and ale that was enforced at an annual lawday.[105] Controlling the weight and quality of victuals was also a matter of private concern for large households. When in Henry I's reign a charter was composed to spell out the terms on which the bishop of Ely's baker should hold a house and eighteen acres in Ely, it was specified that he and his assistants should make the number and size of loaves from each *summa* of grain 'according to the assize of our household'.[106] The royal household operated according to regulations of this kind. The *Constitutio Domus Regis* of about 1136 stipulates that from a Rouen *muid* of wheat the four bakers of the pantry are to bake 40 superior simnels, 150 salt simnels and 260 bakers' loaves.[107] The earliest text of an assize of bread is one 'proved by the bakers of the lord king Henry II' and copied into a large compendium of English laws compiled for the guildhall of London sometime between 1206 and 1216.[108] The document probably concerned only the verge of the court; there is no statement in the text to imply that it had relevance to the whole kingdom.[109]

Occasionally a king gave his blessing to trading rules formulated in grants of borough liberties. Such rules were formulated in the town concerned and submitted to the king for his approval. The major early example is Henry I's charter to Newcastle upon Tyne. Burgesses had to be allowed to buy what they wanted from any ship touching at Tynemouth before it was allowed to leave. Merchandise shipped to the borough had to be brought to land, except for salt and herrings, which were to be sold from the boat. Outsiders were forbidden to buy cloth for dyeing, or to buy raw materials in Newcastle market and the surrounding countryside, or to cut up fish for sale. No other early royal charter has so many regulations of this sort, and this perhaps explains why in later centuries Newcastle merchants were exceptionally aggressive

---

[104] *DB*, I, fo. 262c.   [105] *BBC, 1042–1216*, pp. 157–8.
[106] E. Miller, *The Abbey and Bishopric of Ely: The Social History of an Ecclesiastical Estate from the Tenth Century to the Early Fourteenth Century* (Cambridge, 1951), p. 283.
[107] *Dialogus de Scaccario*, ed. and trans. C. Johnson (London, 1950), p. 130.
[108] BL, Add. MS 14252, fo. 85v; F. Liebermann, *Über die Leges Anglorum saeculo XIII ineunte Londoniis collectae* (Halle, 1894), pp. 79, 101.
[109] H. G. Richardson and G. O. Sayles, *Law and Legislation from Aethelberht to Magna Carta* (Edinburgh, 1966), pp. 102–3.

towards other northern townsmen.[110] Yet other town charters have individual clauses to protect the trading interests of burgesses, as at Cambridge in the 1120s or Nottingham in 1157.[111] A few seigniorial boroughs also sought permission from their lords to regulate trade in their own interests, as in the already mentioned charter to Burford from Robert Fitz Hamon.

More commonly the details of urban regulation were left to the initiative of burgesses, and received no explicit royal sanction. By the early twelfth century, at least, Londoners had devised quite sophisticated rules relating to local trade. A code of citizens' liberties stipulates that 'within the space of three miles beyond the city on all sides nobody should detain or impede another, nor yet trade with him, if he wishes to come to the city under the city's protection. But when he has reached the city, then both poor and rich alike may trade with him.' This regulation was designed to protect the interests of consumers in the city against the threat of potential monopolists.[112] In many towns the regulating of local trade was one of the functions of merchant gilds, some of which were operating from at least the time of the Conquest. The burgesses of Canterbury and Dover had gilds in 1066, though we have no details of how they functioned. Sometime in the period 1107–18 Count Robert I of Meulan recognised the right of the merchants of Leicester to have a gild as in the time of William I and William II. Other gilds from this period, or only shortly after, are known from Beverley (E.R. Yorks.), Burford (Oxon.), Wilton (Wilts.) and York.[113] When twelfth-century gilds were authorised by the crown the details of their operations did not need to be written out. Between 1100 and 1160 gild merchants were recognised to have customs at Leicester, Lewes (Suss.) and Burford, statutes at Beverley, liberties and customs at Chichester (Suss.), Oxford and York, customs and laws at Wallingford (Berks.).[114] To judge from both current and later evidence, gilds developed a style of control that was to remain characteristic of the urban regulation of trade for the rest of the Middle Ages and beyond. On the one hand, one of their main objects was to restrict trade of certain types to gild members or

[110] *The Percy Chartulary*, ed. M. T. Martin, Surtees Soc., CXVII (Durham, 1911), pp. 334–6; *Select Charters and Other Illustrations of English Constitutional History*, ed. W. Stubbs, 9th edn, revised H. W. C. Davis (Oxford, 1921), pp. 133–4; C. M. Fraser, 'Medieval Trading Restrictions in the North East', *Archaeologia Aeliana*, 4th ser., 39 (1961), pp. 136–8, 140–4.

[111] *BBC, 1042–1216*, pp. 168–9.

[112] R. H. Britnell, '*Forstall*, Forestalling and the Statute of Forestallers', *EHR*, 102 (1987), pp. 90–1.

[113] C. Gross, *The Gild Merchant: A Contribution to British Municipal History*, 2 vols. (Oxford, 1890), I, pp. 9–20, II, p. 136; Tait, *Medieval English Borough*, pp. 119–21.

[114] *BBC, 1042–1216*, pp. 202–4.

burgesses, so that commercial regulation became inextricably identified with particular urban interest groups.[115] In the second place, each town was granted or adopted its own code. The absence of new legislation meant that by 1180 urban policies had very little common basis in the laws of the realm.

[115] *Ibid.*, pp. 207–16.

2   Trade and specialisation

I

Domesday Book dominates any attempt to construct a picture of England in the eleventh century. But the great survey, for all its detail, cannot be expected to give a satisfactory description. The commissioners, in obeying their instructions, asked no questions about economic interdependence or local patterns of exchange. In categorising the rural population – slaves, bordars, villains, sokemen, free men – they used terms that tell us more about the status of tenants in their lords' eyes than about the things they did to make a living and meet their obligations. Payments between tenants and lords, employers and employees, buyers and sellers, lenders and borrowers, do not enter the picture. Money is in evidence in every paragraph, but there is no telling where it came from or how it was spent. Unless we are aware of what Domesday Book does not purport to give, we shall not be adventurous enough in interpreting it and looking outside it.

Enough is known about the Anglo-Norman monetary system for some of its strengths and weaknesses to be assessed. It was simpler than modern systems because it lacked bank or paper money and depended entirely on coinage. The total currency circulating in England probably did not exceed £120,000 at any point during the period 1000–1180 – no more than 1s for each man, woman and child. The English system was even more straightforward than that of most regions of the continent. No foreign currency was allowed to circulate, and foreign coins entering the realm had to be taken to a mint for remaking as English currency. Until the temporary weakening of royal control in Stephen's reign, kings benefited financially from periodic recoinages at which all existing money had to be renewed. The dies from which coins were struck were supplied by the crown to local mints, and the number of coins to be minted from a pound of silver was centrally determined.[1] When in 1124 Henry I's knights in Normandy protested about the quality of the coins in which their wages had been payed, his moneyers lost their right hands and their testicles.[2] But the strength and simplicity of the system was achieved at the expense of flexibility. There was only one sort of coin, the silver penny, weighing on average 21.5 grains between 1053 and 1083 and 22.5 grains in the Conqueror's last years and under his successors. Its silver content was exceptionally high by European standards. These characteristics account for the high international reputation of *sterling*.[3]

Such strengths had disadvantages when it came to making small payments. The lowest unit of currency was large in relation to the purchases an ordinary household would make. A household servant's daily wage of 1d about the year 1130 might buy him a quarter of a sheep's carcase, but would not help him buy a pound of neck. Occasionally a few halfpennies were minted, but they were never widely circulated, and very few survive.[4] It became more acceptable in the course of the period to cut pennies into halves or quarters to make small payments, but this had the disadvantage of creating fragments of silver that were unattractively small.[5] The medium of exchange in local commercial transactions at this period falls almost entirely out of view; there are no sources from which it could ever be perceived. But we can deduce from the character of the coinage itself that barter remained a normal way of obtaining household supplies in small quantities. The rigidity of the currency system was an obstacle to trade by small households, and in English villages the use of cash was probably limited to a minority of the transactions necessary for daily life.

Domesday Book suggests the extent to which exchanges were necessary amongst peasant tenants of the eleventh century. The commissioners recorded countrymen by categories partly related to the size of their holdings of land. The 41 per cent described as villains produced most of their own requirements of basic foodstuffs. A further 11 per cent were

---

[1] P. Grierson, 'Sterling', in R. H. M. Dolley, ed., *Anglo-Saxon Coins: Studies Presented to F. M. Stenton on the Occasion of his Seventieth Birthday* (London, 1961), p. 273; P. H. Sawyer, 'The Wealth of England in the Eleventh Century', *TRHS*, 5th ser., 15 (1965), p. 152; P. Spufford, *Money and its Use in Medieval Europe* (Cambridge, 1988), pp. 92–4.
[2] J. A. Green, *The Government of England under Henry I* (Cambridge, 1986), p. 90.
[3] Brooke, *English Coins*, p. 82; Grierson, 'Sterling', pp. 273–8.
[4] F. Barlow, *Edward the Confessor* (London, 1970), pp. 181, 183; F. Barlow, *William Rufus* (London, 1983), pp. 259; Green, *Government*, p. 89.
[5] S. E. Rigold, 'Small Change in the Light of Medieval Site-Finds', in N. J. Mayhew, ed., *Edwardian Monetary Affairs (1269–1344)*, BAR, XXXVI (Oxford, 1977), pp. 78–9.

slaves, oxherds or swineherds who presumably received their requirements from their owners and employers. This suggests that at least half the recorded population was largely independent of the market for its subsistence.[6] Of the remainder, as we have seen, a third were cottagers who were unlikely to be self-sufficient. Yet even this does not imply that so large a proportion of the population depended upon monetised exchange for its normal supplies. In later periods even hired labourers took much of their remuneration in grain.[7]

The best evidence of non-monetary transactions is in the history of rent. For this purpose we have to distinguish between manorial leases, feudal tenures and peasant tenures, the three types of tenure most commonly to be found in England during the eleventh and twelfth centuries. Manorial leases were contractual in character and were the usual means by which landlords managed their estates. Whole manors, both the income and services from peasant tenures and the demesne land under direct seigniorial control, were leased, often for one or more lives at a fixed rent.[8] Unlike feudal tenures, receipts from manorial leases were geared directly to supplying the households of the king, bishops, abbots, barons and other greater landlords. Feudal tenures were those created originally as contracts to provide for a lord's personal service, usually of a military kind. They were of many different sizes. At the top end, from the Conqueror's reign onwards, whole baronies were held from the crown for the service of a stipulated number of knights, though the lands of the barony had to maintain the baron himself as well as his knights. At the lower end of the scale were individual knights' fiefs (the lands given to knights to support them). Such fiefs were often taken out of the demesne land of a baron or a wealthy church burdened with military service. A few of the larger ones became new manors in their own right, though this was unusual in the eleventh century.[9] Peasant tenures were those held by the various categories of villager who owed rents and services at a manor house; they were mostly family holdings of fifty acres or less and the terms of tenure were all customary in some degree. Most manors had some tenants of this kind.

---

[6] Darby, *Domesday England*, p.63.

[7] M. M. Postan, *The Famulus: The Estate Labourer in the XIIth and XIIIth Centuries*, *EcHR* supplement II (Cambridge, 1954), pp. 29–30.

[8] Lennard, *Rural England*, pp.105–212.

[9] The size of eleventh-century knights' fees remains a debated matter. See S. P. J. Harvey, 'The Knight and the Knight's Fee in England', in R. H. Hilton, ed., *Peasants, Knights and Heretics: Studies in Medieval English Social History* (Cambridge, 1976), pp. 145–52; R. A. Brown, 'The Status of Norman Knights', in J. Gillingham and J. C. Holt, eds., *War and Government in the Middle Ages* (Woodbridge, 1984), pp. 22–3.

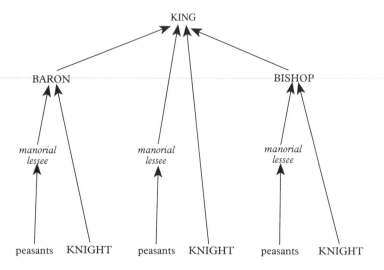

Figure 1   Types of land tenure, *c*. 1070–1180

Capitals indicate a feudal tenure, italics a manorial lease and lower case letters a peasant tenure. The arrows indicate who receive rent and services from whom. Although peasant tenures were held from the manorial lord (king, baron, bishop) they paid rent to a manorial lessee under the terms of his lease.

The interrelationship between the three forms of rent is illustrated in Figure 1. The diagram concerns only three principal manors, one held directly by the king, one held as part of a barony and one held as part of a bishopric. The king receives income as a manorial lord from his manorial lessee, but he also receives feudal service from his own knight, from his baron and from the bishop. The baron and bishop derive manorial income from their lessees, but also receive feudal service from their knights. The knights' lands represented in the diagram may be big enough to be thought of as manors or sub-manors, but not necessarily so. The large number of differently structured manors in the hands of the king and other landlords meant that in reality there were many variations in the overall pattern.

The terms of manorial leases were frequently indifferent to marketing possibilities because produce was used to supply the lord's household. On some estates in the eleventh century, particularly on those of monasteries, demesne agriculture was most fully developed near the household. There are instances, too, where landlords appear to have sited their castles to take advantage of large adjacent demesnes that could be used as a source of supply.[10] Some estates operated an elaborate system of produce rents by which different manors in turn sent the lord's household agricultural produce over long distances. At Canterbury Cathedral Priory in 1086 the estates were divided between food manors and dress manors. The organisation had recently been overhauled by Archbishop Lanfranc to ensure adequate supplies in each week of the year.[11] Similar means were employed on the estates of the monastic cathedral of Rochester, the dean and canons of St Paul's and the abbeys of Ely, Ramsey, Bury St Edmunds and St Albans. There were traces of the system still on the monastic estates of Westminster, Worcester and Abingdon.[12] Food rents were not restricted to monastic estates; any large household was likely to have difficulties with supplies if it stayed long in any one place. Part of the royal estate operated in this way in Edward the Confessor's reign.[13] In Wiltshire, Somerset and Dorset almost all royal manors were organised, either singly or in groups, to supply the royal court with cash and provisions for a twenty-four-hour period, and a few manors preserved the system in Hampshire, Sussex and Gloucestershire. Such organisation had once stretched to manors in Devon, Shropshire and perhaps Oxfordshire as well, though by 1066 it had been abandoned in these counties.[14] A similar system for supplying the court was in operation on royal manors in Cambridgeshire, Norfolk and Suffolk, where the provisions were specified as deliveries of cash, honey, grain and malt.[15]

The persistence of such arrangements was not usually evidence of conservatism. Large households, like the king's, moved around the country for reasons of sanitation and health, to supervise widely scattered properties and to enjoy a variety of leisure activities. Such wanderings inhibited the development of predictable patterns of local supply. Migratory households could not be sure that enough foodstuffs would be marked just where and when they needed them. But this cannot be the sole reason for the self-sufficiency of large households, since monasteries, which provide the best examples of self-sufficiency, did not migrate. The principal explanation is probably that to transport foodstuffs according to a predictable schedule cost landlords no more

[10] S. P. J. Harvey, 'The Extent and Profitability of Demesne Agriculture in England in the Later Eleventh Century', in Aston and others, eds., *Social Relations and Ideas*, pp. 54–5.

[11] R. A. L. Smith, *Canterbury Cathedral Priory: A Study in Monastic Administration* (Cambridge, 1943), pp. 128–9.

[12] Lennard, *Rural England*, p. 131; Miller, *Abbey and Bishopric*, pp. 36–43, 282.

[13] P. A. Stafford, 'The "Farm of One Night" and the Organization of King Edward's Estates in Domesday', *EcHR*, 2nd ser., 33 (1980), p. 492.

[14] Lennard, *Rural England*, p. 130; Stafford, '"Farm of One Night"', pp. 492–5.

[15] Stafford, '"Farm of One Night"', pp. 495–6

than the effort of selling grain and buying supplies as they needed them. This was particularly the case where demesnes were near the household.

Feudal tenures also illustrate non-monetary forms of tenurial obligation, of which military service is the best known. Military tenures were more than an impersonal contract, and a large part of medieval secular literature is devoted to emphasising the personal obligations which vassals incurred in taking their oaths of fealty and homage. Tenures of this kind were created to support members of the lord's family, or to forge alliances of interest with other families, without any question of the feudal superior calculating a commercial rent. English barons and bishops, and the abbots of the greater monasteries, held far more land than was required to support the military service they owed to the king. They could meet their obligations by subletting a small part of their lands to professional knights while retaining the remainder for their own purposes.[16] For such tenants military service was not an economic rent for their estates. Other fiefs, commonly called serjeanties, were constituted to provide for the officials of great households, and again the value of the services performed was not expected to be an exact equivalent of the property's rentable value. Besides service contracts of these sorts there were numerous forms of render in kind. Between 1146 and 1148 Hugh Tirel sold the manor of Langham (Essex) to Gervase of Cornhill, on the condition that the latter should pay an annual rent of a silver cup. Gervase was one of the wealthiest Londoners of his day, a man who lent money to royalty and who accumulated landed property in London, Essex and Suffolk.[17]

One of the characteristic features of peasant tenures was the payment of obligations in labour or in kind. Throughout most of southern and central England villains owed assistance on the lord's demesne lands at key periods of the agrarian year when labour might otherwise be hard to get – at ploughing, at weeding and at harvesting. And particularly in south-eastern England it was common for tenants to owe a certain number of days' work every week – week work, as it is often called.[18] Domesday Book itself does not go into details of such service, but the *Rectitudines Singularum Personarum* from earlier in the eleventh century shows the prominence of labour services in the rent of the *gebur*.[19] The

---

[16] Harvey, 'Knight and Knight's Fee', pp. 135–44.
[17] *Sir Christopher Hatton's Book of Seals*, ed. L. C. Loyd and D. M. Stenton, Northants. Rec. Soc., XV (Oxford, 1950), no. 84, pp. 58–9.
[18] There is inadequate information from the period 1000–1180 to make any generalisation, but later evidence is summarised in E. A. Kosminsky, *Studies in the Agrarian History of England*, trans. R. Kisch (Oxford, 1956), pp. 191–6.
[19] Maitland, *Domesday Book*, p.37.

twelfth-century surveys of the estates of Caen Abbey, Peterborough Abbey, Shaftesbury Abbey and Burton Abbey show week work in different parts of the kingdom.[20] On Peterborough Abbey estates three days' service were owed from full villain holdings on those manors which owed a delivery of produce to the abbey as well as a money rent. Here the pattern of tenants' services that was to characterise the thirteenth and earlier fourteenth centuries was already established by the 1120s.[21]

Demesne agriculture, and perhaps the cultivation of some larger tenant lands as well, required permanent servants both for managerial roles and to take care of livestock. The labour services of tenants were inappropriate for such continuous and responsible duties. Domesday Book records the existence of 28,235 slaves, who were mostly employed in agricultural work of this kind. Yet slaves were not the most common labour force, as their recorded distribution shows. Slavery was concentrated in the Marches of Wales, the west midlands and the south-west, and was virtually absent from the north and from much of East Anglia. It was mostly found on large estates.[22] The institution was in any case dying out, so that slaves are difficult to find in twelfth-century sources. A commonly adopted alternative arrangement similarly avoided clear-cut dependence on hired labour. Domesday Book itself records men with smallholdings who evidently held their land in return for agriculture work, such as the 759 oxherds, 556 swineherds and 64 smiths.[23] Smallholdings tied to particular employments such as these are more conspicuous in twelfth-century estate surveys.

On this showing a large number of dues from all kinds of tenant were paid without the use of money. These preliminary observations, tentative though they must be, seem to call into question the availability of money as a means of payment. Arguments to this effect are not lacking amongst sociological discussions of the period. 'Eleventh-century England was dominated by the non-commodity enterprise.'[24]

---

[20] *Charters and Custumals of the Abbey of Holy Trinity Caen*, ed. M. Chibnall, BARSEH, new ser., V (London, 1982), pp. 39–74; *Chronicon Petroburgense*, ed. T. Stapleton, Camden Soc., 1st ser., XLVII (London, 1849), pp. 157–66; 'Burton Abbey Surveys', ed. Bridgeman, pp. 212–47; Lennard, *Rural England*, pp. 382–4.

[21] E. King, *Peterborough Abbey, 1086–1310: A Study in the Land Market* (Cambridge, 1973), p. 143.

[22] Darby, *Domesday England*, pp. 76, 337–8; Harvey, 'Extent and Profitability', pp. 56, 60–1, 69.

[23] Darby, *Domesday England*, p. 337.

[24] J. E. Martin, *Feudalism to Capitalism: Peasant and Landlord in English Agrarian Development*, 2nd edn (London, 1986), p. 26.

II

This conclusion is nevertheless unsatisfying. It does not adequately represent the importance of money in the structure of social relationships. Given that there was an extensive field of non-monetary exchanges, the next, and more difficult, step must be to account for the apparent ubiquity of money in the Domesday Survey, in estate records of the twelfth century, and in surviving charters. Money may have been of subordinate importance for the distribution of commodities within and between communities, but it was essential to normal relationships between different ranks of society during what Marc Bloch called the Second Feudal Age. To represent this society as one where monetised relationships were unimportant is to eliminate from the scene one of the ways in which power was typically exercised. The ability to extract cash from dependants was a defining criterion of power.[25] Eleventh-century England was particularly rich in silver in comparison with much of France, to judge both from the number of coins that have survived and from the references to money payments in documentary sources.[26] Money was already necessary in dealings between the king and his subjects and between landlords and tenants, and it became more so in the twelfth century.

In this society it was the king and landlords who were best able to benefit from the greater freedom that monetary wealth had to offer. From the tenth century the word *rice*, the modern English 'rich', was being used to mean 'wealthy' rather than 'powerful', which was its earlier sense.[27] It is a commonplace of contemporary chronicle writing that powerful men of the day were greedy for money and hoarded it. The Conqueror's unflattering obituary in the Peterborough Chronicle starts off with his financial oppression.[28] The reputation of William Rufus was no better; he 'vexed the people with military service and excessive taxes' and he exploited the income of the church.[29] He was aided in his rapacity by Ranulph Flambard who is said to have fleeced the rich, destroyed the poor and stolen other men's inheritances.[30] The great store

25 G. Duby, *The Early Growth of the European Economy: Warriors and Peasants from the Seventh to the Twelfth Century*, trans. H. B. Clarke (London, 1974), pp. 211–32; M. Bloch, *Feudal Society*, trans. L. A. Manyon (London, 1961), pp. 69–71.

26 Sawyer, 'Wealth of England', pp. 156–8.

27 M. R. Godden, 'Money, Power and Morality in Late Anglo-Saxon England', *Anglo-Saxon England*, 19 (1990), pp. 42–54.

28 *The Peterborough Chronicle, 1070–1154*, ed. C. Clark, 2nd edn (Oxford, 1970), p. 13.

29 *Two of the Saxon Chronicles Parallel*, ed. C. Plummer and J. Earle, 2 vols. (Oxford, 1892), I. p. 235.

30 William of Malmesbury, *De Gestis Regum Anglorum*, ed. W. Stubbs, RS, 2 vols. (London, 1887–9), II, p. 369.

of coin left by Henry I at his death was estimated, so William of Malmesbury tells us, at nearly £100,000, and when Stephen laid his hands on this sum it buttressed his political fortunes, at least for a while.[31] The Anglo-Norman kings were doing no more than their leading subjects did. Churchmen were amongst those roundly condemned for extortion. Gerard, archbishop of York (1100–8) was 'expert at emptying the purses of those beneath him, even by improper means'.[32] William de Corbeil, archbishop of Canterbury (1123–36), was 'more greedy in keeping the money he had got than lavish in spending it'.[33] William Cumin, who usurped the see of Durham in 1141 with the support of David I of Scotland, plundered the city and tortured its inhabitants for money.[34]

The fact that some kings and lords are overtly described as extortionate by writers of the period reminds us that condemnation of avarice was explicit in the teaching of the church. But the issues were obscured by the legal vagueness of property rights and by the centrality of lordship in thinking about social obligation. Lordship always implied, at some point, a moral claim to call upon the resources of dependants. Arbitrary exactions like tallages were not conceptually distinguished from other rights of lordship that were fixed but customary (like some money rents), or fixed and contractual (like leasehold rents). The idea that rights of lordship ought to be bound by rules was not commonly expressed in the period 1000–1180. It is only with hindsight, and in some danger of anachronism, that we can separate out payments which were 'regular' from those which were 'arbitrary'. It is easy to show, however, that the payment of regular dues (by any definition) contributed greatly to the flow of cash upwards through the ranks of society.

The crown was a major beneficiary of the monetised sector of the economy. The most remarkable source of royal finance was a national system of taxation, unique in Europe, that depended upon a flow of silver from the heart of the countryside and from all over the kingdom except the far north. This was geld, also known anachronistically as danegeld because its prototype in 991 was a source of tribute money to buy off a Danish invasion. Its status as a regular royal tax dated from

---

[31] William of Malmesbury, *Historia Novella*, ed. and trans. K. R. Potter, OMT (Oxford, 1955), p.17.

[32] William of Newburgh, Historia Rerum Anglicarum, 1, cc. 3, 9: *Chronicles of the Reigns of Stephen, Henry II and Richard I*, ed. R. Howlett, RS, 4 vols. (London, 1884–9), I, p. 28.

[33] *Gesta Stephani*, ed. and trans. K. R. Potter and R. H. C. Davies, 2nd edn, OMT (Oxford 1976), pp. 10–11

[34] *Dialogi Laurentii Dunelmensis Monachi ac Prioris*, ed. J. Raine, Surtees Soc., LXX (Durham, 1880), lines 245–58; pp. 7–8.

1021.[35] Geld may not have been collected between 1051 and 1066, though the evidence for this is disputed.[36] But after the Conquest William I adopted it as a normal royal resource.[37] He received geld from all the burgesses of Stafford each year.[38] The Northamptonshire Geld Roll is a valuable record of the system of collection during the decade after the Conquest, and Domesday Book contains the geld assessment of most of the kingdom in 1086.[39] The survey also supplies evidence of a failed attempt to reassess the basis on which geld was collected.[40]

For purposes of levying this tax the lands of every estate, both the lord's demesne and the holdings of tenants, were assessed in taxable units. In most of the country these were in hides and virgates, but the northern and eastern counties (Yorkshire, Lincolnshire, Nottinghamshire, Derbyshire, Norfolk, Suffolk) were assessed in carucates and bovates, and Kent was assessed in sulungs and yokes. A virgate was usually a quarter of a hide, a bovate was an eighth of a carucate, and a yoke was a quarter of a sulung.[41] The collectors of geld received most of their money from manorial officers, who were responsible both for the geld due from the lord's demesne and from subtenants, though some outlying dependencies of manors were responsible for making their own geld payment. Villains, and some free men as well, paid their dues through the lord's hall. Maitland surmised that they also paid the geld due from the demesne land unless their lord was exempted.[42] Failure to pay geld could result in the offender's having to forfeit his land.[43] In the early eleventh century a single geld could raise more than £20,000, and perhaps much more; this is a debatable issue because of the astoundingly high figures stated in the Anglo-Saxon Chronicle.[44] A levy of £20,000

[35] Stenton, *Anglo-Saxon England*, pp. 371, 406.
[36] Barlow, *Edward the Confessor*, pp. 106n, 155.
[37] A. L. Poole, *From Domesday Book to Magna Carta, 1087–1216*, 2nd edn (Oxford, 1954), p. 418.
[38] *DB*, I, fo. 246a
[39] D. C. Douglas, *William the Conqueror: The Norman Impact upon England* (London, 1964), pp. 299–300.
[40] S. P. J. Harvey, 'Taxation and the Ploughland in Domesday Book', in P. Sawyer, ed., *Domesday Book: A Reassessment* (London, 1985), pp. 86–103.
[41] Maitland, *Domesday Book*, pp. 388, 393–5, 399; P. Vinogradoff, *English Society in the Eleventh Century* (Oxford, 1908), p. 146.
[42] Maitland, *Domesday Book*, pp. 54–5; R. W. Finn, *Domesday Studies: The Liber Exoniensis* (London, 1964), pp. 16–17.
[43] M. K. Lawson, 'The Collection of Danegeld and Heregeld in the Reigns of Aethelred II and Cnut', *EHR*, 99 (1984), pp. 723–5.
[44] J. Gillingham, '"The Most Precious Jewel in the English Crown": Levels of Danegeld and Heregeld in the Early Eleventh Century', *EHR*, 104 (1989), pp. 373–84; J. Gillingham, 'Chronicles and Coins as Evidence for Levels of Taxation in Late Tenth- and Early Eleventh-Century England', *EHR*, 105 (1990), pp. 939–50; M. K. Lawson,

was the equivalent of at least a sixth of the currency in circulation. Once geld was established as a royal tax, it was usually collected at the rate of 2s 0d a hide, though sometimes it was 4s 0d, and William I's exceptional levy of 1084 reached 6s 0d.[45] In the Confessor's reign a levy of 2s 0d a hide could be expected to raise about £5,000 – £6,000 for the crown after allowing for exemptions and the costs of collection.[46] By 1130 numerous additional exemptions had reduced that sum to £2,400.[47]

The earliest surviving royal pipe roll is that of 1129–30. This is the account drawn up in the king's exchequer, where the sheriffs and certain other royal officers were obliged to have their accounts audited and enrolled. The roll records a total income due for the year, excluding sums pardoned, of just under £24,000, of which geld contributed around a tenth. Other sources of the crown's income illustrate to varying degrees the monetisation of rural life. The largest element was from the king's own estates, which accounted for about half his money income. Income from the administration of justice rose under Henry I to the point that in 1129–30 it was almost equal to the year's income from geld.[48] The pipe roll demonstrates that some of the income raised by the eyres of 1129 came from very modest households. For example, the sum of £68 was due from 'little men' amerced because of deficient representation from the hundreds of Sussex.[49]

Even more demanding than royal dues was the regular use of money in payments from tenants to landlords, the sum total of which for the whole kingdom must have exceeded the crown's £24,000 a year. In 1086 the income of Robert, count of Mortain, from 623 manors in Wiltshire, Dorset, Devon and Cornwall was about £1,400. Orderic Vitalis reported that as earl of Surrey, William II de Warenne could expect to receive £1,000 a year.[50] The income of the archbishop of Canterbury ranged between £1,200 and £1,600 in the period 1086–1180. Other bishoprics and the bigger abbeys all collected hundreds of pounds annually.

'"Those Stories Look True": Levels of Taxation in the Reigns of Aethelred II and Cnut', *EHR*, 104 (1989), pp. 385–406; M. K. Lawson, 'Danegeld and Heregeld Once More', *EHR*, 105 (1990), pp. 951–61.

[45] J. A. Green, 'The Last Century of Danegeld', *EHR*, 96 (1981), pp. 252–3; Poole, *From Domesday Book to Magna Carta*, p. 418.

[46] Barlow, *Edward the Confessor*, p. 157   [47] Green, *Government*, p. 69.

[48] *Ibid.*, p. 223.

[49] H. G. Richardson and G. O. Sayles, *The Governance of Medieval England from the Conquest to Magna Carta* (Edinburgh, 1963), p. 179.

[50] A. R. Bridbury, 'Domesday Book: A Reinterpretation', *EHR*, 105 (1990), p. 302; D. Crouch, *The Beaumont Twins: The Roots and Branches of Power in the Twelfth Century* (Cambridge, 1986), p. 178.

Westminster Abbey received some £515 a year in 1086.[51] Even in northern England coinage entered regularly into landlords' incomes. Although there were only two mints in the north, at York and Durham, this was partly a matter of administrative convenience and partly the result of the level and direction of overseas trade. The distribution of mints did not correspond to local variations in the volume of currency in circulation.[52] The massive choir, nave and transepts of Durham Cathedral could not have been built between 1093 and 1133 without a partially monetised local economy. Simeon of Durham mentions the mass of coin that used to pile up from the visitors' offerings at St Cuthbert's tomb.[53] The king was said to be receiving over £300 a year from the bishopric when it was in his custody between 1096 and 1099. When the temporalities of the see came into the king's hands after Ranulph Flambard's death in 1128, their lease, together with receipts from cornage of cattle, raised £539 3s 5d a year, and within the first two years of the vacancy £104 12s 0d on top of that was levied as 'gifts' from knights, thegns and drengs.[54] The survey of the bishopric estates compiled in 1183, though only known from late copies, implies that money was then available in the most remote parts of the estate. The bishop received £1 4s 0d from Consett and 6s 8d from Blanchland. Stanhope, a large manor in central Weardale, remote from town life, rendered in all £8 6s 1d.[55]

Though many manorial leases might be used, as we have seen, to secure a landlord's self-sufficiency in basic provisions, no landlord could be satisfied with such a bare existence. A dignified lifestyle meant more than a well-fed household. Private landlords, like the king, depended upon their estates for cash as well as for produce. Many manors on large, scattered estates were leased to tenants who paid an annual money rent, and many of the values of manors recorded in Domesday Book were probably the monetary sums for which they were actually leased.[56] In 1086 the manors of Ralph de Tosny in South Greenhoe Hundred

[51] F. R. H. Du Boulay, *The Lordship of Canterbury: An Essay on Medieval Society* (London, 1966), p. 243; C. Dyer, *Lords and Peasants in a Changing Society: The Estates of the Bishopric of Worcester, 680–1540* (Cambridge 1980), p. 53; B. F. Harvey, *Westminster Abbey and its Estates in the Middle Ages* (Oxford, 1977), p. 28; Miller, *Abbey and Bishopric*, p. 94.

[52] Astill, 'Towns and Town Hierarchies', pp. 97–100; Brooke, *English Coins*, pp. 83–6; S. Reynolds, *An Introduction to the History of English Medieval Towns* (Oxford, 1977), p. 34.

[53] Simeon of Durham, *Opera Omnia*, ed. T. Arnold, RS, 2 vols. (London, 1882, 1885), I, p. 96.

[54] *Ibid.*, I, p. 135; *PR, 31 Henry I*, pp. 130–2.

[55] *Boldon Buke*, ed. W. Greenwell, Surtees Soc., XXV (Durham, 1852), pp. 29–32.

[56] Lennard, *Rural Society*, pp. 123–8; Harvey, 'Extent and Profitability', pp. 46–52.

(Norf.) together paid £60 by weight instead of the six nights' farm they had paid to Harold before the Conquest. This implies that the properties were leased as a group. This same lease was renegotiated between 1102 and 1126, when Ralph de Tosny II granted all that he had in the soke of Necton, except Pickenham, for £80 a year, to William son of Estangrin 'just as his father Estangrin held in feefarm from my father'.[57] This system was particularly appropriate on the estates of landlords whose households were wholly or partly in Normandy, or whose manors were remote from where the household was likely to reside, or whose estates produced cereals and meat in excess of their household requirements. The king's own estate administration was affected by these consider-ations. On one occasion William I showed that he expected to receive the full Domesday values of his manors, with only some adjustment for the weight of the coinage, implying that he expected to be paid in cash.[58] To the extent that leasing manors for money was a commonplace of eleventh- and twelfth-century estate management, the circulation of money in the countryside is attested as a matter of course.

During the century after Domesday Book, as the internal market for agricultural produce grew and commerce increasingly pervaded every-day life, the importance of money in estate management increased. In the course of the twelfth century the food-farm system was often abandoned altogether. The leases of Canterbury Cathedral Priory manors in the twelfth century show a tendency for the money com-ponent to increase even though the food-farm system survived.[59] The *Dialogus de Scaccario*, written by Richard Fitz Nigel about the years 1177–9, gives a striking if over-schematic account of this development in the administration of the royal demesne. He envisages the royal demesne as characterised by produce rents in the late eleventh century, and then comments that the need for cash to finance his wars overseas persuaded Henry I to substitute money rents for produce rents. Henry was also moved, he says, by the 'crowd of aggrieved farmers', who 'beset the court or (what was even more annoying) the king himself on his progresses ... For they suffered countless inconveniences in having to bring the victuals from their own homes to all parts of England.'[60] This report contains elements of mythologising, but the chronology is essen-tially correct; it was in Henry I's reign that the surviving royal food farms were converted to cash payments.[61]

[57] *DB*, II, fo. 235b; *The Beauchamp Cartulary Charters 1100–1268*, ed. E. Mason, Pipe Roll Soc., LXXXI (London, 1980), no. 356, pp. 202–3.
[58] Harvey, 'Extent and Profitability', p. 51   [59] Lennard, *Rural England*, p. 136.
[60] *Dialogus de Scaccario*, ed. Johnson, pp. 40–1.
[61] M. Chibnall, *Anglo-Norman England, 1066–1166* (Oxford, 1986), pp. 119–20.

Money payments also entered into relations between lords and feudal tenants, even where these were principally defined in terms of personal service. Crown, nobility and churchmen all valued military tenures and sergeanties to some extent as a source of cash. According to one interpretation, the Conqueror's monitoring of such revenues was the main reason for Domesday Book's compilation. The ordering of the Domesday record, county by county and then tenant-in-chief by tenant-in-chief, suggests that the survey was designed to enable the king to exploit his seigniorial rights.[62] He was entitled to receive a payment called relief when a tenant took over a feudal tenement from his father. Though the relief on a knight's fee was commonly lower than the £5 which later became traditional,[63] that from baronial fiefs was often very much larger. In 1129–30 Geoffrey de Mandeville owed £866 13s 4d for land that had been his father's.[64] Besides relief, the king was owed three feudal aids payable in coin, for the knighting of his elder son, the marriage of his elder daughter and the ransoming of his person. He was also entitled to take occasional common aids when in need of additional cash.[65] When the military service due from a military tenure was not performed, either because the tenant was not able to do so, or because the king did not require his service, a money payment called scutage was paid. In the early twelfth century this was either 13s 4d or 20s for each knight's fee.[66] The king's tenants-in-chief similarly assumed the wardship of children of deceased vassals, took reliefs from new tenants, levied feudal aids from time to time and took scutage from those whose military service was not performed in person. Armies never depended wholly upon the performance of military obligations; both the king and his barons were always able to employ hired knights. Tenured knights often performed additional services for pay, so that the difference between feudal obligation and paid employment hardly amounted to two separate systems of recruitment. On these grounds it has been strenuously argued that classical feudalism did not exist in England.[67]

Since Anglo-Norman lords received large amounts of cash from their estates in the normal course of events, and since a lot of military service depended upon paid service, it is hard to believe that military tenures were created because magnates lacked the means to pay money wages. In some cases a landlord gave up demesne land, and probably money

[62] V. H. Galbraith, *Domesday Book: Its Place in Administrative History* (Oxford, 1974), p. 172.

[63] Stenton, *First Century*, pp. 163–4.   [64] Barlow, *William Rufus*, p. 254

[65] Stenton, *First Century*, pp. 173–5.   [66] Richardson and Sayles, *Governance*, p. 87.

[67] C.W. Hollister, *The Military Organization of Norman England* (Oxford, 1965), pp. 171–90; Richardson and Sayles, *Governance*, pp. 62–91.

income, in order to create them.[68] Feudal tenures suited the dignity of a lord and some of his men by implying a degree of permanency in a relationship that both felt to be desirable and meaningful. Although military fiefs and serjeanties illustrate the non-monetary character of many social bonds, they are not good evidence of imperfections in the market economy.

Relations between lords and peasants also involved cash flows that were significant for maintaining aristocratic lifestyles. Although labour services and payment in kind were characteristic of manorial economy, money was paid over by peasant producers in large amounts. Domesday Book itself sometimes records money as an element in customary rents. For example, the villains attached to the royal manor of Leominster (Herefs.) paid altogether £12 4s 8½d a year.[69] Although labour services and payments in produce were often the major component of customary rents, money payments were widespread as an additional component. As the example of Leominster suggests, money rents were not peculiar to the southern and eastern counties. Most of Burton Abbey's tenants in Staffordshire and Derbyshire owed some money in 1114–15, and there were many *censarii* who owed little else. Even in the northern counties some tenants are described as *censores*, meaning that their rents were paid in coin. Domesday Book greatly underrepresents the number of tenants of this type.[70].

Mills were commonly a source of cash. The outstanding example in Domesday Book is the complex of seven mills at Battersea, milling for the London market, which rendered an annual £42 9s 8d or corn of that value.[71] But money payments are also found even in small and remote villages, and are everywhere more normal then renders of grain or flour. A mill belonging to the king's manor of Hope in the Derbyshire Peak District rendered 5s 4d in 1086.[72] On Burton Abbey estates in 1114–15 two mills at Burton itself paid 50s, two at Stretton (Staffs.) were leased for three years for 35s a year and some salmon, and other mills paid smaller money rents at Okeover, Ilam, Leigh and Darlaston (Staffs.) and at Littleover, Willington, Stapenhill and Winshill (Derb.).[73] The capacity of such mills to raise cash is also evident from the frequency with which laymen created annuities out of mill revenues for the benefit

---

[68] Harvey, 'Knight and Knight's Fee', pp. 152–3.   [69] *DB*, I, fo. 180a.
[70] Lennard, *Rural England*, pp. 372–4; D. Roffe, 'Domesday Book and Northern Society: A Reassessment', *EHR*, 105 (1990), p. 332; Sawyer, 'Wealth of England', pp. 154–5; J. F. R. Walmsley, 'The "Censarii" of Burton Abbey and the Domesday Population', *North Staffs. J. of Field Stud.*, 8 (1968), pp. 74–8.
[71] Lennard, *Rural England*, pp. 279, 283.   [72] *DB*, I, fo. 273a.
[73] 'Burton Abbey Rentals', ed. Bridgeman, pp. 214, 218, 224, 228, 233, 237, 240, 243.

of religious houses. In about 1142–3 Roger de Mowbray gave the monks of Byland a rent of 20s from his mill of Coxwold (N.R. Yorks.), standing about a mile away from the abbey.[74] In 1172–7 Roger de Esketot gave the monks of Haughmond 4s a year from his mill of Bitterley (Salop.) between Ludlow and the Clee Hills.[75]

On the estates of the abbey of Caen in the first quarter of the twelfth century the money payments from tenants are recorded in a series of manorial surveys. At Felstead (Essex), a village with an early market, the two mills owed 15s and each market stall owed 2d. Five sokemen owed 17s 7d between them and were responsible for carrying the abbey's income to Winchester in readiness for its shipment to Caen. Each of twenty-four virgaters owed 6d a year in cash in addition to labour services, and four of them owed extra sums amounting to 4s 4d. Each of thirty-nine smallholders owed 2d a head for himself, his wife and any working servant and another 2d for any cow which was in milk. Even a slave was obliged to pay 2d a year if his wife was a free woman and another 2d if he had a free servant. The annual total was at least £3. The annual money payment to the abbey from its manor of Horstead (Norf.) totalled £15 9s 11d from three mills and a fishery, demesne lands and the dues from four sokemen, twenty-three villains and five bordars.[76]

On manors with little or no demesne land, as in much of eastern England, the cash income of manorial lords depended upon sales by peasant farmers. Though much of England was remote from towns, estate officers were not the only ones who marketed produce, and their role was often secondary. At Pucklechurch (Glos.) in 1189 it was the custom that if the abbot of Glastonbury wanted to sell his corn his tenants had to buy it from him or pay a fine of 20s.[77] This implies that tenants were able to dispose of the demesne surplus. The number of carrying services owed by manorial tenants similarly implies that they owned a large proportion of the oxen and horses, and particularly of the latter, that were needed for marketing purposes.[78]

This is illustrated by an example from the twelfth-century charters of the honour of Mowbray. In the 1120s Nigel d'Aubigny committed himself to assist the newly established Augustinian priory of Nostell (W.R. Yorks.) by endowing a dependent cell at Hirst in the Isle of Axholme. This region, lying along the marshy western bank of the River

74 *Charters of the Honour of Mowbray*, ed. Greenway, no. 39, p. 32.
75 *The Cartulary of Haughmond Abbey*, ed. U. Rees (Cardiff, 1985), no. 204, p. 58.
76 *Charters and Custumals of the Abbey of Holy Trinity Caen*, ed. Chibnall, pp. 33–4, 36.
77 *Liber Henrici de Soliaco Abbatis Glastoniensis*, ed. J. E. Jackson, Roxburghe Club (London, 1882), p. 101.
78 J. Langdon, *Horses, Oxen and Technological Innovation: The Use of Draught Animals in English Farming from 1066 to 1500* (Cambridge, 1986), pp. 60–2.

Table 2 *Alms due from Belton to Hirst Priory,*
1148–66

| | Cash | | Malt |
	s	d	sesters
Ketel	5	0	—
Macus	5	0	0.5
Lefwin and Wlmar	5	0	—
Baredchrakin	5	0	—
Gamel s. Norman	3	9	—
Elwin de Humelt	4	1	—
Ernui s. Spratlin	2	2	—
Lefwin Basei	—		2.0
Eilward	—		2.0
William s. Swen	—		2.0
Wlmar Rudda	—		0.5

Source: Charters of the Honour of Mowbray, 1107–1191, ed.
D. E. Greenway, BARSEH, new ser., I (Oxford, 1972),
pp. 17–18, 151–2, 154–5.

Trent in the extreme north-west of Lincolnshire, was at the time wild,
wet and only lightly settled even in its drier portions. This gift was
subsequently increased, sometime between 1138 and 1148, by Roger de
Mowbray. Hirst Priory was now to receive annually a money rent of 30s,
eight sesters of malt and a thousand eels to be paid from his manor of
Belton out of the rent of designated tenants. The manorial officers were
forbidden to interfere with the arrangement. The reeves made themselves responsible for making the payment to the priory as intermediar-
ies, but they did so erratically and carelessly, so that before long a more
explicit plan had to be made. A new document was drawn up, sometime
between 1148 and 1166.[79] Roger de Mowbray's tenants at Belton were
made directly liable for handing over the alms due to the priory, and
their obligations were distributed as in Table 2. The details imply that
even in this outlying part of the country the marketing of produce by
small tenants was an expected feature of village life, and that the lord's
cash receipts depended upon sales by tenants rather than sales of
demesne produce by the farmer of the manor.

On many estates the money component in villagers' rents increased
during the twelfth century as a result of the commutation of services.
This was associated with a contraction of the size of the manorial
demesnes to which the labour services in question had hitherto been

[79] *Charters of the Honour of Mowbray,* ed. Greenway, nos. 15, 215, 219, pp. 17–18, 151–2,
154–5.

attached. By implication it was increasingly normal and necessary for ordinary villagers to obtain money every year and the marketing activities of peasants increased while those of demesne lessees decreased. Former villains owing money rents, commonly called molmen, formed an intermediary group between customary and free tenants.[80] Such tenants were not confined to parts of the kingdom where town life was most developed – they were numerous on Burton Abbey estates in 1114–15 and on those of the bishopric of Durham in 1130.[81] Commutation of services was a response to hunger for cash on the part of the nobility for building, fighting, hoarding and other purposes. The pressure fell on the peasantry chiefly because of the absence of direct seigniorial control over demesne agriculture and the vested interests of manorial lessees. Some of the increase in rents went to lessees rather than to their lords.[82]

Since manor houses collected cash both from demesne produce and from tenants, lords could make money grants to religious houses from their manors. Sometimes the source of a rent was specified, as in Aubrey de Vere's grant to Colne Priory (Essex) of about 1160, which lists rents of £4 2s 0d from four mills in Aldham, Earls Colne and Great Canfield, and two rents totalling 18s 0d from the land of Litlefrid and the land of Aluric the smith in Great Canfield.[83] Other grants were a charge on the whole manor. Between 1124 and 1135 David I of Scotland granted St Margaret's Hospital in Huntingdon a rent of £8 from six virgates in Conington (Hunts.).[84] Early in Stephen's reign the abbey of Bec was given £6 13s 4d a year from Langham (Essex) and £5 a year from East Hendred (Berks.).[85]

The importance of money payments to lords from the urban economies of England is also impressive. At least seventeen boroughs owed £50 or more each year to the crown in 1086, and in some cases the borough farm was in three figures – £300 from London, £100 by weight from York, £100 by tale (that is, 24,000 pennies) from Lincoln.[86] For other landlords, too, one of the chief advantages of seigniorial authority over a town, or part of a town, was the ease with which cash could be

[80] Vinogradoff, *Villainage*, pp. 182–3.
[81] Lennard, *Rural England*, pp. 376–8; G. T. Lapsley, 'Boldon Book', *VCH co. Dur.*, I. p. 281.
[82] Dyer, *Lords and Peasants*, pp. 62, 98; Miller and Hatcher, *Medieval England*, pp. 125, 208–9; J. A. Raftis, *The Estates of Ramsey Abbey: A Study in Economic Growth and Organization*, PIMSST, III (Toronto, 1957), pp. 85–9.
[83] *Cartularium Prioratus de Colne*, ed. J. L. Fisher, Essex Archl. Soc. (Colchester, 1946), no. 36, p. 21.
[84] *RRS*, I, no. 58, p. 165.
[85] *Select Documents of the English Lands of the Abbey of Bec*, ed. M. Chibnall, Camden Soc., 3rd ser., LXXIII (London, 1951), charters 44, 45, pp. 23–4.
[86] Tait, *Medieval English Borough*, p. 184.

taken from its inhabitants through tolls, rents, fines and tallages. A townsman with property could not escape owing money, since money rents were one of the defining characteristics of burgage tenures. Their incidence at an early date can be seen in detail in Canterbury, where the monks of Christ Church Priory probably drew £34 from rents in the years 1163–7; the smallest house, workshop or corner of land owed a penny or two. Renders in kind, in salt or in poultry, were there to be found, but they were barely significant for the monks' income from the city.[87]

III

A strong outflow of cash from the countryside implied a strong inflow as well. It is possible to envisage several different patterns of circulation by which this would have been possible. One, which may be termed seigniorial cash outlay, arose from payments by the king or other lords to villagers, particularly in wages. This requires serious consideration as a possibility in a period when landlords' incomes were much bigger than those of merchants and townsmen. A second, mercantile cash outlay, arose from the bulk purchase of foodstuffs and raw materials in the countryside by merchants who wanted them for export, for sale to a large household or for supplying a distant town. A third, urban cash outlay, was the flow of money into the countryside in exchange for such purchases of food and raw materials by townsmen as were not offset by reciprocal sales of manufactures and services to countrymen. It is difficult to imagine any forms of circulation other than these three that can have been significant for monetary circulation in villages of this period. The distinction between the second and third of these patterns cannot always be clear, but is nevertheless worth making. It corresponds to the difference between inter-regional specialisation and local speciali-sation. Mercantile cash outlay related to commodities whose produc-tion depended upon localised resources but which had a wide poten-tial market: certain sorts of fish or game, high-quality wools, metals, certain sorts of pottery and textile. Urban cash outlay involved com-modities such as grain and meat which were locally supplied all over the kingdom.

The chief form of wage payments in the countryside, as we have seen, was perhaps wages in kind for agricultural work. Cash payments to labourers may have been a significant supplementary source of cash for small households, and rural craftsmen were probably paid partly in cash

[87] W. Urry, *Canterbury under the Angevin Kings* (London, 1967), pp. 34, 226–43.

as well. But as in later times such cash injections into village households depended directly upon the selling of produce to merchants or townsmen, and were therefore dependent upon the mercantile or urban cash flows which we shall be examining shortly. Royal or seigniorial expenditure can only be thought of as having autonomous importance when it was independent of manorial sales. Payment for military service is unlikely to have brought significant sums of cash into villages since recruits were expected to be supported by their local communities.[88] The building of cathedrals, castles and bridges in the early twelfth century was a more prominent feature of seigniorial expenditure than it had been during most of the eleventh, since this was a prevalent form of extravagance. Roger of Salisbury used his fortune to build lavish manor houses on all his estates as well as to fund building at his cathedral.[89] But most large projects of this type had little lasting effect on local patterns of expenditure. On balance it is improbable that seigniorial cash outlay can have had much independent effect in structuring the normal flow of cash into the countryside.

England in the eleventh century already had some of the regional specialisations that are so marked a characteristic of the thirteenth. The principal evidence for mercantile cash outlay in rural areas is provided by sheep farming. In some areas there were as many sheep in 1086 as there were in the thirteenth century.[90] The most impressive examples were to be found on heathlands or on estuary lands and marsh lands. Domesday Book records a demesne flock of 1,037 on the downs at Cranborne (Dors.) and another of 1,300 at West Walton on the fen edge in Norfolk. Flocks of several hundred sheep are recorded in 1086 in other pastoral areas. Twelfth-century documents occasionally record flocks as large or larger. The nuns of Caen had 1,012 sheep at Avening (Glos.) in the southern Costswolds in the early twelfth century, and in 1171 Glastonbury Abbey had 2,500 sheep at Damerham (Hants.).[91] Exports of wool, though smaller than they became in the final decades of the twelfth century, probably earned much of England's silver supply from abroad.[92] But inevitably this type of bulk purchasing was more relevant to the biggest producers than to the smallest. Mercantile cash outlay benefited the famers of demesnes rather than the smaller tenant

[88] Hollister, *Military Organization*, pp. 232–3.
[89] William of Malmesbury, *Historia Novella*, ed. Potter, p. 38.
[90] P. D. A. Harvey, 'The English Trade in Wool and Cloth, 1150–1250: Some Problems and Suggestions', in Istituto Internazionale di Storia Economica 'F. Datini', *Produzione, commercio e consumo dei panni di lana* (Florence, 1976), pp. 372–3; Sawyer, 'Wealth of England', pp. 162–3.
[91] Lennard, *Rural England*, pp. 262–4.
[92] Sawyer, 'Wealth of England', pp. 159–63.

population whose small market surpluses would have been difficult to buy up by informal means.

The case was similar with mineral activities, which brought cash into upland parts of the kingdom whose agricultural land was poor. References to iron in Domesday Book give no impression of the real extent of the industry, though they indicate some activity in the Forest of Dean and the West Riding of Yorkshire.[93] From other sources iron working is known from near Egremont (Cumb.) in the first half of the twelfth century.[94] Domesday Book records lead mines in Derbyshire which paid a money income to the king, and there was probably some silver mining in the shire as well.[95] The lead mines at Alston (Cumb.) were in operation by 1133.[96] The Durham rocks were rich in metals, and the bishop was able to exploit veins of silver on his estates to get 'three great talents' every year.[97] From the early 1130s Carlisle was the scene of a boom in silver mining that reached its peak in the early 1140s, and in the middle of the century new mines were opened up to exploit silver deposits at Blanchland (co. Dur.) and in Weardale.[98] Tin production in Devon and Cornwall was sufficiently large in 1156 for the tax on the output to be farmed by the crown for £16 13s 4d, a sum which indicates an annual output of at least 1,000–1,300 cwt and a workforce of several hundreds of men, some of whom were presumably part-timers.[99].

It remains to examine urban cash outlay, to which historians of this period usually give pride of place. English urban population, by a generous definition of the word urban, may have been as large as one tenth of the total in 1086.[100] Even so, difficulties remain with urban cash outlay as a solution to the problem of rural money supplies. The impact of eleventh-century English towns on the countryside was restricted by their semi-rural character. A town was understood not simply as a collection of streets and houses but as a tract of territory as well, and within this territory much of the land was in the hands of townsmen. Most towns were sufficiently small to have been fed from their own fields, or from fields within the radius of a few miles. It was

[93] Darby, *Domesday England*, pp. 266–7.
[94] A. J. L. Winchester, *Landscape and Society in Medieval Cumbria* (Edinburgh, 1987), p. 120.
[95] Sawyer, 'Wealth of England', p. 159; Darby, *Domesday England*, p. 268.
[96] Winchester, *Landscape and Society*, p. 120.
[97] *Dialogi Laurentii Dunelmensis*, ed. Raine, book 2, lines 109–10, 169–70, pp. 19, 20.
[98] I. S. W. Blanchard, 'Lothian and Beyond: The Economy of the "English Empire" of David I', in R. H. Britnell and J. Hatcher, eds., *Progress and Problems in Medieval England: Essays in Honour of Edward Miller* (Cambridge, 1996), pp. 23–45.
[99] J. Hatcher, *English Tin Production and Trade before 1500* (Oxford, 1973), pp. 152–3 (cf. pp. 84–5).
[100] Sawyer, 'Wealth of England', p. 163; Darby, *Domesday England*, p. 89.

common for some burgesses to own property near the town, to supply themselves with agricultural produce and to sell their surpluses in the market. Some urban cash returned, by this route, to urban purses. Even in London the fields were a matter of economic importance to the inhabitants of the city. When William Fitz Stephen wrote his *Description* of the city in the 1170s, he said that the town fields were like the fat fields of Asia that grow joyful crops and fill barns.[101] If countrymen spent any of the proceeds of their sales in town on manufactures or services, this would further reduce the amount retained in the countryside for payment of rents and taxes. There are even better grounds for doubting the force of urban cash outlay in the many regions where urban life was little developed, notably in the northern counties.

The relative importance of seigniorial cash outlay, mercantile cash outlay and urban cash outlay differed from one village to another, and their contribution to the local money supply varied between regions of the kingdom. Between them these monetary channels must account for the monetary circulation in the countryside between 1000 and 1180. From what we have seen of their limitations it is likely that the flow of cash into the countryside was uneven and often unreliable. In places where opportunities to acquire it were restricted people were presumably stretched to meet monetary obligations. Cash in this period should be thought of not so much a convenient medium of exchange as a commodity to be obtained from particular people by particular transactions. It was available everywhere, but the various aspects of society that we have examined imply that the circulation of money into most country areas was restricted to a few barely reliable channels.

The powerful evidence of money as the medium in which the crown and other landlords exacted their dues, when set against the restricted means for money to enter the countryside, has implications for the role of trade. As we have seen, the fact that the economy was incompletely monetised did not mean that coin was unnecessary for the fulfilment of social obligations. It was used everywhere to meet essential and in part predictable requirements. Every family in the kingdom had some monetised relationships, and for the most part it was custom which dictated which these should be. While in some relationships, such as those between the clergy and their parishioners, the use of money was infrequent, in others it was recurrent and indispensable, as in those between taxpayers and the crown. Other payments were made in a mixed form, as in many relationships between lords and their tenants, and sometimes between neighbours or between employers and

---

[101] John Stow, *A Survey of London*, ed. C. L. Kingsford, 2 vols. (Oxford, 1908), II, p. 220.

employees. Most families sought money to fulfil particular obligations or to satisfy particular needs rather than as the prime object of their labours.

Money payments can be divided into two categories, those representing the exchange of equivalents and those representing an acknowledgement of dependence. This distinction corresponds to that between symmetrical and asymmetrical exchanges, the former being a payment for an equivalent, the latter being a payment with no equivalent. Payments to the crown may at times have brought some reciprocal benefits in the form of better law and order, but taxes in this period were not primarily spent to the advantage of taxpayers. Payments to landlords in part represented rent, and as such brought some benefit to the tenant that he could not otherwise have enjoyed, but many cash payments, such as tallage, were asymmetric impositions that brought no reciprocal advantage to the payer. Payments to the crown and landlords were predominant amongst the various purposes for which rural households needed money. The impetus to put produce on the market was in most instances the need to pay taxes and other levies to social superiors. This means that amongst the rural population of England in the eleventh and twelfth centuries symmetrical transactions were often performed in order to be able to make asymmetrical payments. To that extent, facilities for trade had little relevance to material welfare. In the modern world the chief advantage of money income is the range of choice it permits. For most people in the eleventh and twelfth centuries the advantages of a money income were not as clear-cut.

Along these lines we can understand the monetary compensation for violent crimes which remained characteristic of English law into the twelfth century. Murder could be compensated with a monetary *wer* according to the victim's social rank. There was a set *bot* for wounding each member of the body – £4 for the loss of a right hand, for example, and £4 for loss of testicles, from which it may be calculated that Henry I punished false moneyers to the extent of £8.[102] These monetary penalties were abandoned with the growth of local commerce and the increasing use of money in the later twelfth century. This development seems the very reverse of Durkheim's principle that forms of punishment have been more penal in less advanced economies and more restitutory in advanced ones. It can be understood better if we appreciate that money payments were a substitute for private feuds rather than for public penalties.[103] In addition, we may think of money less as

[102] *Leges Henrici Primi*, ed. and trans. L. J. Downer (Oxford, 1972), cc. 93.24, 93.25, p. 297.
[103] W. S. Holdsworth, *A History of English Law*, II, 3rd edn (London, 1923), p. 45.

a means of exchange and more as a form of tribute, and can add to this that for most people its availability in large quantities was fraught with uncertainty. The sums of money implied in the *Leges Henrici Primi* would have represented an impossible challenge to all but a minority of the population.[104]

---

[104] F. Pollock and F. W. Maitland, *The History of English Law before the Time of Edward I*, 2nd edn, 2 vols. (Cambridge, 1898), II, p. 460.

3 Lordship

Because of the constraints of inequality of opportunity, market relationships determine occupational careers only to a limited extent even in
economies that pay lip-service to the ideals of a market economy. They
were less important in this respect during the period 1000–1180, when
the distribution of wealth was more unequal, the division of labour was
less advanced and prejudices against social mobility were stronger. The
economy was more developed than appears at first sight, but commercial
and contractual behaviour at all levels was affected by the exercise of
seigniorial authority and the accompanying hierocratic value system.

Landlords before the Conquest were subject to few restrictions on
their freedom to dispose of land. They held their estates either as
folkland or as bookland. Folkland was subject to public obligations to
the crown and communal obligations. It lacked the privileged status that
a written charter conferred, and litigation concerning it was normally
conducted in the shire court. Bookland was exempt from public obligations by chartered privilege, and its tenure, if disputed, could be
defended before the king and his council. Bookland could be freely
leased, bequeathed or transmitted to another. But even tenure of
folkland allowed some freedom of alienation, since inheritance customs
were loosely formulated. Property was not irrevocably tied to a particular family. The virtue of endowing new churches in perpetuity had been
universally recognised. So had the appropriateness of rewarding faithful
service with a gift of land. Estates were split up not only between
relations but also to the advantage of bishops, priests, monks and valued
friends.[1]

The land law of the Anglo-Norman period seemed to impose more
restraints on landowners. Procedures for conveying land were encum-

---

[1] V. H. Galbraith, *The Latin Charters of the Anglo-Saxon Period* (Oxford, 1955), pp. 62–
5; H. R. Lyon, *Anglo-Saxon England and the Norman Conquest* (London, 1962), pp.
171–9; P. H. Sawyer, *From Roman Britain to Norman England* (London, 1978), pp.
155–6; Stenton, *Anglo-Saxon England*, pp. 306–8.

bered by the need to take account of the wishes of the lord from whom it was held and to gain his assent to any alienation that might affect his interests.[2] The members of a landowner's family could also restrict his freedom to dispose of property, so that gifts and sales of land had to be carefully secured against possible counter-claims.[3] The Anglo-Norman family expected a more restricted devolution of its property than English families had done before the Conquest. On the other hand, these procedures were not incompatible with the alienation of land. Gifts to relatives other than the principal heir were not unusual.[4] Nor were landlords committed to retaining property in the family, or to preventing the fragmentation of the estates of their feudal tenants. Anglo-Norman society would have looked very different had the heads of families not been free to endow monasteries or to enfeoff knights.[5] No subsequent generations gave away so much so rapidly. In this respect Anglo-Norman families were more like their English precursors than their late twelfth- and thirteenth-century successors.

The recognised procedures for alienating property were compatible with occasional sales. Some deeds of sale survive from the twelfth century, like the charter made towards the end of Stephen's reign recording that for £20 Robert le Waleis had sold all his land in Wrabton and Peasenhall (Suff.) to Sibton Abbey, with the assent of his lord, William the sheriff.[6] Even subinfeudations of property were sometimes in effect sales, as when William Fitz Robert granted two and a half acres from his park in Ubbeston (Suff.) as a fortieth part of a knight's fee in exchange for three bezants, two for himself and one for his wife. When land was subinfeudated, the payment for it might be described as an entry fine (*gersuma*) rather than as a selling price. Some time before 1179 Hugh the chamberlain gave 20s and a rouncey worth 5s as an entry fine for a grove and land to be held from Manasser de Dammartin.[7] But in fact outright sales of land were uncommon, and this was the result of current attitudes to property. Transfers of land or rent were rarely made in cold blood, and usually involved the granter's readjustment of his loyalties to his family, to his feudal superior or to God.

Gifts of land often had a symbolic value whose precise content is

[2] Pollock and Maitland, *History of English Law*, I, pp. 340–4.
[3] D. Postles, 'Securing the Gift in Oxfordshire Charters in the Twelfth and Early Thirteenth Centuries', *Archives*, 84 (1990), pp. 183–91.
[4] J. C. Holt, 'Feudal Society and the Family in Early Medieval England', parts 1 and 3, *TRHS*, 5th ser., 32 (1982), pp. 195–9, and 34 (1984), pp. 8–10.
[5] Pollock and Maitland, *History of English Law*, I, pp. 343–4.
[6] *Sibton Abbey Cartularies and Charters*, ed. P. Brown, 4 vols., Suff. Recs. Soc., Suff. Charters, VII–X (Woodbridge, 1985–8), III, no. 477, p. 7.
[7] *Sir Christopher Hatton's Book of Seals*, ed. Loyd and Stenton, nos. 305, 332, pp. 211, 229–30.

difficult to recover. Feudal contracts rarely restricted the freedom of tenants very greatly. The military tenures introduced after the Conquest tied a tenant for only part of the year. At most a knight of the early twelfth century was likely to owe host duty for two months, castle guard for three months, and occasional attendance at his lord's court. Already by Henry I's reign castle guard was coming to be commuted for cash and there were numerous circumstances in which feudal tenants could free themselves from the performance of host service by funding a substitute or by paying a sum of money instead.[8] The nobility and the knightly class were able to resist being tied down by tenurial obligations, and became more free in this respect in the course of the period.

Yet the social ties within large baronies also created important social groupings, of which the honour court was the most formal expression. The honour court was a better guarantor of justice, for many men, than the king's court. At least some of the greater barons had councils, whose membership included feudal subordinates.[9] The honour was also a patronage structure. Lords often chose their leading household officers – their constables and their stewards – from the ranks of their feudal tenants. Constables were responsible for overseeing the military functions of the barony, and it was only appropriate to choose a fief-holder for the post. The steward was responsible for managing a great lord's household and his estate, and for this work too a feudal dependant was desirable.[10] When William Peverel of Dover gave Gidding (Hunts.) and Daywell (Salop.) to his steward Thurstan in 1121–2 they were to be held by the service of half a knight.[11] The baronial honour could offer a full-time career to those with military or administrative talents. Even clerks were sometimes drawn from the military tenants of a great lord.[12] Some household posts became hereditary, and were associated with the tenure of particular fiefs. A famous example of this was the land belonging to the office of the king's hereditary chamberlains.[13]

It was common for even the more menial officers of large households to be rewarded with land.[14] But the tenurial link was rarely the only one

---

[8] Hollister, *Military Organization*, pp. 89–100, 155, 204–13.

[9] Stenton, *First Century*, pp. 42–6, 74–5.

[10] *Charters of the Honour of Mowbray*, ed. Greenway, pp. lix–lxii; W. E. Wightman, *The Lacy Family in England and Normandy, 1066–1194* (Oxford, 1966), p. 229.

[11] Stenton, *First Century*, p. 274.

[12] *Earldom of Gloucester Charters*, ed. Patterson, p. 10.

[13] *Beauchamp Cartulary Charters*, ed. Mason, no. 167, p. 99; Crouch, *Beaumont Twins*, pp. 143, 146–7; Richardson and Sayles, *Governance*, pp. 422–37.

[14] E.g. *Charters of the Honour of Mowbray*, ed. Greenway, no. 380, p. 244; *Earldom of Gloucester Charters*, ed. Patterson, p. 12, and no. 183, pp. 163–4; Miller, *Abbey and Bishopric*, p. 283; Stenton, *First Century*, pp. 105, 272; Wightman, *Lacy Family*, p. 229.

between a lord and his servants, and in economic terms it was inessential. The king often used his influence to obtain for his servants land on monastic or baronial estates. The range of patronage at the disposal of the crown was outstandingly varied. Some offices, such as that of sheriff, carried their own profits. Clerks were often rewarded with ecclesiastical preferment. The chancellor, and some other clerks, were allowed to charge fees for their services. Laymen might be given leases of manors or escheated lands for a period of years. Others might be granted exemption from geld, or judicial privileges, or privileges in the king's forest. One of the most valuable sources of patronage was the king's feudal superiority. Marriage to the heiress or the widow of one of the king's tenants, or the guardianship of one of the king's wards, could be the making of a new fortune. Where the law was poorly defined the ambiguity was turned to the advantage of the king and his servants, as in the frequent event of disputable baronial inheritances. This remained a source of rich pickings long after 1180.[15] In addition, money wages and other perquisites were given to the king's household staff from the senior officers downwards.[16]

The higher nobility could easily afford to support servants without giving them land, and often did so. Household officers might be rewarded with annuities out of estate income, or free milling for their grain, or exemption from tolls and other seigniorial impositions.[17] The great families had their own ecclesiastical patronage with which to remunerate chaplains and clerks.[18] The feudal link between a lord and his household officers, as between the king and his officers, had symbolic value, because in this society a fief was the most acceptable pledge of loyalty, but it was not the only resource by which power was maintained. Towards the end of the period there were clear signs of the administrative apparatus of large households becoming more elaborate, and less dependent upon feudal tenure even in senior positions, so that the opportunities for careerism were widening.[19]

The exercise of lordship required an administrative apparatus employing a number of different skills. As intermediate lords between the king and his subjects the nobility exercised independent authority over villages and towns. Their rights were often defined as liberties or

[15] Green, *Government*, pp. 171–87; R. V. Turner, 'Exercise of King's Will in Inheritance of Baronies: The Example of King John and William Briwerre', *Albion*, 22 (1990), pp. 383–401.

[16] Constitutio Domus Regis, in *Dialogus de Scaccario*, ed. Johnson, pp. 129–35.

[17] Crouch, *Beaumont Twins*, pp. 147–8.

[18] *Charters of the Honour of Mowbray*, ed. Greenway, pp. lxv–lxvi; *Earldom of Gloucester Charters*, ed. Patterson, pp. 10–13; Crouch, *Beaumont Twins*, pp. 148–55.

[19] *Charters of the Honour of Mowbray*, ed. Greenway, pp. lix, lxii, lxvi–vii.

franchises. They shared in the king's government of his kingdom, and collected money for their private use by exercising powers we should regard as those of a public authority, as when they had jurisdiction in hundred courts.[20] For his armed forces the king also depended to a considerable extent upon the private retinues of his leading barons and churchmen. From the reign of William I onwards barons, bishops and the abbots of major monasteries were responsible for supplying the king with a stipulated amount of military support, or its money equivalent, in time of need, but the amount of service they owed did not restrict the number of knights they might retain from their own resources.[21]

The government of estates in this period, like the government of the realm, was nevertheless remote from any bureaucratic ideal. Lordship was exercised in two superficially distinct ways, through the enforcement of custom or law, and through unpredictable lordly will. If we stress the overriding force of the former, the frequent arbitrariness with which lordship was exercised must be viewed as deviant. But given the amount of arbitrary rule in the Anglo-Norman period we may rather attribute to lordly will a status more parallel to that of law, and define the maintenance of authority by arbitrary means as a normal aristocratic practice. In an age when laws were ambiguous, when a lord's will could decide legal disputes between his men and when personal disloyalty gave a sufficient pretext for disappropriating a tenant, it is hard to distinguish between regular and irregular conduct.[22] This does not imply that lords were arbitrary simply because law and custom were still in their infancy. Custom and law were ill defined in this period not because England was a country still to be tamed by sound education, but because in practice kings and noblemen were not prepared to be bound by an excessive number of rules.

Even the upper clergy and the nobility were exposed to the arbitrary exercise of power. There were no firm rules governing the relations between tenants-in-chief and the crown. Eleventh-century kings at times imposed taxation so heavy that their leading subjects were obliged to sell or mortgage parts of their estates. The richest churches had to dispose of their treasures.[23] There was no supreme judiciary distinct

---

[20] H. M. Cam, *Liberties and Communities in Medieval England: Collected Studies in Local Administration and Topography* (Cambridge, 1933), pp. 64–90.

[21] R. A. Brown, *The Normans and the Norman Conquest*, 2nd edn (Woodbridge, 1985), pp. 188–201.

[22] J. C. Holt, 'Politics and Property in Early Medieval England', in T. H. Aston, ed. *Landlords, Peasants and Politics in Medieval England* (Cambridge, 1987), pp. 71–5; E. King, 'The Tenurial Crisis of the Early Twelfth Century', in *ibid.*, p. 117; S. D. White, 'Succession to Fiefs in Early Medieval England', in *ibid.*, pp. 130–1.

[23] Lawson, 'Collection', pp. 726–31.

from the king's executive authority. Though a king's rule depended upon the co-operation of a sufficient number of his leading subjects, this left the status of individual tenants subject to political changes of fortune. The apparent strength of the nobility was offset by their vulnerability to the king's arbitrariness in dealing with outsiders and dissidents. Even succession to the throne was an issue where might and right complemented each other in the absence of any clear rules.

In any period of the Middle Ages variations in the income of noble families depended more upon their dynastic and political fortunes than upon commercial opportunities and the astuteness with which they were pursued. This was even more so in the eleventh and earlier twelfth centuries than later on. Cnut's victory at the Battle of Ashingdon in 1016 was followed by the transfer of some estates to his followers. Some at least of the property owners with Scandinavian names recorded in Domesday Book were probably the heirs of those who had benefited from this redistribution of wealth.[24] In the west midlands the shires of Worcester, Gloucester and Hereford were subjected to Danish earls, and Danes were settled on the land.[25] In the Fenlands Cnut confiscated the estates of English noble families and gave them to his followers.[26] Fifty years later, the decade following the Battle of Hastings saw the greatest discontinuity in the history of English lay landownership as a result of the defeat of King Harold and subsequent rebellions against the Conqueror. Thurkill of Arden and Colswein of Lincoln were the only English tenants-in-chief of any significance in 1087.[27] After that, the consequences of divided political loyalties were sufficiently disruptive during the years 1087–1107 and 1138–54 for these to be described as periods of tenurial crisis.[28] And all property rights were vulnerable, in times of weak central authority, to the offensive and defensive stratagems of local magnates.

This characteristic of the age is particularly evident in the history of ecclesiastical estates. Just as the major acquisitions by churches came from gifts rather than purchases, so their chief losses came by the violent or subversive misappropriation of their properties rather than through sales. Churchmen were often obliged to protect their estates against intrusions by predators, and to restore them after the ravages of military campaigns. In Huntingdonshire, Yelling, Hemmingford and Sawtrey,

[24] Stenton, *Anglo-Saxon England*, pp. 407–8.
[25] A. Williams, 'Cockles among the Wheat: Danes and English in the West Midlands in the First Half of the Eleventh Century', *MH*, 11 (1986), pp. 2, 11–16.
[26] *Chronicon Abbatiae Ramesiensis*, ed. W. D. Macray, RS (London, 1886), p. 129.
[27] Brown, *Normans*, p. 177.
[28] Holt, 'Politics and Property', pp. 83–4, 103; J. C. Holt, 'A Rejoinder', in Aston, ed., *Landlords, Peasants and Politics*, p. 132.

three of Ramsey Abbey's manors, were described in 1086 as having been seized by the Conqueror's men. Ely Abbey's involvement in resistance to the Conqueror made the monastic estates exceptionally vulnerable, and some of the properties lost in the course of Hereward's revolt were never restored. The Chronicle of Glastonbury Abbey tells how various properties were lost and then painstakingly recovered.[29] Yet ecclesiastical losses were not only the result of invasions from overseas. Both before the Norman Conquest and after, estates were liable to depredation and loss in periods of political unrest or of antagonism between neighbours.[30] Many estates were devastated during the civil wars of Stephen's reign, and some churches lost control of outlying manors.[31] Church property was also vulnerable to long periods of exploitation by the crown during vacancies, notably in the reign of William Rufus.[32]

Apart from political hazards, which might be considered a special case, there were other occasions for arbitrariness in relations between the crown and its tenants, and between other lords and their men. The Normans were used to the language of hereditary right, and this notion was already being applied to their English fiefs by the early twelfth century. Yet it is debatable just how clearly defined expectations governing inheritance were.[33] When Pleines of St Ives (Hunts.) with his two sons gave part of his fee to Ramsey Abbey between 1091 and 1102, the monks received the family into their fraternity, granted that the rest of his fee should be held by hereditary right and allowed him to choose which of his sons should be his heir.[34] Such precision was unusual. For a long time there were neither clear general principles governing the tenure and heritability of property, nor definite contracts relating to each tenure individually. The right to inherit had sometimes to be fought for in defiance of the intentions of the landlord who had created the tenure.[35] Terms of tenure were also a source of disagreement, since for a long time they too were neither standardised nor well recorded. When

[29] John of Glastonbury, *Cronica*, ed. J. P. Carley, BAR, XLVII, 2 vols. (Oxford, 1978), II, pp. 187, 198–201; Miller, *Abbey and Bishopric*, p. 66; S. Raban, *The Estates of Thorney and Crowland: A Study in Medieval Monastic Land Tenure*, University of Cambridge Department of Land Economy, Occasional Paper VII (Cambridge, 1977), pp. 23–4; Raftis, *Estates*, p. 23.

[30] Dyer, *Lords and Peasants*, pp. 17–18; Raftis, *Estates*, pp. 14–15.

[31] R. H. C. Davis, *King Stephen, 1135–1154* (London, 1967), pp. 83–8; E. King, 'The Anarchy of Stephen's Reign', *TRHS*, 5th ser., 34 (1984), pp. 133–8; Raftis, *Estates*, p. 86.

[32] Barlow, *William Rufus*, pp. 234–9.

[33] Holt, 'Politics and Property', pp. 65–114; Holt, 'Rejoinder', pp. 132–40; Holt, 'Feudal Society and the Family', part 2, *TRHS*, 5th ser., 33 (1983), pp. 197–218; King, 'Tenurial Crisis', pp. 115–22; White, 'Succession', pp. 123–32.

[34] *Cartularium Monasterii de Rameseia*, ed. Hart and Lyons, I, p. 129.

[35] Holt, 'Feudal Society', part 2, pp. 193–7.

the monks of Ramsey granted Whiston (Northants.) to Henry Fitz William between 1114 and 1130 they recognised his hereditary right, but they recorded nothing of his terms of tenure except that they should be the same as those his father had had.[36] Feudal tenures created scope for disagreements between lords and tenants. There were recurrent uncertainties and disagreements about the services owed for baronies and knights' fees, as for example concerning the issue of service overseas. There was also scope for disagreement when a tenant died and neither the succession to his land nor the amount of relief to be paid to the lord were governed by recognised rules. The authority of lords was limited by the countervailing power of their subordinates rather than by legal restraints.

II

Relations between landlords and their tenants were distant. The estate organisation prevailing in the eleventh and twelfth centuries required little central direction in detail. As long as the rents came in when they were due, administration could be satisfactorily left to local initiative. The system rested on the assumption that market opportunities and prices would remain similar from year to year and that no great opportunities were being lost by leaving rents fixed for long periods. The disadvantage of such disengagement was that lords were likely to lose control of property to self-seeking dependants. At a time when the difference between hereditary and non-hereditary tenures was difficult to determine, and when terms of tenure were often a matter of verbal agreement, lessees of manors lost nothing by trying to establish a permanent right at the expense of their landlords. The century after the Conquest was one when many large estates had problems in maintaining their rights intact.[37]

Relationships between lords and peasants were regulated by custom much of the time. Had it not been so, regional traditions would not have survived the imposition of a French landowning class. At any given moment custom was largely independent of the will of the current lord, whose interests were often barely distinguishable from those of the peasant family in the regulation of inheritance, or of the village community as a whole in the regulation of land use. Village traditions were not usually written down, and it was often necessary for lords to hold

[36] *Cartularium Monasterii de Rameseia*, ed. Hart and Lyons, I, pp. 136–7.
[37] F. Barlow, *Thomas Becket* (London, 1986), pp. 83–4; Chibnall, *Anglo-Norman England*, pp. 146–7; E. Miller, 'England in the Twelfth and Thirteenth Centuries: An Economic Contrast?', *EcHR*, 2nd ser., 24 (1971), pp. 9–10; Raftis, *Estates*, pp. 85–9.

local inquests to find out what they were. In the absence of maps, for example, custom determined the boundaries of jurisdictions and property rights. Even bookland estates whose bounds were recorded in writing could be perambulated only by those with local knowledge of landmarks and place-names.[38]

Yet custom did not and could not regulate everything. It was sometimes uncertain and sometimes set no precedent. Sometimes, too, custom itself was unfavourable to the security of tenants. On the estates of Abingdon Abbey when Rainald became abbot the rustics were literally tenants-at-will. They could be expelled from their holdings if an attractive alternative tenant presented himself, and after a tenant's death his wife and children had no automatic right to retain his land.[39] When lords or their agents wanted to intervene in local affairs they had plenty of scope for arbitrary action.

As a guide to legal relations between landlords and tenants, the Domesday classification of rural population needs some interpretation. This is, in particular, because of ambiguities concerning eleventh-century concepts of freedom. If a man who is not a slave is free, then some 90 per cent of the tenants recorded in Domesday Book were free men. In reality most villagers were subject to a great deal of enforced dependence. Tenants specifically called 'free men' made up only 5 per cent of the recorded population, and were concentrated in East Anglia. By implication the 84 per cent of the population who were neither slaves nor 'free men' were something less than free. Some members of the large class of sokemen, most of whom were in Lincolnshire and Norfolk, were comparable to free men in their status. But many of them were subject to manorial authority, owing services that would later be classed as servile. Some owed regular week work or other labour services on their lord's demesne and some paid merchet when their daughters married.[40]

The concept of freedom in Anglo-Norman England was associated with the notion of social hierarchy and the exercise of power. A lord was by definition free, but lower down the social scale there were ambiguities and inconsistencies. The *Leges Henrici Primi* describes how a slave should be publicly freed before witnesses. He should be given a spear and sword, and a ritual should be enacted to demonstrate that he could go where he pleased.[41] The conjunction of ideas here includes some-

[38] *Cartularium Monasterii de Rameseia*, ed. Hart and Lyons, I, pp. 160–6.
[39] *Chronicon Monasterii de Abingdon* (A.D. *201–1189*), ed. J. Stevenson, RS, 2 vols. (London, 1858), II, p. 25.
[40] G. Platts, *Land and People in Medieval Lincolnshire*, Hist. of Lincs., IV (Lincoln, 1985), pp. 61–2, 66–8.
[41] *Leges Henrici Primi*, ed. Downer, c. 78.1, pp. 242–?

thing akin to our notion of freedom, namely freedom of movement. The sword and spear, symbols of the warrior, show that freedom was status-linked. Freedom was a relative matter, whose different grades corresponded to different degrees of social status and to corresponding degrees of freedom to do different things. One clause of Magna Carta uses the expression 'free man' to describe a lord with rights of jurisdiction.[42] Villains, who made up the majority of the recorded population in 1086 in most regions of England, came low down in the order of social rank and were only free relative to slaves.

By derivation the word villain (Latin *villanus*) means 'villager'. For the Domesday commissioners the villain had a particular social status, since he was distinguished from the slave, cotter, bordar, free man, sokeman and other categories of countrymen. But the word was not a technical one in ordinary administrative usage. It was used more broadly in other contexts. About 1100 St Helen's church in Worcester owned tithes in Northwick (Worcs.) from the lands of the bishop's tenants, both free men and villains, implying that villains included all who were not free.[43] Other terms used to describe the ordinary villager were 'rustic' (Latin *rusticus*) and 'native' (Latin *nativus*). The latter term came easily to a Norman aristocracy as a general term for their English dependants. It implied that a tenant's current status was determined by birth.[44]

Even though manorial lords may have intervened little in the management of their lands, villagers of the Anglo-Norman period were vulnerable to the arbitrary exercise of seigniorial authority when knights or monks were to be provided for. When we find that one of the wealthiest knights enfeoffed by Abingdon Abbey occurs holding five hides of villain land, we can relate it to the vulnerability of tenures on this estate before the early twelfth century. How could so much land – the equivalent of a medium-sized manor – have become available except by the expropriation of sitting tenants? There are many examples in the Domesday survey of knights who held blocks of villain land.[45] Some service holdings of other types were created out of villain land in the twelfth century. Between 1109 and 1131 Bishop Harvey of Ely gave Alfric his reeve at Fen Ditton (Cambs.) three virgates and three houses that had been held before him by three rustics called Hunning, Wulnoth

[42] Magna Carta (1215), c. 34: *Select Charters*, ed. Stubbs, p. 297.
[43] *The Cartulary of Worcester Cathedral Priory (Register 1)*, ed. R. R. Darlington, Pipe Roll Soc., LXXVI (London, 1968), no. 53, pp. 32–3.
[44] R. H. Hilton, 'Freedom and Villeinage in England', in *idem*, ed., *Peasants, Knights and Heretics*, p. 179.
[45] Harvey, 'Knight and Knight's Fee', p. 153; Harvey, 'Domesday England', p. 117.

and Aedwin Cacabred.[46] Even where there was no question of dispossessing tenants, custom offered them little protection against arbitrary financial pressure. Norman lords were more successful at squeezing cash out of tenants than in raising their incomes from demesne agriculture.[47]

The effects of William I's creation of the New Forest were exaggerated in contemporary report, but the most reliable assessment of the evidence suggests that about 500 families were evicted from the land. For those who remained the imposition of forest law was a source of inconvenience and loss. At Downton (Wilts.), on the periphery of the area directly affected, two hides of the bishop of Winchester's land were lying waste 'on account of the king's forest'.[48]

There are numerous examples of high-handedness associated with the endowment of new monastic houses. Cistercian monks in a number of instances created granges, or space around their monasteries, by evicting villagers from their homes and their land, though it was normal for those evicted to be compensated with new land or money. The modern village of Old Byland (N.R. Yorks.) stands where inhabitants of an even older Byland were resettled between 1142 and 1147 so that their original homes could be cleared away by Byland Abbey. The Domesday village of *Melse* (E.R. Yorks.) was destroyed between 1151 and 1154 to make way for Meaux Abbey's North Grange. In these instances, as in most others, we do not know the terms on which tenants were compelled to move.[49] In one instance we do. When Revesby Abbey (Lincs.) was founded in 1142 the rustics of three villages were given the alternatives of accepting other land from the founder, William de Roumare, or going away freely with all their chattels.[50] The implication here is that to allow a tenant to depart with his chattels was akin to giving him freedom. We know of one rather later example of depopulation where the tenants fought back, though unsuccessfully. At Accrington (Lancs.) about 1200 a new grange built by Kirkstall Abbey was destroyed by those evicted from the site.[51]

Another hazard for twelfth-century villagers was the arbitrary usur-

[46] Miller, *Abbey and Bishopric*, p. 284.
[47] Harvey, 'Extent and Profitability', pp. 59–60, 65, 70–1.
[48] F. H. Baring, 'The Making of the New Forest', *EHR*, 16 (1901), p. 431; 'Wiltshire Geld Rolls', ed. R. R. Darlington, *VCH Wilts.*, II, p. 208.
[49] D. Knowles, *The Monastic Order in England: A History of its Development from the Times of Saint Dunstan to the Fourth Lateran Council, 943–1216* (Cambridge, 1950), pp. 350–1; R. A. Donkin, 'Settlement and Depopulation on Cistercian Estates during the 12th and 13th Centuries, especially in Yorkshire', *BIHR*, 33 (1960), pp. 143–9, 152–6.
[50] *Facsimiles of Early Charters from Northamptonshire Collections*, ed. F. M. Stenton, Northants. Rec. Soc., IV (Northampton, 1930), no. 1, frontispiece and pp. 1–7.
[51] Donkin, 'Settlement and Depopulation', p. 152.

pation of power by lords and officials. Even in peacetime William II's courtiers, we are told, fattened themselves on the livelihood of the country people and ate up their substance.[52] The absence of the king overseas could provide opportunity for a sheriff to exact money illegally even from royal villains and burgesses,[53] and kings were abroad a lot of the time. For many households periods of civil war meant an increase in arbitrary local authority as lords tightened their grip on the available resources of men and money. In Stephen's reign conflict between members of the nobility frequently implied the imposition of additional pressure on village families to extract resources for the war. The Peterborough Chronicle describes how those who had usurped power imposed arbitrary taxes on the villages. Wartime exactions from churches were in the first instance chiefly at the expense of tenants living on ecclesiastical estates.[54] The oppression of tenants in wartime might be thought an exceptional case, but internal warfare was not as exceptional between 1066 and 1180 as it became in later centuries. And much of the harassment of tenants for which we have evidence was imposed by those who were supposedly maintaining the peace.

A villager's money and movable goods were ultimately at his lord's disposal. The bishop of Winchester's tenants were apparently obliged to buy grain from his demesnes at Taunton (Som.), Downton (Wilts.), Adderbury (Oxon.) and Witney (Oxon.) to save him the costs of marketing it.[55] Lords could tallage their tenants as heavily as they pleased.[56] A wealthy tenant from Middleton-in-Teesdale (co. Dur.) was so oppressed by his lord that he left his land and fled northwards to Lindisfarne.[57] The villager's right to own personal property had been compromised by the devolution of regalian rights to landlords since the tenth century. *Toll* originated as a public due on exchanges. But since the reign of King Edgar grants of toll, like grants of sake and soke, had become a commonplace, so that many lords had the right to exact a levy on certain types of transaction within their estates. Grain sales were apparently unrestricted, but lords taxed sales of livestock and ale by their tenants.[58] This invited the interpretation that the tenant required

---

[52] William of Malmesbury, *De Gestibus Regum Anglorum*, ed. Stubbs, II, p. 369.

[53] Green, *Government*, p. 122.

[54] *Peterborough Chronicle*, ed. Clark, p. 56; King, 'Anarchy', pp. 133–9.

[55] D. L. Farmer, 'Marketing the Produce of the Countryside, 1200–1500', in *AHEW*, III, p. 360.

[56] Vinogradoff, *Villainage*, p. 163; P. R. Hyams, *King, Lords, and Peasants in Medieval England: The Common Law of Villeinage in the Twelfth and Thirteenth Centuries* (Oxford, 1980), p. 192.

[57] Hyams, *King, Lords, and Peasants*, p. 225.

[58] N. S. B. Gras, *The Evolution of the English Corn Market from the Twelfth to the Eighteenth Century* (Cambridge, Mass., 1915), pp. 18–19.

a licence to sell, or that the villain owed the lord compensation for selling. Precariousness of ownership was also implied in the lord's entitlement to a heriot when a villain died. The vulnerability of tenants' property was a publicly accepted feature of their status. The author of the *Dialogus* tells us that within living memory villains had been considered liable for their lord's debts. He recollected a time when if a tenant-in-chief failed to pay scutage, not only his own goods but those of his knights and villains had been sold to satisfy the king. In this context the word villain seems to embrace men who on other occasions might be called free.[59]

The people most vulnerable to the arbitrary decisions of their lords – slaves, villains, bordars, cotters – were tied to their lord's demesne. This was true by definition in the case of slaves, who were full-time farm-workers.[60] Even when slaves were provided with smallholdings, and were called by some other name, the lord's control over them was not immediately relaxed. Many bordars and cotters of Domesday Book were probably little different from slaves in the degree to which their labour was commanded by the lord of the manor to which they were attached. But a large proportion of other villagers owed labour services on their lord's land, and this compromised their personal freedom. Labour services were not merely a form of rent appropriate to an incompletely monetised society. There was no geographical relationship between labour services and difficulties of money supply. In northern England, where monetary circulation cannot have been of above average volume or velocity, there was less demesne agriculture and less labour rent than in the south.[61] This implies that labour services were not merely a feature of commercial backwardness. Some labour services rested on a whole village community rather than on specified properties, as if they were a tribute due to lordship rather than a rent for land. At Higney (Hunts.) in the twelfth century every man in the village whatever his tenure or social status was obliged, if required, to perform three ploughings in winter, three ploughings in Lent and a day's threshing or reaping in August.[62] Labour services were a sign of subordination.[63] Powerful lords were able to exact levels of labour service higher than was normal in the region where their estates lay. For example, the labour services due from the bishop of Durham's estates in 1183 were unchar-

[59] *Dialogus de Scaccario*, ed. Johnson, p. 112.
[60] Harvey, 'Domesday England', p. 65; Harvey, 'Extent and Profitability', pp. 60–2; Postan, *Famulus*, pp. 7–11.
[61] J. E. A. Jolliffe, 'Northumbrian Institutions', *EHR*, 161 (1926), pp. 2, 4–5; E. Miller, 'Social Structure: Northern England', in *AHEW*, II, pp. 692–3.
[62] Raftis, *Estates*, pp. 124–5.   [63] Hilton, 'Freedom and Villeinage', pp. 182–4.

acteristic of the north-east as a whole. The two days a week of labour service due to Peterborough Abbey from its Lincolnshire manors were heavy by local standards.[64]

Manorial control over the labour of villains was compounded by restrictions upon their mobility.[65] The eleventh-century *gebur* normally suffered this disability: he was 'tied to the land no less than to the lord'.[66] Maitland doubted whether the same was true of the Domesday villain.[67] Yet this degree of bondage is evident, for some villains at least, in two writs from the late eleventh century. When William Rufus gave instructions for Deorman's manor of Pete in West Mersea (Essex) to be given to his own steward Eudo, he instructed that all those who had left the manor after Deorman's death should be compelled to return with their possessions.[68] By another writ in favour of Ramsey Abbey he required his sheriffs and ministers to return fugitive villains to their estates wherever possible.[69] These writs take back this aspect of serfdom to within a decade or two of the Domesday Survey. Similar writs were obtained from Henry I by Ranulph Flambard, bishop of Durham; two from the years 1101–3 ordered back all men who had left the bishopric unjustifiably since the death of the previous bishop in 1096, and a third from sometime between 1114 and 1118 reclaimed men who had fled with their goods. There is a similarly early group of writs in favour of Abingdon Abbey, and one for the bishop of Norwich.[70] Most writs of this sort are from ecclesiastical archives,[71] but there are some in favour of laymen. Early in his reign Henry II ordered that his chamberlain William Mauduit should have all his fugitives and 'natives' who had fled since Henry I's death, together with their possessions, wherever they might be found.[72] Writs of this kind are sufficiently widely scattered from the early twelfth century to suggest that restrictions on personal freedom were a normal feature of village life. The terms in which they are expressed show that they are not concerned with a

[64] W. E. Kapelle, *The Norman Conquest of the North: The Region and its Transformation, 1000–1135* (London, 1979), pp. 181–9; King, *Peterborough Abbey*, p. 143n.

[65] J. Hatcher, 'English Serfdom and Villeinage: Towards a Reassessment', in Aston, ed., *Landlords, Peasants and Politics*, pp. 274–7.

[66] Aston, 'Origins', p. 14.   [67] Maitland, *Domesday Book*, pp. 51–2.

[68] R. C. Van Caenegem, *Royal Writs in England from the Conquest to Glanvill: Studies in the Early History of the Common Law*, Selden Soc., LXXVII (London, 1959), no. 66, p. 445; *The Early Charters of Essex: The Norman Period*, ed. C. Hart, Leicester Department of Local History, Occasional Papers, XI (Leicester, 1957), pp. 15, 43–5.

[69] Van Caenegem, *Royal Writs*, no. 105, pp. 467–8.

[70] *Ibid.*, nos. 106–12, pp. 468–72. The Durham writs are discussed in Hyams, *King, Lords, and Peasants*, pp. 226–7.

[71] Van Caenegem, *Royal Writs*, nos. 113–24, pp. 472–7.

[72] *Beauchamp Cartulary Charters*, ed. Mason, no. 173, pp. 101–2; cf. no. 179, p. 104.

narrow sector of the population. Natives and rustics were, after all, the major part of the population of England.[73] The general point is explicit in the archaising *Leis Willelmi*, a compilation of the third quarter of the twelfth century, which states that 'villains may not depart from their lands'.[74] Richard Fitz Nigel, writing in the later 1170s, used the term *ascriptitius* as a synonym for *villanus*, and he was explicit that such a man was not free to depart from his place without his lord's consent.[75]

A charter granted by Henry I to the burgesses of Newcastle upon Tyne left no doubt that the ordinary countryman – 'rustic' in one version, 'villain' in another – was restricted in his movements. If a migrant had lived in the borough for a year and a day, he was to be allowed to remain unless the length of his stay was governed by some prior agreement with his lord. A similar meaning may be read into privileges conceded to the boroughs of Lincoln and Nottingham in 1157. One version of the Newcastle charter makes the migrant's security depend upon tenure of land in the borough, implying that wealthier migrants were more worthy of freedom, and more likely to achieve it, than poorer ones.[76]

Gifts and sales of villagers were common. Adelelm's gift of a villain called Alfric de Fen with all his effects to Eye Priory (Suff.) was confirmed sometime between 1107 and 1125 by the future King Stephen.[77] Gilbert Foliot as bishop of Hereford (1148–63) granted his 'native' William, the son of his vintner at Ledbury (Herefs.), to the abbey of St Peter's in Gloucester,[78] and subsequently as bishop of London he bought Walter Cheriessone, his sons, daughters and all their descendants from Walter son of Robert.[79] About 1150 the priory of Stoke by Clare (Suff.) paid 7s for Aubrey son of Simon and all his progeny,[80] and the Templars paid 23s 4d and 300 masses for Leofwine Ledmeham with his offspring and all his chattels.[81] About 1174–81 William of Windsor gave Godwin the carpenter with his brothers Ranulph and Richard and all their offspring to the dean and chapter of

[73] Hyams, *King, Lords, and Peasants*, p. 239.
[74] Richardson and Sayles, *Law and Legislation*, pp. 141–2.
[75] *Dialogus de Scaccario*, ed. Johnson, p. 53.   [76] *BBC, 1042–1216*, pp. 103–4.
[77] Stenton, *First Century*, p. 265.
[78] *Historia et Cartularium Monasterii Sancti Petri Gloucestriae*, ed. W. H. Hart, RS, 3 vols. (London, 1863–7), II, no. 427, p. 4.
[79] *Early Charters of the Cathedral Church of St. Paul, London*, ed. M. Gibbs, Camden Soc., 3rd ser., LVIII (London, 1939), no. 267, pp. 210–11.
[80] *Stoke by Clare Cartulary*, ed. C. Harper-Bill and R. Mortimer, 3 vols., Suff. Recs. Soc., Suff. Charters, IV–VI (Woodbridge, 1982–4), II, no. 249, p. 188.
[81] *The Cartulary of the Knights of St. John of Jerusalem in England, Secunda Camera: Essex*, ed. M. Gervers, BARSEH, new ser., VI (London, 1982), no. 355, pp. 206–7.

St Paul's in London.[82] Some villains were sold with both their land and their offspring.[83] Other texts imply that villains might be moved to new land. When Hugh de Chesney gave Boycott (Bucks.) to Cirencester Abbey in the 1140s he also gave them four villains whom he had brought and established on the land there, Hubert, Thowi, Edred and Hamelin, together with all their chattels.[84]

The ordinary villager's right to dispose of his land was heavily circumscribed. Before the Conquest there had been free men and some sokemen who could sell their land without licence.[85] By implication, many of these men were still free to sell land in 1086, like the thirty-five free men of Kelsale (Suff.).[86] But such freedom did not extend to all so-called free men,[87] and even those who were attached to lords by commendation could not necessarily sell their land without permission.[88] Sokemen were commonly more restricted than free men in this respect.[89] Most of St Edmund's many sokemen in Suffolk, we are told, could not give or sell their land without the abbot's consent.[90] The Domesday commissioners raised the question of freedom to sell only with free men and sokemen, and their silence with respect to villains and bordars imply that there was no question of these more subordinate ranks selling tenements without permission.

Domesday Book records the exceptional freedom amongst the peasants of the northern Danelaw. From the following hundred years a small group of charters demonstrates that certain sections of the peasantry in this part of the country could give or sell land. About 1160, Robert son of Ecgmund of Coates gave a strip of land three perches wide to Kirkstead Abbey (Lincs.). His gift had the consent of his son-in-law, so the latter's seal was added to the charter as confirmation, and it was witnessed by the incumbent of Gayton le Wold and three others.[91]

---

[82] *Early Charters of the Cathedral Church of St. Paul*, ed. Gibbs, nos. 256, 257, pp. 202–3.
[83] *Cartulary of the Knights of St. John*, ed. Gervers, nos. 281, 282, 377, pp. 173–4, 217–18.
[84] *The Cartulary of Cirencester Abbey, Gloucestershire*, ed. C. D. Ross and M. Devine, 3 vols. (Oxford, 1964–77), II, no. 646, p. 545.
[85] *DB*, II, fos. 356b (free man at Risby), 357b (two free men at Saxham), and more examples on fos. 358a–70a. For sokemen who could sell their land, see fos. 291a (Onehouse), 358b (Herringswell), 359b (Preston), 360a (Bures).
[86] *DB*, II, fo. 330b.
[87] E.g. *DB*, II, fos. 309b (free man in Finningham), 349b (free man at Brockley), 357b (free man at Saxham), 358a (free man at Brockley), 362a (three free men at Bradfield), 367b (free man at Little Fakenham), 368a (free man at Bedingfield), 370b–371a (free woman at Oakley).
[88] Maitland, *Domesday Book*, p. 73.
[89] *DB*, II, fos. 317a (five sokemen in Hollesley), 318b (Godric, a sokeman in 'Halgestou').
[90] *DB*, II, fos. 356b–60a, 364a–5a, 368b.
[91] F. M. Stenton, *The Free Peasantry of the Northern Danelaw*, 2nd edn (Oxford, 1969), no. 181, pp. 93, 150–1.

Amongst the village populations elsewhere in England, however, manorial constraints were tighter than they had been before 1066. Some free men lost part of their independence by being added to manors, and many free men and sokemen were replaced or depressed in status.[92] Large numbers lost their independence through the Conqueror's ravaging of the north in the winter of 1069.[93] Surviving free peasants often required seigniorial ratification of their land grants, and this was true in Lincolnshire as well as in the rest of the country.[94]

Even from Lincolnshire transfers of land out of peasant hands were rare before 1180. The buying and selling of land was nowhere characteristic of village life. If it was unusual even for unmanorialised peasants to give or sell their property, it is improbable that more subordinate classes of countrymen would do so. In the early thirteenth century the buying and selling of land amongst the peasantry was probably confined to East Anglia and Kent.[95] Seigniorial controls were not the only constraint affecting the land market, since family interests were also restrictive. Yet particularly in the case of customary tenants the interests of landlords were probably a dominant factor in preventing the splitting up of family holdings.

The strength of the constraints on the buying and selling of tenant land is evident from the standardised form of some peasant tenements. In much of England, villain land was measured in virgate units, often containing as many as thirty acres. In the north holdings were commonly measured in bovates of about fifteen acres. In East Anglia the standard unit was the *tenementum* usually holding twelve acres. Such regular holdings imply ordered creation by a superior authority,[96] and their persistence suggests the continuing exercise of sanctions to thwart the giving and selling of land. Standard units are everywhere in evidence in Domesday Book. In Middlesex almost all villains had either virgates or half virgates.[97] Again, in the estate surveys of Henry I's reign from the abbeys of Burton, Peterborough and Shaftesbury, standard holdings were the normal units of villain tenure. Even when not all villains were equal, the differences were expressed in the division and multiplication of hides and virgates rather in their uncontrolled fragmentation.[98] Surveying the estates of Holy Trinity, Caen, was greatly simplified by

---

[92] Maitland, *Domesday Book*, pp. 61–5.   [93] Kapelle, *Norman Conquest*, pp. 176–90.
[94] Stenton, *Free Peasantry*, nos. 55, 65, pp. 48, 51–2, 147–8.
[95] P. R. Hyams, 'The Origins of a Peasant Land Market in England', *EcHR*, 2nd ser., 23 (1970), pp. 24–5.
[96] Aston, 'Origins', p. 13; P. D. A. Harvey, 'Introduction', in *idem*, ed., *The Peasant Land Market in Medieval England* (Oxford, 1984), pp. 12–19.
[97] Lennard, *Rural England*, p. 341.   [98] *Ibid.*, p. 358.

the existence of virgate units. At Felstead (Essex) there were twenty-five virgates, of which one was used to maintain the pig herd and the other twenty-four all owed identical labour services and money rents. At both Minchinhampton and Avening (Glos.) seventeen virgates owed labour services and a smaller number, nine and a half and eight and a half respectively, owed money.[99] On many estates, like those of the bishopric of Durham surveyed in 1183 or those of the abbot of Glastonbury, surveyed in 1189, intact standard holdings were still numerous at the end of the period we are discussing.[100]

The Norman Conquest probably had a detrimental effect on the freedom of the peasantry in most parts of the country. The new landlords had no liberal inhibitions about the rights of the natives, and in many respects – the destruction of property, the redefinition of tenures, the imposition of forest law – the late eleventh century was a time of increased uncertainty and seigniorial pressure. But though the institution of villainage survived through the twelfth century with little change there were some developments which ultimately meant greater freedom. Chief of these was the increasing number of money-paying tenants as a result of the commutation of labour services. This development cannot be narrowly related to a particular region or to a particular period, which implies that it was not the consequence of temporary or local disruptions or disasters. On the estates of Burton Abbey and the bishopric of Durham there had been considerable commutation by the end of Henry I's reign. On Ramsey and Glastonbury estates there was some commutation as early as this, but it came mostly in the reigns of Stephen and Henry II. On the bishop of Worcester's manors commutation is mostly associated with the years 1125–60.[101]

There can be little doubt that this change was a response to initiative from above rather than from below. A new passion for monumental architecture was one of the main causes of the hunger for cash on the part of ecclesiastical landlords. Amongst the laity military requirements of manpower and castle-building were another recurrent source of financial pressure. Such tastes could only be indulged by exploiting landed estates in new ways. Manorial lessees, too, were more willing for villagers to grow produce, market it and supply them with cash than to

[99] *Charters and Custumals of the Abbey of Holy Trinity Caen*, ed. Chibnall, pp. 33–8.

[100] *Boldon Buke*, ed. Greenwell, pp. 1–42; *Liber Henrici de Soliaco*, ed. Jackson, pp. 1–142.

[101] Dyer, *Lords and Peasants*, p. 98; M. M. Postan, *Essays on Medieval Agriculture and General Problems of the Medieval Economy* (Cambridge, 1973), pp. 93–100, 257–9; Raftis, *Estates*, pp. 86–9.

take the responsibility or do the work themselves. To respond to their new rent requirements villagers had to produce more if they were not to consume less, and their standards of living may have suffered. Yet tenants who owed money rents were considered more free than those who owed labour services.[102] They made gains in personal status, the significance of which increased with the passage of time. So, with reservations, the movement towards commutation may be regarded as one in the direction of greater peasant freedom.

Another development of peripheral relevance to the legal condition of villagers was the multiplication of rent-paying lands that resulted from the reduction in the size of demesnes and the exploitation of new arable lands created from forest and marsh. Weak central control sometimes meant that such developments were illicit, and brought no service at all to the landlord. Such were the new tenures recorded about 1170 on the estates of the abbey of Caen, which were subsequently held for money rents.[103] But even where lords retained control of their estates the amount of land in the hands of peasant farmers increased, and any additional rent was usually in money rather than labour. At Cranfield (Beds.) in Henry II's reign there were about 350 acres of tenants' land carved from woodland 'which never owed labour services', and there had perhaps been earlier deforestation of the same kind in Pegsdon and Crawley (Beds.).[104] Land of this sort is to be found in the earliest charters by which peasants granted land to religious houses.[105]

The commercialisation of rural life did indirectly, therefore, have the effect of expanding the area of land which was held for money rent. By implication it had some effect in increasing the amount of freedom, in this rather narrow sense. But the changes did not transform the character of villainage in England, and did nothing to weaken the power of landlords over large numbers of villagers who continued to hold lands on traditional terms. Tenants who still held land by customary terms in Henry II's reign were subject to the same impositions as those of the earlier twelfth century, and learned lawyers were soon to bracket them with the slaves of Roman Law because of their legal disabilities.[106]

[102] Hilton, 'Freedom and Villeinage', pp. 182–4.
[103] *Charters and Custumals of the Abbey of Holy Trinity Caen*, ed. Chibnall, pp. 44–5, 55–6, 100–1, 105–31.
[104] *Cartularium Monasterii de Rameseia*, ed. Hart and Lyons, III, pp. 302–4; Raftis, *Estates*, p. 72.
[105] H. E. Hallam, *Settlement and Society: A Study of the Early Agrarian History of South Lincolnshire* (Cambridge, 1965), pp. 6, 9, 20.
[106] Vinogradoff, *Villainage*, pp. 47–8.

III

Towns were not much freer from seigniorial exactions than the countryside, even where their administration was separated off from that of the
county in which they lay. They were subject to royal or seigniorial
jurisdiction and were periodically fleeced by their lords by way of aids
and tallages.[107] In 1086 the main English royal boroughs were governed
by a sheriff in the joint interests of the crown and local earl.[108] The
crown used its rights over county towns as a source of political
patronage, and by implication they were subject to predatory lordship.
Some were alienated from the crown to become part of noble estates and
others were leased to sheriffs or to barons.[109] In Stephen's reign, for
example, the Beaumont twins Robert and Waleran had lordship over a
number of towns. From 1118 Robert was lord of Leicester by virtue of
the earldom created for his father in about 1107. Waleran acquired
rights over Worcester in 1136 as a royal favour, and had his rights
augmented about 1138 as Stephen's new earl of Worcester. Their
younger brother Hugh was given Bedford about the same time, though
he was unable to hold his position.[110] Other towns were firmly attached
to lay or ecclesiastical lordship from their origins. Such was the new
market town of Hungerford (Berks.) that belonged to the estate of
Robert Beaumont.[111] Other representative examples are the monastic
towns of Bury St Edmunds (Suff.), Durham, Evesham (Worcs.), Peterborough (Northants.) and Tewkesbury (Glos.),[112] or the seigniorial
boroughs founded by baronial castles such as Chepstow (Monms.),
Ludlow (Salop.) and Richmond (N.R. Yorks.).[113]

In towns, perhaps more than in the countryside, the Norman Conquest entailed considerable contempt for established property rights.
Castle-building overrode responsibility to local residents, as the burgesses had already discovered by 1086 at Wallingford (Berks.), Cambridge, Gloucester, Huntingdon, Lincoln, Stamford (Lincs.), Norwich
(Norf.), Shrewsbury (Salop.), Warwick and York. In Lincoln the
destruction was equivalent to about a seventh of the city houses. One of

[107] Pollock and Maitland, *History of English Law*, I, pp. 295–6; Maitland, *Domesday Book*,
198–9; Reynolds, *Introduction*, pp. 43, 95–6.
[108] Maitland, *Domesday Book*, pp. 204–6.
[109] Tait, *Medieval English Borough*, pp. 154–6.
[110] Crouch, *Beaumont Twins*, pp. 8, 30, 39–41, 178; Davis, *King Stephen*, pp. 134–7.
[111] Beresford, *New Towns*, p. 395; Crouch, *Beaumont Twins*, pp. 178.
[112] Bonney, *Lordship*, pp. 41–9; R. H. Hilton, *Class Conflict and the Crisis of Feudalism:
Essays in Medieval Social History* (London, 1985), pp. 187–93; E. King, 'The Town of
Peterborough in the Early Middle Ages', *Northants. Past and Present*, 6 (1980), pp. 187–
95; Lobel, *Borough of Bury St. Edmund's*, pp. 16–59.
[113] Beresford, *New Towns*, pp. 481, 518, 559; Wightman, *Lacy Family*, p. 204.

the seven wards of the city of York was cleared to make way for two castles, one on either side of the River Ouse. In Canterbury houses were cleared away to make a new residence for the archbishop. There were waste properties in many other towns for reasons which are not divulged by the Domesday commissioners.[114] Later examples of Norman high-handedness with tenants who got in the way of favoured projects are not unknown. Palace Green in Durham was cleared of tenants by Ranulph Flambard in the early twelfth century.[115]

Urban self-government of any sort was rare between 1000 and 1180. Urban freedom had no unambiguous meaning. The expression might relate to the free tenure of individual burgage properties, as in the liberties granted to Tewkesbury by the earls of Gloucester. Alternatively the burgesses of royal boroughs might be free in the sense that they were subject to the jurisdiction of no lord but the king, as in charters granted to Lincoln and Nottingham in 1157. Or the idea of burghal freedom might be vague and relative, as in Henry I's grant that a youth living with his father in Newcastle upon Tyne should have the same liberty as his father.[116] By the end of Henry I's reign modest concessions of self-government had been made to Lincoln and, temporarily, to London.[117] Some seigniorial boroughs gained a similar independence, as when the earl of Richmond granted the fee farm of Richmond to the burgesses in the period 1136–45.[118] But it was not until the last two decades of the twelfth century that there were many royal and seigniorial grants of this kind.

However, the townsman, like the tenant of free land, was able to buy and sell his urban property as he pleased. And mercantile occupations depended upon the individual burgess being free to travel with his goods and to have recognised property rights over them. Henry I's charter to Newcastle upon Tyne links the two liberties together: 'Any burgess may sell his land and go where he will, unless the land is in dispute.' Even in seigniorial boroughs these rights were an essential feature of borough status.[119] There were numerous crudities in the laws and customs by which a townsman's freedom was defined. A merchant away from home might have to answer for the debts of a fellow townsman, and in this event was likely to have his goods distrained and confiscated.[120] A burgess's liberty was in some respects restricted to his own town. His

[114] Darby, *Domesday England*, pp. 364–8; Hill, *Medieval Lincoln*, pp. 53–5.
[115] *VCH co. Dur.*, III, p. 11.   [116] *BBC, 1042–1216*, pp. 101–4.
[117] Hill, *Medieval Lincoln*, p. 184; Tait, *Medieval English Borough*, pp. 157–61.
[118] *BBC, 1042–1216*, p. 220.   [119] *Ibid.*, pp. 64–6.
[120] E. Lipson, *The Economic History of England, I: The Middle Ages*, 12th edn (London, 1959), pp. 287–9.

rights were severely reduced when he went to trade elsewhere and confronted the monopolistic privileges of other merchant gilds.[121] Nevertheless, in the few narrow respects we have described, the multiplication of towns and the increase in the total number of townsmen in the eleventh and twelfth centuries represented an expanding area of personal freedom.

IV

One explanation for the continuing high degree of seigniorial control over the villagers of England between 1050 and 1180 is that tenants were hard to come by and labour was difficult to obtain for demesne husbandry, so that it was in the interests of lords to tie countrymen to the land in various ways. But there are difficulties with this argument. Scarcity of tenants and labourers might be expected to lead to an improvement in their lot unless they were subjected to a ruthlessly efficient use of force. So the ability of lords to maintain their authority under these circumstances would imply willingness to pursue corporate rather than individual interests, since it would have benefited individuals to compete for tenants and labourers and to lure men away from their neighbours. It would also imply a surprisingly comprehensive efficacy of seigniorial control at a time when the policing apparatus at the disposal of manorial lords was of a very local and ramshackle kind. Apart from occasionally granting licenses to authorise sheriffs to return fugitive neifs to particular estates, English kings did nothing to facilitate tying villains to the soil. It is not obvious, in other words, why lords should have had any success in imposing their will on their tenants.

To explain the authority of landlords something other than their willpower is wanted. The best explanation has nothing to do with shortages of tenants and labourers, since these were not characteristic of the period as a whole. In most of the country, for most of the period between 1000 and 1180, there is more likely to have been slow growth of population than a problem of underpopulation.[122] In relationship to the cultivated demesne and the available tenant land the size of the English population remained high enough, through most of the twelfth century at least, to supply the labour that was wanted and to place pressure on resources. In villages where the demand for new land to cultivate arose from the inhabitants themselves, even quite large areas of newly cleared land were taken up by families already resident. In short, the intake of

---

[121] *BBC, 1042–1216*, pp. 207–14.
[122] Miller, 'England in the Twelfth and Thirteenth Centuries', pp. 5–7.

new land was the result of pressure of demand rather than the result of increased availability of land.

This had implications for the situation of families that had inherited land, whatever their legal status. To run away from a medieval village was not difficult. Landlords were never very successful in getting determined fugitives to return. But if demand for land was high, to abandon a family virgate or half virgate was to exchange the likelihood of economic security for the certainty of insecurity. Even if he was sore pressed by the exactions of his lord, custom would normally ensure that a hereditary tenant could feed his family from year to year. To abandon that hereditary right was to commit himself to a life dependent upon wage-earning. It would not be easy to accumulate a new holding of free land at a time when earnings were low, and when the market in peasant land was little developed. Escaping from villainage did not have the optimistic prospects it acquired in the late Middle Ages, and was attempted only under severe provocation from an unacceptable lord. Natives could be tied to the land only because they were so little tempted by liberty.

Part 2

1180–1330

4   Markets and rules

I

The growth of English commerce accelerated in the last decades of the twelfth century. This was partly because of an expansion of England's overseas trade in wool, cloth and tin.[1] It was also a response to an increase of population, the development of new agricultural land from forest and marsh and an increase in the number of landless people looking for work.[2] More families became dependent upon the market economy, sometimes having to find customers for their services from many different villages.[3] Many depended upon casual work. At the same time, expansion of demand encouraged the development of some specialised occupations. Such were those of the sieve-makers of the Forest of Dean (Glos.) recorded in 1255, of Robert the grease-seller who had a shop at Chipping Hill in Witham (Essex) about the year 1258, of John the salt-carter who committed some misdemeanour at the fair of Stratton St Margaret (Wilts.) in 1279 and of William the locksmith who was taxed in Alnwick (Northumb.) in 1296.[4]

Not surprisingly, occupational specialisation was more advanced in towns than in villages, though even there craftsmen and their families were not always uniquely dependent on a single skill. Bristol's tallage list of 1312 and subsidy list of 1327 record between them ninety-two different occupational surnames. In Winchester we know of seventy-two different crafts from the period 1300–39. In Durham fifty-three trades

---

[1] E. M. Carus-Wilson, *Medieval Merchant Venturers*, 2nd edn (London, 1967), pp. 211–14; Harvey, 'English Trade in Wool and Cloth', pp. 371–2, 374–5; Hatcher, *English Tin Production*, pp. 19–25; R. Van Uytven, 'Cloth in Medieval Literature of Western Europe', in N. B. Harte and K. G. Ponting, eds., *Cloth and Clothing in Medieval Europe* (London, 1983), pp. 161–2.

[2] Miller and Hatcher, *Medieval England*, pp. 28–53.

[3] J. A. Raftis, *Warboys: Two Hundred Years in the Life of an English Medieval Village*, PIMSST, XXIX (Toronto, 1974), p. 210.

[4] *CPR, 1247–58*, p. 450; PRO, D.L.43/14/1, m.9; *The Rolls of Highworth Hundred, 1275–1287*, ed. B. Farr, Wilts. Rec. Soc., 2 vols., XXI, XXII (Devizes, 1966–8), I, p. 128; *The Northumberland Lay Subsidy Roll of 1296*, ed. C. M. Fraser, Soc. of Antiquaries of Newcastle upon Tyne, Rec. Ser., I (Newcastle upon Tyne, 1968), p. 96.

and crafts are known from thirteenth-century deeds. In the small borough of Halesowen (Worcs.) there were some thirty-five different non-agrarian specialisations, about half in manufacturing and the other half in the victualling trades.[5] Even in the smallest market towns the tenants of plots, shops or stalls were commonly specialised craftsmen or tradesmen.[6]

Dependence on commerce encouraged innovation. The best known instances are in the manufacture of woollen cloth. Though the finer branches of clothmaking suffered in the latter part of the period from foreign competition, a growing sector of the industry made cheaper fabrics for sale in the home market. Local specialisation created new commercial lines, like Colchester russets. The finishing of cheaper cloths was transformed after 1180 by the diffusion of water-powered fulling mills.[7] From the late twelfth century growing demand for ironware permitted both regional specialisation and occupational diversification. It seems likely that iron was being applied to a wider range of uses. In York the market for armour and cutlery was great enough to allow workers to specialise in these manufactures, even though there was no rigid demarkation between skills.[8] The leather industry, which already by 1180 included numerous different products, was further subdivided between different crafts. In London the cordwainers, skinners and curriers were all distinct interests by the 1260s.[9]

One instance of occupational specialisation is particularly well known to us because its products survive in large quantities. An increasing volume of record-keeping from the late twelfth century permitted the expansion and diversification of clerical employment, even in the countryside. From about 1270 manorial accounts were often prepared locally. The accounts of Cuxham (Oxon.) between 1302 and 1321 were written by Robert the clerk, the resident son of a former miller. Then for many years from 1323 they were the work of Robert ate Elme of Chalgrove, a village adjoining Cuxham.[10] Such employment required instruction in

5   D. Keene, *Survey of Medieval Winchester*, 2 vols. (Oxford, 1985), I, pp. 352–65, 368; S. A. C. Penn, 'Social and Economic Aspects of Fourteenth-Century Bristol', PhD thesis, Birmingham, 1989, p. 73; Bonney, *Lordship*, p. 269; Hilton, *Class Conflict*, p. 201.

6   Britnell, 'Making of Witham', pp. 17–18; J. H. Clapham, 'A Thirteenth-Century Market Town: Linton, Cambs.', *Cambridge Hist. J.*, 4 (1933), pp. 198–9.

7   Carus-Wilson, *Medieval Merchant Venturers*, pp. 183–210, 213–14; *English Historical Documents, III: 1189–1327*, ed. H. Rothwell (London, 1975), p. 881.

8   J. L. Bolton, *The Medieval English Economy, 1150–1500* (London, 1980), pp. 163–4; H. Swanson, *Medieval Artisans: An Urban Class in Late Medieval England* (Oxford, 1989), p. 68.

9   Swanson, *Medieval Artisans*, pp. 53–5; G. A. Williams, *Medieval London: From Commune to Capital*, 2nd edn (London, 1970), pp. 183–6.

10 *Manorial Records of Cuxham, Oxfordshire, circa 1200–1359*, ed. P. D. A. Harvey, HMC, JP23 (London, 1976), pp. 16–17, 29, 37–9.

basic clerical Latin. There were schoolmasters in Battle (Suss.) by 1253. At Witham (Essex) about 1262 there was a 'land of the Scolhus'. Chelmsford (Essex) had a schoolmaster in 1327. Lincolnshire had at least eleven grammar schools by the second quarter of the fourteenth century.[11]

Illegitimate activities were as much affected by new opportunities as legitimate ones. Plundering those on their way to or from market was nothing new, but opportunities multiplied as the number of traders increased.[12] Edward I's Statute of Winchester (1285), recognising this problem, provided that verges of highways were to be kept broad and clear.[13] Many criminals chose market places or fairgrounds for their operations, risking the terrible revenge that might ensue if they were caught. On 22 February 1275 Thomas Kek of Oxford was pilloried, mutilated and killed after being caught in Shefford market (Beds.) with 7s in a purse belonging to Walter Sparuwe of Meppershall. A thief found with 8d in his possession at the time of the fair of Stratton St Margaret (Wilts.) in 1277 was immediately hanged.[14]

Changes in occupational practice were so numerous in thirteenth-century society as to transform it. The capacity of people to find out new ways to earn a living explains why changing relationships between population and natural resources are of limited relevance.

II

The institutional framework for commercial activity was also transformed. Landlords were encouraged to found new markets and fairs. From Norfolk alone sixty-two new licences are known from the thirteenth century.[15] Some apparently new markets may have had an earlier form. Often, however, a market charter authorised a new enterprise.

---

[11] PRO, D.L.43/14/1, m.1; E. Searle, *Lordship and Community: Battle Abbey and its Banlieu, 1066–1538*, PIMSST, XXVI (Toronto, 1974), p. 426n; H. Grieve, *The Sleepers and the Shadows. Chelmsford: A Town, its People and its Past, I: The Medieval and Tudor Story*, Essex RO Publication c (Chelmsford, 1988), p. 25; Platts, *Land and People*, p. 265.

[12] E.g. *Bedfordshire Coroners' Rolls*, ed. R. F. Hunnisett, Beds. Histl. Rec. Soc., XLI (Streatley, 1961), pp. 1, 66.

[13] *SR*, I, p. 97.

[14] *Bedfordshire Coroners' Rolls*, ed. Hunnisett, pp. 79–80; *Rolls of Highworth Hundred*, ed. Farr, I, p. 69.

[15] R. H. Britnell, 'The Proliferation of Markets in England, 1200–1349', *EcHR*, 2nd ser., 34 (1981), p. 210. For counties other than Norfolk, see Britnell, 'Essex Markets', pp. 15–21; B. Coates, 'The Origin and Distribution of Markets and Fairs in Medieval Derbyshire', *Derb. Archl. J.*, 85 (1965), pp. 92–111; A. Kondo, 'The Rise of Market Economy in Rural Wiltshire, 1086–1461', *Stud. in Market Hist.*, 5 (1988), pp. 35–53; D. Postles, 'Markets for Rural Produce in Oxfordshire, 1086–1350', *MH*, 12 (1987), pp. 14–26; D. M. Palliser and A. C. Pinnock, 'The Markets of Medieval Staffordshire',

Shortly after the abbot of Waltham Holy Cross was granted a market and fair at Epping Heath (Essex) in 1253 the king instructed the steward of the Forest of Essex to allow him to take timber for making stalls, shops and other things. Within two years of a similar grant for Elsdon (Northumb.), William de Umfraville complained in 1283 that a pillory and tumbrel set up as appurtenances to his market and fair had been demolished by his enemies.[16] Important new markets and fairs continued to be created until the 1250s. After that new foundations, though still numerous, made less impact because the countryside was already well provided with trading outlets.[17]

New markets varied in the scale on which they were conceived and in their potential for growth. Many were intended only for local transactions between small households.[18] However, landlords often established plots for artisans and tradesmen even in small market places.[19] Some modest settlements were described as boroughs because they had burgage tenure. For example, South Zeal (Devon), founded about 1264, had twenty burgesses in 1315.[20] Such places required small but regular supplies of food and raw materials, and their proliferation increased the range of opportunities for local farmers. New towns were even more numerous between 1180 and 1310 than during the period of equivalent length between 1050 and 1180.[21] Some new foundations became large and important. One of the best known is Stratford-upon-Avon (Warws.), set out with building plots in 1196 by the bishop of Worcester, after he had received a market charter from Richard I.[22] Other distinguished new towns were Birmingham (from 1166), Hull (1160–93), Portsmouth (1194), Leeds (1207), Liverpool (also 1207) and Salisbury (1219).[23]

Bulky foodstuffs did not travel far overland because of the high costs

North Staffs. J. of Field Stud., 11 (1971), pp. 49–63; Platts, *Land and People*, pp. 296–304; M. Reed, 'Markets and Fairs in Medieval Buckinghamshire', *Recs. of Bucks.*, 20 (1975–8), pp. 563–85; G. H. Tupling, 'An Alphabetical List of Markets and Fairs of Lancashire Recorded before the Year 1701', *Trans. of the Lancs. and Ches. Antiquarian Soc.*, 51 (1936), pp. 86–110; T. Unwin, 'Rural Marketing in Medieval Nottinghamshire', *J. of Histl. Geography*, 7 (1981), pp. 231–51.

[16] *CChR*, I, p. 427, and *CR Henry III, 1251–3*, p. 472 (Epping Heath); *CChR*, II, p. 257 and *CPR, 1281–92*, p. 65 (Elsdon).
[17] Britnell, 'Proliferation', pp. 218–19.   [18] *Ibid.*, pp. 213–18.
[19] R. H. Britnell, 'Burghal Characteristics of Market Towns in Medieval England', *Dur. Univ. J.*, new ser., 42 (1981), pp. 147–51.
[20] Beresford, *New Towns*, p. 426.   [21] *Ibid.*, p. 330.
[22] E. M. Carus-Wilson, 'The First Half-Century of the Borough of Stratford-upon-Avon', *EcHR*, 2nd ser., 18 (1965), pp. 49–50.
[23] Beresford, *New Towns*, pp. 447–9, 461, 506–8, 515–16, 524; R. Holt, *The Early History of the Town of Birmingham*, Dugdale Soc., Occasional Paper XXX (Oxford, 1985), pp. 3–7.

of road transport.[24] But the majority of rural markets had no communications except by road. The legal treatise called Bracton compiled in the years 1235–59 defines 'neighbouring' by arguing that six and two-third miles would normally be a limit for such short-haul marketing; if the journey was any longer the seller would not get to market and back in a single day.[25] This understates the distance people were prepared to travel to good markets in decent weather. Wheat and barley from Kennet (Cambs.) was sold ten miles away in Bury St Edmunds in the early 1270s. Grain from Holywell, in the suburbs of Oxford, was sometimes carted fourteen miles to be sold in Wallingford or twenty-six miles to be sold in Reading.[26] But it was unusual for manorial officers to send produce to market by land as far as this. Grain from the manors of Longbridge Deverill and Monkton Deverill (Wilts.) was mostly traded within ten miles. More distant markets were patronised only in years of high prices, and even then twenty miles was the outside limit.[27] The resources at the disposal of manorial officers often favoured small sales over relatively short distances rather than a large consignment sent a long way.[28]

Good communications helped determine where new markets could be profitable. Some markets grew as collecting points for larger centres and handled exceptional quantities of produce. Such, for example, were Henley-on-Thames (Oxon.), Ware (Herts.) and Stratford (Essex), all of which were sources of supply for London. Henley was the main market for Merton College's manor of Cuxham (Oxon.).[29] In the Severn valley Bewdley (Worcs.) and Tewkesbury (Glos.) were collecting points for Bristol's provisions, and so were some nearer markets inland, like Sherston (Wilts.), Hawkesbury (Glos.) and Marshfield (Glos.).[30] Some new towns acquired a reputation for manufacturing specialisations.[31] Well-situated roadside communities developed as staging posts, like

[24] C. Dyer, 'The Consumer and the Market in the Later Middle Ages', *EcHR*, 2nd ser., 42 (1989), p. 309.

[25] Bracton, fo. 235: *Bracton De Legibus et Consuetudinibus Anglie*, ed. G. E. Woodbine, 4 vols. (New Haven, 1915–42), III, pp. 198–9.

[26] Farmer, 'Marketing', p. 364; D. Postles, 'The Perception of Profit before the Leasing of Demesnes', *AHR*, 34 (1986), pp. 16–17.

[27] D. L. Farmer, 'Two Wiltshire Manors and their Markets', *AHR*, 37 (1989), pp. 5–7.

[28] P. D. A. Harvey, *A Medieval Oxfordshire Village: Cuxham, 1240 to 1400* (Oxford, 1965), p. 103; Farmer, 'Two Wiltshire Manors', p. 3.

[29] K. McDonnell, *Medieval London Suburbs* (Chichester, 1978), pp. 69–70, 73; Harvey, *Medieval Oxfordshire Village*, pp. 54n, 103; Williams, *Medieval London*, pp. 162–4.

[30] Farmer, 'Marketing', p. 335; Penn, 'Fourteenth-Century Bristol', p. 56.

[31] R. H. Hilton, *A Medieval Society: The West Midlands at the End of the Thirteenth Century*, 2nd edn (Cambridge, 1983), p. 199; D. Dymond and A. Betterton, *Lavenham: 700 Years of Textile Making* (Woodbridge, 1982), pp. 3–5; K. C. Newton, *Thaxted in the Fourteenth Century* (Chelmsford, 1960), pp. 20–2.

Stratford-upon-Avon (Warws.) and Stony Stratford (Bucks.), whose names record the Roman streets passing through them.[32] The success of new markets often diverted trade from older ones, as when Salisbury (Wilts.) grew at the expense of Old Sarum, Chelmsford (Essex) at the expense of Writtle, Witham (Essex) at the expense of Chipping Hill, or Abingdon and Reading (Berks.) at the expense of Wallingford.[33]

The expansion of the marketing system was accompanied by the triumph of legal formality. The crown finally established effective control over outlying parts of the kingdom. The earliest known royal market charters for northern England, apart from that for Norton (co. Dur.), are those granted by John in 1200 and 1201 for markets and fairs at Hartlepool (co. Dur.), Morpeth (Northumb.), Bridlington (E.R. Yorks.), Brough (Westmld.) and at an unnamed place in Cumberland. A three-day fair at Darlington (co. Dur.) was also licensed that year.[34] The king's ministers and justices also formulated clear opinions concerning the rights of existing institutions. From 1200 new foundations were authorised only conditionally; they might be suppressed by process of law if they were damaging to neighbouring markets and fairs.[35] This in turn created new problems of definition. What was a market, and what did 'neighbouring' mean? The courts became more suspicious of trading assemblies that were less than formal markets and fairs. Landlords were under pressure either to forbid irregular assemblies on their estates or to develop them more formally. The market at Moretonhampstead (Devon), licensed in 1207, reconstituted an irregular earlier assembly.[36]

Another break with the past arose from the more rigid attitudes of churchmen towards trading assemblies that coincided with church services or met in churchyards. A number of markets were moved to unconsecrated ground.[37] Hostility to Sunday trading was fomented by Eustace, abbot of St Germer de Fly in the diocese of Beauvais (Normandy), who preached at several places in southern England in 1200 and returned in 1201 to spread his mission to the north. Twenty-

[32] Carus-Wilson, 'First Half-Century', p. 46; R. H. Britnell, 'The Origins of Stony Stratford', *Recs. of Bucks.*, 20 (1977), pp. 451–3.

[33] Beresford, *New Towns*, pp. 436–7, 506–8; K. C. Newton, *The Manor of Writtle* (Chichester, 1970), pp. 16–18; Grieve, *Sleepers and the Shadows*, pp. 14–15; D. M. Stenton, *English Society in the Early Middle Ages (1066–1307)*, 4th edn (Harmondsworth, 1965), p. 189; Harvey, *Medieval Oxfordshire Village*, pp. 102–3.

[34] *PR, 2 John*, pp. 5, 111, 244; *PR, 3 John*, pp. 249–50, 252, 257.

[35] R. H. Britnell, 'King John's Early Grants of Markets and Fairs', *EHR*, 94 (1979), pp. 90–6.

[36] Salzman, 'Legal Status', p. 208.

[37] *PR, 2 John*, p. 248; *RLC*, I, pp. 536b, 547b; L. F. Salzman, *English Trade in the Middle Ages* (Oxford, 1931), pp. 124–5.

two markets are known to have changed to a weekday during John's reign, and many more during the following decades.[38] No similar objection was made to the holding of fairs on saints' days – every day was some festival – so an association between fairs and liturgical festivities remained the usual practice.

III

While new centres were being founded, older ones grew, chiefly by the influx of people from the countryside. The romance of *Havelock the Dane* tells how Grim the fisherman, the legendary founder of Grimsby (Lincs.), used to sell fish in Lincoln, helped by his five children and Havelock his protégé, until there came a famine so severe that he could not feed his family. So Havelock went to Lincoln, and being of heroic disposition succeeded in getting a job.[39] The story epitomises the plight of thousands who drifted into towns in search of work. In the process the difference in size between the smallest English towns and the largest increased. While the rural base of the urban hierarchy was broadening, the summit was rising.

Market towns usually had a central market place. We know of markets that were moved because they were inconveniently situated; in 1203, for example, the prior of Coventry shifted his market to a position nearer the earl of Chester's castle.[40] The degree of centralisation varied according to the volume of local trade and the amount of available space. In larger towns, as in Lincoln and Oxford, the central market was divided into different sections, and some trades were located elsewhere.[41] Even some small towns, like Stratford-upon-Avon, had a fragmented marketing structure, so that different trades occupied different streets. Wholesale trades, particularly in livestock, were separated off from the main area. Stratford had different market areas for cattle, sheep and pigs. Canterbury's cattle market was in Dover Street outside the eastern wall of the city. A paved cattle market is recorded in

---

[38] *RLC*, I, pp. 355b bis, 361a, 366b bis, 368b ter, 381b bis, 385a, 386a, 387a, 399b, 412b, 515a, 543a bis, 561a, 599b, 622a, 647b; J. L. Cate, 'The English Mission of Eustace de Flay (1200–1)', in *Etudes d'histoire dédiées à la mémoire de Henri Pirenne par ses anciens élèves* (Brussels, 1937), pp. 73–6, 88.

[39] *The Lay of Havelock the Dane*, ed. W. W. Skeat and K. Sisam, 2nd edn (Oxford, 1915), lines 824–926, pp. 31–4.

[40] *PR, 5 John*, p. 38; *The Early Records of Medieval Coventry*, ed. P. R. Coss, BARSEH, new ser., IX (London, 1986), p. xxx.

[41] Hill, *Medieval Lincoln*, pp. 153–4; O. Ogle, 'The Oxford Market', in M. Burrows, ed., *Collectanea II*, Oxford Hist. Soc., XVI (Oxford, 1890), pp. 13–27, 119–20, map facing p. 13.

Leicester from 1341.[42] Cattle markets must have been a prominent feature of those provincial towns like Bolton or Pontefract that served a wide area.[43]

Provincial towns often depended on water-borne transport for the supply of foodstuffs, and had hithes as well as central markets. Of the three largest provincial cities, Bristol had quays on the Avon and the Frome, York on the Ouse and Norwich on the Wensum.[44] The main coastal ports – Southampton, Great Yarmouth, Lynn, Newcastle upon Tyne – had quays where purchases could be made from moored vessels or from adjacent markets.[45] Cities beside estuaries made similar provision. Cargoes for Exeter were traded at Topsham, four miles away. Colchester had wharves on the Colne estuary at Hythe, about a mile from the town centre. An extreme case of dependence upon water transport was the new town of Hull, which had no access by road in the late thirteenth century.[46] Waterfront markets supplied goods wholesale to local retailers, though householders were usually given the chance to bypass middlemen if they arrived in good time. The same pattern repeated itself in towns far inland if they were beside navigable rivers. By 1300 there was a string of specialised hithes in Cambridge, including a corn hithe.[47] The Severn was a major line of communication for the supply of west-country towns.[48] Waterways permitted areas of supply to be larger and more varied than they would otherwise have been. Outside the London area it was nevertheless unusual to find specialised cornmongers. The size of the long-distance trade in normal years was too small to justify such a commitment of trading capital.[49]

---

[42] Carus-Wilson, 'First Half-Century', pp. 61–2; M. K. Dale, 'The City of Leicester: Social and Economic History', *VCH Leics.*, IV, p. 46; Urry, *Canterbury*, p. 203.

[43] G. H. Tupling, *The Economic History of Rossendale*, Chetham Soc., new ser., 86 (Manchester, 1927), p. 25.

[44] E. Miller, 'Medieval York', in *VCH Yorks.: The City of York*, p. 97; J. W. Sherborne, *The Port of Bristol in the Middle Ages* (Bristol, 1965), pp. 4–7; *The Records of the City of Norwich*, ed. W. Hudson and J. C. Tingey, 2 vols. (Norwich and London, 1906–10), II, p. cxxix.

[45] Gross, *Gild Merchant*, II, pp. 182, 227; *The Making of King's Lynn: A Documentary Survey*, ed. D. M. Owen, BARSEH, new ser., IX (London, 1984), pp. 14–18, 22–3, 426; H. Swinden, *The History and Antiquities of Great Yarmouth* (Norwich, 1772), pp. 17–23.

[46] M. Kowaleski, 'Local Markets and Merchants in Late Fourteenth-Century Exeter', PhD thesis, Toronto, 1982, pp. 240, 285, 287; R. H. Britnell, *Growth and Decline in Colchester, 1300–1525* (Cambridge, 1986), p. 11; E. Gillett and K. A. MacMahon, *A History of Hull* (Hull, 1980), pp. 2, 7.

[47] H. M. Cam, 'The City of Cambridge', *VCH Cambs.*, III, p. 88; P. H. Reaney, ed., *The Place-Names of Cambridgeshire and the Isle of Ely*, EPNS, XIX (Cambridge, 1943), p. 42.

[48] Hilton, *Medieval Society*, p. 181.   [49] Britnell, *Growth and Decline*, p. 39.

At the apex of the urban hierarchy came London, whose population around 1300 may have been as large as 80–100,000.[50] It was by far the largest source of demand for agricultural produce in England, and its marketing organisation was correspondingly complex. During the thirteenth century the old chain of markets stretching across the middle of the city was supplemented by new trading areas.[51] London and Westminster increased their share of the luxury trades as a growing establishment of resident landowners and royal servants attracted a complementary settlement of resident merchants. The Westminster fairs were developed in the thirteenth century and attracted numerous French and Flemish merchants.[52] But not all luxury trade depended upon fairs. Shops and warehouses traded through the year. In 1264–5 about a quarter of the royal wardrobe's purchases of cloth, furs and spices were made in London, and that share increased in Edward I's reign. By 1300 almost any imported luxury was obtainable in the city. It was for this reason that the king's wardrobe maintained an increasingly large establishment in London and Wesminster, and eventually in Edward II's reign established a main storehouse in the city.[53] London was simultaneously gaining ground at the expense of provincial ports in its share of the wool and wine trades.[54]

Supplies came in to London by road over distances up to twenty miles.[55] Grain brought by road from the west side of the city was sold inside the walls on the pavement by Grey Friars, Newgate. Grain from western parts was sold on the pavement at Gracechurch.[56] But London did not have to depend solely on road carriage. In 1224–5 merchants of the Cinque Ports were required to carry their grain to Queenhithe.[57] Westminster Abbey usually shipped its surplus from Feering manor in Essex to London.[58] Further north, Londoners were occasional buyers of grain and fish from the East Anglian coast and from the Fenland regions of Norfolk and Cambridgeshire, using Lynn as the major collecting

[50] D. Keene, 'A New Study of London before the Great Fire', *Urban Hist. Yearbook, 1984*, p. 20; D. Keene, 'Medieval London and its Region', *London J.*, 14 (1989), pp. 101, 107.

[51] Williams, *Medieval London*, pp. 86, 185.

[52] G. Rosser, *Medieval Westminster, 1200–1540* (Oxford, 1989), pp. 17–32, 97–109.

[53] E. W. Moore, *The Fairs of Medieval England: An Introductory Study*, PIMSST, LXXII (Toronto, 1985), pp. 214–16; Williams, *Medieval London*, pp. 107–8.

[54] Williams, *Medieval London*, pp. 110–26.

[55] Keene, 'Medieval London', pp. 104–5; McDonnell, *Medieval London Suburbs*, pp. 69–70; M. Morgan, *The English Lands of the Abbey of Bec* (Oxford, 1946), pp. 49, 93.

[56] *Calendar of Letter-Books Preserved among the Archives of the Corporation of the City of London, 1275–1498*, ed. R. R. Sharpe, 11 vols. (London, 1899–1912), book E, pp. 56–7, book F, pp. 100–2, book G, p. 103; Gras, *Evolution*, pp. 66–7.

[57] Stow, *Survey of London*, ed. Kingsford, II, p. 7.

[58] PRO, S.C.6/841/6d, 7d, 8d, 9d; Harvey, *Westminster Abbey*, p. 148.

port.[59] London also had a river trade along the Thames. Henley (Oxon.) is first heard of in 1179 and thereafter developed rapidly.[60] River trade also contributed to the growth of Maidenhead (Berks.), originally Maidenhythe, whose name first occurs in 1202.[61] The River Lea was another means of access to London markets, and through Ware London drew supplies from the east midland counties.[62] The more distant effects of London's demands were confined to land near the coast and the navigable rivers. The two main waterside markets were Queenhithe below London Bridge and Billingsgate above it. The price of grain in these markets was acknowledged as a just standard in a recognition of debt between two London citizens in 1309.[63]

A good deal of incoming produce was sold directly to householders in the principal markets. But the London by-laws show that special arrangements were made for wholesale trade.[64] Many butchers, bakers, brewers, innkeepers and cooks were occupied in feeding the city, and they required regular supplies. The provisioning of London and Westminster also created opportunities for cornmongers, otherwise called bladers, who came to include some of the city's wealthiest men. They bought in bulk and sold both to householders and to middlemen. London's bladers reached the peak of their political influence about 1300 when there were at least thirty-eight of them. Supplying the capital also provided a living for cornmongers from market towns of the London region and the Thames Valley.[65] Londoners often ate bread made of materials which had passed through the hands of both a merchant and a baker after leaving the grower.

IV

As the number of market places increased between 1180 and 1330, so did the number of fairs, most of which were held in the summer months between May and September.[66] These too required authorisation by the crown. The business of rural fairs was rarely recorded even where

[59] Morgan, *English Lands*, pp. 49–50; Williams, *Medieval London*, p. 161.
[60] Beresford, *New Towns*, pp. 476–7.
[61] M. Gelling, ed., *The Place-Names of Berkshire*, EPNS, 3 vols., XLIX–LI (London, 1973–6), I, p. 53; *VCH Berks.*, III, p. 97; Beresford, *New Towns*, p. 395.
[62] McDonnell, *Medieval London Suburbs*, p. 73.
[63] *Calendar of Letter-Books*, ed. Sharpe, book B, p. 219, book E, p. 56, and book F, pp. 100–2; Gras, *Evolution*, pp. 66–7.
[64] *Calendar of Pleas and Memoranda Rolls Preserved among the Archives of the Corporation of the City of London, A.D. 1323–64*, ed. A. H. Thomas (Cambridge, 1926), p. 160; *Calendar of Letter-Books*, ed. Sharpe, book G, p. 103.
[65] Gras, *Evolution*, pp. 164–6; Williams, *Medieval London*, pp. 161–3.
[66] Farmer, 'Marketing', p. 341.

their value to their owners is known in some detail.[67] One of their main
purposes was the sale of livestock, both for farm work and butchers'
meat.[68] In 1332–3 the abbot of Westminster's officer from Feering
(Essex) bought a bay horse at a fair held by the prior of Tiptree on the
edge of Tiptree Heath.[69] The reeve of Cuxham (Oxon.) bought ten foals
at Winchcombe fair for the bursar of Merton College in 1320–1.[70] In
1320–1 Bolton Priory (W.R. Yorks.) sold horses at a fair at Nostell
Priory and bought others at Settle fair.[71] On the third day of the fair of
Stratton St Margaret (Wilts.) in 1282 a horse and three mares were
separately 'claimed and proved' in the associated hundred court.[72]
Some minor summer fairs, like those of St Osyth and Coggeshall in
Essex, traded the wool clip of local sheep farmers.[73] Other fairs were
outlets for the products of local industries. In 1280 Adam Hoget was
said to have sold four ells of linen 'where the linen merchants were' at
Stratton St Margaret fair.[74] All sorts of other specialisations found an
outlet in small fairs. Cuxham demesne acquired a pair of cartwheels
from Crowmarsh fair.[75]

Like new markets, fairs encouraged new patterns of itinerant marketing. Amongst those appearing in Highworth Hundred court at the time
of Stratton St Margaret fair in 1282, and probably on account of it, was
Richard the chapman of Aldbourne (Wilts.).[76] Because they came but
once a year, and brought people and money together, fairs were often
occasions for entertainment as well as sober commerce. *The Tale of
Gamelyn*, written in the mid-fourteenth century, tells of a wrestling
competition at a country fair.[77] The reeve of Sevenhampton (Wilts.) was
fined in 1284 for having stayed too long at Highworth fair, presumably
for pleasure rather than duty's sake.[78]

At the apex of the hierarchy of fairs were those of international
significance, where native merchants and buyers from the largest households met importers of foreign goods. The fairs of this class were at

---

[67] Kershaw, *Bolton Priory*, p. 29.
[68] Farmer, 'Marketing', p. 343; Farmer, 'Two Wiltshire Manors', p. 9.
[69] PRO, S.C.6/841/6; Morant, *History and Antiquities*, II, p. 141.
[70] Harvey, *Medieval Oxfordshire Village*, p. 66.   [71] Kershaw, *Bolton Priory*, p. 105.
[72] *Rolls of Highworth Hundred*, ed. Farr, II, p. 214; *Accounts and Surveys of the Wiltshire Lands of Adam de Stratton*, ed. M. W. Farr, Wilts. Archl. and Nat. Hist. Soc. Recs. Branch, XIV (Devizes, 1959), p. xiii.
[73] Britnell, *Growth and Decline*, p. 45.
[74] *Rolls of Highworth Hundred*, ed. Farr, I, pp. 165–6.
[75] Farmer, 'Marketing', pp. 343–4; Harvey, *Medieval Oxfordshire Village*, p. 60n.
[76] *Rolls of Highworth Hundred*, ed. Farr, II, p. 213.
[77] M. H. Keen, *The Outlaws of Medieval Legend* (London, 1961), pp. 81–2.
[78] *Court Rolls of the Wiltshire Manors of Adam de Stratton*, ed. R. B. Pugh, Wilts. Rec. Soc., XXIV (Devizes, 1970), p. 86.

Winchester, Boston (Lincs.), Stamford (Lincs.), St Ives (Hunts.), Northampton and Bury St Edmunds (Suff.). Here wool was sold in bulk to Flemish buyers. In exchange, foreign merchants brought luxury goods for the consumption of the rich.[79] A big fair also offered an exceptional opportunity for local residents to sell ale and prepared foods. The women of Bridge Street in St Ives augmented their income annually from this source.[80] In contrast to the history of urban growth, however, the multiplication of fairs was not accompanied by the expansion of business in older ones. In the hierarchy of English fairs there were problems at the top. By 1300 the larger towns, and notably London, offered all-year trading in commodities that had previously been available only in periodic fairs. This inevitably reduced the importance of the larger fairs for the wholesale and luxury trades.[81]

V

Markets and fairs, multiplying and expanding as the division of labour became more marked, created many problems of organisation that had to be tackled in the interests of fairness or public order. Regulation of local trade was the foundation of a complex body of statutes and by-laws. Some were promulgated for the whole kingdom, to regulate weights, measures, currency and prices. Other developments, even if backed by royal authorisation, were only of local relevance. Local regulation was chiefly concerned with the manner and place in which trade should be conducted. In reality different market authorities interpreted even national regulations differently, so that there was little uniformity of practice.

England was unusual in the Middle Ages for the extent to which government attempted to enforce standard weights and measures.[82] The king's court had some interest in the question because of its position as a buyer of provisions. In the years 1180 and 1181 royal justices exacted penalties for the use of false measures from the townsmen of Chichester (Suss.), Arundel (Suss.) and Rochester (Kent), implying perhaps that their local standard was not good enough.[83] Both wine and grain measures were scrutinised in Henry II's last years, and from this period the crown began to pursue the ideal of national uniformity more actively.[84] Roger of Howden's chronicle preserves the text of the Assize

[79] Moore, *Fairs*, pp. 24–62; Kershaw, *Bolton Priory*, pp. 136, 148, 151.
[80] Moore, *Fairs*, p. 259.
[81] *Ibid.*, pp. 43, 214–17, 220; Williams, *Medieval London*, pp. 107–8.
[82] Cf. W. Kula, *Measures and Men*, trans. R. Szreter (New Jersey, 1986), pp. 114–19.
[83] *PR, 26 Henry II*, p. 31; *PR, 27 Henry II*, pp. 144, 149.
[84] *PR, 32 Henry II*, pp. 8, 176 (wine); *PR, 33 Henry II*, pp. 103, 199 (wine), p. 132 (grain).

of Measures of 1196 which established that standard measures should be used throughout England for cereals and liquids, that weights should be similarly standardised and that woollen cloths should all have the same width, measured by a standard ell.[85] The assize specified 'a good horse load' as the measure for cereals. Measures remained an issue under King John, and a clause requiring standard measures of wine, ale and grain, this time affirming the status of the London quarter, was incorporated in Magna Carta. The size of cloths was also regulated.[86] From time to time later governments enquired into the way these regulations were enforced. Henry III sent out commissions for the purpose between 1255 and 1257 and again in 1270. As if to advertise the virtues of good kingship, both Edward I and his son held a nationwide scrutiny of weights and measures at the start of their reigns.[87] Where the standard measures in use were deficient townsmen were fined and made to replace them.[88]

Apart from the problem of ensuring that weights and measures were of the required standard, local authorities had to check how they were employed. Regulating the capacity of measures was not enough to ensure standardisation. A bushel measure was like a large bowl. Measures of the same capacity could give different results depending upon whether grain in the measure was levelled or heaped.[89] Measuring a quarter of grain as eight separate bushels gave scope for yet further variation, depending upon whether every bushel was heaped or only one in eight.[90] English legislation tried to achieve standardisation. The Assize of Measures of 1196 required that grain should be sold by level measure. This requirement was repeated in a thirteenth-century ordinance, the *Statutum de Pistoribus*, except for sales of oats, malt and flour. These rules came to be part of normal practice in some markets. A man was fined in Norwich in 1293 for refusing the king's level measure.[91]

The wider problems of securing a competitive market price and preventing monopoly were tackled by urban authorities in different ways. It was normal to restrict certain trades to market places. In 1264,

[85] Roger of Howden, *Chronica*, ed. W. Stubbs, RS, 4 vols. (London, 1868–71), IV, pp. 33–4.
[86] Magna Carta (1215), c. 35: *Select Charters*, ed. Stubbs, p. 297.
[87] Britnell, '*Forstall*', pp. 95, 100.
[88] 'Annales Prioratus de Dunstaplia', in *Annales Monastici*, ed. H. R. Luard, RS, 5 vols. (London, 1864–9), III, p. 263.
[89] Harvey, *Medieval Oxfordshire Village*, pp. 54–6.
[90] *Walter of Henley and Other Treatises on Estate Management and Accounting*, ed. D. Oschinsky (Oxford, 1971), pp. 168–70; Harvey, *Medieval Oxfordshire Village*, p. 54; Searle, *Lordship and Community*, pp. 318–19.
[91] R. H. Britnell, '*Advantagium Mercatoris*: A Custom in Medieval English Trade', *Nottingham Med. Stud.*, 24 (1980), p. 39.

for example, Roger de Asse was fined in Exeter for having bought eels in a churchyard. It was also normal to insist that trade in the market should take place between certain set times, and to limit the times when middlemen could buy up produce.[92] The pricing policies of market authorities are obscure. There was often some element of rationing to protect household purchasers. At Andover (Hants.) in 1279 'no regrater should buy hens, eggs, capons, geese, foals, meat or fish, until the good men of the town and country have bought'. Southampton customs of 1327 forbade regraters to buy produce before a set hour.[93] At York cooks had to hold back from buying their materials until ordinary consumers had bought what they wanted.[94] But there are also cases of stricter rationing whereby members of a merchant gild, or the burgesses of a borough, had some claim on incoming supplies at a publicly agreed price. In Colchester all burgesses were allowed to share in cargoes coming into port. Newly arrived cargoes were officially proclaimed in public, together with the offer price.[95] At Newcastle upon Tyne in 1342 all burgesses might buy what they wanted from ships entering the port. If a wholesaler was asked by an ordinary consumer for a share he needed to feed his household, the former had to concede it at the price he had agreed on board ship.[96] The auctioning of produce was unknown. Normal practice gave priority to securing low prices for consumers.

The problems of regulating supply were complex. On the one hand, merchants who went to find grain or fish in large quantities, or merchants from other towns who brought in large supplies for sale, were performing an important function, and one which minor tradesmen could not emulate. On the other hand, authorities were suspicious of middlemen who intercepted produce already on the way to market. Such forestalling might adversely affect prices by creating a monopoly. A systematic operator with enough capital might finish up with a hold over the market sufficiently strong to be able to raise prices in his favour. This problem had already been confronted, as we have seen, in twelfth-century London. Another threat to the urban market came from interlopers who set out to sabotage the system of market pricing. In any town, an insider who knew that the market was badly supplied could use this information to his own advantage. He could buy up produce and put it on sale at a higher price than the original vendor would have asked, or alternatively he could take the outsider into his confidence in exchange for a share of the resulting higher profit.

[92] Britnell, 'Forstall', p. 90.   [93] Gross, Gild Merchant, II, pp. 228, 291.
[94] Miller, 'Medieval York', p. 99.   [95] Britnell, Growth and Decline, p. 36.
[96] Gross, Gild Merchant, II, pp. 184–5. A similar rule was known in the Bristol fish trade: Penn, 'Fourteenth-Century Bristol', p. 120.

From the mid-thirteenth century it became more common for urban authorities to tackle these problems in the interests of consumers. New rules were added to the regulations of merchant gilds, or included in charters of liberties purchased from the crown. In 1256 the Suffolk towns of Great Yarmouth, Dunwich and Ipswich all secured charters in which open trade was enhanced by a rule making brokerage illegal. Similar customs were granted to Grimsby (Lincs.) in 1258. In 1268 a charter to London granted that 'no merchant or anyone else should meet merchants coming by land or by water with their merchandise or victuals towards the city to buy or resell until they have reached the said city and put their wares up for sale', and this clause was repeated in charters to Melcombe Regis (Dors.) in 1280, Lyme Regis (Dors.) in 1285, Newton near Poole (Dors.) in 1286 and Berwick-upon-Tweed (Northumb.) in 1302.[97] These measures against brokerage and the interception of goods came together in 1274–5 in rules issued by the king's marshalsea to prohibit what they termed forestalling. At first these rules had only temporary authority in the interests of the king's court, though some local courts began to apply them. For example, in 1294 the leet court at Ramsey reported a forestaller in terms which are borrowed from the marshalsea rules.[98] But in 1307 Edward II instructed commissioners to enforce them, together with the laws relating to weights and measures. From that time onward forestalling was penalised by local authorities as a statutory offence.[99]

In exceptional circumstances English kings issued price ordinances to restrain inflation brought about by local or general dearth. In 1301, at a time when York was the administrative capital of England, Edward I fixed the prices of a wide range of foodstuffs and manufactures in the city in an effort to check local inflation.[100] In an impending national emergency during the spring of 1315, Edward II was induced by parliamentary pressure to fix prices for some livestock and foodstuffs, though not for grain.[101] However, neither crown nor urban authorities adopted price fixing as a normal way to tackle problems of supply. It was assumed that the price of goods would fluctuate. From the late twelfth century the main form of price regulation was designed to eliminate excessive profits in retail trades rather than to stabilise prices.

[97] *BBC, 1216–1307*, p. 297.
[98] *Court Rolls of the Abbey of Ramsey and of the Honor of Clare*, ed. W. O. Ault (New Haven, 1928), p. 204.
[99] Britnell, '*Forstall*', pp. 100–2.
[100] *York Civic Ordinances, 1301*, ed. M. C. Prestwich, Borthwick Paper XLIX (York, 1976), pp. 11, 14–15.
[101] I. Kershaw, 'The Great Famine and Agrarian Crisis in England, 1315–1322', in Hilton, ed., *Peasants, Knights and Heretics*, p. 88.

An assize of wine was introduced in Henry II's reign. The pipe rolls of 1176 and afterwards show amercements by the king's justices for breach of this assize in all parts of the kingdom.[102] The judicial visitations which began in September 1194 required jurors from each hundred to report, amongst other things, wines sold against the assize.[103] Offences against the assize are recorded in thirteenth-century eyres.[104] The assize of wine, like other examples of basic policing, passed into the hands of the lords of private hundreds and the elected officers of chartered boroughs.[105] It was primarily a matter of regulating prices. The *Composicio* of 1274–5 speaks of a fixed price of 12d a sester.[106] Later texts imply that the assize price of wine in the provinces was taken from that in London.[107] Some texts imply an associated check on quality.[108]

Grain prices were expected to fluctuate according to market forces. Attempts to fix them were never more than temporary responses to fears of profiteering.[109] Prepared foodstuffs, however, were subject to more controls. They were regulated to rise and fall in accordance with grain prices. Earlier local or private forms of regulation were brought together sometime between 1193 and 1199 to create an assize of bread and ale made 'in the presence of Hubert Walter, archbishop of Canterbury, and in the presence of bishops and all the English at Canterbury by King Richard'. This declaration implies that the document was relevant to the whole kingdom. A standard loaf was to be achieved by weighing loaves against coins, whose weight was regulated by the crown. This remained a feature of later assizes of bread.[110] No penalties were specified in the 1190s, but Matthew Paris records another assize of bread issued in 1202 to be kept on pain of the pillory. It had been approved 'by the baker of Geoffrey Fitz Peter, justiciar of England, and the baker of Robert de

---

[102] *PR, 22 Henry II*, pp. 126, 184; *PR, 23 Henry II*, pp. 30, 171, 178, 190.
[103] Roger of Howden, *Chronica*, ed. Stubbs, III, p. 264.
[104] *The Roll and Writ File of the Berkshire Eyre of 1248*, ed. M. T. Clanchy, Selden Soc., XC (London, 1973), pp. 311, 315, 322, 348, 376–7, 380, 396, 398; *Cartularium Monasterii de Rameseia*, ed. Hart and Lyons, III, p. 36.
[105] Essex RO, Colchester Muniments, CR 2/2d, 6d, 10r; CR 3/1d, 3d; *Records of the City of Norwich*, ed. Hudson and Tingey, I, p. 176; *Select Pleas in Manorial and Other Seignorial Courts*, ed. F. W. Maitland, Selden Soc., II (London, 1889), pp. xxxi–xxxvii; Keene, *Survey*, I, pp. 270–1; D. W. Sutherland, *Quo Warranto Proceedings in the Reign of Edward I, 1268–1294* (Oxford, 1963), pp. 3–4.
[106] *SR*, I, p. 203.
[107] Essex RO, Colchester Muniments, Red Paper Book, fo. 124r.
[108] As in the *Justicium Pillorie*: *SR*, I, p. 202.
[109] M. C. Prestwich, *War, Politics and Finance under Edward I* (London, 1972), p. 128.
[110] *The Red Book of the Exchequer*, ed. H. Hall, RS, 3 vols. (London, 1896), II, p. 750.

Turnham'.[111] This assize occurs in a sufficiently large number of sources to imply that it was widely disseminated.[112]

Another text of John's reign, probably from after 1202, is the first royal ordinance to associate the assize of bread with an assize of ale. In these regulations the scale of wheat prices rises higher than in 1202 – to 8s 0d rather than 6s 0d a quarter. Each wheat price is associated with a mandatory price for a gallon of ale. So, for example, with wheat at 8s 0d a quarter, a white farthing loaf should weigh 18s 0d and a gallon of ale should sell for 1d. Though the prices of different cereals tracked each other quite closely, this attachment of the price of ale to the price of wheat was unsatisfactory, since ale was made from barley or oats. The two assizes were never again linked so closely. They were nevertheless generally enforced in all parts of the kingdom from this time. About 1202 Richard de Lucy granted his burgesses of Egremont (Cumb.) the assize of bread and ale to be held by twelve burgesses. In 1205 the assize of victuals was required to be observed at Shrewsbury. In 1206 the abbot of Bury granted 'the cucking-stool and justice of trangressors against the assize of bread and ale' in Worlington (Suff.). The assize was enforced on at least some of the bishop of Winchester's manors at the time of the earliest pipe roll of 1208–9.[113]

After John's reign the assizes of bread and ale occur in many different forms. This was partly because the text was a difficult one for bored copyists to get right, partly because local courts added their own variations and partly because there were changes in the official rules. In 1237 the mayor and bailiffs of Oxford were instructed to observe the assizes of bread and ale 'provided in the king's presence at Woodstock'. The court in its travels imposed the current marshalsea scale on towns it passed through.[114] Henry III drew fines into the exchequer from this source – £10 from Oxford and £20 from Worcester in 1241. The rules enforced were not very stable. An assize imposed on Nottingham by officers of the crown in 1249 is unlike either that of John or those

[111] Matthew Paris, *Chronica Majora*, ed. H. R. Luard, RS, 7 vols. (London, 1872–83), II, pp. 480–1. The text is one of Paris's own additions: A. S. Ross, 'The Assize of Bread', *EcHR*, 2nd ser., 9 (1956–7), p. 335.
[112] *Registrum Malmesburiense*, ed. Brewer and Martin, I, pp. 134–6; BL, Add. MS 24066, fo. 220r; CUL, Kk.5.33, fo. 99r, v. Versions other than Matthew Paris's say the baker(s) of Stephen de Turnham.
[113] *A Terrier of Fleet Lincolnshire*, ed. N. Neilson, BARSEH, 1st ser., IV (London, 1920), p. 106; *BBC, 1042–1216*, p. 159; *The Kalendar of Abbot Samson of Bury St. Edmunds and Related Documents*, ed. R. H. C. Davis, Camden Soc., 3rd ser., LXXXIV (London, 1954), charter 105, pp. 135–6; *The Pipe Roll of the Bishopric of Winchester, 1208–9*, ed. H. Hall (London, 1903), pp. 45, 47, 49, 65.
[114] *CR Henry III, 1234–7*, p. 519; *CR Henry III, 1237–42*, pp. 180, 221, 242, 274, 276.

known from later times.[115] The most commonly found text is described on one occasion as 'the assize of bread in the Great Hall of Westminster from the bakers of the lord king of England the Tuesday next the three weeks of Easter in the year of our Lord 1253 in the Ides of May', that is on 13 May.[116] In this instance the scale of wheat prices runs from 1s 0d to 12s 0d a quarter. This scale was imposed on Chester in 1261.[117] In practice the adoption of different variants in different places meant that the assizes of bread and ale were absorbed into local custom.[118] The assize of ale became a sort of tax on brewing rather than a serious attempt to regulate prices.[119]

Although most of the time the enforcement of these petty regulations was left to local courts, the king's officers could, and did, step in to punish offenders on numerous occasions. Justices in eyre punished breaches of the assize in the vicinity of their sessions.[120] From time to time kings appointed special commissions to go round the shires scrutinising weights and measures and other matters, as in the years 1255–7, 1273–5 and 1307–11.[121] In addition, the duties of the clerk of the market, an officer of the king's household, included visiting towns and markets in areas through which the court was passing or about to pass and to empanel juries to report on the enforcement of marketing regulations.[122] Many market towns were fined for such offences in the course of a year; forty-two were amerced for defective measures in 1299–1300.[123] One of the duties of the clerk of the market was to check up on the efficiency of policing. On 30 September 1315 he made the first inspection of Haverhill (Suff.) for twenty years, but a jury reported that measures were checked annually and that bakers and brewers were duly fined for their misdemeanours. The jury at Freckenham (Suff.) on the following 12 October said that no clerk of the market had visited them for eighteen years, but that brewers, bakers and users of false measures were corrected once a year.[124]

---

[115] BL, Add. MS 35179, fo. 90v.   [116] BL, Egerton MS 2733, fos. 175v–6v.

[117] BL, Add. MS 35179, fo. 89r.

[118] E.g. *Early Records of Medieval Coventry*, ed. Coss, no. 31, pp. 41–2.

[119] H. M. Cam, *The Hundred and the Hundred Rolls: An Outline of Local Government in Medieval England* (London, 1930), pp. 211–12.

[120] *Britton*, ed. F. M. Nichols, 2 vols. (Oxford, 1865), I, p. 84.

[121] Britnell, 'Forstall', pp. 95, 100.

[122] *Records of the Wardrobe and Household, 1285–1286*, ed. B. F. Byerly and C. R. Byerly (London, 1977), p. xxv; J. H. Johnson, 'The King's Wardrobe and Household', in J. F. Willard, W. A. Morris, J. R. Strayer and W. H. Dunham, eds., *The English Government at Work, 1327–1336*, The Mediaeval Academy of America, 3 vols., XXXVII, XLVIII, LVI (Cambridge, Mass., 1940–50), I, pp. 245–6.

[123] *Liber Quotidianus Contrarotulatoris Garderobae Anno Regni Regis Edwardi Primi Vicesimo Octavo*, ed. J. Topham (London, 1787), pp. 1–3.

[124] BL, Harleian MS 230, fos. 91v, 92r.

The efficacy of these royal policies is difficult to assess. The law relating to weights and measures had some influence in formal markets. There are frequent examples in the court rolls of boroughs and market towns of individual tradesmen being accused of using unjust measures.[125] Royal policy achieved considerable success. Manorial reeves rarely made adjustments for differences of measures in their accounts, either for transactions between manors or for those involving outside parties, and this implies that neither they nor the auditors who supervised them thought there was much significant variation. But there remained some discrepancies between standard urban measures and those on country farms, and standardisation within towns was better than standardisation between them.[126] The assize of bread and ale was less relevant to the real interests of consumers, since competition between bakers and brewers was likely to eliminate excessive profits. In small towns it was not difficult for bakers to conspire together to raise their profits.[127] Yet a lot of baking was still carried on in private houses and even a successful monopolistic operation by bakers was unlikely to have very deleterious effects upon food supplies.

VI

Despite these developments in formal marketing, a great deal of trading remained a matter between neighbours, between lords and tenants, or between villagers and pedlars. In a region like the palatinate of Durham where there were few formal markets, chiefly because bishops would not authorise them, there was nevertheless trade between villagers. An agreement made in 1303 between the bishop and the commonalty of Durham records that the bishop's officers had been taking tolls illegally on purchases made in country villages.[128] Small traders might make purchases and sales wherever they could. *Havelock the Dane* describes how Grim exchanged fish for other foodstuffs by door-to-door sales.[129] Many villages depended on regular visits from such itinerant pedlars for a variety of their regular needs.[130]

[125] E.g. Essex RO, Colchester Muniments, CR 1/1d, 6r, CR 2/2d; *Leet Jurisdiction in the City of Norwich during the XIIIth and XIVth Centuries*, ed. W. Hudson, Selden Soc., V (London, 1892), pp. 5, 6, 13, 14, 30; Gross, *Gild Merchant*, II, p. 310; *Court Rolls of the Wiltshire Manors of Adam de Stratton*, ed. Pugh, pp. 156–7.

[126] D. L. Farmer, 'Some Grain Price Movements in Thirteenth-Century England', *EcHR*, 2nd ser., 10 (1957–8), pp. 208–9; Salzman, *English Trade*, pp. 45–7.

[127] Britnell, *Growth and Decline*, pp. 38–9.

[128] *Records of Anthony Bek, Bishop and Patriarch, 1283–1311*, ed. C. M. Fraser, Surtees Soc., CLXII (Durham, 1953), no. 89, p. 95.

[129] *Lay of Havelock the Dane*, ed. Skeat and Sisam, lines 760–70, pp. 28–9.

[130] J. M. Bennett, *Women in the Medieval English Countryside: Gender and Household in Brigstock before the Plague* (Oxford, 1987), p. 52.

Most evidence relating to retail trade outside markets concerns bread, ale and meat. Because these trades were regulated by the law of the realm, policing authorities everywhere fined brewers, bakers and butchers who broke the rules. In many villages without markets like Downham (Cambs.), Holywell (Hunts.) and Brigstock (Northants.) the manor court regularly amerced ale-sellers. Brewers are recorded in all the abbot of Ramsey's villages. Most ale-sellers were women, and breach of the assize was the commonest reason for women coming before the courts, even though most of them sold ale only sporadically. Bread and meat were also sold in ordinary villages. There was usually a butcher in Holywell between 1286 and 1339, and butchers from outside the village are also recorded to have traded there.[131]

In the grain trade, too, small transactions were often informal. Villagers with too little land to feed themselves bought food from neighbours or from nearby manor houses. The accounts of manorial bailiffs sometimes record such sales with the observation that grain has been sold 'in the country', as opposed to 'in the market'.[132] In such instances the latter commonly outweigh the former.[133] On the small Essex manor of Langenhoe those who purchased wheat directly from the demesne granary included the lord's cowman, Richard the herd, who bought two quarters in 1324–5. John Lytebery, shepherd and cowman in 1338–9, bought two bushels in 1344–5, and the manor's smith, Thomas, bought two quarters in the same year. Some occasional labourers on the manor were among the grain buyers. John atte Hathe, a reaper in 1342, and John Certayn, who cleaned out a pond in 1344–5, bought one bushel and two bushels respectively in the latter year.[134] Large quantities of grain were similarly sold to the abbot of Glastonbury's tenants from his demesnes at Longbridge Deverill and Monkton Deverill (Wilts.)[135] Manorial accounts rarely report local transactions in detail; they usually record where a sale was made only if transport had had to be organised.[136]

The informal market also operated in relations between neighbouring

[131] *Ibid.*, pp. 120–9, 190–1; M. C. Coleman, *Downham-in-the-Isle: A Study of an Ecclesiastical Manor in the Thirteenth and Fourteenth Centuries* (Woodbridge, 1984), pp. 8, 116–19; E. B. Dewindt, *Land and People in Holywell-cum-Needingworth: Structures of Tenure and Patterns of Social Organization in an East Midlands Village, 1252–1457*, PIMSST, XXII (Toronto, 1971), pp. 235–9; Moore, *Fairs*, p. 258.
[132] The Latin terms are *in patria* and *in foro*.
[133] Dyer, 'Consumer', p. 321.
[134] R. H. Britnell, 'Production for the Market on a Small Fourteenth-Century Estate', *EcHR*, 2nd ser., 19 (1966), p. 382; Essex RO, D/DC 2/11, 12; D/DE1 M220, M221, M222.
[135] Farmer, 'Two Wiltshire Manors', p. 8.
[136] Harvey, *Medieval Oxfordshire Village*, p. 104.

landlords. In 1293–4 Worcester Priory obtained only 3 per cent of its wheat purchases in the nearby market, the remainder coming from more informal systems of trading.[137] From time to time Bolton Priory bought quantities of 100 or more quarters of wheat from the dean of York.[138] William Inge's small manor at Rippingale (Lincs.) sold a large part of its surplus grain to the nearby household of John Gubaud in the famine year 1316–17.[139] Local transactions also took place to enable the lords of neighbouring demesne farms to acquire new seed or livestock.[140]

The best examples of trade outside markets are those relating to transactions in grain, wool and other demesne produce between landlords and merchants. Surpluses of demesne produce from the demesnes of the bishop of Ely were often collected together in order to be sold in bulk. Grain was sold in large lots at Fen Ditton and Wisbech Barton (Cambs.), both of which had the advantage of easy communications with Lynn.[141] Near towns landlords could sell grain in bulk to local middlemen, sometimes even before it was threshed.[142] In 1339–40, a year of high prices, the tenants of Longbridge Deverill (Wilts.) carried wheat twenty miles to the home of a buyer in Wells.[143] The growth of town life had the effect of encouraging the informal market in grain at the same time as it increased opportunities for formal marketing. Though village markets and provincial towns could not support a merchant class, many middlemen combined dealing in grain with other local trades or with the preparation of food and drink. Urban brewers and bakers went out into the countryside to find supplies and bought them directly from the producers.[144] The purchases of this kind by London bladers could be considerable. A London recognisance of 1291 shows a merchant owing £118 17s 6d for grain to a single landlord.[145] At current prices this represents the value of 340 quarters of wheat.

The informal market in grain was encouraged by war. From the late thirteenth century it is illustrated in the sheriffs' accounts recording the purveyance of grain for the king's armies. Supplies were obtained mostly by a direct approach to sellers rather than through markets, where the available lots would have been only small. In 1296 tax assessments were used to estimate how much grain might be taken from

[137] Dyer, 'Consumer', p. 323.   [138] Kershaw, *Bolton Priory*, pp. 73–4.
[139] Platts, *Land and People*, pp. 141–2.
[140] Harvey, *Medieval Oxfordshire Village*, p. 51; Smith, *Canterbury Cathedral Priory*, pp. 134–5.
[141] Miller, *Abbey and Bishopric*, p. 86.   [142] Britnell, *Growth and Decline*, p. 38.
[143] Farmer, 'Two Wiltshire Manors', pp. 7–8.
[144] Britnell, *Growth and Decline*, pp. 38–9.
[145] *Calendar of Letter-Books*, ed. Sharpe, book A, pp. 129–30.

each taxpayer. More commonly in Edward I's reign local juries were asked to make an independent assessment of what each man might be expected to supply. Subsequently the procedure became more arbitrary; the sheriff's officer descended on a village and took what he could. Bigger producers were sometimes able to pay the officer to go away, or to buy letters of protection, but the system could not have operated had bribery and avoidance been the general rule. Some large landowners negotiated directly with the crown. In 1304 Walter Langton undertook to supply 100 quarters of wheat and 200 quarters of malt from Barton-on-Humber (Lincs.).[146]

Despite the large number of formal institutions of trade grain markets were poorly integrated across the country. High transport and weak mercantile organisation meant that prices varied erratically between different regions.[147] Nevertheless, the multiplication of marketing centres strengthened the confidence of rural sellers of grain in their knowledge of current local prices. On 14 April 1275 Luffield Priory (Bucks.) agreed with William de Plumpton, clerk, that wheat received from him should be paid for on 17 June 'according to what a quarter of that wheat happened to be sold for in Towcester on three market days preceding the feast of St John the Baptist'. The contract was drawn up in this way as a means of avoiding usury; wheat prices could confidently be expected to rise during the two months after Easter, and around the feast of St John the Baptist (Midsummer Day, 24 June) they could be expected to reach their peak. This procedure would have been impossible had there been any doubt that a local price could be cited when the time came.[148] The same confidence is evident in the practice of giving favourable terms to bulk purchasers who bought direct from the manor, a concession depending on the existence of a known market price in relation to which fine adjustments could be made.[149]

The wool trade has long been famous for the enterprise displayed by landlords and merchants alike. Bigger producers often bypassed formal markets by collecting wool together at some central point on their estate and selling it to a contractor. Such a policy had probably been adopted by some Cistercian houses in the twelfth century. It was taken up by

[146] Prestwich, *War, Politics and Finance*, pp. 118–36; J. R. Maddicott, 'The English Peasantry and the Demands of the Crown, 1294–1341', in Aston, ed., *Landlords, Peasants and Politics*, pp. 299–318.

[147] Gras, *Evolution*, pp. 42–64; D. L. Farmer, 'Prices and Wages [1000–1355]', in *AHEW*, II, pp. 743–4.

[148] *Luffield Priory Charters*, ed. G. R. Elvey, Bucks. and Northants. Rec. Socs., 2 vols. (1968–75), II, no. A1, p. 436.

[149] Britnell, '*Advantagium*', pp. 37–50; Postles, 'Markets', p. 21.

other big estates as the wool trade expanded.[150] There are many
instances from the later thirteenth and early fourteenth centuries. Some
abbeys took advantage of the informal market to buy wool from their
neighbours for inclusion with their own in deals contracted with wool
merchants.[151] But not all centralised control depended on a central
depot. Wool from Glastonbury Abbey's manors in Wiltshire was sold in
bulk to merchants who visited the manors to view it and bargain for it
there.[152] In the early fourteenth century even some small landlords
centralised their wool sales.[153] The purchase of wool in bulk, often long
in advance of the shearing, was the characteristic operation of Flemish
merchants before the 1270s, but during the reigns of Edward I and
Edward II a similar strategy was adopted by the Italian companies
trading in England.[154] The famous list of wool-producing abbeys and
wool prices drawn up by Franceso Pegolotti, probably about 1320,
would have been useless to merchants who expected to buy wool in
formal markets.[155]

[150] T. H. Lloyd, *The Movement of Wool Prices in Medieval England*, *EcHR* supplement VI
(Cambridge, 1973), pp. 6–8; T. H. Lloyd, *The English Wool Trade in the Middle Ages*
(Cambridge, 1977), pp. 288–9; Postles, 'Markets', p. 20; Smith, *Canterbury Cathedral
Priory*, p. 149.
[151] N. Denholm-Young, *Seignorial Administration in England* (Oxford, 1937), pp. 53–7;
Kershaw, *Bolton Priory*, pp. 85–8.
[152] Farmer, 'Two Wiltshire Manors', p. 10.
[153] R. H. Britnell, 'Minor Landlords and Medieval Agrarian Capitalism', in Aston, ed.,
Landlords, Peasants and Politics, p. 238; N. Saul, *Scenes from Provincial Life: Knightly
Families in Sussex, 1280–1400* (Oxford, 1986), pp. 117, 134.
[154] Lloyd, *English Wool Trade*, pp. 290–1.
[155] Lloyd, *Movement of Wool Prices*, pp. 8–10.

5   Trade and specialisation

I

During the forty years following 1180 the currency in circulation
increased many times over. During the 1160s and 1170s a normal year's
minting was less than 1m pennies. Annual mint output then rose to 4m
pennies between 1180 and 1204, to 10m, between 1234 and 1247 and to
15m in the 1250s.[1] Coinage in circulation rose from probably less that
£125,000 in 1180 to £300,000 or more in 1218 and £400,000 in 1247.[2]
By 1311 it was about £1,100,000.[3] At any given moment a large
proportion of this money stock lay idle in hoards. When Adam Stratton,
chamberlain of the exchequer, was arrested for corruption in 1290 his
house in London was found to contain £11,333 in current coin and
£1,317 in old currency.[4] The elder Despenser held at least £2,800 in
cash deposits in 1326.[5] However, a rapid increase in circulation is
confirmed by archaeological evidence. Finds of isolated coins, which
must mostly have been lost while in use, are more frequently from the
years 1279–1351 than from any other period of the Middle Ages.[6]
Growth of the money supply was made possible chiefly by England's
capacity to export wool and other produce. European silver mining
increased from the 1180s,[7] and merchants brought in bullion to the
mints usually by way of ports in the Netherlands.

English population probably doubled or trebled between 1180 and
1330 – perhaps from 2m or 3m in 1180 to 6m in 1330.[8] By implication

[1] Spufford, *Money*, pp. 196–7, 202–3.
[2] N. J. Mayhew, 'Money and Prices in England from Henry II to Edward III', *AHR*, 35
     (1987), p. 125.
[3] N. J. Mayhew, 'Numismatic Evidence and Falling Prices in the Fourteenth Century',
     EcHR, 2nd ser., 27 (1974), p. 7; Mayhew, 'Money and Prices', p. 125.
[4] M. C. Prestwich, *Edward I* (London, 1988), p. 341.
[5] E. B. Fryde, 'The Deposits of Hugh Despenser the Younger with Italian Bankers',
     EcHR, 2nd ser., 3 (1951), p. 358.
[6] Rigold, 'Small Change', pp. 59–80.
[7] Spufford, *Money*, pp. 109–13.
[8] J. Hatcher, *Plague, Population and the English Economy, 1348–1530* (London, 1977),
     p. 68.

currency per head of the population more than trebled, from no more than 1s in 1180 to between 3s and 4s in 1330. At times, notably between 1180 and 1220, circulation increased more rapidly than the value of market transactions, and the consequences were inflationary. The average price of wheat more than doubled between the 1170s and the 1220s.[9] But probably even in these years most additional currency was absorbed in a growing number of transactions. Periods of exceptionally high prices in the later thirteenth and early fourteenth centuries were caused by bad harvests rather than by monetary inflation.

The demand for currency to meet everyday needs was enhanced by monetary change. As the value of the silver penny fell its usefulness for small transactions increased, and this encouraged the substitution of money payments for barter. Smaller denominations of currency became more common at the same time. Edward I was obliged to make it unlawful to reject halfpennies and farthings made by cutting pennies.[10] From 1279 the mints frequently issued ready-made fractional currency for purposes of everyday retail trade. During Edward I's recoinage of 1279–81 the Tower mint alone struck 72m pennies, 20m halfpennies and 13m farthings.[11]

England's population growth in this period must imply some increase in the productivity of land. The amount of arable cannot possibly have doubled, except perhaps north of the Humber.[12] In southern England the ploughed area was already in 1086 as large as it was on the eve of the First World War.[13] The clearance of forests and drainage of marshes could make only modest additions to crop acreages. On the estates of the bishopric of Worcester some 2,000 acres were cleared between 1150 and 1299; this was only 5 to 7 per cent of the whole area in cultivation at the latter date.[14] It was rarely feasible to expand the sown area by converting from two-field to three-field systems.[15] Additional food supplies must have been produced by some forms of technical adaptation. Existing fields could often be made to yield more. Additional

---

[9] Farmer, 'Prices and Wages [1000–1355]', pp. 787–8; P. D. A. Harvey, 'The English Inflation of 1180–1220', in Hilton, ed., *Peasants, Knights and Heretics*, pp. 57–8, 79–84.

[10] *SR*, I, p. 204n. For an early text, see BL, Harleian MS 645, fo. 148v.

[11] Rigold, 'Small change', p. 69; D. M. Metcalf, 'A Survey of Numismatic Research into the Pennies of the First Three Edwards (1279–1344) and their Continental Imitations', in Mayhew, ed., *Edwardian Monetary Affairs*, p. 5.

[12] E. Miller, 'New Settlement: Northern England', in *AHEW*, II, pp. 247–56; Miller and Hatcher, *Medieval England*, p. 32.

[13] Maitland, *Domesday Book*, pp. 435–6; Lennard, *Rural England*, p. 393.

[14] Dyer, *Lords and Peasants*, p. 96.

[15] H. S. A. Fox, 'The Alleged Transformation from Two-Field to Three-Field Systems in Medieval England', *EcHR*, 2nd ser., 39 (1986), pp. 538–48.

families were accommodated by subdividing older tenements, and the land was worked more intensively.[16]

However, an increasing number of families could not be fed from their own land. Beyond a certain point – which varied with the quality of the soil and the knowledge of the cultivators – the subdivision of holdings and the multiplication of cottages was possible only if new occupational opportunities were available. One option was self-employment and dependence upon trade, and this is what the growth and multiplication of English towns and markets between 1180 and 1330 demonstrates. We cannot be sure how far the number of craftsmen and traders grew as a proportion of the total population. A doubling of population would account for much of the development observed in the previous chapter. But at least between 1180 and 1260 the combined effect of new market towns, expanding older ones and the multiplication of artisans in the countryside is likely to have raised the number of those occupied outside agriculture by more than the increase in population.[17] Probably a rising share of the kingdom's output of goods and services was bought and sold.

Another consequence of population growth was greater availability of wage labour. Landlords continued to use tied holdings as a way of accommodating some permanent staff and they often used the labour services of their villains, but as population growth created a superabundance of labour many preferred to hire workers for a regular wage.[18] Full-time servants were paid mostly in kind. It was not unusual for a ploughman or a carter to receive only grain and an allocation from the standing crops of the demesne.[19] When they received a cash sum it rarely accounted for more than a fifth of the total value of their wage (Table 3). More casual work – the sort of work that often substituted for labour services – was remunerated in cash. At Cuxham (Oxon.) in 1296–7, for example, full-time employees received 12s 6d in coin and other workers received about £5.[20] On large manors the wage bill could be much larger than this, especially where there were few or no labour services, as at monastic granges. At Peterborough Abbey's Biggin

[16] B. M. S. Campbell, 'Agricultural Progress in Medieval England: Some Evidence from Eastern Norfolk', *EcHR*, 2nd ser., 36 (1983), pp. 39–41.

[17] K. G. Persson, *Pre-Industrial Economic Growth: Social Organization and Technical Progress in Europe* (Oxford, 1988), pp. 73–88.

[18] Miller, *Abbey and Bishopric*, pp. 92–3; Morgan, *English Lands*, pp. 87–94; Postan, *Famulus*, pp. 16–18.

[19] Postan, *Famulus*, pp. 20–1.

[20] *Manorial Records of Cuxham*, ed. Harvey, pp. 268–72; Harvey, *Medieval Oxfordshire Village*, pp. 75–81.

Grange (Oundle, Northants.) the permanent demesne staff received £6 3s 9d in 1310, and cash payments to other workers came to £20 3s 6d.[21]

II

A rising outflow of cash from villages can be illustrated unambiguously from the history of taxation. In 1129–30 the total receipt from a geld of 2s on the hide was about £2,400. But this tax was not raised very frequently after the reign of Henry I, and the total annual burden up to its last collection in 1162 was well below £1,000.[22] After 1162 the main imposition on rural areas was tallage, which was restricted to royal demesne and collected only five times between 1168 and 1193; the burden averaged £377 a year over this twenty-five-year period. Other income that Henry II derived from his subjects depended on his powers as feudal overlord and on judicial fines.[23] The direct taxation of the countryside increased under the Angevins by a series of improvisations, of which the most successful was a tax on the assessed value of movable goods. The landmarks here were Richard I's so-called Saladin tithe of 1188, said to have raised over £70,000 from Christians and £60,000 from Jews, and John's thirteenth of 1207 which raised about £60,000.[24] The levying of sums of this magnitude imposed a strain at any period of the Middle Ages, and could not be repeated frequently. Even so, the normal burden of taxation in the thirteenth century increased considerably above that of the twelfth. In the five financial years from 1240–1 to 1244–5 Henry III's recorded annual cash income from taxation averaged £2,236.[25] During the following hundred years levels of taxation rose yet higher. Six levies assessed on movable wealth were granted between 1294 and 1306; averaged over the twelve years they represent an annual burden of about £22,473. Even in the relatively peaceful interval between Edward I's campaigns and the outbreak of the Hundred Years War levels of taxation were higher than earlier in the thirteenth century. Between 1307 and 1335 there were ten taxes on movables, averaging about £12,524 annually over these years, even though the northern

---

[21] T. A. M. Bishop, 'Monastic Granges in Yorkshire', *EHR*, 51 (1936), p. 206; King, *Peterborough Abbey*, pp. 163–4 For wage bills at some other granges, see F. M. Page, *The Estates of Crowland Abbey: A Study in Manorial Organization* (Cambridge, 1934), pp. 187–93.

[22] Green, 'Last Century', pp. 242, 254.

[23] S. K. Mitchell, *Taxation in Medieval England* (New Haven, 1951), p. 273.

[24] *Ibid.*, p. 119; W. L. Warren, *King John* (Harmondsworth, 1966), p. 167.

[25] R. Stacey, *Politics, Policy and Finance under Henry III, 1216–1245* (Oxford, 1987), p. 208.

Table 3 *Some examples of ploughmen's wages (fifty-two weeks) in 1296–7*

Place	Description of ploughman	Cash component s	Cash component d	Grain component bushels	Composition of grain component (in descending order of quantity)
Witney (Oxon.)	carucarius	1	0[a]	42	barley, currall
Howden (E.R. Yorks.)	carucarius	1	0[b]	34	maslin
Ivinghoe (Bucks.)	carucarius	1	4[c]	52	maslin, barley, bear, currall, beans
Morton (Bucks.)	bovarius	2	0[d]	52	currall, barley, beans, dredge
West Wycombe (Bucks.)	carucarius	2	0[e]	52	bear, maslin, barley
	tinctor	2	0[e]	52	barley
Cuxham (Oxon.)	carucarius	2	0[b]	41½	currall, barley, dredge, peas
Harewell (Berks.)	carucarius	2	2[f]	42	barley
Farnham (Surr.)	fugator	2	6	52	barley
Poundisford (Som.)[g]	bovarius	2	6	34½	currall
Fonthill (Wilts.)	bovarius	3	0	52	barley
Knoyle (Wilts.)	bovarius	3	0	52	barley, bear
Alresford (Hants.)[h]	bovarius	3	0	52	barley
Droxford (Hants.)	fugator	3	0	46	barley, currall, bear
	carucarius	3	0	46	barley, currall, bear
Bishopstone (Wilts.)	carucarius	3	0	42	barley, currall
Twyford and Marwell (Hants.)	fugator	3	0	41½	barley
Ashmansworth (Hants.)	bovarius	3	0	41	bear
Wellingborough (Northants.)	carucarius	3	4[j]	34	barley, bullimong, oats, rye
Roecliffe (W.R. Yorks.)	carucarius	4	0	34⅔	rye, peas, barley
Billingbear (Berks.)	carucarius	4	6	42	bear
	fugator	4	6	42	bear
Culham (Berks.)	fugator	4	6	42	bear
Isleworth (Mdx.)	carucarius	5	0	46	maslin, barley
East Meon (Hants.)	fugator	5	0	42	barley
Upton Knoyle (Wilts.)	bovarius	5	0	38	barley, bear
Ketton (co. Dur.)	carucarius	5	0	34⅔	wheat, barley
Newport (Essex)	fugator[k]	5	0	34	millcorn
Mere (Wilts.)	carucarius	5	0	34	barley

				(..., ...)	rye, barley
Berkhamsted (Herts.)	fugator	4	8	41½	maslin, currall
	carucarius	5	8	46	maslin, currall
Watlington (Oxon.)	fugator	4	4	46	maslin, millcorn, wheat
Iver (Bucks.)	carucarius	5	8	41½	rye
	ten(at)or	6	0	46	rye
Sundon (Beds.)	fugator	5	6	41½	barley, dredge, currall
	tenator	6	0	46	barley, dredge, currall
	fugator	4	6	46	barley
Esher (Surr.)	carucarius	6	0	52	barley
	fugator	6	0	52	

[a]The wage also included the crop of an acre of wheat.

[b]This low wage was presumably supplemented by some unrecorded perquisite. See P. D. A. Harvey, *A Medieval Oxfordshire Village: Cuxham, 1240 to 1400* (Oxford, 1965), p. 77.

[c]The wage also included the crop of half an acre of wheat and half an acre of oats.

[d]The wage also included 72 sheaves of wheat (about 10 bushels) and 72 sheaves of oats (about 8 bushels).

[e]The wage also included 61 sheaves of wheat (about 8 bushels) and 61 sheaves of oats (about 10 bushels).

[f]The money payment is described as *compinag(ium)*, and was assessed at ¾d a week. The wage also included the crop of an acre of barley (about 14 bushels).

[g]Similarly at the other Taunton dependencies (Kingston, Nailsbourne, Holway, Hull, Staplegrove). At the last three of these, however, the grain livery was paid in maslin.

[h]Similarly on the Hampshire manors of Bentley, Bitterne, Crawley, Fareham, Mardon, East Meon Church, Overton, North Waltham, Bishop's Waltham, Wield. In some of these manors bear and currall were a more important part of the grain liveries.

[i]Similarly on the Hampshire manors of Burghclere, High Clere, Ecchinswell and Woodhay.

[j]Estimated from the accounts of 1294–5 and 1297–8.

[k]*fugator* in cash account, *carectarius* in grain account.

Note: Currall was wheat of inferior quality, and bear, otherwise known as mancorn, was an inferior species of barley. Dredge (barley and oats), maslin (wheat and rye) and bullimong (peas and oats) were mixtures of two grains sown together.

Sources: Hants. RO, 11M59 131/53: Durham D. and C. Muniments, Ketton account, 1296–7; *Ministers' Accounts of the Earldom of Cornwall, 1296–1297*, ed. L. M. Midgley, Camden Soc., 3rd ser., 2 vols., LXVI, LXVIII (London, 1942, 1945), pp. 9–10, 20–4, 29–30, 36–8, 51–2, 62–6, 87–90, 197–8, 209–11; *Manorial Records of Cuxham, Oxfordshire, c. 1200–1359*, ed. P. D. A. Harvey, HMC, JP23 (London, 1976), pp. 271–5; *Wellingborough Manorial Accounts, A.D. 1258–1323*, ed. F. M. Page, Northants. Rec. Soc., VIII (Northampton, 1936), pp. xlii, 67, 72–3, 76.

counties of Cumberland, Westmorland and Northumberland could not be taxed because of their devastation by the Scots.[26]

The cash landlords could obtain from their lordships was also increasing. Commercial development affected many dues which had not been monetised earlier, and the period 1180–1330 had its own distinctive characteristics, particularly in the management of demesne lands. The extent to which landlords' total cash incomes rose between 1180 and 1330 varied from estate to estate, according to economic opportunity and the preferred system of estate management. The net cash income of Canterbury Cathedral Priory rose by four-fifths from about £1,406 at the beginning of the thirteenth century to £2,540 in 1331. More strikingly, the bishopric of Worcester tripled its net revenues from £330 in 1185–6 to £1,307 in 1312–13. Increases on other ecclesiastical estates whose income can be assessed were within these extremes.[27].

Feudal tenures had already before 1180 involved a mix of financial and non-financial obligations. Of all the forms of rent and service existing in the twelfth century these were the least amenable to alteration at a landlord's whim. In the early thirteenth century the provision of knight service was renegotiated downwards, so that feudal obligations were no longer related to the older structure of knights' fees. The military services available to the crown survived more as symbols of loyalty or status than for their practical utility. If they were to fight at all the king's principal tenants preferred the superior dignity of feudal service at their own expense, with the prospect of a share in any conquered territory, to the renunciation of independence that the acceptance of wages implied. Not before Edward II's reign did magnates accept the principle of paid service, by which time the unreliability of feudal military service had long become irksome to the crown.[28] Though the formation of armies eventually responded to the more commercial character of the times, the same was not true of feudal tenure. There was no question of replacing it with a tenure of a more commercial kind. A superior lord could derive little in the way of regular income from dependent feudal tenants, and his right to exploit wardships and marriages, and to levy a relief from an incoming heir, were more circumscribed by tenant right in the thirteenth century than before.

The second form of rent we examined from the period 1000–1180 was

---

[26] J. F. Willard, *Parliamentary Taxes on Personal Property, 1290 to 1334: A Study in Medieval English Financial Administration* (Cambridge, Mass., 1934), pp. 343–5.

[27] C. Dyer, *Standards of Living in the Later Middle Ages: Social Change in England, c. 1200–1520* (Cambridge, 1989), p. 36.

[28] Prestwich, *War, Politics and Finance*, pp. 72, 78–9; M. C. Prestwich, *The Three Edwards: War and State in England, 1272–1377* (London, 1980), pp. 63–6.

that from manorial leases, many of which required deliveries of agricultural produce. It remained normal practice between 1180 and 1330 for monasteries to take supplies from their own manors, sometimes over long distances.[29] Similar observations can be made from lay estates. The countess of Leicester's household accounts from 1265, for example, show that most of her requirements for grain were met from estates near where she was staying at any given moment.[30] Despite such continuity with the past the method by which households obtained their grain and cash had changed. From the 1170s it became increasingly common for landlords and their councils to assume direct responsibility for demesne lands and for commercial policies to be co-ordinated from estate centres.[31] Manors were no longer put out to rent; demesnes were administered by servants who accounted for all the profits, and tenants' rents were paid directly to an agent of the landlord. The new order is illustrated in Figure 2, which shows the substitution of manorial officers for the lessees previously shown in Figure 1. The crown's own demesne land is represented in the old way because it remained normal for royal manors to be leased for a term of years or for one or more lives.[32]

Two different circumstances had brought about the abandonment of leasing by most landlords. The first was the price rise of the decades after 1180 which discouraged landlords from making contracts that would fix their income for a long time.[33] Short leases were a feasible alternative, and were indeed tried on many estates, but it was difficult for fair rents to be assessed for this purpose because prices of agricultural products fluctuated so greatly. Short-term leases were also unattractive to potential lessees from the upper ranks of landed society because at this period they were considered demeaning.[34] The second circumstance was the development of royal justice under Henry II which had the effect of making it more dangerous than before to grant the sorts of lease that tenants preferred. The security of occupiers of

---

[29] King, *Peterborough Abbey*, p. 148; Raftis, *Estates*, pp. 178–83.
[30] M. W. Labarge, *A Baronial Household of the Thirteenth Century* (London, 1965), p. 74.
[31] P. D. A. Harvey, 'The Pipe Rolls and the Adoption of Demesne Farming in England', *EcHR*, 2nd ser., 27 (1974), pp. 353–8; Harvey, 'English Inflation', pp. 58–9.
[32] B. P. Wolffe, *The Royal Demesne in English History: The Crown Estate in the Governance of the Realm from the Conquest to 1509* (London, 1971), pp. 61–2.
[33] Harvey, 'English Inflation', pp. 58–63; E. Miller, 'Farming of Manors and Direct Management', *EcHR*, 2nd ser., 26 (1973), p. 138; C. G. Reed and T. L. Anderson, 'An Economic Explanation of English Agricultural Organization in the Twelfth and Thirteenth Centuries', *EcHR*, 2nd ser., 26 (1973), pp. 135–6.
[34] Harvey, 'English Inflation', pp. 61–3; Harvey, 'Pipe Rolls', p. 353; Harvey, *Westminster Abbey*, p. 82.

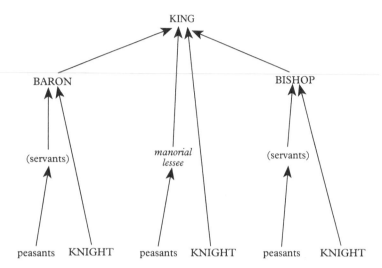

Figure 2   Types of land tenure, *c.* 1220–1330

Capitals indicate a feudal tenure, italics a manorial lease, brackets an employed officer and lower case letters a peasant tenure. The arrows indicate who receive rent and services from whom.

land, even if only for terms or for life, had been enhanced to the point that landlords feared losing control of their manors.[35]

The new system of estate management allowed landlords to reap the benefit of rising demand for food and raw materials. A considerable increase in the income of Peterborough Abbey accompanied the transition to direct management between 1176 and 1210. Over the course of the thirteenth century revenue from ecclesiastical demesnes was rising everywhere. The importance of renders of money rather than produce increased on estates which retained the food-farm system, such as those of Ramsey Abbey. The monks of Canterbury Cathedral Priory in the 1290s allowed large amounts of grain to be sold in local markets even when this meant that demesnes were unable to send their produce quotas to the monks.[36] Twelfth-century aristocrats had undoubtedly had some interest in developing their property, as the founding of new markets demonstrates. Sometimes, like Waleran, count of Meulan, they

---

[35] Harvey, *Westminster Abbey*, p. 82; Stacey, *Politics, Policy and Finance*, pp. 70–2; S. L. Waugh, 'Tenure to Contract: Lordship and Clientage in Thirteenth-Century England', *EHR*, 401 (1986), pp. 813–14.

[36] King, *Peterborough Abbey*, p. 145; Miller, *Abbey and Bishopric*, p. 94; Raftis, *Estates*, pp. 114–15, 178–9; Smith, *Canterbury Cathedral Priory*, pp. 132–3.

had deliberately developed the assets of their estates, employing men with relevant expertise where necessary. William Marshal, the paragon of Angevin chivalry, had commercial interests his admirers had to ignore.[37] Direct demesne management brought the importance of commerce more to the attention of landowners – which is not to say that it drove out other concerns.

Coinage exacted from rural tenants remained an essential part of landlords' incomes, and it too was increasing in amount. By 1279 money rents were predominant over labour and produce rents.[38] The older money component of villain rents known as the assized rent was to some extent protected by custom against the upward pressure of market forces, but examples of increasing rents are not uncommon.[39] Meanwhile other money dues were not protected at all. It is possible that payment of aid was made general on the bishop of Worcester's manors between 1170 and 1250. Landlords were able to increase their revenues from court fines, particularly from the fines paid by new tenants on their purchase or inheritance of customary property.[40]

Some features of peasant tenures continued to resist commercialisation. In the most prosperous parts of England landlords were reluctant to abandon their right to labour services, and in some instances the amount of labour to which they were entitled was increased.[41] This was partly because labour rent might be used as a defining characteristic of villainage in the king's courts; a landlord who commuted services for a fixed money rent might be giving up more than he intended.[42] Landlords also preferred to retain labour because it guaranteed workers for the principal operations of the agricultural year and for other tasks needing ready hands at particular moments. Ploughing services and boons at haymaking and harvest time were often indispensable, and of all labour rents they were the least likely to be relinquished.[43] Week work remained a significant source of labour on some demesnes. How-

[37] Crouch, *Beaumont Twins*, pp. 186–8; D. Crouch, *William Marshal: Court, Career and Chivalry in the Angevin Empire, 1147–1219* (London, 1990), pp. 169–70.

[38] Kosminsky, *Studies*, pp. 152–96.

[39] P. R. Coss, *Lordship, Knighthood and Locality: A Study in English Society, c. 1180–c. 1280* (Cambridge, 1991), pp. 124–6; Dyer, *Lords and Peasants*, p. 74; R. H. Hilton, 'Medieval Agrarian History', *VCH Leics.*, II, p. 179; Miller, *Abbey and Bishopric*, p. 107.

[40] Dyer, *Lords and Peasants*, p. 103; King, *Peterborough Abbey*, pp. 166–7; J. Z. Titow, *English Rural Society, 1200–1350* (London, 1969), pp. 73–8.

[41] Postan, *Essays*, pp. 101–3; Dyer, *Lords and Peasants*, p. 102; Miller, *Abbey and Bishopric*, pp. 101–2.

[42] Hyams, *King, Lords and Peasants*, pp. 185, 195–7; Vinogradoff, *Villainage*, p. 215.

[43] Hilton, *Medieval Society*, pp. 135–6; T. H. Lloyd, 'Ploughing Services on the Demesnes of the Bishop of Worcester in the Late Thirteenth Century', *University of Birmingham Hist. J.*, 8 (1962), pp. 191–4.

ever, it became common for labour services to be acquitted by cash payments, at the convenience of estate officials. In manorial surveys of the late thirteenth century lists of services are accompanied by a tariff of the payments for which they might be sold – 3d for a day's ploughing and harrowing, a farthing for a day's washing and shearing sheep, 1d for an ordinary day's work, and so on.[44] Manorial accounts often include among their cash receipts a sum for 'sold works', particularly in the late thirteenth century and the early fourteenth.[45] On the estates of the bishopric of Worcester perhaps one third of all labour services were sold in 1302–3.[46] Because services could be converted to cash, the upward shift in the burden of labour services which has been observed for the thirteenth century meant in practice an increase in seigniorial cash incomes.[47]

Not all the cash from villages went into the royal treasury or the coffers of landlords. Urban growth must to some extent be considered further evidence of an outflow of payments from the rural population. However careful villagers may have been in re-using iron, a regular demand for new supplies was created by the wearing out of ploughs, cart rims, horseshoes, nails and door fittings. Axes and knives were in everday use for a variety of tasks. Many peasant households had pots and pans which were not the products of village industry.[48] Some types of fabric were also bought in from the outside world. In March 1271 a thief broke into the house of Reynold de le Schaler in Harrold (Beds.) and stole a surcoat of burnet, two sets of linen cloths and a sheet. In 1275 a thief stole linen from Robert of Soltonstall of Sowerby (W.R. Yorks.).[49] The purchase of salt was essential to preserve meat for the gradual consumption of small farmers, and if sea fish was any part of the rural

[44] E.g. *Accounts and Surveys of the Wiltshire Lands of Adam de Stratton*, ed. Farr, pp. 7–12 18–21, 27–30; 'A Transcript of "The Red Book" of the Bishopric of Hereford (*c*1290)', ed. A. T. Bannister, in *The Camden Miscellany, XV*, Camden Soc., 3rd ser., XLI (London, 1929), pp. 1–33.

[45] F. G. Davenport, *The Economic Development of a Norfolk Manor, 1085–1565* (Cambridge, 1906), pp. 47–8; Harvey, *Westminister Abbey*, pp. 233–4; King, *Peterborough Abbey*, pp. 162–6; Miller, *Abbey and Bishopric*, pp. 93–4, 110; Raftis, *Estates*, pp. 222–3, 242–4; W. Rees, *South Wales and the March, 1284–1415: A Social and Agrarian Study* (Oxford, 1924), pp. 176–8.

[46] Dyer, *Lords and Peasants*, p. 100

[47] Miller, *Abbey and Bishopric*, p. 102; Dyer, *Lords and Peasants*, p. 103.

[48] H. S. Bennett, *Life on the English Manor: A Study of Peasant Conditions, 1150–1400* (Cambridge, 1937), p. 233; Dyer, *Standards of Living*, pp. 170–3; Hilton, *Medieval Society*, p. 104.

[49] *Bedfordshire Coroners' Rolls*, ed. Hunnisett, no. 121, p. 54; *Court Rolls of the Manor of Wakefield (1274–1331)*, ed. W. P. Baildon, J. Lister and J. W. Walker, Yorks. Archl. Soc. Rec. Ser., 5 vols., XXIX, XXXVI, LVII, LXXVIII, CIX (1901–45), I, p. 38; Dyer, *Standards of Living*, pp. 170, 175–6.

diet it had to come in by trade. Some villagers probably bought ointments, or tar and pitch, to apply to their sheep during outbreaks of scab.[50]

Circulation of currency back into rural life was impeded by the vagaries of government expenditure, especially because of war. It has been estimated that between June 1294 and November 1295 Edward I's expenditure was equivalent to a quarter of the total English currency.[51] Eventually most of the money spent on troops, or amassed by royal officials, re-entered circulation at some point, but the disposal of such large sums by the government inevitably affected who had money to spend, where it was spent and what it was spent on.[52] Such disruptions of the normal pattern of circulation interrupted regular patterns of demand. When that happened townsmen and countrymen alike complained of shortage of money.[53]

Up to the early fourteenth century, however, the quantity of currency entering the countryside was normally growing. The growth of mercantile activity was a major source of cash in many rural areas, including some that would have been unpromising if dependent upon arable husbandry alone. Some particular resources of land, water or minerals created opportunities for regional specialisation. Pastoral areas are perhaps the most obvious case in point, as in the twelfth century. Inland trade in wool grew both because of the expansion of exports up to the end of Edward I's reign and because of the simultaneous expansion of industry to clothe a rising population.[54] Even peasant wool was bought up by some large producers to fulfil contracts with merchants, and some peasants dealt with merchants directly.[55] There was also long-distance trade in cattle. In 1258 Welsh drovers were regularly bringing cattle through Ross (Herefs.) and Newent (Glos.) to sell in Gloucestershire. In the Pennine valleys of Blackburnshire and upper Swaledale whole

---

[50] The practice was widespread in demesne sheep farming. E.g. *Select Documents of the English Lands of the Abbey of Bec*, ed. Chibnall, pp. 149, 162; *Accounts and Surveys of the Wiltshire Lands of Adam de Stratton*, ed. Farr, pp. 102, 111, 120, etc.

[51] M. C. Prestwich, 'The Crown and the Currency: The Circulation of Money in Late Thirteenth- and Early Fourteenth-Century England', *Numismatic Chronicle*, 142 (1982), p. 56.

[52] *Ibid*, pp. 60–4.   [53] Maddicott, 'English Peasantry', pp. 296–9, 351–4.

[54] E. M. Carus-Wilson and O. Coleman, *England's Export Trade, 1275–1547* (Oxford, 1963), pp. 36–41, 122; Carus-Wilson, *Medieval Merchant Venturers*, pp. 208–9; H. Summerson, 'The Place of Carlisle in the Commerce of Northern England in the Thirteenth Century', in P. R. Coss and S. D. Lloyd, eds., *Thirteenth Century England*, 3 vols. (Woodbridge, 1986–91), I, pp. 143–4.

[55] *Court Rolls of the Abbey of Ramsey*, ed. Ault, p. 249; M. Bailey, *A Marginal Economy? East Anglian Breckland in the Later Middle Ages* (Cambridge, 1989), p. 173; E. Power, *The Wool Trade in English Medieval History* (Oxford, 1941), pp. 44–6.

villages specialised in cattle breeding and dairy farming. The earl of Lincoln alone had 2,400 cattle in his Pennine vaccaries in 1300.[56]

Much country cloth was sold locally, but the large number of fulling mills in sparsely populated regions where there was water power suggests dependence upon merchant trade. They were numerous in the Lake District, the Pennines, the Welsh Marches and in Cornwall and Devon. In Cumberland it has been observed that the fulling mills recorded before 1350 were in upland communities rather than in more densely settled parts of the county.[57] Forest regions gave work to charcoal burners, to craftsmen needing plenty of fuel (potters and iron-makers) and to those who needed wood as a raw material – carpenters, coopers, wheelwrights, cartwrights and makers of bows and arrows.[58] The Forest of Dean in 1282 had at least fifty-eight forges for the manufacture of bar iron and well over 900 charcoal burners' hearths. The charcoal burners sold their produce to forgemasters, when they were not forgemasters themselves, and the latter hired labour and sold the iron that they produced.[59] Other minerals similarly permitted the commercial growth of otherwise unpromising areas of countryside. In Cornwall there were probably over 2,000 people employed in tin mining in 1307, producing on average over 800,000lb of tin, and accounting perhaps for the incomes of over a tenth of the population of the county.[60] The Fenland economy was a highly diversified one in which fishing, fowling and reed-gathering were all occupations whose output was orientated to markets far away.[61] Similar occupations were important in the Breckland of Suffolk and Norfolk, where there was additional employment in flint mining, the custody of warrens, the preparation of skins and the manufacture of cloth from local wool.[62] Quarrying and stonecutting, pottery and tile-making brought trade to many villages.[63] In the villages on estuaries and the coast shipping and

---

[56] H. P. R. Finberg, 'An Early Reference to the Welsh Cattle Trade', *AHR*, 2 (1954), p. 13; J. McDonnell, 'Upland Pennine Hamlets', *NH*, 26 (1990), pp. 22–9; E. Miller, 'Farming in Northern England during the Eleventh and Twelfth Centuries', *NH*, 11 (1976), pp. 12–13; Tupling, *Economic History*, pp. 17–27.

[57] Carus–Wilson, *Medieval Merchant Venturers*, pp. 195–8; Winchester, *Landscape and Society*, pp. 118–19.

[58] J. R. Birrell, 'Peasant Craftsmen in the Medieval Forest', *AHR*, 17 (1969), pp. 91–107.

[59] Hilton, *Medieval Society*, pp. 215–16; Birrell, 'Peasant Craftsmen', pp. 97–9.

[60] J. Hatcher, *Rural Economy and Society in the Duchy of Cornwall, 1300–1500* (Cambridge, 1970), p. 31; Hatcher, *English Tin Production*, p. 47.

[61] H. C. Darby, *The Medieval Fenland* (Cambridge, 1940), pp. 21–42; J. R. Ravensdale, *Liable to Floods: Village Landscape on the Edge of the Fens, A.D. 450–1850* (Cambridge, 1974), pp. 48–51.

[62] Bailey, *Marginal Economy?*, pp. 158–91.

[63] C. Platt, *Medieval England: A Social History and Archaeology from the Conquest to A.D. 1600* (London, 1978), pp. 118–25; Platts, *Land and People*, p. 132.

fishing were major sources of employment.[64] Salt-making was another coastal specialisation, particularly in Lincolnshire.[65]

Finally, there can be no doubt of the impact of urban expansion as a source of cash for rural producers, though in part purchase from market communities represented simple local systems of circulation, through which the money that villagers spent on services and manufactures came back in exchange for agricultural produce. The size of the urban sector in the early fourteenth century is impossible to ascertain with any certainty. We may assign 80–100,000 people to London, at least 50,000 to the next four largest towns (Norwich, Bristol, York and Winchester), perhaps 250,000 to a further 50–100 towns with 3,000 or more people,[66] and perhaps 500,000 to a further 350–400 recorded boroughs together with over 1,000 other market towns and villages whose populations were below 3,000. This would account for perhaps 15 per cent of the total English population. Taking account of the large number of craftsmen and traders in village communities, perhaps one fifth of the population earned its living partly or wholly in the production and trading of goods and services. The proportion of English incomes that these people earned would have been smaller than their share of employment, since these occupations were characteristically those of the relatively less well-remunerated sections of the community. Some townsmen, too, had land of their own, particularly in the smaller towns. As we have seen, few English towns grew large enough to need to bring foodstuffs for more than ten miles or so overland. Nevertheless, urban demand figures in our records as a prominent source of cash in rural communities. The multiplication of small towns meant that by the mid-thirteenth century few villages were beyond a few miles of at least one.

III

In the twelfth century landlord enterprise had contracted as tenant commercial activity increased. In the thirteenth century the situation was reversed. The bigger institutional landlords, like Westminster, Ramsey, Peterborough and Thorney Abbeys, purchased land, sometimes from tenants, and added it to their demesnes.[67] The extent of demesne cultivation peaked between 1240 and 1315. Individual

[64] Hatcher, *Rural Economy and Society*, p. 32; Platts, *Land and People*, pp. 125–6, 217–18.
[65] A. R. Bridbury, *England and the Salt Trade in the Later Middle Ages* (Oxford, 1955), pp. 20–1; Hallam, *Settlement and Society*, pp. 77–80; Platts, *Land and People*, pp. 134–5.
[66] R. H. Britnell, 'The Towns of England and Northern Italy in the Early Fourteenth Century', *EcHR*, 2nd ser., 44 (1991), pp. 22–3.
[67] Harvey, *Westminister Abbey*, pp. 120–2; King, *Peterborough Abbey*, pp. 66–9; Raban, *Estates of Thorney and Crowland*, pp. 62–5; Raftis, *Estates*, pp. 109–12.

demesnes rarely contained more than a few hundred acres; on Peterborough estates in 1301 the acreage of demesne under crops averaged 234 acres on twenty-one manors, and the largest demesne had only 560. But in terms of overall management there were some large concentrations of enterprise. Peterborough Abbey had about 5,437 acres under crops in 1301.[68] By 1299 the bishop of Worcester had 6,969 acres of arable land in demesne, so presumably about 4,500 acres under crops in any one year.[69] The archbishop of Canterbury had all told nearly 7,000 acres under crops in 1274.[70] By 1322 the monks of Christchurch, Canterbury, had 8,373 acres of demesne land under crops in Kent, Surrey and Essex.[71]

The commercial role of local servants who administered demesnes was similar to that of the lessees who had preceded them. They often used their position to develop as minor entrepreneurs in their own right.[72] Accounts such as those from Glastonbury Abbey's manors of Longbridge Deverill and Monkton Deverill show the ingenuity and enterprise of which they were capable.[73] The main difference from times past was that a manorial servant was more answerable for his conduct than the lessee had been. He had to record his activities in detail. The most important records in this respect were accounts, whose use spread slowly before 1250 and more rapidly thereafter.[74] By 1300 we have good accounts from numerous monastic estates (Canterbury Cathedral Priory, Westminster Abbey, Norwich Cathedral Priory, Peterborough Abbey, the abbey of Bury St Edmunds, Ramsey Abbey, Durham Priory), and from some lay estates (the Bigod estates, the Lacy estates, the estates of the earldom of Cornwall). Normally each manor of a large estate had its own annual account, usually drawn up at Michaelmas.[75] Records from small estates are much less common, but some examples exist from the earlier fourteenth century.[76]

The accounting tradition of the thirteenth century was a remarkable achievement. Towards the end of this period Italian merchants were devising new forms of book-keeping which were a landmark in the development of accounting methods. The records of English estate management have been less highly considered by historians of account-

---

[68] King, *Peterborough Abbey*, p. 151.   [69] Dyer, *Lords and Peasants*, p. 67.

[70] Miller and Hatcher, *Medieval England*, p. 182.

[71] Smith, *Canterbury Cathedral Priory*, pp. 140–1.

[72] Britnell, 'Production for the Market', pp. 381–2; Farmer, 'Two Wiltshire Manors', p. 8.

[73] Farmer, 'Two Wiltshire Manors', p. 11.

[74] P. D. A. Harvey, *Manorial Records*, British Records Association: Archives and the User, V (London, 1984), p. 25.

[75] *Ibid.*, pp. 31–5.

[76] Britnell, 'Minor Landlords', pp. 226–31; Saul, *Scenes*, pp. 104–7.

ancy because they showed less concern with the calculation of profit and did not not anticipate modern commercial practice.[77] Yet the degree of commercial rationality behind the two systems is more comparable than these contrasts would imply. The calculation of agricultural profit was conceptually more difficult than anything the Italians attempted. The concept of capital is particularly problematic in an agricultural context. The calculation of receipts and expenditures was further complicated by a large number of non-monetary transactions. The English system of manorial accounts failed to develop because of later changes in the structure of estates rather than because of any deficiency in the method. So long as demesnes were directly administered the associated accounting system became more elaborate and more informative.

Detailed accounts required new habits of accuracy and observation. Written information may not have assisted the day-to-day conduct of demesne management, since past records would not have been available to a manorial officer even in the unlikely event of his being able to read them. The heavy hand of conservative auditors may even in some circumstances have reduced the freedom of manorial officers to make intelligent changes in the structure of farming operations. But the recorded information helped lords and their counsellors to decide how demesnes should be managed.[78] Details such as particulars of the furlongs or fields in which crops were sown allowed for more than a simple check on a reeve's good faith.[79] Written records encouraged a calculating carefulness with money and stores that can be regarded as one of the characteristics of a commercial frame of mind.

How alert were estate managers to the market? Over short periods they could not learn very much. Demesne officials lacked the advantage of a stable structure of prices. For example, in 1288 the price of wheat in Hampshire was 3s 6d at its peak but in 1289 it reached 4s 0d, in 1290 6s 0d and 1291 8s 0d.[80] These fluctuations were the result of the varying quality of the harvest, which in turn was chiefly affected by the weather.[81] The movement of cereal prices was no guide in the short term to changes in demand. Thirteenth-century farmers were less

---

[77] But see Postles, 'Perception of Profit', pp., 12–28 , and E. Stone, 'Profit-and-Loss Accountancy at Norwich Cathedral Priory', *TRHS*, 5th ser., 12 (1962), pp. 26–39.

[78] Stone, 'Profit-and-Loss Accountancy', pp. 40–6.

[79] T. A. M. Bishop, 'The Rotation of Crops at Westerham, 1297–1350', *EcHR*, 9 (1938–9), p. 38; P. F. Brandon, 'Demesne Arable Farming in Coastal Sussex during the Later Middle Ages', *AHR*, 19 (1971), p. 126; R. H. Britnell, 'Agriculture in a Region of Ancient Enclosure, 1185–1500', *Nottingham Med. Stud.*, 27 (1983), pp. 46–7.

[80] Titow, *English Rural Society*, p. 97.

[81] J. Z. Titow, 'Evidence of Weather in the Account Rolls of the Bishopric of Winchester, 1209–1350', *EcHR*, 2nd ser., 12 (1960), p. 363.

responsive to prices than modern farmers are. Wool prices also fluctuated from year to year. Sheep were vulnerable to epidemics that killed
many and damaged the skins of survivors, and in years when output was
lower than usual growers were able to get more for their fleeces. But
wool prices reflected fluctuations in demand more than grain prices, and
may have had more immediate impact on production.[82]

In the longer term, response to commercial incentives was blunted by
conflicting objectives and by the traditional character of technical
knowledge. These constraints both weighed more heavily than they
would with a modern business enterprise. Managerial objectives were
mixed because most estate officers had to give considerable attention to
supplying a large household before they could start thinking of commercial profit. Though greater flexibility was encouraged by the growth of
marketing opportunities, estate officers adopted *ad hoc* strategies that are
likely to have fallen far short of optimising their returns. The accounting
technique available was, as we have seen, only partly orientated to the
assessment of performance. Traditional technology, the other constraint
upon adaptability, restricted the capacity of estate officers to respond to
changing relative prices. They were often locked into practices of
pasturing and crop rotation that meant many agricultural commodities
were joint products. It required technical change to adjust the composition of cropping in favour of more profitable crops. Even so, commercial development between 1180 and 1330 did affect the composition
of output and methods of production. The varied farming systems
revealed in manorial accounts of the period 1250–1349 imply widespread adaptation to market opportunities in different parts of the
country.[83]

The commercial intentions of estate managers are particularly visible
in livestock husbandry. In sheep farming, for example, individual
demesnes were often subordinated to a larger scheme of estate policy in
an attempt to use pasture resources as productively as possible. In 1260
the Holderness flocks of Isabella de Forz, countess of Devon and
Aumale, were organised as a single scheme of management under a
stock-keeper with ten or so subordinate shepherds; there were about
7,000 sheep all told and the wool was sold centrally. Similar large
integrated systems from the late thirteenth century are well recorded on

---

[82] Lloyd, *Movement of Wool Prices*, pp. 13–14.
[83] R. H. Britnell, 'Agricultural Technology and the Margin of Cultivation in the
Fourteenth Century', *EcHR*, 2nd ser., 30 (1977), p. 55; B. M. S. Campbell and J. P.
Power, 'Mapping the Agricultural Geography of Medieval England', *J. of Histl. Geog.*,
15 (1989), pp. 30–8; M. Mate, 'Medieval Agrarian Practices: The Determining
Factors?', *AHR*, 33 (1985), pp. 30–1.

the estates of the abbeys of Crowland and Peterborough.[84] Both the size of sheep flocks and their importance for estate incomes was particularly great in northern England.[85]

The extent to which arable husbandry responded to commercial stimuli is more problematic. We have little evidence from the principal phase of urban expansion, between about 1180 and 1250. Slow technical change in agriculture is in any case difficult to observe. But manorial accounts suggest that between 1250 and 1349 wheat, the principal winter-sown crop, increased its share of sown demesne arable. Barley and dredge, too, expanded at the expense of oats.[86] In eastern Norfolk the reduction of fallowing to cultivate barley for sale was already so advanced that on eleven demesnes for which there is evidence from before 1350 three-quarters of the arable land was under crops each year. A similar intensive husbandry was developed in parts of Kent and coastal Sussex. In Norfolk too, as in some other regions, the cultivation of peas, beans and vetches expanded in the later thirteenth and earlier fourteenth centuries. Besides producing a more valuable and higher-yielding crop than previously, this innovation had beneficial consequences for the soil by diversifying rotations excessively dependent upon cereal crops.[87] More frequent cropping of the land in response to rising urban demand also encouraged the switch from oxen to horses as plough beasts, a development in which Norfolk led the rest of the country.[88]

The high quality of evidence available for manorial demesnes can lead to an exaggerated view of their significance for the marketing of agricultural produce. They probably accounted for most of the wool that went abroad as well as some that was used in English manufactures. But their contribution to the grain trade was more modest. In the shires of

---

[84] K. Biddick, *The Other Economy: Pastoral Husbandry on a Medieval Estate* (Berkeley and Los Angeles, 1989), pp. 100–9; Denholm-Young, *Seignorial Administration*, pp. 58–60; F. M. Page, 'Bidentes Hoylandie (A Medieval Sheep Farm)', *Economic Hist.*, 1 (1926–9), pp. 603–10.

[85] Miller, 'Farming in Northern England', pp. 11–12; B. Waites, *Moorland and Vale-Land Farming in North-East Yorkshire: The Monastic Contribution to the Thirteenth and Fourteenth Centuries*, Borthwick Paper XXXII (York, 1967), pp. 26–35.

[86] B. M. S. Campbell, 'Land, Labour, Livestock and Productivity Trends in English Seignorial Agriculture, 1208–1450', in B. M. S. Campbell and M. Overton, eds., *Land, Labour and Livestock: Historical Studies in European Agricultural Productivity* (Manchester, 1991), pp. 165–70.

[87] Bishop, 'Rotation of Crops', pp. 43–4; Brandon, 'Demesne Arable Farming', pp. 123–8; P. F. Brandon, 'Farming Techniques: South-Eastern England', in *AHEW*, II, pp. 317–25; Campbell, 'Agricultural Progress', pp. 29, 31–3, 43; B. M. S. Campbell, 'The Diffusion of Vetches in Medieval England', *EcHR*, 2nd ser., 41 (1988), pp. 193–208.

[88] B. M. S. Campbell, 'Towards an Agricultural Geography of Medieval England', *AHR*, 36 (1988), pp. 90–8; Langdon, *Horses*, pp. 47, 104–5.

Huntingdon, Cambridge, Bedford, Buckingham, Oxford and Warwick in 1279 demesne land occupied only about a third of the recorded arable acreage.[89] This land grew food for landlords, their families, their servants, their horses and their working beasts. In addition it supplied seedcorn, a variable proportion of the crop but often over a fifth even after a normal harvest.[90] It was unusual for an estate to be able to sell more than a half of its total harvest of bread grain, even if individual manors exceeded this, and the proportion of the oat yield sold was even lower. The share of the total arable acreage devoted to producing marketable demesne crops each year is unlikely to have exceeded 10 per cent. Table 4 gives examples from a variety of estates showing the contrast between three whose grain policy was dominated by marketing (the earldom of Cornwall, the bishopric of Winchester, the abbey of Bec), one which operated a mixed strategy (Beaulieu Abbey) and two which provisioned monastic communities (the priory of Durham and the abbey of Crowland). On the estates of Durham Priory most of the demesnes were leased in 1299–1300, so the figures give an incomplete picture of the total demesne arable economy.[91]

Meanwhile, in the counties surveyed in 1279, 68 per cent of all arable land was held by non-seigniorial occupiers. This area was divided into family units which often left little surplus. The evidence of the Hundred Rolls of 1279 suggests that 46.0 per cent of the serf and free tenant population had less than fifteen acres, about 26.0 per cent hovered around the subsistence level and only some 28.0 per cent of all holdings were clearly above this mark. Similar conclusions emerge from a survey of the estates of the bishopric of Worcester in 1299.[92] The structure of herd-ownership amongst the tenantry was similarly less conducive than that of demesne farming to commercial enterprise. Sheep farming was associated chiefly with the wealthiest peasants. Out of 961 taxpayers in a traditionally pastoral area of Wiltshire in 1225, 338 had no sheep at all, and these were concentrated among the smallholders.[93] There were evidently great differences in the capacity of peasants to engage in commerce for the sake of the profits that they could earn. Differences of wealth in rural communities implied different marketable assets and different marketing strategies. Amongst Bedfordshire taxpayers in 1297,

[89] Kosminsky, *Studies*, pp. 90–1.
[90] D. L. Farmer, 'Grain Yields on Westminster Abbey Manors, 1271–1410', *Canadian J. of Hist.*, 18 (1983), p. 335; Kershaw, *Bolton Priory*, p. 41; M. Mate, 'Profit and Productivity on the Estates of Isabella de Forz (1260–92)', *EcHR*, 2nd ser., 33 (1980), p. 332; J. Z. Titow, *Winchester Yields: A Study in Medieval Agricultural Productivity* (Cambridge, 1972), pp. 121–35.
[91] R. A. Lomas, 'The Priory of Durham and its Demesnes in the Fourteenth and Fifteenth Centuries', *EcHR*, 2nd ser., 31 (1978), pp. 341–2.
[92] Kosminsky, *Studies*, pp. 92, 228; Dyer, *Lords and Peasants*, p. 89.
[93] Postan, *Essays*, p. 243

Table 4 *Proportions of available grain sold on six thirteenth-century estates*

Estate	Year	No. of demesnes	Wheat %	Rye and Maslin %	Barley and Dredge %	Legumes %	Oats %
Earldom of Cornwall	1296–7	11	72.5	16.6	55.7	68.3	41.0
Bishopric of Winchester	1208–9	32	49.1	39.7	27.9	36.0	17.0
Abbey of Bec	1288–9	16	47.7	41.6	41.8	23.4	4.0
Abbey of Beaulieu	1269–70	14[a]	27.7	51.8	45.5	13.1	14.3
Priory of Durham	1299–1300	7	3.0	0.0	2.7	0.4	1.0
Abbey of Crowland	1258–9	14	0.0	2.1	1.6	0.0	0.1

[a]The percentages also take account of grain received and sold from the tithes of Faringdon, Inglesham and Coxwell and from the mill at 'Kyndelwere'. This has the effect of raising all the percentages slightly above what they would have been had demesne produce alone been available for sale.
Sources: Ministers' Accounts of the Earldom of Cornwall, 1296–1297, ed. L. M. Midgley, Camden Soc., 3rd ser., 2 vols., LXVI, LXVIII (London, 1942, 1945), pp. 1–277; *The Pipe Roll of the Bishopric of Winchester, 1208–9*, ed. H. Hall (London, 1903), pp. 1–84; M. Morgan, *The English Lands of the Abbey of Bec* (Oxford, 1946), pp. 50–2; Durham D. and C. Muniments, Enrolled Manors, 1299–1303; F. M. Page, *The Estates of Crowland Abbey: A Study in Manorial Organisation* (Cambridge, 1934), pp. 174–212; *The Account-Book of Beaulieu Abbey*, ed. S. F. Hockey, Camden Soc., 4th ser., XVI (London, 1975), pp. 46–319.

for example, wool and malting grains were associated with the wealthier peasantry.[94] Potential entrepreneurs were a small minority.

Left to their own devices most rural households would have eaten most of what they produced.[95] But tenant farmers had no more freedom of choice than in past centuries. They had to make payments to landlords that forced their produce into the market place. The raising of taxes and the purveyance of grain, too, compelled both free and unfree tenants to market produce, especially in the period of heavier wartime expenditure after 1294. Although there was a lower exemption limit for the payment of taxes on property it did not exclude the wealthier peasant families.[96] Many tenants had to sell between a quarter and a half of their output of grain to pay these compulsory levies in cash.[97] It

[94] K. Biddick, 'Missing Links: Taxable Wealth, Markets, and Stratification among Medieval English Peasants', *J. of Interdisciplinary Hist.*, 18 (1987), pp. 284–91.
[95] Maddicott, 'English Peasantry', pp. 297–9; E. Miller, 'The English Economy in the Thirteenth Century: Implications of Recent Research', *PP*, 28 (1964), p.26.
[96] Willard, *Parliamentary Taxes*, pp. 87–92; Maddicott, 'English Peasantry', pp. 290–4.
[97] Dyer, *Standards of Living*, pp. 135–6, 113; M. M. Postan, 'Medieval Agrarian Society in its Prime: England', in *idem*, ed., *The Cambridge Economic History of Europe*, I: *The Agrarian Life of the Middle Ages*, 2nd edn (Cambridge, 1966), pp. 603–4.

is likely that over 10 per cent of the total arable area was devoted to producing marketable crops by tenants, and that peasant husbandry made a greater contribution to feeding the landless than demesne husbandry.

Differences in conduct between landlords and peasants were not only a matter of attitude of mind and scale of operations. Scope for profit-making was affected by differences in the circumstances of the two classes of producer. Large landlords in particular depended upon rents and other seigniorial dues for a large part of their income, and sometimes for the major part.[98] Two of the commonest quarter days were Michael-mas and Christmas. This meant that the larger estates had cash flowing in early in the accounting year without having to market their own produce, while tenants had to sell a part of their marketable surplus within a few months of the harvest. Large estates were also better able to equip themselves with storage facilities to keep grain in good condition through the winter. So while small producers marketed grain soon after the harvest, bringing prices down because of the inflow of new supplies, large estates could hold their surpluses back until prices rose above their autumn levels. It was a point of policy on large estates to wait until the spring, when alternative supplies of food became increasingly less obtainable. This was not a hard and fast distinction between lords and tenants, however, since many small landlords had only a small income from rents, and were consequently as dependent as the peasantry on sales of agricultural produce.[99]

A source of marketed produce which has received little attention from historians was ecclesiastical tithes. These presumably accounted for the produce of something over 5 per cent of the cultivated area, which passed both from manorial demesnes and from peasant lands into the hands of the rectors of English parishes. Wool, too, was tithed. By the thirteenth century many rectories had been appropriated by monaster-ies, who were able to manage the disposal of the grain and other produce as they thought best. Some, like Bolton, used their tithe grain for their own consumption.[100] Yet it was also common for tithes to be leased or sold. Some tithe produce was simply taken to one of the tithe-owner's nearby demesnes and used to increase the marketable surplus there.[101]

---

[98] Dyer, *Lords and Peasants*, pp. 72–4; G. A. Holmes, *The Estates of the Higher Nobility in Fourteenth-Century England* (Cambridge, 1957), pp. 145–7; N. Saul, *Knights and Esquires: The Gloucestershire Gentry in the Fourteenth Century* (Oxford, 1981), pp. 67–8.

[99] Britnell, 'Minor Landlords', pp. 242–4.   [100] Kershaw, *Bolton Abbey*, pp. 63–7.

[101] R. H. Hilton, *The Economic Development of Some Leicestershire Estates in the Fourteenth and Fifteenth Centuries* (Oxford, 1947), pp. 21–7; *The Account-Book of Beaulieu Abbey*, ed. S. F. Hockey, Camden Soc., 4th ser., 16 (London, 1975), pp. 55–8, 71, 93; R. Graham, *English Ecclesiastical Studies* (London, 1929), p. 266; Lomas, 'Priory of Durham', p. 342n.

The amounts of grain involved in large parishes, like those of southern Lincolnshire, could be considerable; at Pinchbeck in 1274 the tithe of grain was valued at £40, and at Weston in 1287 the estate was £46 13s 4d.[102] The marketing of tithes of demesne produce meant that they were sold by the rectors of parishes rather than by producers. The tithe of peasant crops represented a route by which grain came on to the market by compulsion rather than through the voluntary enterprise of producers.

If commercialisation is defined in quantitative terms, any estimate of its progress in agriculture by 1330 must be a rough approximation. Most of the wool produced came from demesne flocks and the flocks of larger tenants' farms, and it was nearly all sold. So sheep farming may confidently be categorised as predominantly a commercial branch of agriculture. In grain cultivation the situation was more complex, but it is possible that 20–30 per cent of all bread grains produced was sold. The market for these sales is easily accounted for if tradesmen and craftsmen constituted a fifth of the population and if as much as 45 per cent of the rural population was only partially self-sufficient in producing food. Grain production was less commercialised than that of wool, partly because all farmers needed to retain grain for seed (but had no corresponding need to keep wool), partly because farmworkers' wages were often paid in grain (but never in wool), and partly because all farmers, farmworkers and their families had to eat bread or porridge (but did not necessarily spin).

If commercialisation is defined in terms of a spirit of enterprise, there is a contrast to be drawn between larger and smaller producers. Only manorial lords and a small minority of their tenants could afford the luxury of an entrepreneurial frame of mind and sell produce from their demesnes in order to increase their consumption or investment. Smaller farmers benefited from a larger number of local markets and fairs to choose from, and it was in their interests to make the best choices they could. But their marketing was still more a matter of response to compulsion. The sale of produce was often detrimental to their consumption and investment, and consequently to the productivity of their farming.

IV

The commercialisation of rural life was the outcome of millions of separate decisions by landlords, peasants and labourers seeking to improve their lot. It was possible to achieve so much because of the

---

[102] Hallam, *Settlement and Society*, pp. 237–8.

availability of untapped resources, both material and organisational, within the technical grasp of medieval men. To the extent that it succeeded, available resources of land and communications were used more intensively than in the past, and the amount of available employment increased. Interpretations of medieval economic development which underplay this aspect of development lead to unresolvable problems. The discovery that about 45 per cent of the rural population lived on smallholdings that would not support a family does indeed suggest that this proportion of the population lived precariously.[103] But for the situation to persist over many decades there must have been opportunities for employment, on and off the land, which our sources do not adequately disclose. The fact that the poor were vulnerable to famine in years of scarcity and high prices does not dispose of the need to explain how they lived in normal years.

Undervaluing the importance of commercialisation leads to an excessive emphasis on arable husbandry in the thirteenth-century economy. There is no doubt cereals were the largest single category of output. But thirteenth-century England was a diversified economy in which even regions of poor soil were able to exploit such resources as they had. This depended on inter-regional trade. Regions of good agricultural land were more densely populated than others. East Anglia, in particular, achieved some of the highest recorded densities in medieval Europe.[104] Yet average incomes were not necessarily lower in regions of sparser settlement where mining, metal working or weaving were important occupations. Regions of infertile soil could be described as marginal to the English economy only on the assumption that inter-regional specialisation was of trivial significance. Close observation of different types of medieval countryside shows that this was not the case.[105] The denser populations of the towns and the better arable regions had come to depend, by 1300, on iron, cloth, hides and even fuel brought from regions of a different character.

In the twelfth and thirteenth centuries, as in modern periods, technological and occupational adaptation was necessary to accommodate larger numbers of people into existing economic structures. It does not follow that there was a general improvement in standards of living. All the technological change and urban development of the later eighteenth

[103] Postan, 'Medieval Agrarian Society', p. 619.
[104] B. M. S. Campbell, 'Population Pressure, Inheritance and the Land Market in a Fourteenth-Century Peasant Community', in R. M. Smith, ed., Land, Kinship and Life-Cycle (Cambridge, 1984), pp. 91–2; R. M. Smith, 'Human Resources', in G. Astill and A. Grant, eds., The Countryside of Medieval England (Oxford, 1988), pp. 196–8.
[105] M. Bailey. 'The Concept of the Margin in the Medieval Economy', EcHR, 2nd ser., 43 (1989), pp. 10–14.

century – so apparent at the time that it transformed people's attitudes to the age in which they lived – had little immediate impact upon the average income of the population. It is improbable that the changes of the period 1180–1330, when neither urbanisation nor technical change were so rapid, had even as many beneficial effects as the early Industrial Revolution. Two comments about the welfare implications of economic development will be enough to show the need for caution. The first concerns the social distribution of the gains. The second concerns the extent to which they were continuous throughout the period.

First, then, the distribution of gains. There are good grounds for rejecting the supposition that standards of living improved for the whole population between 1180 and 1330. Estimated budgets for smallholders in the countryside during the late thirteenth century show that even their basic supplies of food and fuel must have been problematic, and leave no room for optimism about their capacity to purchase manufactures.[106] Amongst those without land the margin of income available for anything other than food was never more than slender, and it disappeared in years following poor harvests. The earnings of manorial *famuli*, though to some extent protected by custom, left little margin for purchases of manufactures.[107] It is harder to document change, but such evidence as we have is not optimistic. The subdivision of holdings and competition for employment pushed living standards downwards for the poorest families.[108] Piece rates deteriorated during the period of commercial growth between about 1270 and 1320.[109] We cannot estimate changes in the earnings of whole households, but in periods when workers were unable to maintain current wage rates it is unlikely that there was compensation to be had through increased participation by women and children in the workforce. Smallholders and their families were particularly vulnerable to famine when prices rose because of poor harvests.[110]

On balance, any conspicuous increases in household consumption must have been confined to the crown, landlords, churchmen, some merchants and a small minority of the peasantry. We have already seen that the incomes of crown and nobility rose in the course of the period. The merchant class, though still tiny as a proportion of the total

[106] Titow, *English Rural Society*, pp. 78–90; Dyer, *Standards of Living*, pp. 117–18.
[107] Postan, *Famulus*, p. 20.
[108] Dyer, *Lords and Peasants*, pp. 110–12; Farmer, 'Prices and Wages [1000–1355]', pp. 763–4.
[109] Farmer, 'Prices and Wages [1000–1355]' pp. 772–9.
[110] M. M. Postan and J. Z. Titow, 'Heriots and Prices on Winchester Manors', *EcHR*, 2nd ser., 11 (1959), pp. 383–411; Z. Razi, *Life, Marriage and Death in a Medieval Parish: Economy, Society and Demography in Halesowen, 1270–1400* (Cambridge, 1980), pp. 34–45.

population, was larger and wealthier in 1330 than in 1180.[111] Some improvement in the living conditions of richer peasants is indicated in the development of village housing registered by archaeological research.[112] The narrow social basis of these higher real incomes discourages any enthusiastic assessment of changes in economic welfare for the country as a whole.

Famine threatened the poorer inhabitants of both town and countryside more frequently between 1258 and 1320 than before. The famines and murrains of the years 1315–18 were the most severe in the recorded history of England.[113] Famine conditions indicate the limits to which the development of a market order of society could proceed, since it was the degree of market dependence, rather than the size of the population as such, that determined how many people were at risk. The economic achievements of the age had depended upon the growth of a large sector of society dependent upon buying basic foodstuffs. And yet the economy could not guarantee adequate subsistence to the whole population. The economic weakness here was no doubt partly in the institutions of trade. The way urban regulations protected insiders against outsiders complicated the gathering of accurate knowledge about market conditions, and may have inhibited enterprise in the grain trade. The main problem, however, was the low productivity of arable husbandry. Whether on demesnes or on peasant holdings, the proportion of the harvest required for seed, wages and household was so high that even in good years the marketable surplus was a small proportion of the crop. In years of poor harvest shortages were inevitable.

In rural areas, in fact, the safeguard of traditional relationships was more favourable than the advance of commercialisation for the welfare of families able to benefit from them. The existence of a traditional wage in kind protected certain categories of worker against fluctuations in prices. Even in famine years the ploughman received his grain allowance, and might hope to fare better than his more market-dependent neighbours. A traditional wage, low though it was, also gave the farmworker some protection against the tendency for wages to fall as population grew and more men and women were seeking paid work. In the thirteenth and early fourteenth centuries, when the market price of labour often fell below subsistence level, workers with a guaranteed food supply were the lucky ones. The economic implications of rents in kind are, for a number of reasons, more difficult to specify, but maybe a traditional rent in labour or in kind was in the best interest of most

[111] Lloyd, *English Wool Trade*, pp. 50–6, 124–36; Miller, 'English Economy', p. 29.
[112] Dyer, 'Standards of Living', pp. 161–6.
[113] Kershaw, 'Great Famine', pp. 85–132.

families. It was an advantage to tenants in a period of rising prices that their rent should be fixed by custom. In many cases this meant that at least the fixed money component in tenants' renders to their lords declined in real terms between 1180 and 1330.[114] But it was probably to the advantage of most tenants, too, to perform labour services rather than to pay money, since this left the household's food stocks more intact. The alternative was to find paid work, which in the prevailing state of the labour market was more difficult and less convenient than working on the neighbouring demesne. For these reasons it seems likely that tenants were favoured to the extent that the non-market aspects of land tenure survived.

The second comment concerns the chronology of development. It is unlikely that non-agricultural employment expanded steadily through-out the period of 150 years under discussion. The founding of new towns and new markets implies that the possibilities for growth were deteriorating from the third quarter of the thirteenth century. This is about the time when reserves of colonisable land were becoming exhausted in most of the country. It is also unlikely that the older towns grew continuously throughout the period. Central London was more densely populated in 1300 than on the eve of the Black Death.[115] Rents were falling at Winchester before the Black Death, and it is possible that population was falling.[116] Colchester, too, may have contracted in the earlier fourteenth century.[117] On balance any increases in average standards of living which the technology of the age was capable of yielding were probably realised before the end of the thirteenth century, maybe as early as the 1260s. From that time onwards, though there was certainly technical and administrative change, its effect was more to support the existing level of output per head than to increase it.

These reservations about the beneficial effects of commercialisation do not imply that the institutional achievements of the age were of no cultural significance. On the contrary, they suggest that it is a narrow-minded prejudice to evaluate economic progress solely in terms of modern economic growth. The commercial developments of the twelfth and thirteenth centuries permitted a growth in population which was itself a cultural achievement. They also greatly enriched the resources of knowledge and experience which future generations had at their disposal.

[114] Hatcher, 'English Serfdom', pp. 258–65
[115] D. Keene, *Cheapside before the Great Fire*, Economic and Social Research Council (London, 1985), pp. 19–20.
[116] Keene, *Survey*, I, pp. 93, 239, 243.   [117] Britnell, *Growth and Decline*, pp. 20–1.

6   Lordship

Commercial development was relevant both to what kings and lords
might hope to achieve and to the means they adopted for achieving it.
Though they were not managers of profit-making enterprises, and were
more concerned with other values, honour and authority could be gained
or lost as a result of faulty management. Just as artisans and peasants
modified their practices to secure employment or to increase their
incomes, so their masters altered their methods to safeguard or enhance
their power.

An obvious area for examination is the changing character of feudalism. Even in the early twelfth century tenurial relationships that
ostensibly created personal ties of dependence had often achieved much
less. Between 1180 and 1330 such ties became weaker still. Feudal
tenures never wholly lost the personal aspect implied by the lord's right
to the wardship and marriage of an under-age heir – a right which
particularly benefited the crown as a source of patronage and income[1] –
but such rights had few implications for personal loyalty and dependence. The king's right to the allegiance of his tenants was not primarily
dependent upon his status as feudal superior. Lower down the social
scale the relationship between tenure and personal dependence was
looser than that between king and his subjects, partly because even men
of knightly rank often held land from a number of different lords.[2].

Patterns of allegiance were made more complex, and less meaningful,
by the purchase and sale of land, which was more frequent after 1180
than earlier. On the estates of Peterborough Abbey knights' fees which
had hitherto survived as intact tenures were split up in the last quarter of
the twelfth century.[3] The right of lords to prevent the sale of land was

---

[1]   S. L. Waugh, 'The Fiscal Uses of Royal Wardships in the Reign of Edward I', in Coss
   and Lloyd, eds., *Thirteenth Century England*, I, pp. 53–60.
[2]   Du Boulay, *Lordship of Canterbury*, pp. 106–8.
[3]   King, *Peterborough Abbey*, p.52

already unprotected at law by the reign of Henry III. The treatise ascribed to Bracton argues that a lord could not refuse to accept a substitute tenant.[4] Until 1290 a lord could do nothing to prevent the subinfeudation of land by his tenants.

As in the past lords often parted with inherited land in favour of churches and relatives.[5] After 1180, however, alienation of property through financial necessity became more common than in the past. Men who needed cash quickly sold land or took up loans on the security of property, which they then risked losing. Until their expulsion from England in 1290, Jewish moneylenders operated by giving mortgages of this kind. The financial problems of John de Carun of Sherington (Bucks.) stemmed from a long history of family misfortunes, partly inflicted by the crown. He sold eighty-four acres of land in 1234, but he also had to borrow from Elias le Eveske the Jew. This debt was acquitted by the sale of a further thirty acres or so about 1270.[6] Jews were not the only lenders. Landowners who needed money to go on crusade raised it from churchmen, royal servants, merchants, local landowners or members of their own family, often by selling land. Acquired properties, a wife's marriage portion or an outlying property were likely to be disposed of before the core of an inheritance.[7] But once in financial straits a family could lose all its land by slow attrition.

Though the language of fiefs and feudal service survived in legal formulae, the idea of creating new fiefs as a condition of personal service had become anachronistic by 1180. Subinfeudation continued for over a century after this date, but this was a response to the growth of the land market and the reasons for it were financial. A sale of land by subinfeudation created a permanent rent, which might be only nominal, but it contained the possibility of future entry fines, wardships or escheats. For example, twenty-six of the eighty-four acres which John de Carun sold in 1234 were to be held by knight service, and this not only allowed him to take back the land in wardship for a period during the 1250s, but also meant his son could recover the land in 1286 on the grounds that the original grantee's grandson was illegitimate.[8] In 1290 the statute of Quia Emptores made it illegal to subinfeudate land in order to create new fiefs in this way, though it allowed free men to sell their land by substituting new tenants in the feudal chain. The intention here was to

[4] Bracton, fo. 81: *Bracton*, ed. Woodbine, II, p. 235.
[5] King, *Peterborough Abbey*, p. 52.
[6] A. C. Chibnall, *Sherington: Fiefs and Fields of a Buckinghamshire Village* (Cambridge, 1965), pp. 50–3, 59.
[7] S. D. Lloyd, 'Crusader Knights and the Land Market in the Thirteenth Century', in Coss and Lloyd, eds., *Thirteenth Century England*, II, pp. 130–3.
[8] Chibnall, *Sherington*, pp. 52–3, 61–3.

protect the entitlement of the nobility in wardships, marriages and escheats while allowing the market in land to operate as freely as in the past.[9]

The decay of feudal relationships was accompanied by the abandonment of feudal institutions. The growth of the royal law courts gradually undermined the feudal honour as a unit of jurisdiction, even though the Angevin kings did not set out to weaken private jurisdiction, and this was never a major political issue.[10] In practice barons tolerated appeals to the king's courts and used them themselves to proceed against defaulting dependants. Some honorial courts were sufficiently busy to survive. In the reign of Edward I Isabella de Forz had 'knights' courts', at Plympton (Devon), Harewood (W.R. Yorks.), Skipton in Craven (W.R. Yorks), Cockermouth (Cumb.) and Walbrook (London), though only the first two of these had much business. The earl of Cornwall in 1295–6 held courts for the honours of Wallingford (Berks.), Berkhamsted (Herts.), St Valery (centred on Beckley, Oxon.), Eye (Suff.) and Knaresborough (W.R. Yorks.).[11] Until the reign of Edward I Ramsey Abbey and the honour of Clare continued to hold courts for military tenants where matters such as military service could be discussed. There may have been a similar court at St Albans. But the survival of these courts depended upon the exercise of a broader jurisdiction than that for knights alone. They were used as general courts for free tenants and were employed to enforce decisions of manorial courts where necessary, so that some of their jurisdiction concerned the offences of villains.[12] Meanwhile the court of the honour of Peterborough was already decayed by 1200, though it is known to have met again in 1218. The court of the honour of Ely is last known to have met in 1229.[13]

The continued fading of traditional feudal relationships did not mean that the authority of crown and nobility was weakening. Tenurial links had never been the only determinant of social dependence, and they had long been unreliable as a guarantee of good service. Seigniorial authority rested upon entitlement to property and on generally accepted hierarchi-

---

[9] T. F. T. Plucknett, *Legislation of Edward I* (Oxford, 1949), pp. 102–5.

[10] P. R. Coss, 'Bastard Feudalism Revised', *PP*, 125 (1989), pp. 43–5; J. C. Holt, *Magna Carta* (Cambridge, 1965), p. 225.

[11] *Ministers' Accounts of the Earldom of Cornwall, 1296–1297*, ed. L. M. Midgley, Camden Soc., 3rd ser., 2 vols., LXVI, LXVIII (London, 1942, 1945), I, pp. xvii–xxii, 14–15, 113–28, 138–50, II, pp. 172–6; Denholm-Young, *Seignorial Administration*, pp. 96–9.

[12] *Select Pleas*, ed. Maitland, pp. 48–85; *Court Rolls of the Abbey of Ramsey*, ed. Ault, pp. xiv–xxiv, xxviii–xxx; W. O. Ault, *Private Jurisdiction in England* (New Haven, 1923), pp. 327–8; A. E. Levett, *Studies in Manorial History* (Oxford, 1938), pp. 117–29.

[13] King, *Peterborough Abbey*, p. 36; Miller, *Abbey and Bishopric*, pp. 193–4.

cal beliefs and expectations, not – even in moments of political crisis – on the loyalty of a small group of feudal tenants. Nevertheless, it was in the interests of the powerful to be able to bind men to perform regular duties by ties other than feudal tenure. From the 1180s and 1190s magnates were pioneering a form of patronage in which tenure was of little significance. William Marshal (c. 1147–1219) was one of the first magnates to form a private affinity of knights who, for the most part, owed no feudal service.[14] There was no shortage of minor landlords looking for the patronage of the great. From the thirteenth century there is evidence for the formal retaining of dependants by written contract; at least a hundred examples are known by 1300. They stipulated a variety of types of reward for the client's service, of which a cash annuity was about the most common.[15] The word fee (*feodum*) had implied a grant of land in the twelfth century, but by the end of the thirteenth century it had come to be used for an annual money payment, even for estate officers.[16]

The growth of commerce is of little relevance to these changes. As we have seen, the relationship between lords and their feudal tenants in the twelfth century is not evidence of a natural economy, since both the king and other lords had cash and other resources for remunerating the servants they needed. Furthermore, contractual relationships were not always dependent upon cash payments. The main form of remuneration might be maintenance in the lord's household, tenure of office or the promise of good lordship, with money fees as a minor element in the deal.[17] The links between economic change, commercial growth and changing patterns of lordship were very indirect.

Economic development did, however, encourage the multiplication of some types of office. It created new opportunities for the king and other lords to augment their resources, their prestige and their authority. The expansion of the customs administration, for example, can be analysed as a result of a series of successful moves by which the crown came to benefit from the growth of overseas trade. Direct demesne management was in itself a reason for having more officials on large estates.[18] Many developments were the response to particular problems or particular

[14] Crouch, *William Marshal*, pp. 133–42.
[15] Saul, *Knights and Esquires*, pp. 99–101; Waugh, 'Tenure to Contract', pp. 817, 819–22.
[16] E.g. *Two 'Compoti' of the Lanchashire and Cheshire Manors of Henry de Lacy, Earl of Lincoln*, ed. P. A. Lyons, Chetham Soc., CXII (Manchester, 1884), pp. 15, 40, 51, 88, 97; *Accounts and Surveys of the Wiltshire Lands of Adam de Stratton*, ed. Farr, pp. 90, 99, 108, 116, 126, 134, etc.
[17] J. M. W. Bean, *From Lord to Patron: Lordship in Late Medieval England* (Manchester, 1989), p. 32.
[18] Waugh, 'Tenure to Contract', pp. 814–16, 835, 837.

opportunities. But the way in which these problems were solved, through an elaboration of written records and administrative machinery, created a cultural environment in which further innovation was possible. Just as in the world of market-dependent production the pioneering of new skills was a source of greater specialisation, so it was in the command economy of large households. One direct consequence was a broadening of the range of career opportunities for competent servants.

The most eminent source of patronage was the crown, whose growing power led directly to an expansion in the number of men dependent upon the king. A marked elaboration of offices accompanied the expanding scope of government and its extension to a wider territorial area. Royal record-keeping became bulkier and more formal. By the mid-1280s about 570 people were entitled to receive robes in Edward I's household, some for menial work, some for military or clerical services.[19] There was also a growing number of royal servants who operated permanently outside the king's household as justices, chancery clerks, exchequer clerks and customs officials.

There were many parallels between the development of royal administration and that of noble estates. The management of estates became more centralised. The surviving accounts from the earldom of Cornwall, for example, show this development under way between 1270 and 1295, and demonstrate that conciliar control of the estates was established in the interim.[20] Another feature of change was the growing specialisation and multiplication of administrative offices. Where in the twelfth century large households had often been headed by a single steward responsible for both the household and the estate which supported it, by the middle of the thirteenth these two areas of responsibility were separate, and there had to be both an estate steward and a steward for household affairs.[21] The same movement to greater central control and greater complexity can be seen in monastic houses. The subdivision of responsibilities between obedientiaries already existed in the later twelfth century, but with little formal check on their separate activities. In the late twelfth and early thirteenth centuries monastic administration was elaborated to provide tighter central control. Improved systems of accounting were called into play.[22] During the early thirteenth century the monks of Canterbury Cathedral Priory established a centralised audit of their finances and more effective

[19] Prestwich, *Edward I*, p. 136.
[20] N. Denholm–Young, *Richard of Cornwall* (Oxford, 1947), p. 163.
[21] *EYC*, IV, p. 105; Denholm-Young, *Seignorial Administration*, pp. 6–7.
[22] Knowles, *Monastic Order*, pp. 428–31, 435–9; D. Knowles, *The Religious Orders in England*, 3 vols. (Cambridge, 1948–61), I, pp. 55–63.

control over obedientiaries. This was accompanied by the multiplication of offices and subdivision of tasks.[23]

In the later thirteenth century both secular and religious lords appointed councillors to advise on difficult administrative or legal matters. Details of the council of Gilbert de Clare, earl of Gloucester, in 1299 reveal a mixed composition which is likely to be representative of such bodies everywhere. Its members were paid. Some were friends and neighbours. Others were permanent officials of his household, with special responsibilities for overseeing aspects of administration and auditing the accounts. A third category was that of lawyers with expertise greater than the lord's estate officials could command.[24] The retaining of lawyers, in fact, was one of the most important manifestations of the new form of contractual service.[25] Such councils became a more regular part of estate administration during the later thirteenth century.[26] The author of the *Seneschaucy* assumed both that lords had councils and that their duties included the supervision of local estate officials.[27] A case in point is a meeting of the earl marshal's council at Bungay (Suff.) in 1303, where a reeve's account was balanced and an old debt written off.[28] But the duties of councillors might relate to almost any matter of relevance to the lord's welfare. One of the best known from this period is the council of Canterbury Cathedral Priory, which amongst other things advised Prior Henry of Eastry in his purchases and sales of property.[29]

These considerations account for the multiplication of non-tenurial ties between lords and men which has been noted as one of the most important developments in thirteenth-century society. In 1343, towards the end of our period, Elizabeth de Burgh, the lady of Clare, was giving liveries of cloth and fur to 15 knights, 21 principal clerks, 18 lesser clerks, 93 esquires, 100 minor servants, and 12 pages.[30] The resulting pattern of mutual obligations between lords and men, not depending on

---

[23] Smith, *Canterbury Cathedral Priory*, pp. 19–21, 32–3.
[24] Denholm-Young, *Seignorial Administration*, pp. 28–9; Levett, *Studies*, pp. 26–7; Smith, *Canterbury Cathedral Priory*, pp. 70–2; C. M. Fraser, *A History of Anthony Bek, Bishop of Durham, 1283–1311* (Oxford, 1957), pp. 100–5.
[25] J. R. Maddicott, *Law and Lordship: Royal Justices as Retainers in Thirteenth- and Fourteenth-Century England*, PP supplement IV (Oxford, 1978), pp. 10–21; Waugh, 'Tenure to Contract', pp. 822–3.
[26] Du Boulay, *Lordship of Canterbury*, pp. 111–12; Denholm-Young, *Richard of Cornwall*, p. 163; Miller, *Abbey and Bishopric*, pp. 223–4; Smith, *Canterbury Cathedral Priory*, p. 70.
[27] Seneschaucy, I, c.9, in *Walter of Henley*, ed. Oschinsky, pp. 266–7: cf. XII, cc. 77, 78, pp. 290–3.
[28] Denholm-Young, *Seignorial Administration*, p. 29.
[29] Smith, *Canterbury Cathedral Priory*, pp. 77–78.   [30] Holmes, *Estates*, pp. 58–9.

any tenurial relationship, is often called bastard feudalism, though the word bastard is tendentious in this context. For many minor landlords ties of affiliation were little more than an accommodation to the superior power of a local magnate. Perhaps two-thirds of minor landlords, the gentry as they were later to be called, were retained by the earlier fourteenth century.[31] The greater variety of career structures open to both barons and knights allowed many men to consolidate or improve the fortunes of their families.

It is difficult to talk meaningfully about the fortunes of a landowning class, or landowing classes, in a world where there was such rapid turnover as there was in thirteenth-century England. In every part of the kingdom the plight of established families who were losing land and status can be contrasted with the triumphs of those who were accumulating. Rapid accumulation was never possible out of incomes from land alone. The most conspicuously accumulating families were those whose earnings derived from some lucrative office or, less commonly, from the profits of overseas trade. The Braybrook Cartulary records the properties acquired by Robert de Braybrook and his son Henry between 1185 and 1234. Robert was under-sheriff of Bedfordshire and Buckinghamshire between 1197 and 1204, then sheriff, and by the time he died in 1211 he was sheriff of Northamptonshire and Rutland as well. His son took the offices over from him. The two between them built up the Mathias Manor in Great Crawley (Bucks.) by piecemeal purchases. A comparable example from the same region at a slightly later date is that of the Cave family of Sherington (Bucks.). Their first holdings in the village were acquired in the 1240s by John Cave, a lawyer and later a royal justice. In the nearby village of Lavendon (Bucks.), Simon de Norwich, a royal clerk, built up the manor of Uphoe from the 1230s.[32]

II

Both the development of feudal land law and the growth of government and administration affected the amount of activity governed by rules. Lords both high and low accepted some restriction of their freedom of action in exchange for increased authority or income in other respects. Lords were aware that to gain a regular and uncontested advantage from new opportunities they would have to accept new rules to define their

[31] Saul, *Knights and Esquires*, pp. 97–8.
[32] A. C. Chibnall, *Beyond Sherington* (Chichester, 1979), pp. 29, 107–9; Chibnall, *Sherington*, pp. 56–7; *VCH Bucks.*, IV, p. 383. On this subject see further Coss, *Lordship*, pp. 294–304, 312–17, and P. R. Coss, 'Sir Geoffrey de Langley and the Crisis of the Knightly Class in Thirteenth-Century England', in Aston, ed., *Landlords, Peasants and Politics*, pp. 166–202.

rights. Many developments in the common law relating to land tenure, the use of waste land and the conduct of trade can be seen in these terms. So can the tighter codes of conduct relating to relationships between lords and borough communities. Even the traditional rights of kings and other lords led to conflict that could be resolved only by some formal definition of legality. For example, the problems raised by female succession created conflicts both within families and between lords and tenants, but during the Angevin period the king's courts began to adopt routine principles that narrowed the discretion of feudal superiors.[33] The restriction of the king's capacity to levy arbitrary feudal dues or to impose taxes can be seen as further instances of this limitation of conflict. By the early fourteenth century there were writers who seriously considered the possibility of introducing procedures to allow legal redress against the crown.[34] It is likely that the expansion of rule-bound conduct had an independent beneficial effect in the furtherance of economic achievement.

Between 1154 and 1216, the opposing principles of royal arbitrariness and royal justice were more in tension than ever before in English history.[35] On the one hand Henry II displayed unprecedented enthusiasm for enforcing the criminal law, overhauled the English system of private litigation and fought a major battle with the church to define more precisely the boundaries between royal and ecclesiastical jurisdiction. On the other hand the assertion of his will, in defiance of all opposition, came as second nature to him, and he is best known as the king who, in his rage, authorised the murder of an archbishop of Canterbury. King John's respect for the law of the land and insistence on its observance bemused historians in the days when he was castigated as the most tyrannical of all English kings.[36] Throughout the period, kings continued to enforce the law of the land, and expand its scope, while manipulating the courts when political circumstances made this desirable. Henry III's retention of the county of Chester in his own hands after the death of Earl John in 1237 was an instance of royal policy affecting the administration of justice.[37] Edward I was prepared on occasion to fix the process of law to his own advantage, as when he

[33] S. L. Waugh, 'Women's Inheritance and the Growth of Bureaucratic Monarchy in Twelfth- and Thirteenth-Century England', Nottingham Med. Stud., 34 (1990), pp. 71–92.

[34] M. H. Keen, England in the Later Middle Ages (London, 1973), pp. 82–5.

[35] J. E. A. Jolliffe, Angevin Kingship, 2nd edn (London, 1963), pp. 50–86; Holt, Magna Carta, pp. 68–79; W. L. Warren, Henry II (London, 1973), pp. 385–9, 395.

[36] D. M. Stenton, English Justice between the Norman Conquest and the Great Charter, 1066–1215 (London, 1965), pp. 88–9.

[37] R. Eales, 'Henry III and the End of the Norman Earldom of Chester', in Coss and Lloyd, eds., Thirteenth Century England, I, pp. 109–12.

cheated the heirs of Aveline, countess of Aumale, out of their inheritance in 1274.[38] Enforcement of law and the exercise of arbitrary judgement existed side by side in government as different ways of exercising power.

More damaging than anything the crown did to the cause of justice in everyday life was the propensity of royal servants, and other men with local influence, to bend the law to their own advantage.[39] Ordinary villagers had little redress against the frequent arbitrariness of the king's local officers.[40] The traditional pattern of delegating local jurisdiction to landlords remained a feature of English society under the three Edwards. The Hundred Rolls of 1274–5 show that out of about 628 English hundreds 358 were in private hands.[41] The right to such jurisdiction was liable to be scrutinised more closely than it had been in the past, but little was done to supervise its performance. At county court level the bulk of the business was transacted by a small number of men, and their chief concern was to defend local interests rather than to advance justice.[42] Thirteenth-century reform movements attempted to eliminate corruption in the courts. In 1258 commissions were appointed to hear complaints against officials in each county.[43] Edward I in 1274–5 made it easier to transfer cases from the county to the court of Common Pleas, and in 1275 he made it easier to complain about officers of the crown by means of petition to parliament, though historians have agreed with the Dunstable chronicler, who recorded these reforms with the comment that nothing came of them.[44] Edward's reforms involved a concession to local interests concerning the sort of men who were appointed sheriff. Even royal commissions of oyer and terminer appointed to deal with specific complaints could be rigged.[45]

The interests of court groups could be more sinister than those of local caucuses. When the powers of the crown were exercised by a faction, as under the aegis of the Poitevins in 1232–4 or the Despensers in 1321–6, the king's justice was harnessed to servicing the interests of the dominant group.[46] Where kings themselves were prepared to bend rules, it is

[38] K. B. McFarlane, *The Nobility of Later Medieval England* (Oxford, 1973), pp. 256–9.
[39] Chibnall, *Sherington*, pp. 61–5.
[40] R. F. Treharne, *The Baronial Plan of Reform, 1258–1263* (Manchester, 1932), pp. 44–6.
[41] Cam, *Hundred and the Hundred Rolls*, p. 137.
[42] P. R. Coss, 'Knighthood and the Early Thirteenth-Century County Court', in Coss and Lloyd, eds., *Thirteenth Century England*, II, pp. 55–7.
[43] Treharne, *Baronial Plan*, pp. 108–16.
[44] 'Annales Prioratus de Dunstaplia', in *Annales Monastici*, ed. Luard, III, p. 263.
[45] J. R. Maddicott, 'Edward I and the Lessons of Baronial Reform: Local Government, 1258–80', in Coss and Lloyd, eds., *Thirteenth Century England*, I, pp. 11–30.
[46] Stacey, *Politics, Policy and Finance*, pp. 38–9; N. Saul, 'The Despensers and the Downfall of Edward II', *EHR*, 99 (1984), pp. 22–7.

not surprising that members of their families, and others of their leading subjects, should be prepared to do the same thing. Powerful members of the nobility were on occasion blatantly defiant of proper legal procedure. In 1266 Henry of Almain contrived the arrest of Robert de Ferrers, earl of Derby, who was kept in a royal prison until he had agreed to grant away all his estates. Expansion of government administration did not breed traditions of dispassionate public service. It encouraged local interest to compete for control of the system.[47]

There is plenty of scope for scepticism about the bureaucratic disinterestedness of English medieval institutions. But such a response can be carried too far. The development of rule-bound conduct was too pervasive for its social significance to be dismissed out of hand. The important contrast is not with absolute standards but with the preceding period, and such a comparison leaves no doubt that institutional development had had a far-ranging impact upon the security of property.

One relevant facet of changing social relationships was the body of custom concerning feudal dues, both between subtenants and tenants-in-chief and between tenants-in-chief and the crown. Here developments between 1180 and 1330 were conspicuously favourable to tenants. After a long period when many aspects of feudal custom had been arbitrary, and open to abuse by feudal superiors, the thirteenth century was an age of standardisation, partly through deliberate codification and partly through the accumulation of precedents at common law. The drive towards standardisation arose chiefly from opposition to the monarchy. In the revolt against King John in 1215 the king's arbitrary exercise of his feudal rights was one of the principal issues at stake.[48] Magna Carta was an assault on the arbitrary freedom of action as feudal lords which the Angevin kings had inherited from their Norman predecessors. But the settlement of 1215 was not designed to benefit tenants-in-chief alone. The relations between them and their own tenants were also regulated, partly as a result of the political circumstances in which the charter was drawn up. These principles gained the force of law in the thirteenth century not so much by the insecure guarantee of John's seal in 1215 as through the reissue of the Great Charter by the king's friends in 1216, 1217, 1225 and subsequently.[49] They restricted the exploitation of feudal reliefs and arbitrary amerce-

[47] Coss, 'Bastard Feudalism Revised', pp. 50–1, 55; Denholm-Young, *Richard of Cornwall*, pp. 143–4.
[48] J. C. Holt, *The Northerners: A Study in the Reign of King John* (Oxford, 1961), pp. 177–82; Holt, *Magna Carta*, pp. 107–12, 201–2.
[49] Holt, *Magna Carta*, pp. 38, 196–200, 216, 269–76.

ments, and compelled the monarchy to move in other directions to expand its income.[50]

The effective extension of rule-bound behaviour is to be seen most convincingly in the surge of business in the king's courts. The growth of royal jurisdiction was in part the result of an absolute increase in litigation which can be related to economic development. The increased buying and selling of land, and the increased number of credit operations arising from commercial development, would in themselves have had some such effect. But the development of the king's courts was also in part a response to the dependable routine in operation there.[51] New legal actions, *novel disseisin*, *mort d'ancestor* and *darrein presentment*, provided unambiguous procedures for anyone disseised of his property or his expectations of inheriting property without due process of law. They concerned themselves not with the ultimate right to property but with the protection of those currently in possession. Their introduction inhibited some of the lawlessness that arose from self-help amongst the nobility without giving too much independence to the king's local officers.[52]

As time went on, possibilities for litigation continued to be enhanced by new forms of action at common law.[53] Most of these were devised by the courts, but some received statutory authority. Edward I's Statute of Westminster I (1275) extended the availability of the action of *novel disseisin* to the heirs of the injured party, and made it possible to proceed through the courts during periods of the year that had previously been blocked. The Statute of Gloucester (1278) allowed plaintiffs to recover their costs. Westminster II (1285) widened the range of occasions where *novel disseisin* could be used and made it more difficult for defendants to excuse themselves from attending court.[54] The build-up of case law in the king's courts is demonstrated by Bracton's notebook, and later by the Year Books of case reports from 1283 onwards.[55] New devices worked out by the lawyers had further beneficial implications for the security of free tenure. They extended the range of techniques whereby landlords and tenants could control their properties, and removed many of the uncertainties of legal principle which had hitherto

[50] Stacey, *Politics, Policy and Finance*, pp. 43–4, 217.
[51] Stenton, *English Justice*, pp. 91–2.
[52] W. L. Warren, *The Governance of Norman and Angevin England, 1086–1272* (London, 1987), pp. 112–19.
[53] F. W. Maitland, *The Forms of Action at Common Law* (Cambridge, 1936), pp. 31, 41–7.
[54] Prestwich, *Edward I*, pp. 271–2.
[55] A. Harding, *The Law Courts of Medieval England* (London, 1973), p. 79; F. W. Maitland, *Selected Historical Essays*, ed. H. M. Cam (Cambridge, 1957), pp. 104–6.

surrounded such important issues as the inheritance and transfer of land.[56]

All this did nothing to simplify the common law. Legal sophistication increased the complexity of titles to property, and procedures through the courts became increasingly numerous and varied. The same problem could be brought to trial in a variety of ways. Judgements were often only interim solutions. There were so many opportunities for reopening old issues and challenging the results of a previous trial that some disputes were protracted over many generations. The resulting slowness and expense of litigation often encouraged contestants to compromise. In later centuries procedural intricacies became excessive, and weakened the authority of the law. Arguably, though, in the thirteenth century the complexities were well adapted to the values of the landed classes since they allowed feuding with writs to replace feuding with armed men.[57]

The best measure of the crown's achievement in improving the reliability of land law was the development of the final concord, or fine, as a legal instrument. The fine was a record kept by both parties to an action over real estate, and because it originated in the king's court its status came to rival that of charters.[58] They were often recorded in cartularies.[59] On 15 July 1195 copies of all fines began to be filed in the treasury.[60] The many thousands of surviving feet of fines (as such official copies were called) constitute our best source of information about changes of land tenure in the thirteenth century. There are over 2,600 surviving fines from thirteenth-century Essex. Litigation during the eyre of 1198 gave rise to 200 fines in Norfolk alone.[61] The authoritative standing of fines led, perhaps even before Henry II's death, to the practice of initiating fictitious actions in the king's courts simply to establish the claimant's title more securely than a charter could do.[62]

Was the tenure of property better protected in the period 1180–1330 than earlier? Political confiscations were numerous. The loss of Normandy in 1204 caused problems for noble families similar to those which

---

[56] J. M. W. Bean, *The Decline of English Feudalism, 1215–1540* (Manchester, 1968), pp. 104–17.

[57] R. C. Palmer, *The Whilton Dispute, 1264–1380: A Social-Legal Study of Dispute Settlement in Medieval England* (Princeton, 1984), pp. 214–15; Saul, *Scenes*, pp. 90–2.

[58] Richardson and Sayles, *Law and Legislation*, pp. 114–15.

[59] *Cartulary of Cirencester Abbey*, ed. Ross and Devine, I, nos. 186–8, 190–214, pp. 179–201, and numerous others in volumes II and III.

[60] M. T. Clanchy, *From Memory to Written Record: England 1066–1307* (London, 1979), p. 48.

[61] *Feet of Fines for Essex*, ed. R. E. G. Kirk and others, Essex Archl. Soc., 4 vols. (Colchester, 1899–1964); Stenton, *English Justice*, pp. 52, 84.

[62] Warren, *Henry II*, p. 348.

had beset their predecessors in similar circumstances.[63] But there were no great discontinuities in land tenure comparable to those of the eleventh century. Nor was there so much marauding as in the Anglo-Norman period; Henry II's legal reforms had channelled disputes through the courts even if they were not always dealt with even-handedly when they got there. After Henry II's reign, too, ecclesiastical properties were better protected than in earlier times. No period of the later Middle Ages saw the inroads into monastic or episcopal estates that had complicated their histories before 1154. In part this is attributable to the foresight of churchmen themselves. Not for nothing did they store and index their charters, or fill their cupboards with manorial records. But in part the more secure status of church properties was the result of changing codes of behaviour. Depredations upon ecclesiastical estates by the crown in periods of vacancy were also restricted from the later twelfth century as a result of agreements made with the church.

III

None of the economic development of the thirteenth century removed the disabilities of unfree status or made the weight of manorial obligation any lighter. On the contrary, customary tenure was more clearly defined as servile than ever before as a direct result of legal developments that benefited free tenants. An unintended consequence of the growth of business in the king's courts was that for the first time freedom acquired a definite meaning in the law of the land. Free tenures were protected by the various forms of legal action that were made available from the 1160s. However, the king's justices gave no protection to customary tenure, and so created a new rift in status between villains and free men.[64] Some serfs still could be evicted at the lord's will. The property rights of villains were circumscribed by the doctrine that their chattels belonged to their lord. Increasingly in the thirteenth century they were expected to pay an annual fine if they wanted to live away from the manor to which they were attached.[65] They were also subject to fiscal demands from which free men were exempt. From manorial accounts and court rolls we can see that villains were burdened with personal obligations such as the payment of merchet, when a villain's

---

[63] Warren, *King John*, pp. 118–21.
[64] *Select Pleas*, ed. Maitland, pp. lxxii–lxxiii; Hyams, *Kings, Lords, and Peasants*, pp. 134–6.
[65] Coss, *Lordship*, pp. 119, 125; Hyams, *Kings, Lords, and Peasants*, pp. 34–6; Miller, *Abbey and Bishopric*, p. 141; J. A. Raftis, *Tenure and Mobility: Studies in the Social History of the Medieval English Village*, PIMSST, VIII (Toronto, 1964), pp. 139–43.

daughter married, or of leyrwite, when an unmarried girl became pregnant.[66] Thirteenth-century landlords were consequently tenacious of their villains, and conflicts over the legal status of individuals and groups were numerous.[67]

Changes in the burden of dues from villain tenements are difficult to assess. Even the customary components in villain rents were not absolutely frozen, and there is widespread evidence that lords could increase labour services. Some elements of customary tenure were not fixed, so that lords were able to increase the sums they demanded as the value of land increased. The entry fines which villains paid on taking up properties were capable of being raised to take account of changes in land values. The highest entry fines so far recorded are from Somerset on the estates of the abbot of Glastonbury and on the bishop of Winchester's great manor of Taunton.[68] Even where they were appreciably lower, an upward tendency in the later thirteenth century may sometimes be observed.[69] Villains were significantly more vulnerable to seigniorial exactions than free tenants, who mostly paid a fixed money charge at the manor house from which they were held. For villains themselves, comparisons with the lighter burdens on free tenants, and on luckier groups of customary tenants, were undoubtedly the most poignant indicator of their inferior status. Customary rents were less capable of being negotiated than purely contractual ones, and some of them were lower than contractual rents by the early part of the fourteenth century.[70] Yet freehold rents were not contractual rents either, and freeholders were less susceptible to pressure to squeeze extra cash out of them.

Colonisation of new land and urban growth, with their promise of greater personal freedom, created continuing opportunities for migration, particularly in the century before 1260. No more than in the Anglo-Norman period was it feasible for lords to control the movements of serfs determined to escape from the manor of their birth. The non-inheriting children of customary tenants often took advantage of these opportunities to create an independent life for themselves that would otherwise have been impossible, and the total level of migration was high. But economic constraints on migration by villagers with land were even more severe than in the twelfth century. Serfs who surrendered an

[66] E.g. J. R. Ravensdale, 'Population Changes and the Transfer of Customary Land on a Cambridgeshire Manor in the Fourteenth Century', in Smith, ed., *Land, Kinship and Life-Cycle*, pp. 210–11, 217–19; Razi, *Life, Marriage and Death*, pp. 45–50, 64–71.

[67] Hilton, *Class Conflict*, pp. 127–33; Hilton, 'Freedom and Villeinage', pp. 184–90.

[68] Titow, *English Rural Society*, pp. 73–8.   [69] King, *Peterborough Abbey*, p. 166.

[70] Hatcher, 'English Serfdom', pp. 259–65.

inherited holding could not hope to match it by a free equivalent elsewhere. By 1260 the reserves of new agricultural land were running out.[71] Higher grain prices, falling wage rates and recurrent famine made urban employment an even more unattractive alternative to serfdom than it had been before 1180. This accounts for the fact that in spite of continuing commercialisation serfdom remained unshaken in thirteenth-century rural society.

Yet though the king's justices prevented villains from taking advantage of opportunities opening up to their free neighbours, they did not take away legal facilities they had previously enjoyed. In reality, developments in manorial jurisdiction meant that the legal status of customary tenants became more secure than before, even if it had not improved as much as that of free men with land of equivalent extent and even if the financial burden of villainage had increased. One of the clearest indications of this is the practice, well attested from the 1270s though with some earlier examples, of recording the business of manorial courts.[72] From the earliest surviving examples these records are concerned not only with listing fines and amercements but with extending the legal memory of the court. In part this was simply to help estate officials by recording the stage that each piece of business had reached. However, manor court rolls also recorded titles to property and changes of custom affecting whole villages or individual holdings. At the first court recorded at Chalgrave (Beds.) in July 1278 the lord of the manor granted to John son of Richard of Wootton three acres of land to be held for 2s a year with all other accustomed services.[73] This implies that he committed himself to recognising the hereditary and contractual expectations of his tenants-at-will.

Manorial justice had been so transformed in recent times that to reconstruct how halmotes conducted their business in the twelfth century is out of the question. The common influence upon them had been the procedures of royal justice. A litigant had to plead according to a set form of legal action. There were a number of different 'forms of action' at common law, each of which had to be conducted through the court in accordance with precise rules. Pleas of debt and pleas of trespass, as found in manorial records, derived from actions in the king's courts. The same was true even of the procedures for defending a title to

[71] Raftis, *Tenure and Mobility*, pp. 139–52; Miller and Hatcher, *Medieval England*, pp. 41–9.

[72] Harvey, *Manorial Records*, p. 42; R. M. Smith, 'Some Thoughts on "Hereditary" and "Proprietary" Rights in Land under Customary Law in Thirteenth and Early Fourteenth Century England', *Law and Hist. R.*, 1 (1983), pp. 98–9, 114, 126.

[73] *Court Roll of Chalgrave Manor, 1278–1313*, ed. M. K. Dale, Beds. Histl. Rec. Soc., XXVIII (Streatley, 1950), p. 3.

customary land. In the harsh language of lawyers' textbooks nothing could seem further removed from the legal rights of the free tenant than those of the tenant-at-will. Yet early manor court rolls show villains bringing pleas framed in terms devised in Henry II's reign to handle disputes about freehold.[74] At Burton (W.R. Yorks.) in 1275 a woman claimed that she had been forcibly deprived of a barn to which she was the next heir, and an inquest was summoned to enquire whether this was the case. The same year a widow alleged at Wakefield (W.R. Yorks.) that she had been unjustly disseised of a third of a bovate, and she offered to submit to the verdict of a sworn inquest.[75]

Even in the transfer of customary land the procedures of the later thirteenth century were not very old. The normal practice was that on a tenant's death the heir or heirs took up the holding on payment of an entry fine, and performed fealty to the lord. If a piece of customary land was to be exchanged, the existing tenant formally surrendered it to the lord of the manor or his officer, who then granted it to the new tenant. The new tenant paid a money fine on entry and performed fealty. These procedures had been adapted from those relating to seisin in common law, which in turn derived from feudal custom as practised in honorial courts. Their use in manorial courts was the result of a recent process of assimilation, still under way in the later thirteenth century.[76] There had been a revolution in manorial justice hardly less great than that in the king's courts, with major implications for the security of villain tenure.

Other evidence pointing in the same direction is the care with which manorial custom was codified. English lords did not grant their villains the sort of charter by which villagers of France and Italy secured their rights; in English law such documents would have implied their grantees' free status, and would have created intolerable legal anomalies.[77] Charters granting collective rights were only for communities of townsmen whose freedom was unambiguously conceded. On the other hand custumals that recorded tenurial practice in detail were a normal part of estate documentation in the thirteenth century. Though these records were the private archives of landlords, the information they contained was established in public, often with the sworn assent of senior inhabitants of the villages concerned, as in the late twelfth-century custumals of Glastonbury Abbey and the mid-thirteenth-century custumals from

[74] Pollock and Maitland, *History of English Law*, I, p. 588.
[75] *Court Rolls of the Manor of Wakefield*, ed. Baildon and others, I, pp. 43–4, 77.
[76] G. C. Homans, *English Villagers of the Thirteenth Century* (New York, 1960), pp. 129, 130, 144, 150, 201, 203; Raftis, *Tenure and Mobility*, pp. 63–7; Smith, 'Some Thoughts', pp. 108–10.
[77] Hyams, *King, Lords, and Peasants*, pp. 44–5; Pollock and Maitland, *History of English Law*, I, pp. 418–19; Vinogradoff, *Villainage*, p. 73.

the abbeys of Ramsey and Gloucester.[78] This information was presumably available in manorial courts since it is difficult to imagine what other use it might have. The landlord's primary purpose was no doubt to protect himself against the evasion of services to which he was entitled. This defensive spirit was nevertheless a conservative one, and carried favourable implications for the security of villain tenure.

It is significant, in this context, that the arbitrary treatment of ordinary villagers, both free and unfree, became less common after the mid-twelfth century than it had been in the Anglo-Norman period. Even in periods of internal unrest, chroniclers no longer dwell on the cruelties inflicted by the powerful on the poor. The eviction of villagers by Cistercian abbeys became much less common than in the twelfth century.[79] It is difficult to cite evidence to establish what is essentially an argument from negative evidence. Nothing in either the literary or non-literary sources of this period implies the degree of seigniorial ruthlessness associated with the reigns of William I or Stephen. Property was least secure in the far north of England, but this was the result of external aggression. From the late thirteenth century the Scots raided the country, particularly in the period of anarchy that followed England's defeat at Bannockburn.[80]

As in the world of military tenures, many impositions on tenants that had once been arbitrary were moderated or fixed. This continued a development which had certainly begun during the twelfth century.[81] The complex history of tallage remains to be written, but it seems that its capacity to disrupt peasant economies was lower in the thirteenth century than in the early twelfth. Arbitrary tallage was a corroborative indicator of unfree status in thirteenth-century law.[82] Yet on some estates it was transformed into a fixed annual payment, often assessed on a village or manor as a whole and levied at a regular time each year. Even heriots and entry fines underwent a similar process of standardisation.[83]

Another feature of changing estate management was the diminishing

---

[78] *Liber Henrici de Soliaco*, ed. Jackson, pp. 1–142; *Cartularium Monasterii de Rameseia*, ed. Hart and Lyons, I, pp. 281–373, 380–496; *Historia et Cartularium Monasterii Sancti Petri Gloucestriae*, ed. Hart, III, pp. 35, 41, 61, 67.

[79] Donkin, 'Settlement and Depopulation', p. 156.

[80] E. Miller, *War in the North* (Hull, 1960), pp. 5–7; Kershaw, *Bolton Priory*, pp. 14–17; Winchester, *Landscape and Society*, pp. 44–5.

[81] Raftis, *Estates*, p. 118n.

[82] Hyams, *King, Lords, and Peasants*, p. 191; Vinogradoff, *Villainage*, p. 163.

[83] Bennett, *Life on the English Manor*, pp. 140–1; H. P. R. Finberg, *Tavistock Abbey: A Study in the Social and Economic History of Devon* (Cambridge, 1951), p. 254; Hatcher, 'English Serfdom', p. 253; Miller, 'Social Structure', p. 694; Titow, *English Rural Society*, pp. 76–7.

importance of service holdings, the final vestiges of slavery. It is possible still in the thirteenth-century records to trace the route by which slaves were accommodated with land and absorbed into the cotter class. Eleven slaves at Felstead in Henry I's reign correspond to eight ploughman holding smallholdings in the early thirteenth century.[84] Such tied holdings, sometimes called *encheland*, are to be found all through the period, even if the service due from them was sometimes replaced by a money rent.[85] Already by 1200 the distinctive nature of these holdings had frequently been lost because manorial officers were able to supply the labour they needed more satisfactorily by employing men less formally attached to demesne husbandry. Competition amongst skilled men for employment was to the advantage of landlords, and made the old system of retaining labour redundant in most parts of the country by the fourteenth century.[86]

A distinctive feature of village life in the period after 1180 was the development of a market in peasant land. Before then, as we have seen, there is little evidence for the buying and selling of land even amongst freeholders. From the early thirteenth century peasant charters were more numerous in eastern England and Kent, and from the middle of the century they became more numerous everywhere.[87] Amongst the unfree population there were severe constraints on the emergence of a land market. Some landlords resisted the break-up of the old customary tenements against which rents and labour services were charged. In the palatinate of Durham both the bishop's rents and the priory rents from bondland continued to be collected from standard bondlands of two bovates.[88] On Ramsey Abbey estates the virgate remained the basic unit of villain tenure.[89] Villains who acquired a free tenure by charter sometimes found that the land was declared 'soiled', the charter confiscated and an additional rent imposed. This was one way in which landlords could increase their rents.[90] Nevertheless, prosperous villains took advantage of the availability of land, often for the purpose of setting up their sons and daughters. From at least the early thirteenth century landlords were usually prepared to allow land to be sublet, as on the

---

[84] *Charters and Custumals of the Abbey of Holy Trinity Caen*, ed. Chibnall, pp. 33, 98.

[85] Morgan, *English Lands*, pp. 88–92; Du Boulay, *Lordship of Canterbury*, p. 172; Dyer, *Lords and Peasants*, pp. 97–8, 141.

[86] Miller, *Abbey and Bishopric*, pp. 125–6, Postan, *Famulus*, pp. 33–5.

[87] Hyams, 'Origins', pp. 24–5; Harvey, 'Introduction', in *idem*, ed., *Peasant Land Market*, pp. 19–25.

[88] T. Lomas, 'South-East Durham: Late Fourteenth and Fifteenth Centuries', in Harvey, ed., *Peasant Land Market*, pp. 270–1, 274.

[89] Raftis, *Estates*, pp. 267–72.

[90] King, *Peterborough Abbey*, p. 100.

bishop of Winchester's manors in 1208–9.[91] There was also a growing trade both in free land and, with seigniorial consent, in unfree land.[92] In parts of eastern England the pressures for buying and selling land were so strong that lords accepted a need for greater freedom than that tolerated by the bishops of Durham or the abbots of Ramsey. Virgates and other traditional units were split up, to the point that they virtually disappeared.[93]

The importance of customary tenure was diluted by increasing numbers of free tenures. The expansion of cultivation into new lands frequently took the form of free tenures owing money rents. The more recently colonised land on the estates of St Paul's of London in 1222 were listed separately from the customary tenures on the manor, and were held in small parcels for money rents, though sometimes with boon works, and sometimes with slight rents in kind in the case of the older asserts.[94] On the estates of the bishopric of Durham lands colonised after the compilation of Boldon Book 1183 were classed as exchequer lands because they paid a simple money rent to the bishop's exchequer of Palace Green. These rents were more numerous in the hilly western manors of the estate than in the lower-lying land towards the coast. The relative freedom of late-colonised land affected the balance between free and servile tenures over the bishop's estate as a whole.[95] In the west midlands the Hundred Rolls permit us to compare the Warwickshire hundreds of Kineton and Stoneleigh, the former already well-settled arable region in the eleventh century, the latter a forest region whose population grew rapidly between 1086 and 1279. In 1279 free tenants constituted 30 per cent of the recorded population in Kineton Hundred but 50 per cent in Stoneleigh Hundred.[96] The increasing number of free tenures in England was particularly encouraged by the growth of population and the reclamation of land in the eastern counties, a region distinguished by its density of population and the freedom of its

[91] *Carte Nativorum: A Peterborough Abbey Cartulary of the Fourteenth Century*, ed. C. N. L. Brooke and M. M. Postan, Northants. Rec. Soc., XX (Northampton, 1960), pp. xxxvii–xxxviii.

[92] *Ibid.*, pp. xxxvii–lx; Harvey, 'Introduction', in *idem*, ed., *Peasant Land Market*, pp. 19–26; King, *Peterborough Abbey*, pp. 99–125; Raftis, *Tenure and Mobility*, pp. 63–93.

[93] J. Williamson, 'Norfolk: Thirteenth Century', in Harvey, ed., *Peasant Land Market*, pp. 31–105.

[94] *The Domesday of St Paul's of the Year MCCXXII*, ed. W. H. Hale, Camden Soc., 1st ser., LXIX (London, 1858), pp. 6, 11–13, 23–6, 36–7, 78, 80, 91–2.

[95] F. Bradshaw, 'Social and Economic History', *VCH co. Dur.*, II, pp. 183–4; *Bishop Hatfield's Survey*, ed. W. Greenwell, Surtees Soc., XXXII (Durham, 1857), pp. 1–199.

[96] R. H. Hilton, *The English Peasantry in the Later Middle Ages* (Oxford, 1975), pp. 122–8; J. B. Harley, 'Population Trends and Agricultural Developments from the Warwickshire Hundred Rolls of 1279', *EcHR*, 2nd ser., 11 (1958), p. 14.

tenantry. On the estates of the bishopric of Ely the number of new free and semi-free tenants of the twelfth and thirteenth centuries probably exceeded that of old free tenures. Large areas of Fenland were colonised by money-paying tenants, as at Wiggenhall and Wisbech.[97]

The expansion of agrarian freeholds was accompanied by the multiplication of burgage tenures in urban settings of all sizes from London down to the meanest market town. These were characteristically plots of land of about half an acre around or near a market place, held by money rents and freely transferable by charter. The number of new tenures of this kind during the thirteenth century ran in to many thousands, both in old towns and in new ones. During the period from 1180 to 1348 over 300 new boroughs were founded.[98] The number of burgage tenants in the more successful new ventures ran to several hundreds. There were 250 burgages in Stratford-upon-Avon in 1251–2, some fifty-six years after the foundation of the bishop of Worcester's market there.[99] The incidence of such tenures was more widespread than meets the eye in contemporary documentation. Lords created burgage plots not only in the many new communities which we know to have been described as boroughs but also at many other market places around the countryside. The Essex market towns of Barking, Coggeshall, Saffron Walden, Halstead, Great Dunmow and Braintree were never, so far as we know, recognised as boroughs in the Middle Ages, and yet there were many small freehold plots there which had been created on account of the commercial occupations of their populations.[100]

IV

The development of urban privileges illustrates, perhaps more clearly than any other facet of social change, the main themes that have been discussed so far. From about the 1180s the king and other landlords were more willing to recognise formal limitations to their seigniorial rights. The legal constraints which discouraged lords from granting charters to their serfs did not operate in the context of urban societies of free men. From the late twelfth century, following grants to Colchester, Northampton and Nottingham in 1189, it became more common for royal boroughs to be given charters of liberties by the crown. In effect these charters were sets of rules regulating normal relations between burgesses and the king. They allowed burgesses to elect their own

---

[97] Miller, *Abbey and Bishopric*, pp. 119–21.
[98] Beresford and Finberg, *English Medieval Boroughs*, pp. 38–9.
[99] Carus-Wilson, 'First Half-Century', p. 51.
[100] Britnell, 'Burghal Characteristics', p. 149.

officers to replace royal nominees, and to some extent they regulated behaviour amongst burgesses. They prohibited the prosecution of fellow burgesses in courts outside the borough, and fixed the frequency with which borough courts should be held. They often gave details about the selling or bequeathing of burgage tenures, and specified some of the rights and obligations which went with them. Sometimes, too, they confirmed or conceded markets and fairs and sanctioned local rules about the organisation of trade. A charter granted to Cambridge in 1268 required that wines should be sold to clergy and laity alike from the moment that casks were opened.[101] The implementation of rules about town government required some sort of constitutional apparatus, even if only an annual meeting to elect borough officers. Grants of liberties also encouraged burgesses to develop their own institutions and to make their own by-laws.[102] Many seigniorial boroughs were granted similar chartered rights by their lords.[103]

Besides the effects of charters to individual boroughs, townsmen also benefited in this period from changes in the statute law of the realm. Various developments regulated a merchant's entitlement to recover debts better than had ever been the case in the past. One strand of improvement removed the authority of borough courts to recover a debt by distraining upon the goods of someone who was neither the debtor nor a surety. Protection against such distraint had been granted to the men of many individual boroughs by clauses in their charters of liberties.[104] In 1275, however, the first Statute of Westminster gave general protection to English merchants. Another statutory advance facilitated recovery of debts by authorising their official registration – as recognisances of debt – in the records of particular local courts.[105] The Statute of Acton Burnell (1283) and the Statute of Merchants (1285) were the foundations of this procedure, which soon spread to boroughs not authorised under the original legislation.[106] The official registration of debt, which was similarly developed elsewhere in northern Europe during the thirteenth century, can be regarded as a functional substitute for the notarial registration of obligations which was characteristic of the

[101] *BBC, 1042–1216*, pp. 38–100, 115–21, 202–19, 244–7; *BBC, 1216–1307*, pp. 45–131, 148–55, 278–302, 351–7.

[102] Tait, *Medieval English Borough*, pp. 265–85; Hill, *Medieval Lincoln*, pp. 293–301.

[103] These are included in the lists in *BBC, 1042–1216*, pp. xxvi–xxxii; *BBC, 1216–1307*, pp. xxv–xxxiv. For a carefully analysed example, see J. Tait, *Medieval Manchester and the Beginnings of Lancashire* (Manchester, 1904), pp. 60–119.

[104] *BBC, 1216–1307*, pp. 229–33.

[105] T. H. Lloyd, *Alien Merchants in England in the High Middle Ages* (Brighton, 1982), pp. 15–17.

[106] Plucknett, *Legislation of Edward I*, pp. 138–43; Britnell, *Growth and Decline*, pp. 104–5.

Mediterranean world.[107] It greatly extended the amount of debt that was recorded in writing, though unrecorded debt long remained characteristic of urban systems of trading credit.[108]

In spite of the growth of trade between 1180 and 1330 the economic organisation of towns, even at the end of the period, owed little to large accumulations of capital. The textile industries depended too little on long-distance trade to have developed capitalist relationships between merchants and workers to the same extent as in Flanders. Weavers and fullers were sometimes tightly regulated by urban authorities and their trading activities were restricted. Yet urban industry was organised domestically, and craftsmen were usually their own masters.[109] Nor was the ownership of urban property the major determinant of social divisions within towns. Even in boroughs that were not part of some seigniorial estate, landlords were often not townsmen. Institutional property owners increased their stake in urban property throughout the period as a result of gifts and purchases. Some of this property was used to expand the premises of abbeys, friaries, churches, hospitals and colleges, but some was retained for income. Ordinary town dwellers were often subtenants of such institutional landlords.[110] Wealthier burgesses might be significant owners of urban property, but this was not the major divide between urban ruling elites and the rest of the population. Some leading townsmen had little urban estate. Other more conspicuous sources of wealth were the profits of trade, professional fees and the ownership of agricultural land. The resulting inequalities of wealth, though not readily classifiable either as feudal or capitalist in character, were nevertheless formalised into gradations of power. Urban office was restricted to the wealthier groups of burgesses even where there was no clearly defined constitution.[111] Where there was a constitution it was oligarchic, not democratic.[112]

A major social division in borough communities, and one that became more marked in the thirteenth century, was that between the sworn burgesses, who alone had rights under the borough charter, and inhabi-

---

[107] Clanchy, *From Memory to Written Record*, pp. 241–4.

[108] Britnell, *Growth and Decline*, pp. 103–4.

[109] Carus-Wilson, *Medieval Merchant Venturers*, pp. 223–38.

[110] Hill, *Medieval Lincoln*, pp. 149–52; Keene, *Survey*, I, pp. 193–214; M. Rubin, *Charity and Community in Medieval Cambridge* (Cambridge, 1987), pp. 202–12.

[111] Britnell, *Growth and Decline*, pp. 25, 31–3; A. F. Butcher, 'Rent and the Urban Economy: Oxford and Canterbury in the Later Middle Ages', *SH*, 1 (1979), pp. 13–18; Hilton, *Medieval Society*, pp. 202–5; E. Miller, 'Rulers of Thirteenth Century Towns: The Cases of York and Newcastle upon Tyne', in Coss and Lloyd, eds., *Thirteenth Century England*, I, pp. 128–41.

[112] Tait, *Medieval English Borough*, pp. 302–3; Reynolds, *Introduction*, pp. 122–3.

tants who were not burgesses. The former were more free than the latter. This division, implicit in the way urban self-government was constituted, became more definite as towns developed their administrative independence. Many urban residents had no privileges at all.[113] Even for sworn burgesses the chief advantage of town life was easy access to buyers and suppliers. The chartered benefits were often slight and the costs heavy. In 1274 it was reported that because many of the wealthier Northampton burgesses refused to pay their fair share of tallages, many heavily burdened textile workers and other craftsmen had left the town.[114] It is doubtful whether the new institutions of town life brought a significant increase in average prosperity to English townsmen.

Nevertheless, in retrospect the accumulation of urban privileges was of momentous importance in the building of civil society in England. It created a large number of legal communities whose relationship with the government, and with each other, was defined by standard, written rules. The fact that some of those rules might be ambiguous is, from this perspective, of little relevance. Actions which in the past had been simply the exercise of sovereign authority could now be defined as tyrannical if they defied the expectations of ruling urban groups.

V

We have seen that, in the context of economic development between 1180 and 1330 lords retained power by adapting their modes of operation in two principal ways. They increased the number of their dependants, so creating new career structures for lesser men, and they adopted forms of relationship with their subordinates which were more governed by rules than in the past. The implications of these changes for English society can be judged favourably. The second of them, in particular, was generally beneficial. It is intrinsically better that the livelihood of individuals should be protected by rules, especially when their status is an oppressed one. There can also be little doubt that the proportion of the population that was free of heavy seigniorial constraints increased.

On the other hand, as we saw earlier, the economic developments of the period were not analogous to modern growth, and did not promote general improvement in material standards of living. The favourable interpretation that can be placed on the institutional development of English society has accordingly to be dampened, at least with respect to

---

[113] Reynolds, *Introduction*, p. 124.   [114] *RH*, II, pp. 2–3.

the poorest third of the population, by the reflection that thousands of families were left free to be hungry, and that the less immediate considerations of social welfare which we have considered in this chapter could have been of little or no consolation to them.

Part 3

1330–1500

7   Markets and rules

I

In contrast with the two preceding periods we have examined, the third was one in which the size of England's population declined. From the late thirteenth century constraints on the expansion of agricultural production and of occupational specialisation meant that further population growth was severely limited. No coherent pattern of change can be established for England as a whole in the earlier fourteenth century. The far north suffered from Edward II's failure to defend his realm against the Scots.[1] Elsewhere the evidence is more mixed.[2] Without the catastrophe of the Black Death of 1348–9 numbers would probably have oscillated around the high levels of the early fourteenth century without exceeding them.[3] We are in little doubt, however, about the severity of the mid-century crisis. Many areas suffered a loss of about half their inhabitants.[4] During the rest of the period of 170 years with which we are now concerned numbers never recovered to their early fourteenth-century level, and some settlements shrank further as a result of repeated epidemics accompanied by low rates of reproduction. The county of Essex is particularly rich in direct evidence of prolonged demographic recession, but there is complementary evidence from most parts of the

[1] Winchester, *Landscape and Society*, pp. 44–5; Kershaw, *Bolton Priory*, pp. 14–18.
[2] Campbell, 'Population Pressure', pp. 95–9; L. R. Poos, 'The Rural Population of Essex in the Later Middle Ages', *EcHR*, 2nd ser., 38 (1985), pp. 521–3; Razi, *Life, Marriage and Death*, pp. 28–32; R. M. Smith, 'Demographic Developments in Rural England, 1300–48: A Survey', in B. M. S. Campbell, ed., *Before the Black Death: Studies in the 'Crisis' of the Early Fourteenth Century* (Manchester, 1991), pp. 37–47.
[3] B. F. Harvey, 'Introduction: The "Crisis" of the Early Fourteenth Century', in Campbell, ed., *Before the Black Death*, pp. 19–24.
[4] Hatcher, *Plague*, pp. 22–3; R. A. Lomas, 'The Black Death in County Durham', *J. of Med. Hist.*, 15 (1989), pp. 129–31; L. R. Poos, *A Rural Society after the Black Death: Essex, 1350–1525* (Cambridge, 1991), p. 107; Razi, *Life, Marriage and Death*, pp. 99–107.

kingdom.[5] England's population in 1522–5 has been estimated at 2.3m, though that is arguably too high. The number was, in any case, probably similar to what it had been in 1086 and less than half that in Edward I's reign.[6]

The decline in numbers, most of which had occurred by 1400, had complex implications for the volume and composition of trade. On the one hand falling numbers led to a decline in the demand for certain commodities as well as in the employed labour force. The implications of this for commerce and occupational specialisation were unfavourable. On the other hand an improvement in the ratio of resources to the number of people permitted higher productivity and standards of living, and this in turn promoted new trades and specialisations.

One of the best documented features of agriculture after 1349 is a reduction of the area of land under crops. The cultivated acreage of the demesnes of the bishopric of Winchester shrank by a quarter between the second quarter of the fourteenth century and c.1420.[7] On the estates of the bishop of Worcester there were only half as many demesne ploughs in 1389 as in 1303, and the cultivated area had been similarly reduced on most manors. Between 1340 and 1440 the sown acreage was probably halved in many Breckland villages.[8] Even greater reductions are in evidence on particular manors. An extreme case is Writtle (Essex), where by 1440 only about 400 out of the total 1,300 acres of demesne arable were cultivated.[9] Falling receipts from parochial tithes demonstrate that reduction of the acreage under crops was not confined to demesne lands.[10] By implication the decline in arable husbandry, the biggest sector of England's economy, resulted from reduced demand for cereals from a reduced population.

The institutions of retail trade bore the marks of declining activity. A few new market towns came into existence, like Knowle (Warws.). Some older markets increased their business, as at Newmarket (Suff.), where

[5] Hatcher, *Plague*, pp. 21–54; M. K. McIntosh, *Autonomy and Community: The Royal Manor of Havering, 1200–1500* (Cambridge, 1986), pp. 126–8; M. Mate, 'The Occupation of the Land: Kent and Sussex', in *AHEW*, III, pp. 127–8; Newton, *Manor of Writtle*, pp. 79–80; Poos, 'Rural Population', pp. 515–30.

[6] B. M. S. Campbell, 'The Population of Early Tudor England: A Re-Evaluation of the 1522 Muster Returns and 1524 and 1525 Lay Subsidies', *J. of Histl. Geog.*, 7 (1981), pp. 152–4; J. K. C. Cornwall, 'English Population in the Early Sixteenth Century', *EcHR*, 2nd ser., 23 (1970), pp. 39–44.

[7] D. L. Farmer, 'Grain Yields on the Winchester Manors in the Later Middle Ages', *EcHR*, 2nd ser., 30 (1977), pp. 561–2.

[8] Bailey, *Marginal Economy?*, p. 278; Dyer, *Lords and Peasants*, pp. 122–3.

[9] Newton, *Manor of Writtle*, pp. 75–6.

[10] 'Three Carrow Account Rolls', ed. L. J. Redstone, *Norf. Arch.*, 29 (1946), pp. 44–5; Britnell, *Growth and Decline*, pp. 150–1; R. B. Dobson, *Durham Priory, 1400–1450* (Cambridge, 1973), pp. 268–71.

income from stalls and shops more than tripled between 1403 and 1473.[11] But for every such case it is possible to find a dozen whose lords were less fortunate. Many urban markets, though not all, lost business because of the contraction of the populations they served. In some city markets, as at York and Winchester, tolls were abolished in an attempt to arrest this decay.[12] Tolls levied on overland trade in Colchester (Essex) rose slightly in the late fourteenth century but then fell from £18–20 around 1400 to £10 in 1444 and 1449, and by 1520 they were apparently worth only £4 or less.[13] At Gloucester the inhabitants complained in 1487 of a decline of tolls and other regular sources of income.[14] Contraction of urban trade often led to the abandonment of market stalls and shops. At Nottingham there were twelve untenanted stalls in the shambles in 1500.[15] The effects of declining local demand were complemented by those of contracting long-distance trade. Boston (Lincs.) had grown as a port supplying wool, in particular, to various manufacturing centres around the North Sea. This trade dwindled after 1400 and left the port with manifold features of urban decline. Seigniorial income from the market and fair there fell by over two-thirds between 1428 and 1435, and remained at the lower level.[16]

Smaller weekly markets of the thirteenth-century countryside decayed in the same ways. Some were already faltering in the thirteenth and fourteenth centuries, as at Witney (Oxon.) by 1263, Alresford (Hants.) by 1307, Taunton (Som.) by 1300 and Farnham (Hants.) by 1363.[17] All over the kingdom markets had lost business by the 1420s. A manorial account of Dunmow (Essex) from 7 April–29 September 1417 records that the bailiff had received nothing from tolls of the market there and that rents totalling £1 8s 10d had not been collected because various shops and stalls were untenanted.[18] The market tolls of Cheltenham (Glos.) declined from £3 in the reign of Edward III to £1 5s 1d

---

[11] C. Dyer, 'The Hidden Trade of the Middle Ages: Evidence from the West Midlands of England', in *idem, Everyday Life in Medieval England* (London and Rio Grande, 1994), pp. 294–5; P. May, 'Newmarket 500 Years Ago', *Proc. of the Suff. Inst. of Arch.*, 33 (1975), p 263.

[12] *York House Books, 1461–1490*, ed. L. C. Attreed, 2 vols. (Stroud, 1991), I, pp. 282, 291, 391; Keene, *Survey*, I, p. 100.

[13] Britnell, *Growth and Decline*, p. 249.

[14] N. M. Herbert, 'Gloucester's Livelihood in the Middle Ages', in N. M. Herbert, R. A. Griffiths, S. Reynolds and P. Clark, *The 1483 Gloucester Charter in History* (Gloucester, 1983), p. 25.

[15] *Records of the Borough of Nottingham*, ed. W. H. Stevenson, 5 vols. (London, 1882–1900), III, pp. 68–9.

[16] Platts, *Land and People*, pp. 226–7; S. H. Rigby, ' "Sore Decay" and "Fair Dwellings": Boston and Urban Decline in the Later Middle Ages', *MH*, 10 (1985), pp. 51–2.

[17] Farmer, 'Marketing', p. 338; E. Robo, *Mediaeval Farnham: Everyday Life in an Episcopal Manor*, 2nd edn (Farnham, 1939), pp. 179–80.

[18] PRO, S.C.6/840/15.

in 1422 and to 6s 3d in 1466.[19] At Revesby (Lincs.) the market tolls were leased in 1420–1 for £1 6s 8d, having declined by 10s from some earlier time. In the same year the market at Wrangle (Lincs.) produced no income at all.[20] Eleven market stalls were unlet in the market at Clare (Suff.) in 1425.[21] At Whitchurch (Salop.) there were forty unoccupied premises by 1400, and the tolls from the market and fair fell from £29 in 1380 to £8 in 1427.[22]

The decay of England's marketing structure cannot be attributed to the immediate effects of depopulation. Some cattle and sheep markets improved their business as a result of a widespread increase in pasture farming after 1349. At Warminster (Wilts.) the market increased sharply in value in the thirty years following the Black Death, though its profits then slumped from £20 in 1385–6 to £8 10s in the 1440s and 1450s and to £6 in 1462–3.[23] At Mildenhall (Suff.) the first decade of the fifteenth century was one of expansion, when both the number of stalls and their rent rose, but then the stalls let fell from thirteen in 1410–11 to only two in 1464–5, and their total rent fell from 16s 10d to 2s.[24] There is no common pattern to the chronology of change, but it is not difficult to find continuing evidence of markets in decline after the 1420s. On the Percy estates the lease of the tolls of the market at Petworth (Suss.) was adjusted downwards between 1427 and 1439, and the profit of Alnwick market (Northumb.) contracted between 1434–5 and 1442–3. Three shops in Alnwick market were empty for want of tenants in 1471–2 and there were other vacant properties in the town centre.[25] At Middleham (N.R. Yorks.) the tolls declined between 1465 and 1487.[26] The rents of 'chepeacre places' around the market at Deddington (Oxon.) declined in the later fifteenth century.[27] At Blythburgh (Suff.) receipts from the market fell from 12s in 1420 to 6s in the 1460s and 1470s and then to 3s in 1491; by this last date only a single stall was still let.[28] There was also a decline in the value of market at Thetford (Suff.), where the value of

---

[19] G. Hart, *A History of Cheltenham* (Leicester, 1965), p. 42.
[20] W. O. Massingberd, 'Social and Economic History', *VCH Lincs.*, II, pp. 320–1.
[21] PRO, S.C.2/203/67, m. 3d.
[22] A. J. Pollard, 'Estate Management in the Later Middle Ages: The Talbots and Whitchurch, 1383–1525', *EcHR*, 2nd ser., 25 (1972), p. 559.
[23] *VCH Wilts.*, VIII, p. 115.   [24] Bailey, *Marginal Economy?*, pp. 304–5.
[25] *Percy Bailiff's Rolls of the Fifteenth Century*, ed. J. C. Hodgson, Surtees Soc., CXXXIV (Durham, 1921), pp. 5–6; J. M. W. Bean, *The Estates of the Percy Family, 1415–1537* (Oxford, 1958), pp. 19, 30.
[26] A. J. Pollard, *North-Eastern England during the Wars of the Roses: Lay Society, War and Politics, 1450–1500* (Oxford, 1990), p. 40.
[27] *VCH Oxon.*, XI, p. 84.
[28] C. Richmond, *John Hopton: A Fifteenth Century Suffolk Gentleman* (Cambridge, 1981), p. 42.

market tolls in the first decade of the fifteenth century was never attained subsequently.[29] In the Marches of Wales the toll income of Newport (Monms.) fell from £1 8s 0½d in1434/5 to 5s in 1497/8.[30]

Many other English markets have left evidence of contracted activity at some point in the fifteenth century. The market at Charlbury (Oxon.) was described as 'vacant and useless' in 1440. At Banbury (Oxon.) twenty-six stalls and nine workshops were vacant in 1441.[31] Trade at Towcester (Northants.) had contracted by 1468, when three shops were untenanted and ten others were let at a reduced rent.[32] At Alnmouth, on the Northumberland coast, there was no income from toll or anchorage in 1471–2, and the lord of the manor was collecting rents from the grazing in abandoned burgage plots.[33] Many shops and stalls in Battle market were ruinous by the 1470s. There, as elsewhere, parcels of the former trading area were let off for other uses, such as private building.[34]

Deserted medieval markets were as much a feature of the age as deserted medieval villages. Some deserted villages, such as Burton Constable (N.R. Yorks.), had indeed once had markets, though most abandoned settlements had been too small to have attracted any such investment.[35] Discontinued markets were usually in villages that have survived to the present day, like Steeple Ashton (Wilts.). The market here, licensed in 1266, was worth only 8d in the mid-fifteenth century and subsequently disappeared.[36] Most of the redundant markets had never been of much importance. Many were late foundations, licensed after the main period of commercial expansion was over.[37] Such was the Etchingham family's market at Salehurst (Suss.), licensed in 1268.[38] Other disappearing markets had already suffered from competition before the Black Death. All through the thirteenth century the market at Writtle (Essex) had been subject to competition from the nearby market of Chelmsford, founded in 1199. It could still be leased for £1 in 1304, and together with a newly founded fair it was worth £1 6s 8d in 1328, but in 1366 and 1371 it was leased for only 6s 8d, and by 1419 was discontinued. There was no market at Writtle in the sixteenth century.[39]

[29] Bailey, *Marginal Economy?*, p. 305.
[30] *The Marcher Lordships of South Wales, 1415–1536: Select Documents*, ed. T. B. Pugh (Cardiff, 1963), p. 171.
[31] *VCH Oxon.*, X, pp. 27, 145.
[32] *The Grey of Ruthin Valor of 1467–8*, ed. R. I. Jack (Sydney, 1965), pp. 67–8.
[33] *Percy Bailiff's Rolls*, ed. Hodgson, p. 29.
[34] Searle, *Lordship and Community*, p. 365.
[35] *CChR*, III, p. 437; M. Beresford, *The Lost Villages of England* (London, 1954), p. 393.
[36] *VCH Wilts.*, VIII, p. 210.   [37] Britnell, 'Proliferation', p. 219.
[38] Saul, *Scenes*, p. 164.
[39] Newton, *Manor of Writtle*, p. 17; A. Everitt, 'The Marketing of Agricultural Produce', in *AHEW*, IV, p. 474.

The number of markets recorded before the Black Death century can be compared with that recorded in the sixteenth century to give a tentative assessment of the extent of the losses. Apparently only some 37 per cent were still in being. These calculations are a poor guide to the chronology and magnitude of decline in the English marketing structure. Most markets recorded before 1349 are known only from foundation charters. Some may never have been successfully established, and some had already disappeared before 1349. The majority of lost village markets had never been even of local importance, and those that survived were usually the older and larger ones.[40] For these reasons, the evidence of lost markets is less interesting than that of the numerous well-established market towns whose activities and revenues contracted. To offset the disappearance of minor markets the trade of those that survived would have had to increase. It more commonly declined, and this argues against the idea that trade was simply relocating from small markets to big ones. Since formal markets were chiefly of importance for retailing food and raw materials to small households we should perhaps infer that there were fewer such transactions.

Some fairs continued, as in the past, to be valued as sources of pigs, cattle and horses.[41] In 1459–60 the Stanleys of Knowsley (Lancs.) bought forty-one two-year-old cattle at Preston fair and two cows at Wigan fair, though other livestock was bought more informally.[42] Well-known fairs attracted buyers and sellers over large distances. Those at Birmingham and Coventry, together with the weekly markets there, were centres of trade between Welsh cattle drovers and the graziers of the west midlands.[43] Some fairs perhaps increased their trade in the later fourteenth century. Yet many decayed. That at Dunmow (Essex) yielded no income in 1417, and the one at Patrington (E.R. Yorks.) was similarly unprofitable in 1427. Wentford fair, belonging to the manor of Clare (Suff.) was recorded as discontinued in 1425.[44]

[40] A. Dyer, *Decline and Growth in English Towns, 1400–1640* (London, 1991), pp. 18–19; Farmer, 'Marketing', pp. 338–9; R. H. Hilton, 'Medieval Market Towns and Simple Commodity Production', *PP*, 109 (1985), pp. 9–11.

[41] E.g. *Medieval Framlingham: Select Documents, 1270–1524*, ed. J. Ridgard, Suff. Recs. Soc., XXVII (Woodbridge, 1985), p. 97; *The Stonor Letters and Papers, 1290–1483*, ed. C. L. Kingsford, Camden Soc., 3rd ser., 2 vols., XXIX, XXX (London, 1919), I, no. 103, p. 108.

[42] 'A Stanley Account Roll. 1460', ed. R. Sharpe France, *Trans. of the Historic Soc. of Lancs. and Ches.*, 113 (1961), p. 206.

[43] C. Dyer, 'A Small Landowner in the Fifteenth Century', *MH*, 1, part 3 (1972), pp. 6–7; Holt, *Early History*, p. 10.

[44] PRO, S.C.6/840/15 (Dunmow); 'Patrington: A Fifteenth-Century Manorial Account', ed. A. Alexander, F. Casperson, M. Habberjam, M. Hall and M. Pickles, *Yorks. Archl. J.*, 42 (1990), p. 147; G. A. Thornton, *A History of Clare, Suffolk* (Cambridge, 1930), p. 178.

Larger international fairs were less busy than they had been in earlier centuries. Their trade, as we have seen, had been eclipsed by the mercantile development of the towns, notably London. Nothing happened to reverse that decline in the fourteenth and fifteenth centuries. The income from St Ives fair court declined steeply in the later thirteenth century, and the fair was discontinued about 1340.[45] The great St Edward's fair at Westminster, founded in 1245, had yielded £92 to £130 in the decade 1306–16, mostly from rents, but it rapidly declined thereafter, and was a very subdued affair by the fifteenth century. It was discontinued about 1487.[46] St Giles's fair at Winchester was already waning by 1330, and the downward trend continued throughout the fourteenth century. The bishop's total income from the fair fell from an annual average of £43 in the years 1331–5 to £11 in 1396–1400, and was at that low level still at the end of the fifteenth century.[47]

This decline in the institutional structure of trade is not definite evidence for a general contraction of internal commerce. Even in the food trades, as in the past, a considerable share of the total volume of business was conducted away from market places. The practice of giving a discount of 5 per cent on such sales remained common all through the late Middle Ages.[48] Some of the grain acquired in bulk would eventually pass through urban markets.[49] A lot of grain nevertheless bypassed formal institutions altogether. Such were the large quantities purchased for consumption by large households.[50] Wheat, malt and barley were obtained by King's Hall, Cambridge, on contract from producers and dealers in over forty parishes in Cambridgeshire and the Isle of Ely. Some of these contracts represented long-standing arrangements extending for up to fifteen years. Informal though the system was, it was clearly reliable. In spite of the large volume of business transacted by King's Hall there is no recorded example of a contract having been broken.[51]

Wool exporters bought their wool either directly from the growers or

---

[45] *Select Cases concerning the Law Merchant*, ed. C. Gross and H. Hall, Selden Soc., 3 vols., XXIII, XLVI, XLIX (London, 1908–32), I, p. xxx; Moore, *Fairs*, pp. 208–9.
[46] Rosser, *Medieval Westminster*, pp. 97–113.   [47] Keene, *Survey*, II, pp. 1124–7.
[48] E.g. *Paston Letters and Papers of the Fifteenth Century*, ed. N. Davis, 2 vols. out of 3 (Oxford, 1971–6), I, no. 74, p. 136; *Plumpton Correspondence*, ed. T. Stapleton, Camden Soc., 1st ser., IV (London, 1839), p. 21.
[49] R. H. Britnell, 'Bailiffs and Burgesses in Colchester, 1400–1525', *Essex Arch. and Hist.*, 21 (1990), p. 104; Britnell, *Growth and Decline*, pp. 246–7.
[50] Dyer, 'Consumer', pp. 311–12.
[51] A. B. Cobban, *The King's Hall within the University of Cambridge in the Later Middle Ages* (Cambridge, 1969), pp. 214–15.

from brokers. The Cely family acquired most of theirs from Cotswold middlemen, who in turn had purchased it from local producers after sheep-shearing in June. Growers sold their wool to these brokers directly from manor houses and substantial tenant farms rather than through any formal marketing organisation. Sometimes wool was sold on approval in advance of shearing. Having purchased their wool, the brokers stored it in warehouses at Northleach (Glos.), Chipping Campden (Glos.), Chipping Norton (Oxon.) and elswhere, until the export merchants came to buy. On some occasions, however, brokers contracted to supply wool to exporters and to transport it to London.[52] Though Cotswold trade between brokers and merchants was centred in market towns, it did not make use of market places. All over the country abbeys and priories continued to sell wool to wholesale buyers. In 1363–4 Sibton Abbey sold the wool from its manors of Sibton (Suff.) and Croxton (Norf.) to Robert Gaude, and the lambs' wool of the previous year to John Hardyng.[53] All the wool clip of Finchale Priory (co. Dur.) was sold to Alice Bird of Newcastle upon Tyne each year between 1458 and 1461 and again in 1467.[54] Italian merchants bought large consignments in this way as in the thirteenth century, though their share of the export trade was smaller than it had been.[55]

The supply of fuel was another trade that did not normally make use of markets or fairs. In inland areas faggots cut from the undergrowth could be purchased directly from the owners of woodland. In the Fenlands, where dried turves were available, King's Hall acquired them from farmers and dealers in Waterbeach, Swaffham and Orwell (Cambs.). At Waterbeach attempts were made to restrict the number of turves from the common turbary that could be sold to non-commoners, but even if the rules were obeyed they allowed for the sale of 10,000 turves each year in the mid-fifteenth century.[56] In the coalfields, a large

---

[52] A. Hanham, *The Celys and their World: An English Merchant Family of the Fifteenth Century* (Cambridge, 1985), pp. 112, 115; Lloyd, *English Wool Trade*, p. 313; E. Power, 'The Wool Trade in the Fifteenth Century', in E. Power and M. M. Postan, eds., *Studies in English Trade in the Fifteenth Century* (London, 1933), pp. 51–6.

[53] *The Sibton Abbey Estates: Select Documents 1325–1509*, ed. A. H. Denney, Suff. Recs. Soc., II (Ipswich, 1960), p. 114.

[54] *The Charters of Endowment, Inventories and Account Rolls of the Priory of Finchale*, ed. J. Raine, Surtees Soc., II (Durham, 1837), pp. cclxvi, cclxx, cclxxiv, cclxxviii, ccci.

[55] E. B. Fryde, 'Italian Maritime Trade with Medieval England (c. 1270–c. 1530)', *Recueils de la Société Jean Bodin*, 32 (1974), pp. 327–30; Power, 'The Wool Trade', p. 52.

[56] Cobban, *King's Hall*, pp. 212, 215; Farmer, 'Marketing', p. 412; Ravensdale, *Liable to Floods*, p. 53. Some sources suggest that this trade was contracting in the later Middle Ages: Bailey, *Marginal Economy?*, p. 304; Hatcher, *Rural Economy and Society*, pp. 186–9.

part of the mined output was for seigniorial consumption, and much of what was left was sold to local people at the pit head.[57] There were also extensive inland and external trades in coal which depended on the ability of merchants or the accredited agents of large consumers to buy in bulk from producers. The king's large requirements of coal for limeburning, a necessary part of building operations, were usually negotiated through local sheriffs. Shipments from Newcastle upon Tyne to other English ports were organised by wholesale merchants. Larger households that needed coal would acquire it from a dealer rather than through a public market.[58]

Trade in building materials was similar. The construction of a new bridge at Rochester (Kent) between 1383 and 1391, and its subsequent maintenance by appointed bridge wardens, required the purchase of hundreds of trees, large quantities of stone, lime and sand and numerous iron utensils. We know from the bridge accounts that hardly any of these things were bought in markets. Trees were purchased from local landlords and stone was dug in local quarries. Iron was bought direct from smiths in Chatham. The wardens resorted to Maidstone fairs for some special laths they needed, but these purchases were a minute proportion of their total spending on materials. In 1414–15 the auditors allowed the expenses incurred 'on several occasions in taverns for buying timber', which indicates one of the less formal, but important, institutions of medieval commerce.[59] The numerous landlords who developed quarrying, tile-making or brick-making to exploit the resources of their estates traded their manufactures privately. In 1468, for instance, the gild of Stratford-upon-Avon purchased 20,000 tiles from John Brome's tile works at Baddesley Clinton (Warws.).[60]

These are only a few examples of the wide range of important local trades that were conducted informally. They show well enough why the decay of markets and fairs does not in itself prove that England's total internal trade was contracting. Increasing dispersal of manufacturing in villages may even have contributed to the contraction of trade in formal

[57] Dobson, *Durham Priory*, pp. 278–9; Pollard, *North-Eastern England*, p. 76.
[58] J. B. Blake, 'The Medieval Coal Trade of the North-East: Some Fourteenth-Century Evidence', *NH*, 2 (1967), pp. 3–4, 9–12; Carus-Wilson, *Medieval Merchant Venturers*, pp. 5, 8, 11; Cobban, *King's Hall*, p. 212; C. Platt, *Medieval Southampton: The Port and Trading Community*, A.D. *1000–1600* (London, 1973), p. 159.
[59] M. J. Becker, *Rochester Bridge, 1387–1856: A History of its Early Years* (London, 1930), pp. 67–78.
[60] Dyer, 'Small Landowner', p. 9; D. Moss, 'The Economic Development of a Middlesex Village', *AHR*, 28 (1980), p. 112.

markets.[61] We have no aggregate statistical evidence to work with. Even trends in the total volume of the wool sales are a matter of considerable uncertainty. The export trade declined from an annual average of about 36,000 sacks at its peak in the first decade of the fourteenth century to 8,000 sacks in the last decade of the fifteenth, but this decline was offset, to some extent, by the growth of clothmaking in England. Commercial wool production on large estates declined, but that of smaller producers increased.[62] The best argument that England's internal trade was contracting depends neither upon institutional evidence nor upon commercial statistics but upon what is known of the quantity of currency in circulation. That evidence, however, must wait for the next chapter.

II

In the wake of declining population, demand for many products also decreased, and these included basic necessities likely to be sold in public market places. However, rising standards of living brought about changes in patterns of expenditure that favoured some manufactures and services. Between 1050 and 1330 the chief social benefit of commercialisation had been to support a growing number of people, and the effects upon standards of living had been confined to the upper ranks of society and a minority of the peasantry. Between 1330 and 1500 the pattern of internal trade altered to supply a better standard of comfort to a declining population.

As in the past, occupational specialisation remained less clear-cut than in the modern world. Many men had more than one occupation, especially in the countryside, where the available employment changed with the seasons.[63] In towns merchants often followed several trades, and craftsmen engaged in several manufactures, either concurrently or sequentially.[64] By a statute of 1363 merchants were required to restrict

---

[61] P. D. A. Harvey, 'Non-Agrarian Activities in the Rural Communities of Late-Medieval England', in Istituto Internazionale di Storia Economica 'F. Datini', Settimana di Studio XIV (forthcoming).

[62] Carus-Wilson and Coleman, *England's Export Trade*, pp. 40–1, 69–70; Lloyd, *Movement of Wool Prices*, pp. 27–8.

[63] I. S. W. Blanchard, 'Labour Productivity and Work Psychology in the English Mining Industry, 1400–1600', *EcHR*, 2nd ser., 31 (1978), pp. 2–3; S. A. C. Penn and C. Dyer, 'Wages and Earnings in Late Medieval England: Evidence from the Enforcement of the Labour Laws', *EcHR*, 2nd ser., 43 (1990), pp. 361–2.

[64] M. K. James, *Studies in the Medieval Wine Trade* (Oxford, 1971), pp. 196, 199–203; Swanson, *Medieval Artisans*, pp. 6, 117; S. Thrupp, 'The Grocers of London: A Study of Distributive Trade', in Power and Postan, eds., *Studies*, pp. 289–92; S. L. Thrupp, *The Merchant Class of Medieval London* (Chicago, 1948), pp. 5–6, 12.

their trading to one kind of merchandise and craftsmen were restricted to a single craft, the object here being to control monopolistic practices.[65] In reality urban authorities enforced this legislation only when it was useful for the solution of particular industrial problems or the disciplining of particular troublesome individuals. It is likely, nevertheless, that in the late Middle Ages an increased proportion of the male workforce depended upon particular specialised skills. This can be attributed to greater regularity of employment. Urban regulations placing emphasis on rules governing apprenticeship, hours of work and the manner of working, imply that many craftsmen were dependent upon a single craft.

Opportunities for female employment were better after the Black Death as a result of the general scarcity of labour.[66] Women and children might be occupied in different activities from their menfolk, and each might develop a variety of marketable skills. Women assisted their husbands in urban workshops, but they traded in their own right as brewers or spinners. In the countryside women's employment, like that of men, depended on the time of year; it included some types of agricultural work, especially at harvest time. Women were less likely than men to be specialised in a single occupation.[67]

In circumstances of labour shortage families abandoned activities which were considered degrading and those whose productivity was low. This in itself probably implied the abandonment of some part-time activities. Many of the ways in which people had made ends meet in the earlier fourteenth century were no longer the best available. In Colchester, for example, fewer people were recognised in the borough courts as 'common forestallers'. These were smaller traders, many of them women, who made a living by buying up small consignments of poultry, rabbits or other foodstuffs on their way to market and retailing them at a profit in the town market, a degrading occupation associated with poorer families. The number of common forestallers was higher in the early decades of the fourteenth century than at any later time, and after 1412 the borough authorities stopped bothering about them as a group to be

---

[65] 37 Edward III, cc. 5, 6; *SR*, I, pp. 379–80.

[66] P. J. P. Goldberg, 'Mortality and Economic Change in the Diocese of York, 1390–1514', *NH*, 24 (1988), pp. 51–2.

[67] P. J. P. Goldberg, 'Women's Work, Women's Role in the Late Medieval North', in M. A. Hicks, ed., *Profit, Piety and the Professions in Later Medieval England* (Gloucester, 1990), pp. 40–7; M. Kowaleski, 'Women's Work in a Market Town: Exeter in the Late Fourteenth Century', in B. A. Hanawalt, ed., *Women and Work in Pre-Industrial Europe* (Bloomington, 1986), p. 157; S. Penn, 'Female Wage-Earners in Late Fourteenth-Century England', *AHR*, 35 (1987), pp. 6–7; Thrupp, *Merchant Class*, pp. 170–1.

systematically investigated.[68] Many women abandoned small-scale brewing, leaving the industry to the larger operators.[69] Other workers migrated as more lucrative opportunities presented themselves. Small markets, which had always catered for the needs of rural craftsmen, were abandoned when a better living was to be made elswhere.[70]

There is ample evidence from manorial court rolls, and from the records of justices entrusted with the enforcement of the mid-fourteenth-century labour laws that prospering trades attracted employees away from agriculture. Ploughmen abandoned tillage to go into urban employment.[71] Even the tenants of hereditary lands sometimes did better for themselves by leaving the land to begin a new life as urban craftsmen.[72] The generations after the Black Death experienced a thorough restructuring of the labour market as workers migrated to more remunerative employment. Some occupations contracted or disappeared while others drew new recruits. The wages of unskilled workers rose particularly fast. It was easier for men to move from labouring into skilled employment because of the scarcity of trained workers.[73] This encouraged further the upward mobility of the poorer ranks of the population. The period in which the implications of depopulation were worked out saw an unprecedented increase in the productivity of the workforce and was in this respect unique in medieval social history.

In spite of the contraction of the structure of markets, England did not return after 1349 to the trading pattern that had existed in the eleventh century. The development of commercial and legal practice during the twelfth and thirteenth centuries meant that the marketing system remained more clearly defined than it had been earlier. In addition, competition between trading centres meant that marketing facilities remained superior to those of 1000. Many foundations of the twelfth and thirteenth centuries survived. The north particularly benefited from a structure of marketing unknown in the eleventh century. Lancashire, Yorkshire and the shires to the north can be credited with 124 market towns in the early modern period.[74] In most parts of the country main roads were of greater significance than they had been 300 years earlier, to judge from the frequent survival of roadside markets and the economic

---

[68] Britnell, *Growth and Decline*, pp. 131–2, 276.
[69] Dyer, *Lords and Peasants*, pp. 346–9.   [70] Britnell, *Growth and Decline*, p. 97.
[71] Penn and Dyer, 'Wages and Earnings', p. 362.
[72] Britnell, *Growth and Decline*, p. 149.
[73] M. Mate, 'Labour and Labour Services on the Estates of Canterbury Cathedral Priory in the Fourteenth Century', *SH*, 7 (1985), p. 61; Postan, *Essays*, p. 202.
[74] Everitt, 'Marketing', pp. 468–9.

importance of wheeled transport.[75] The continuing use of ports founded since 1000 – Newcastle upon Tyne, Hull, King's Lynn, Southampton, Portsmouth – was another aspect of the way in which the pattern of urbanisation had altered permanently. England continued to benefit more than it had done in the eleventh century from the advantages of international specialisation.

An important feature of these differences between England in the eleventh and the fifteenth centuries was that the kingdom had become more urbanised. Having grown through the twelfth and thirteenth centuries, many towns remained larger than before in spite of some late medieval contraction. This is self-evident in northern England, but is also arguable for some towns in the southern part of the kingdom. Though less populous than in Edward I's reign, London was nevertheless bigger than any plausible estimate of its size in 1086. For that date estimates of 10–20,000 are the most acceptable. Around 1500, however, the population of the city was around 50–60,000.[76] A similar case can be supported by best estimates from some other towns, such as Cambridge, Canterbury, Chester, Colchester, Exeter, Ipswich, Northampton and Norwich, though none of these show the increase postulated for London.[77] Some towns, like Gloucester, Lincoln, Nottingham and Oxford, may not have been larger than they were in 1086. On the other hand, in addition to the towns of Norman England there were now many of the boroughs and market towns that had been founded in the intervening period.

These contrasts demonstrate the qualitative changes in the English economy during the twelfth and thirteenth centuries. Technology and organisational techniques had improved and resources were used more productively. New patterns of craftsmanship were retained, and were sometimes developed further. For example, the prosperity of cloth workers in the later fourteenth century often depended upon the construction of fulling mills.[78] In agriculture the advanced rotations of the twelfth and thirteenth centuries continued to be used even after the demand for cereals had contracted.[79] Institutional innovations were also

---

[75] Farmer, 'Marketing', pp. 351–2.

[76] J. K. C. Cornwall, *Wealth and Society in Early Sixteenth Century England* (London, 1988), p. 64; Darby, *Domesday England*, p. 303.

[77] Darby, *Domesday England*, p. 302–9; C. Phythian-Adams, *Desolation of a City: Coventry and the Urban Crisis of the Late Middle Ages* (Cambridge, 1979), p. 12.

[78] Bailey, *Marginal Economy?*, pp. 176–7, 262; Britnell, *Growth and Decline*, pp. 76, 157; Dyer, *Lords and Peasants*, p. 345; Poos, *Rural Society*, pp. 61, 71; Winchester, *Landscape and Society*, pp. 118–20.

[79] R. H. Britnell, 'Farming Practice and Techniques: Eastern England', in *AHEW*, III, pp. 199, 202.

lasting. The legal system and the credit system created since 1180 remained available to farmers, merchants and craftsmen alike. Because of these advantages productive resources could be used more effectively than in the past. Falling population released potential that had been held back before 1330 by the large number of people who had lived on the margins of subsistence, working fitfully at low levels of productivity, or dependent upon charity to keep alive.

The productivity of labour, and average standards of living, rose as population fell, particularly between the 1360s and the early fifteenth century. For many manufactures demand per head of the population increased. This was the main reason why the range of occupational specialisations remained higher than it had been in Norman England. Even in country areas there were large numbers of craftsmen and tradesmen, often producing manufactures of good quality to be distributed by merchants, as in the case of the scattered textile workers of central Gloucestershire, west Wiltshire and northern Essex.[80]

In industries whose products were in greater demand, specialisation was even more advanced in the late Middle Ages than earlier. This can be illustrated from the history of the leather industry. High average meat consumption, another indirect consequence of declining population, had favourable implications for supplies of hides. The price of leather held low relative to rising incomes. This encouraged the consumption of a variety of leather goods. Besides skinners, tanners, shoe-makers, saddlers and glovers, late medieval fashions gave work to curriers, whittawers, coffer-makers, girdlers, point-makers, pouch-makers, sheath-makers and scabbard-makers.[81] This did not always save town leather industries from declining numbers, as at Winchester.[82] In spite of the contraction of population in fifteenth-century York, however, the number of glovers in the city was greater in the second half of the century than it had been in the fourteenth century.[83]

The textile trades, too, benefited from rising standards of living. The total number employed may not have exceeded thirteenth-century

---

[80] E. M. Carus-Wilson, 'Evidences of Industrial Growth on Some Fifteenth-Century Manors', *EcHR*, 2nd ser., 12 (1959), pp. 190–205; Dyer, *Lords and Peasants*, pp. 345–9; J. N. Hare, 'The Wiltshire Risings of 1450: Political and Economic Discontent in Mid-Fifteenth Century England', *SH*, 4 (1982), pp. 16–19; Harvey, *Medieval Oxfordshire Village*, pp. 143–5; Harvey, 'Non-Agrarian Activities in the Rural Communities of Late-Medieval England'; Poos, *Rural Society*, pp. 64–72.

[81] M. Kowaleski, 'Town and Country in Late Medieval England: The Hide and Leather Trade', in P. J. Corfield and D. Keene, eds., *Work in Towns, 850–1850* (Leicester, 1990), pp. 64–5.

[82] Keene, *Survey*, I, pp. 356–7.

[83] Swanson, *Medieval Artisans*, pp. 59–60.

levels, but the range of skills was probably wider. Demand shifted from locally produced fabrics of low quality towards better qualities made in recognised centres of clothmaking and marketed by merchants. It was observed that, in spite of the consumption laws, labourers and servants were dressing in more expensive cloth. One preacher of the early fifteenth century was dismayed that a ploughman who would once have been satisfied with a white kirtle and russet gown was now to be seen as proudly dressed as a squire. Peter Idley, writing about 1445–50, grumbled that 'a man shall not now ken a knave from a knight'.[84]

The local effects of increasing standards of living upon economic specialisation were seen at their best in London and Westminster, which were distinguished for both the wealth of their inhabitants and the multiplicity of their links with the outside world. A list of 111 London crafts compiled in 1422 includes parchmenters, bookbinders, paternosterers, jewellers, organ-makers, quilters, mirrorers, feathermongers and seal-engravers.[85] Andreas Franciscius, an Italian visitor to the city in 1497, wrote that 'throughout the town are to be seen many workshops of craftsmen in all sorts of mechanical arts, to such an extent that there is hardly a street which is not graced by some shop or the like'.[86] About eighty crafts are known from Westminster in the late Middle Ages, including goldsmiths, armourers and bookbinders. A reconstruction of the residential pattern in King Street about 1508 shows both sides of the road lined with the residences of different craftsmen and tradesmen. Westminster's economy 'was based primarily on the entrapment of the consumer'.[87]

The ability of manufacturers to compete more effectively in overseas markets created a secondary, but locally important, source of urban employment after the Black Death. Manufacturing had always been strongly associated with town life, but this was particularly true of superior grades of work appropriate to foreign trade. The importance of exports was in this respect at its peak between about 1330 and 1415. The reasons for England's international success in this period have never been satisfactorily explained, though it is likely that Edward III's

---

[84] V. J. Scattergood, *Politics and Poetry in the Fifteenth Century* (London, 1971), pp. 346–7.

[85] E. M. Veale, 'Craftsmen and the Economy of London in the Fourteenth Century', in A. E. J. Hollaender and W. Kellaway, eds., *Studies in London History Presented to Philip Edmund Jones* (London, 1969), pp. 139–41.

[86] *English Historical Documents, V: 1485–1558*, ed. C. H. Williams (London, 1971), p. 189.

[87] Rosser, *Medieval Westminster*, pp. 124–5, 161.

wartime duties on wool exports gave English textile entrepreneurs cost advantages over their closest competitors. Export performance was particularly important for cloth-manufacturing towns, some of which gained international reputations for their fabrics. Salisbury was known for a striped fabric manufactured to narrower specifications than standard broadcloth, Colchester for russet 'dozens' about half the length of standard broadcloth, Coventry for its blue broadcloth, Norwich for its worsteds, York for both worsteds and broadcloths.[88] As a result of their manufacturing successes a number of fortunate towns, like Colchester, Coventry and York, enjoyed intervals of vigorous economic growth between 1350 and 1500.[89] Meanwhile a number of villages grew into small manufacturing towns, no doubt by fits and starts. Crediton (Devon) seems to be a case in point. Its population rose from about 550 to about 2,815 between 1377 and 1525.[90] Some other towns had no comparable luck but contracted less than their rural surroundings. So though the total number of townsmen remained lower than it had been before the Black Death, the urban sector was larger relative to the whole population. Tax assessment suggests that the urban share of England's wealth was higher in the early sixteenth century than in 1334.[91]

The economic changes we have discussed explain why historians debate whether medieval towns were in decay after 1350. Some of the arguments are about obscure matters of fact, but some have arisen because 'economic decay' and 'economic decline' are ambiguous expressions. Most towns were decayed by 1500 in the sense that their population was smaller than some earlier level. Population decline led to visible decay whenever abandoned houses, many of them fragile constructions, fell into ruin.[92] Employment in some occupations had contracted, and in some towns the total range of occupational specialisa-

---

[88] A. R. Bridbury, *Medieval English Clothmaking: An Economic Survey* (London, 1982), pp. 68–9; Britnell, *Growth and Decline*, pp. 55–60; E. M. Carus-Wilson, 'The Oversea Trade of Late Medieval Coventry', in *Economies et sociétés au Moyen Age: Mélanges offerts à Edouard Perroy* (Paris, 1973), p. 372; Lipson, *Economic History*, I, pp. 491–2; Miller, 'Medieval York', p. 89.

[89] J. N. Bartlett, 'The Expansion and Decline of York in the Later Middle Ages', *EcHR*, 2nd ser., 12 (1959–60), pp. 21–7; Britnell, *Growth and Decline*, pp. 53–114, 266; Dyer, *Decline and Growth*, p. 72; Phythian-Adams, *Desolation*, pp. 33–5.

[90] Dyer, *Decline and Growth*, p. 72.

[91] A. R. Bridbury, *Economic Growth: England in the Later Middle Ages* (London, 1962), pp. 79–82, 111. This interpretation is, however, questioned by S. H. Rigby, 'Late Medieval Urban Prosperity: The Evidence of the Lay Subsidies', *EcHR*, 2nd ser., 39 (1986), pp. 411–16.

[92] R. B. Dobson, 'Urban Decline in Late Medieval England', *TRHS*, 27 (1977), pp. 1, 11.

tion had narrowed.[93] Contraction in certain food trades affected the profitability of markets adversely. But some towns were not decayed in this sense before the mid-fifteenth century. Some crafts offered more scope for skilled specialisation than in the past. And even if total income had declined families were more prosperous than they had ever been.[94]

A higher standard of living was evident in the material conditions of everyday life, such as housing, dress and diet, and in the surplus funds available for maintaining gilds and building churches. The abandonment of properties meant that there was more empty space but did not always lead to unsightly ruins. Some sites were newly developed by speculators. Sometimes, too, wealthier townsmen constructed large houses or house rows across a number of former plots.[95] The urban fabric and culture that remained was more comfortable and more interesting than what it replaced. For many historians it goes against the grain to talk about 'urban decay' in these circumstances.

III

In the late fourteenth century the implications of the division of labour were a matter for comment and wonder. This was to some extent a measure of the extent to which trading activity, and more particularly the growth of employment outside agriculture, had forced itself upon people's attention. It also resulted in part from the higher standards of living in the population at large, which meant that writers interested in lax morality had a wide range of current observation on which to draw. Langland's *Piers the Plowman* opens with a dream in which 'all manner of men, the mean and the rich' are seen working and sinning in various ways.[96] He builds into the scene many varieties of secular activity, rural and urban, as well as different forms of religious life. In some instances the occupation and the sin he describes were inextricably connected. Langland was sceptical of the honesty of those who lived by

---

[93] Bonney, *Lordship*, pp. 148–9, 269–71; Keene, *Survey*, I, pp. 352–65.
[94] A. R. Bridbury, 'Dr. Rigby's Comment: A Reply', *EcHR*, 2nd ser., 39 (1986), p. 420.
[95] G. G. Astill, 'Economic Change in Later Medieval England: An Archaeological Review', in Aston and others, *Social Relations and Ideas*, p. 238; R. Holt, 'Gloucester in the Century after the Black Death', in R. Holt and G. Rosser, eds., *The Medieval Town: A Reader in English Urban History, 1200–1540* (London, 1990), pp. 152–3; Keene, *Survey*, I, pp. 143–7; Keene, *Cheapside*, pp. 13–14; S. R. Rees Jones, 'Property, Tenure and Rents: Some Aspects of the Topography and Economy of Medieval York', PhD thesis, York, 1987, pp. 253–70; Rosser, *Medieval Westminster*, pp. 81–92; Searle, *Lordship and Community*, pp. 363–6; *VCH Oxon.*, X, p. 6.
[96] Piers the Plowman, A-text, prologue, lines 17–109: *The Vision of William concerning Piers the Plowman*, ed. W. W. Skeat, 2 vols. (Oxford, 1886), I, pp. 3–19.

trade, though he was no less scathing about the other orders of society. He saw tradesmen, professional men and churchmen alike living by craft and cunning. The growth of occupational specialisation away from the simplicity of rural life implied the decay of Christian standards of behaviour. Amidst much soul-searching, he saw Piers the Plowman, an archetype of old-fashioned, honest toil, as a symbol of Christ himself.

Chaucer's *Canterbury Tales* elaborates another view of the variety to be found in late fourteenth-century English society. Observing differences between men and women with different worldly concerns is intrinsic to the pattern of the work. Chaucer's attitude to specialisation was in some respects similar to Langland's. His ploughman and village parson exemplify Christian conduct. The clerk of Oxford and the prioress represent other valid forms of moral living. Most other pilgrims are characterised by their preoccupation with material things. Some are flawed by the way they earn their living. The shipman and the miller cheat their clients. The moral weakness of some pilgrims, like the merchant and the sergeant of the law, was almost a necessary consequence of their work, because their minds were given up to worldly affairs. The learned doctor of physic is a fourteenth-century specialist academic: 'His study was but little on the Bible.'[97]

Awareness of specialisation and market dependence brought not the celebration of economic individualism but an uneasy feeling that private virtue and the social order were under threat.[98] Such a view is exemplified in the policies of public authorities. Fifteenth-century attitudes to occupational specialisation are apparent from the way craft organisation were deployed for civic ceremonial. The feast of Corpus Christi was authorised in a papal letter published in 1317, and introduced into England the following year.[99] Though originally conceived in predominantly liturgical terms, Corpus Christi processions were elaborated to make occupational specialisation a central element in public perception of the way communities were structured. The significance of other social distinctions was so disregarded that the image of urban society presented in these processions can only be regarded as a distorted one. Women and children were hardly represented.[100] The symbolism of these festivals stressed the interdependence of the differ-

---

[97] Geoffrey Chaucer, The Canterbury Tales, A, line 438: *The Works of Geoffrey Chaucer*, ed. F. N. Robinson, 2nd edn (Oxford, 1957), p. 21.

[98] Hilton, 'Medieval Market Towns', p. 22.

[99] M. Rubin, *Corpus Christi: The Eucharist in Late Medieval Culture* (Cambridge, 1991), pp. 181–4, 199–200.

[100] Swanson, *Medieval Artisans*, p. 111; Rubin, *Corpus Christi*, p. 266.

ent occupations represented in them. Just as a living body is composed of different members functioning together to sustain life, comfort and efficiency, so the body of Christ, the church on earth, comprises men of different crafts, all of whom are necessary to the well being of the whole, whatever conflicting interests there may be between them.

Corpus Christi ritual implied that without charity the effect of occupational specialisation would be to tear society apart. Some larger towns introduced Corpus Christi play cycles, whose production required co-operation between the crafts. Often there was some particular connection between the stage properties which a play required and the craft to which it was allocated. At York the goldsmiths, together with the masons, were responsible for the Herod and the Three Kings, and the pinners, who made pins and nails, were charged with the Crucifixion.[101] Participation in the cycle of mystery plays was a compulsory obligation. Several crafts might have to share the costs of a production that would have strained their individual resources. In 1428 the smiths of Coventry were required against their will to take responsibility for the cutlers' Corpus Christi pageant, and in 1435 the saddlers and painters were required to contribute to that of the card-makers. A standard fine of £5 for failure to produce a play was introduced in 1461.[102] These ceremonies are better thought of as the representation of a social ideal than as a mirror of social reality.[103]

Urban authorities did not rely on goodwill to achieve social harmony in everyday life any more than in civic ritual. It was a commonplace of political thinking that concord in the state depended upon each person knowing his place and his duties.[104] Upholding justice in urban life implied the regulation of craft activities. Town officers assumed that individual crafts would conspire against the public interest. To bring the various crafts into harmony with each other, and thereby to promote the health of the whole body of a community, was accordingly one of the tasks of government.

As in the thirteenth century, responsibility for regulating trade for the common good was divided between the crown and local communities. Statutory regulation of the market economy increased after 1330. Older

---

[101] *The York Plays*, ed. R. Beadle (London, 1982), pp. 134–48, 315–23.
[102] *The Coventry Leet Book*, ed. M. D. Harris, EETS, 4 vols., CXXXIV–CXXXV, CXXXVIII, CXLVI (London, 1907–13), I, pp. 115–16, 172, 205–7, and II, p. 312.
[103] M. E. James, *Society, Politics and Culture: Studies in Early Modern England* (Cambridge, 1986), pp. 18–27; Rubin, *Corpus Christi*, pp. 260–86.
[104] 'Justice is, every person to do his office that he is put in according to his estate or degree' (Robert Stillington, bishop of Bath, 1467), cited in S. B. Chrimes, *English Constitutional Ideas in the Fifteenth Century* (Cambridge, 1936), p. 121.

regulations concerning standard measures were renewed,[105] though even in the later fifteenth century there were still local discrepancies; for example, a Lancashire account of 1460 refers to eleven quarters of wheat bought by Lancaster measure.[106] Legislation concerning forestalling was elaborated to cover a number of specific cases.[107] The government intervened to counter rising wages after 1349. By the Ordinance of Labourers of 1349 workers were required to demand no more than they had received before the Black Death, and some agricultural rates were fixed by the Statute of Labourers of 1351.[108] The Ordinance of 1349 also gave urban authorities powers to regulate profits in the victualling trades according to their whim. Butchers, fishmongers, innkeepers, brewers, bakers, poulterers and all other sellers of food were bound to sell their wares 'for a reasonable price, having regard to the price for which such victuals are sold in nearby places, so that such sellers may have a moderate, not excessive, profit such as is reasonably to be expected according to the distance of the places from which such victuals are carried'.[109] The Statute of 1351 went further in trying to regulate the profits of cordwainers, shoe-makers, goldsmiths, saddlers, blacksmiths, spurriers, tanners, curriers, tawers of leather, tailors and other craftsmen.[110] The list of fixed rates in agriculture was lengthened in 1388.[111] The powers of justices of the peace were extended by allowing them to regulate the food allowances given to workmen (1390), to summon and examine wage-earners, craftsmen and victuallers concerning infringements of statutory regulations (1414) and to proclaim wage rates and food allowances in full sessions of local courts (1427).[112]

Late medieval economic legislation was loosely drafted and of uncertain purpose. It enabled juries to bring poorly founded charges against individuals or groups held responsible for raising prices. It gave respectability to prejudice and occasionally indulged occupational rivalries. Its implementation could be harmful to the provisioning of the townspeople, since authorities could not easily distinguish between monopoly and scarcity as the reason for high prices, so that in years of dearth merchants were liable to be punished for profiteering.[113] The enterprise needed to seek out scarce supplies was made morally dubious.

[105] 34 Edward III, cc. 5, 6, 13 Richard II, c. 9; *SR*, I, pp. 365–6, II, pp. 63–4.
[106] 'Stanley Account Roll', ed. Sharpe France, p. 205.
[107] 25 Edward III, 3, c. 3, 31 Edward III, 2, cc. 1, 2; *SR*, I, pp. 315, 354.
[108] 23 Edward III, c. 1, 25 Edward III, cc. 1, 2; *SR*, I, pp. 307, 311.
[109] 23 Edward III, c. 6; *SR*, I, p. 308.   [110] 25 Edward III, c. 4; *SR*, p. 312.
[111] 12 Richard II, c. 4; *SR*, II, p. 57.
[112] 13 Richard II, 1, c. 8, 2 Henry V, 1, c. 4, 6 Henry VI, c. 3; *SR*, II, pp. 63, 176–7, 234.
[113] Britnell, *Growth and Decline*, pp. 237–8.

In practice the imposition of heavy fines was sporadic. More commonly controls on trade were used to provide local authorities with additional income from fines that did nothing to deter offenders.[114] The statutes concerning prices and profits joined the assize of bread and ale, and the so-called Statute of Forestallers, as legitimation for local taxes on trade. Market forces established wage rates substantially above those of the earlier fourteenth century, and it is likely that the profits of victuallers and self-employed craftsmen were also proportionately higher.

Meanwhile, most new regulations after 1330 were the affair of urban communities resolving their own problems. Many concerned individual crafts rather than the whole community of burgesses. Craft gilds were not autonomous agents. As the ethos of the Corpus Christi festivities implied, their conflicting interests were harmonised through the intervention of town councils. To all intents and purposes gilds were agencies of urban government responsible for administering rules either initiated or at least approved by higher authority.[115] At Coventry in 1421 the wardens of all the crafts were commanded to bring their ordinances before a committee of borough officers and councillors so that the contents could be scrutinised in the public interest. The crafts were not allowed to alter their rules without the assent of the mayor and council.[116] The city of Norwich in 1415 formally required all newly enfranchised burgesses to become members of a craft, and in 1449 took the initiative in reconstructing the system to provide for crafts with too few members to constitute viable gilds on their own.[117] The increased prominence of craft gilds in the late medieval period is direct evidence that urban authorities regulated internal trade more actively than in earlier times.[118]

Many trading regulations can be regarded as valid responses to the interests of consumers. Such were rules to maintain the quality of meat and fish, which are little more than elaborations of statute law. For example, in 1421 John Leeder, the mayor of Coventry, proclaimed a lengthy set of by-laws relating to the food trades which ordained among other things that fish brought for sale by outside victuallers should be inspected to ensure that it was fit for human consumption, that butchers

---

[114] Grieve, *Sleepers and the Shadows*, p. 63.

[115] A. S. Green, *Town Life in the Fifteenth Century*, 2 vols. (London, 1894), II, pp. 145–52; Phythian-Adams, *Desolation*, p. 105; Swanson, *Medieval Artisans*, pp. 111–14.

[116] *Coventry Leet Book*, ed. Harris, I, pp. 32, 170.

[117] Swanson, *Medieval Artisans*, p. 112.

[118] A. B. Hibbert, 'The Economic Policies of Towns', in M. M. Postan, E. E. Rich and E. Miller, eds., *The Cambridge Economic History of Europe, III: Economic Organisation and Policies in the Middle Ages* (Cambridge, 1963), pp. 211–14.

should not sell diseased or tainted meat and that no cooks should sell warmed-up meat or leave feathers, hair or entrails under their stalls or in the high street. The location of trade was often minutely specified. John Leeder's ordinances required all badgers coming to Coventry with corn to sell to set their pitches 'at the West orchard end', and those bringing oatmeal from the country were to stand near the door of the gaol with the sellers of bread. Weights were regulated in the interests of consumers, and sometimes in the interests of workers. Spinsters, in particular, needed the weights by which wool was weighed to be strictly controlled. Suppliers of services were regulated in response to customers' complaints, as when the Coventry tilers were prohibited from using half tiles or broken tiles in 1447. The quality of manufactured goods was regulated when there were grounds for thinking that fraud was difficult to detect. In 1435 the mayor and court leet of Coventry regulated the cardwire drawers and girdlemen on complaint from the clothmakers that the deceitful quality of wire used in the making of cards for carding cloth was causing loss.[119] Gild ordinances might set up machinery by which unsatisfied consumers could obtain redress without the inconvenience of having to prosecute through the ordinary courts.[120]

Other regulation arose from the need to standardise export goods at a time when the individual artisan's livelihood depended upon the reputation of his town. In this respect town authorities were monitoring quality the way a modern firm would do. At Winchester the supervision of weaving was tightened up in 1408 because of complaints against unskilled workmen who were harming the reputation of the city's cloth.[121] Ten years later the Colchester cloth industry was regulated by gild ordinances for similar reasons; merchants there were trying to promote cloth of a higher quality than the old russets that had made the town's fortune in the later fourteenth century.[122] In 1451 Coventry weavers were ordered not to make a 'dozen' cloth with less than 30lb of yarn.[123]

The dividing line between public interest and sectional interest was often hard to draw. Much of the local economic regulation of this period suffered from a deficient concept of what the public interest was. Burgesses – the acknowledged free men of each borough – invariably defined the public interest as the strengthening of their own privileges at the expense of countrymen and merchants from other towns. Often, however, they turned against particular groups of traders and craftsmen.

[119] *Coventry Leet Book*, ed. Harris, I, pp. 23–33, 180–4, 232, 243, 255, and II, p. 271.
[120] Britnell, *Growth and Decline*, p. 243.   [121] Keene, *Survey*, I, p. 302.
[122] Britnell, *Growth and Decline*, pp. 165–7, 186.
[123] *Coventry Leet Book*, ed. Harris, II, p. 262.

After a storm which ruined many roofs in London in 1362, the tilers were forbidden to raise their prices.[124] Often, too, the privileges of burgesses were enforced at the expense of fellow townsmen who were not free men. Towns varied considerably in the narrowness with which they defined their common interest.[125] Some towns, like Exeter, deliberately restricted freedom of the borough to a small group in order to protect the commercial privileges of existing burgesses.[126]

One consequence of the multiplication of by-laws and gild regulations was that minor offices concerned with enforcing rules and regulations multiplied.[127] Even in Westminster, a manor of Westminster Abbey where there was no formally constituted urban government, there was a remarkable increase in the number of constables and other ward officers.[128] The election of craft officers was often surrounded by expensive inaugural ceremonies comparable to those of the senior officers of the borough.[129] The Coventry masters' fellowships each had between two and four elected officers. For exceptionally successful townsmen office in a craft was a first step for a higher rank in urban government.[130] The multiplication of offices in the lower rungs of urban establishments is the other side to the increasing oligarchy typical of urban government in this period.

Prevailing attitudes in local government were in these ways ambivalent about commercial freedom. On the one hand monopolistic practices were a constant source of alarm, and were technically outlawed. On the other hand townsmen were subject to increasing intervention by local government in what was supposed to be their common interest. Occupational specialisation increased the economic dependence of individuals upon the rest of society not only in that they needed to make exchanges with other people, but also in the sense that they were compelled to accept a whole framework of controls imposed by those in authority. It is difficult to tell how far entrepreneurial ambition was deterred by public intervention of this kind. It is likely that by the later fifteenth century profit-making was easier in smaller, less regulated communities than in the older boroughs. Some of the most ambitious industrial entrepreneurs of the early sixteenth century were to be found in villages and

---

[124] Green, *Town Life*, II, p. 152.   [125] Swanson, *Medieval Artisans*, p. 108.

[126] M. Kowaleski, 'The Commercial Dominance of a Medieval Provincial Oligarchy: Exeter in the Late Fourteenth Century', *Med. Stud.*, 46 (1984), pp. 358–9.

[127] Britnell, *Growth and Decline*, p. 245.

[128] Rosser, *Medieval Westminster*, pp. 236–7.

[129] C. Phythian-Adams, 'Ceremony and the Citizen: The Communal Year at Coventry, 1450–1550', in P. Clark and P. Slack, eds., *Crisis and Order in English Towns, 1500–1700* (London, 1972), pp. 60–3.

[130] Phythian-Adams, *Desolation*, pp. 112–14.

small market towns, like Lavenham (Suff.), Coggeshall (Essex), Tiverton and Cullompton (Devon).[131] The newer cloth towns had their gilds and gild halls, but these were of a religious and social character rather than for the regulation of trade.[132]

---

[131] E. M. Carus-Wilson, *The Expansion of Exeter at the Close of the Middle Ages* (Exeter, 1963), pp. 18–19; Dymond and Betterton, *Lavenham*, pp. 4–8; E. Power, *Medieval People* (London, 1924), pp. 12–14, 24–7.

[132] Dymond and Betterton, *Lavenham*, p. 21.

8   Trade and specialisation

I

The English money stock, having stood at about £1.1m in 1324, subsequently diminished. By the early 1330s prices were falling as silver flowed out of domestic circulation.[1] The more severe deflation of the later 1330s was the result of Edward III's overseas expenditure on diplomacy and war, compounded by exchange rates that encouraged the export of silver.[2] These were temporary fluctuations, and the situation was partly reversed in the 1350s. However, the former level of circulation was not regained for over a century.[3] Coinage in circulation in the years 1351–6 was less than four-fifths of what it had been in the period 1311–24, and it later declined further. In 1417 it was only three-fifths of its peak level. The coinage in circulation increased again in the later fifteenth century (Table 5). Evidence from the time of Edward IV's recoinage of 1464–75 supplies a maximum estimate as high as £0.9m for the money stock around 1470. However, that figure is an unreliable guide to the levels and trends of monetary circulation during the previous fifty years because of the circumstances of the recoinage.[4] Moreover, the reduction of the effective currency for retail trade was more severe than these aggregated estimates imply, since the composition of the coinage was transformed by the establishment of a gold currency from 1344. Gold soon accounted for the major share of the currency by value. The smallest gold coin, the quarter noble, valued at 1s 8d between 1344 and 1464, was equivalent to five days' wages for a labourer in the mid-fifteenth century and was inappropriate for the normal expenditure of most households.[5]

[1] M. Mate, 'High Prices in Early Fourteenth-Century England: Causes and Consequences', *EcHR*, 2nd ser., 28 (1975), p. 14; Mayhew, 'Numismatic Evidence', p. 7.
[2] M. C. Prestwich, 'Currency and the Economy of Early Fourteenth Century England', in Mayhew, ed., *Edwardian Monetary Affairs*, pp. 46–7.
[3] J. Day, *The Medieval Market Economy* (Oxford, 1987), p. 64.
[4] Mayhew, 'Population, Money Supply', p. 243.
[5] H. B. Brown and S. V. Hopkins, *A Perspective of Wages and Prices* (London, 1981), p. 11; Dyer, *Standards of Living*, p. 215; Spufford, *Money*, pp. 282, 409.

Table 5 *Estimates of English currency in circulation, 1324-1544*

	£'000
1324	1,100
1350	500[a]
1356	788
1417	639[b]
1470	900[c]
1544	1,190

[a] Recoinage of 1351–6.
[b] Recoinage of 1412–17.
[c] Recoinage of 1464–75.

Sources: C. E. Challis, 'Currency and the Economy in Mid-
Tudor England', *EcHR*, 2nd ser., 25 (1972), p. 318; J. Craig,
The Mint: A History of the London Mint from A.D. 287 to 1948
(Cambridge, 1953), pp. 412–13; J. Day, *The Medieval Market
Economy* (Oxford, 1987), p. 70; N. J. Mayhew, 'Money and
Prices in England from Henry II to Edward III', *AHR*, 35
(1987), p. 125; *idem*, 'Population, Money Supply and the
Velocity of Circulation in England, 1300–1700', *EcHR*, 48
(1995), p. 244.

Maybe figures of money stock estimated from mint output exaggerate
the decline in active circulation. Conceivably fashion among the wealthy
had shifted to holding more wealth in plate and jewellery rather than in
coin, so that less currency was immobilised in hoards. Plate was
undoubtedly a store of wealth, particularly amongst the rich.[6] An
Italian writer at the end of the fifteenth century described the wealth of
silver and gold plate in English households, even, so he said, in the
meanest inn. The goldsmiths in the Strand, he thought, had more silver
vessels in their shops than all those of Milan, Rome, Venice and Florence
put together.[7] Yet there was nothing new about accumulated plate as a
mark of status either in town or country. Wealthier townsmen held a
certain amount of silver already in the thirteenth century, as we know
from taxation assessments. Nor are the Italian's comments evidence for
growth in the goldsmiths' trade. In Winchester the number of goldsmiths fell during the fourteenth and fifteenth centuries from a higher
level in the thirteenth. Goldsmiths are mentioned in Durham deeds

[6]   Spufford, *Money*, pp. 345–7.
[7]   *A Relation of the Island of England about the Year 1500*, ed. C. A. Sneyd, Camden Soc.,
1st ser., XXXVII (London, 1847), pp. 28–9, 42–3.

of the thirteenth and fourteenth centuries, but not in those of the fifteenth.[8]

Even if evidence for increased holding of plate could be properly substantiated, it would not dislodge the independent archaeological evidence of coin finds, which suggests a severe reduction in the currency. At 100 sampled sites the number of stray finds of small denominations from the period 1412–64 – half groats and below – turns out to be only about a fifth of the number from the period 1279–1351.[9] For the local trading economy to be unaffected by such a reduction of the coinage in everyday use there would have had to be some revolutionary developments in monetary institutions, either in the form of substitute currencies or in the creation of new types of credit. The evidence does not point in either of these directions.

Jettons and lead tokens were to some extent substituted for small change. They are more numerous from the fourteenth century than from the fifteenth century, however, so they do not offset the evidence for monetary contraction very effectively. There is no record of the circumstances in which they were used, but they cannot have done more than alleviate problems of local retail trade.[10] From the late thirteenth century institutional development of commercial credit perhaps modified the relationship between the size of the mercantile sector of the economy and the quantity of coined money, so that a given volume of trade required less currency in circulation. This was because in some circumstances obligations cancelled out and obviated the need for cash transactions, However, there was no institutionalised substitution of paper claims for coined money. Nor did credit continuously expand as the stock of money contracted; it shrank with the diminution of the money supply in the fifteenth century. In London the monetary disorders of the late fourteenth century brought about a contraction of credit after a financial crisis in 1397. In Colchester the level of credit was at its peak in the 1380s, and from the 1390s, fell to a lower level.[11]

How did monetary contraction make itself felt in reality? People complained repeatedly of 'scarcity of money', but the relationship

[8] Bonney, *Lordship*, pp. 269–71; Dyer, *Standards of Living*, p. 206; J. F. Hadwin, 'Evidence on the Possession of "Treasure" from the Lay Subsidy Rolls', in Mayhew, ed., *Edwardian Monetary Affairs*, pp. 147–65; Keene, *Survey*, I, pp. 280–1.

[9] Rigold, 'Small Change', pp. 67–78.

[10] N. J. Palmer and N. J. Mayhew, 'Medieval Coins and Jettons from Oxford Excavations', in Mayhew, ed., *Edwardian Monetary Affairs*, pp. 87–9.

[11] Britnell, *Growth and Decline*, pp. 206–8; 281; P. Nightingale, 'Monetary Contraction and Mercantile Credit in Later Medieval England', *EcHR*, 2nd ser., 43 (1990), pp. 569–74; M. M. Postan, *Medieval Trade and Finance* (Cambridge, 1973), pp. 37–8.

between their experience and the contraction of the money stock was complex. There were two main sorts of problem. One had to do with the availability of particular forms of currency. A bimetallic currency brought problems which medieval governments found difficult. Silver and gold coins could be sold abroad as bullion. That meant that if either silver or gold coinage were undervalued relative to the other, merchants were induced to export it. In this way monetary disorders could arise as a result of mismanagement by the government. The silver currency suffered most. Gold currency contracted by 18 per cent between c. 1353 and c. 1467, but silver contracted by 64 per cent. Even the situation in the 1460s was a marked improvement on that in Henry V's reign; at the time of the battle of Agincourt silver constituted only about one seventeenth of the total value of the English currency.[12] 'Scarcity of money' in these circumstances might relate specifically to the problems of the retail trade, because the money in circulation was unsuitable for small transactions, though it is surprisingly difficult to find examples of local trade suffering from such problems.

Secondly, and more commonly, 'scarcity of money' was equivalent to our concept of deflation caused by deficient market demand. Over the period as a whole the relationship between declining circulation and declining prices was weak. The current price of a representative basket of consumables in 1465–9 was only seven per cent below what it had been in 1311–15.[13] Yet the problem of economic depression was a recurrent one. One such episode occurred between 1322 and 1344, particularly in the last seven years of this period when low prices were correctly attributed to monetary problems caused by the war.[14] Monetary problems were less an issue during the remainder of Edward III's reign, but recurred under his successors, first in the period of high taxation between 1377 and 1381 and then during the general European crisis of c. 1395–c. 1415, which Day calls the first bullion famine. In England this phase of discontent culminated in the debasement of 1411. In 1419 and 1420 parliament was again alerted to the danger of deficient currency.[15] Another long contraction of the currency in circulation occurred between about 1440 and 1465.[16] The worst period of this depression, well documented in the *Paston Letters*, came in the early

[12] Day, *Medieval Market Economy*, p. 70
[13] Brown and Hopkins, *Perspective*, pp. 28–9.
[14] Mayhew, 'Numismatic Evidence', p. 12; Prestwich, 'Currency', pp. 51–2.
[15] Day, *Medieval Market Economy*, pp. 1, 47; J. H. Munro, *Wool, Cloth and Gold: The Struggle for Bullion in Anglo-Burgundian Trade, 1340–1478* (Toronto, 1978), pp. 43–4, 56–61, 72.
[16] J. Hatcher, 'The Great Slump of the Mid Fifteenth Century', in Britnell and Hatcher, eds., *Progress and Problems*, pp. 237–72.

1460s.[17] These problems did not end with the 1460s. A servant of Sir William Plumpton wrote to him from Nottinghamshire in 1469 complaining of his lack of ready money, and it is plain that one of the problems was low prices: 'I was on St Lawrence day at Melton with forty of your sheep to sell, and could sell none of them but if I would have selled twenty of the best of them for 13d a piece, and therefore I selled none.'[18] Norfolk was said to be 'barren of money' in 1475, and the problem was again low prices.[19]

Problems of deficient demand were sometimes the result of particular patterns of internal taxation and government expenditure. War with France was at times a drain on English purses, and there were periods where depressed domestic demand was a direct consequence of heavy taxation and high expenditure abroad, as in 1337–44 and 1377–81. Levies in kind, because they lowered the current earning of farming communities, were just as much a cause of 'shortage of money' in this sense as the heavy taxes in coin.[20] At other times economic depression arose from crises of international trade, when falling sales of English exports meant that merchants had to lay off workers and export bullion – if allowed to do so – to pay for imported goods. The depression of 1395–1415 was apparently of this latter sort, and so was that of 1440–65; in both these periods English exports sagged because of flagging demand from the continent.[21]

Some problems arising from the composition of the money stock, and some of the problems of economic depression, were resolved by demanding or permitting payments in kind. Edward III himself took goods rather than cash from taxpayers in the early years of his war with France, probably because spending power in England was known to be reduced.[22] Payment in kind was institutionalised in the barley-growing regions of fifteenth-century Norfolk, where rents were often paid in barley.[23] Landlords were often willing to offset goods and services against rent.[24] This is much in evidence in the north-east, where from the late fourteenth century onwards tenants were recorded to be paying their dues in grain and livestock. The Durham Priory Bursar's Rent

---

[17] R. H. Britnell, 'The Pastons and their Norfolk', *AHR*, 36 (1988), pp. 137–42; Munro, *Wool, Cloth and Gold*, pp. 139, 155, 160–1.

[18] *Plumpton Correspondence*, ed. Stapleton, p. 21.

[19] *Paston Letters*, ed. Davies, I, nos. 224–5, pp. 375–7.

[20] Maddicott, 'English Peasantry', pp. 329–51; W. M. Ormrod, 'The Crown and the English Economy, 1290–1348', in Campbell, ed., *Before the Black Death*, pp. 175–81, 183.

[21] Carus-Wilson and Coleman, *England's Export Trade*, pp. 122–3, 138–9.

[22] Ormrod, 'Crown and the English Economy', p. 166.

[23] Britnell, 'Pastons', p. 134.   [24] Dyer, 'Consumer', p. 322.

Book of 1495–6 is full of examples of tenants whose rent was acquitted partly in some non–monetary form. Even many Durham city house-holders paid their rents in merchandise or agricultural work.[25].

Such payments in kind were more in evidence in asymmetrical exchanges – representing acknowledgements of dependence – than in commercial transactions. They occur only in a few local contexts, and do not imply a general retreat from monetised relationships between landlords and tenants. Indeed, their significance was offset, as we shall see, by the widespread substitution of cash payments for former labour services. Sometimes, as in Edward III's wartime taxation, the compulsory confiscation of goods by those in authority exacerbated problems rather than solving them. At all times there were many circumstances in which payment in kind offered no solution to temporary problems of liquidity. 'As for fish,' wrote Hugh Unton in 1482 to Sir William Stonor, 'I can none buy without money.'[26]

The history of money, and the related history of economic depressions, is an essential part of our evidence relating to later medieval commercial history. Contracting population does not necessarily imply a diminution of output or trade. The contraction in arable husbandry makes the case for declining internal commerce stronger, though it is open to the objection that the English economy in the later Middle Ages had more to it than growing of crops.[27] When we add shrinkage in the marketing network the argument for contracting trade is stronger still, particularly for the fifteenth century, though a great deal of trade was conducted outside formal marketing institutions. Add to all this a severe reduction of the currency in circulation, however, and the compound argument for some degree of commercial contraction is difficult to escape.

There are two important qualifications to be added to this conclusion. The first is that the contraction of trade was not continuous. It is more appropriate to think of the period 1330–1500 as one in which severe trading depressions recurred than as one of sustained contraction. Some decades experienced commercial recovery – notably the decades following the Black Death. There was no clear relationship between commercial depressions and changes in population. Secondly, the value of currency in circulation – and by implication the volume of trade – did not decline as severely as population. At a rough guess the ratio rose

[25] *Durham Cathedral Priory Rentals, I: Bursars Rentals*, ed. R. A. Lomas and A. J. Piper, Surtees Soc. (Durham, 1989), pp. 129–97; Bonney, *Lordship*, pp. 115–19; Lomas, 'Priory of Durham', pp. 343–4; Pollard, *North-Eastern England*, pp. 77–8.

[26] *Stonor Letters*, ed. Kingsford, II, no. 313, p. 146.

[27] This, essentially, is the argument in Bridbury, *Economic Growth*.

from between 3s and 4s a head in 1324 to 8s a head in 1470. The availability of coin was another substantial difference between fifteenth-century society and that of the eleventh century.

II

The crown's income from taxation was undoubtedly affected adversely by the contraction of monetary circulation in spite of some far-reaching adaptations to the changed circumstances of the age. After 1334 the principle on which direct taxes were levied was altered. Up to this time personal wealth had been reassessed for each tax on movable property, and people had been liable for tax in proportion to their assessments. After 1334, however, no new assessments were made. The assessed wealth of each town and village was fixed, and as a result the sums they owed rapidly became independent of the real wealth of their inhabitants. Cumberland, Westmorland and Northumberland, three counties which had not been taxed in 1334, were rated according to assessments made in 1336, bringing the yield of a fifteenth and tenth to £38,500.[28] It was up to the authorities in each settlement to levy taxes in some acceptable way. In practice this meant that the burden was spread over a larger number of people than in the past. This development was apparent within a few years of 1334.[29] Poorer families were now drawn into ranks of the taxpayers, and direct taxes came to be paid by most house-holders.[30] Since at the upper end of society there were conspicuous accumulations of wealth, many taxpayers were very lightly burdened. Local developments of this sort later encouraged Edward III's government to think that the basis of lay taxation could be converted to an easily assessed poll tax.

The changing level of taxation did not closely reflect changes in national income. The success with which kings could raise money depended upon how well they could persuade parliaments that it was needed for a good cause. Since overseas aggression could induce willingness to give more than usual, taxation reached high levels under the most belligerent kings of the period, Edward III and Henry V. In the opening phases of the Hundred Years War between 1336 and 1348 parliaments authorised the collection of twelve fifteenths and tenths and a ninth. The yield of these taxes was equivalent to an average burden of

[28] W. M. Ormrod, *The Reign of Edward III: Crown and Political Society in England 1327–1377* (New Haven, 1990), p. 165.

[29] *Ibid.*, p. 179; Willard, *Parliamentary Taxes*, p. 177.

[30] *Dunwitch Bailiffs' Minute Book, 1404–1430*, ed. M. Bailey, Suff. Recs. Soc., XXXIV (Woodbridge 1992); Britnell, *Growth and Decline*, pp. 227–8.

£37,800 a year. There were also two taxes in wool, which together raised the average to £53,000 a year, a burden over twice that of direct taxes in Edward I's busiest period between 1294 and 1306.[31] Henry V's victory at Agincourt inspired another temporary surge of patriotic fervour that allowed him to collect seven and three-quarter fifteenths and tenths between 1415 and 1422, implying an average yield of about £41,800 a year.[32]

However, parliaments were not normally so generous and in the long run the crown had difficulty in maintaining its income from direct taxation. Taxation was particularly light in the later fifteenth century. In the 1470s Sir John Fortescue was in no doubt that Englishmen were better off than Frenchmen, and that this was because they paid fewer taxes.[33] Even in the reign of Henry VII fifteenths and tenths together with lay subsidies raised on average less than £12,000 a year.[34] These figures take account of concessions made in 1433 and 1446 to communities that had pleaded poverty. The yield of a fifteenth and tenth had been reduced to about £31,000. Aggregate national income, and perhaps national wealth as well, had declined, and the strength of the English parliament had ensured that taxation assessments should decline as well.[35]

The extent to which the flow of cash from the countryside into landlords' coffers sagged in the later Middle Ages remains a debated matter. It is not difficult to find examples of families whose incomes from land increased during some part of this period, either because they had accumulated property through marriage or inheritance,[36] or because they had successfully tightened the administration of their estates. Even some ecclesiastical estates, like those of Battle Abbey, Westminster Abbey and the archbishopric of Canterbury, returned a larger cash income in 1500 than in 1330.[37] What matters here, however, is not whether individual families or institutions experienced rising or falling incomes from time to time but whether total money income from landowning was rising or falling. One way of examining this question is to ask what commonly happened to individual sources of income. This can

[31] Ormrod, *Reign of Edward III*, p. 204.
[32] E. F. Jacob, *The Fifteenth Century, 1399–1485* (Oxford, 1961), p. 203.
[33] John Fortescue, *The Governance of England*, ed. C. Plummer (Oxford, 1885), pp. 113–16.
[34] Figures from R. S. Schofield, cited in R. Lockyer, *Henry VII*, 2nd edn (London, 1983), p. 47.
[35] Bridbury, 'Dr. Rigby's Comment', p. 420; R. A. Griffiths, *The Reign of King Henry VI: The Exercise of Royal Authority, 1422–1461* (London, 1981), pp. 117, 378–9; J. R. Lander, *Government and Community: England, 1450–1509* (London, 1980), p. 80.
[36] McFarlane, *Nobility*, pp. 59–60.
[37] Du Boulay, *Lordship of Canterbury*, p. 243; Dyer, *Standards of Living*, p. 36.

best be done by examining in turn the different types of income – from feudal rights, from demesne management and from peasant tenures.

Feudal income became less important in this period than it had been in the thirteenth century, even for the king. Edward III proved willing to relax his feudal rights to strengthen his political position, He collected no tallage and scutage after 1340, and agreed in 1352 that parliament's consent was required for the levying of feudal aids.[38] Even more destructive of feudal dependence was the more widespread application of legal devices to enhance the private control of fiefs. From Edward I's reign tenants-in-chief were allowed to create joint tenures, called jointures, to protect their wives in their widowhood. Other developments affected the wardship of tenants who inherited property as children, one of the most valuable rights of a feudal lord. Kings had often granted the wardship and marriage of his young tenants to others, either as a form of patronage or in exchange for cash. Between the 1340s and 1370s, however, it became a common practice for lords to avoid such loss of control by their families and friends. They created trusts to hold and manage their estates on the heir's behalf; such a trust became known as a use. This expedient was adopted not only by tenants-in chief but by their feudal subtenants as well. Although the crown had the necessary legal powers to control the creation of uses it did not employ them to any coherent effect, and administrative vigilance deteriorated from the late fourteenth century. The creation of uses had significantly reduced the value of feudal rights over land by the fifteenth century.[39]

Estate records of the later Middle Ages still retained the old distinction between demesne and tenant lands. In the course of the fourteenth century, though, the significance of the distinction changed. The problems of managing demesne farms discouraged landlords from maintaining direct demesne management. Money wage rates went up between the Black Death and at least the second decade of the fifteenth century as a result of labour scarcities.[40] Work was reduced, and perhaps skimped, in order to lower costs.[41] The productivity of demesne arable declined

[38] Ormrod, *Reign of Edward III*, p. 47.
[39] Bean, *Decline of English Feudalism*, pp. 104–5, 120–6, 210–34; McFarlane, *Nobility*, pp. 64–78, 217–19.
[40] W. Beveridge, 'Wages in the Winchester Manors', *EcHR*, 7 (1936), pp. 38–43; W. Beveridge, 'Westminster Wages in the Manorial Era', *EcHR*, 2nd ser., 8 (1955), pp. 20–9; Brown and Hopkins, *Perspective*, pp. 3–4, 11; Hatcher, *Rural Economy and Society*, pp. 290–1; Mate, 'Labour', pp. 59–61, 64–6.
[41] Campbell, 'Land, Labour, Livestock and Productivity Trends', pp. 165–78; Dyer, *Lords and Peasants*, pp. 125–6; C. Dyer, *Warwickshire Farming, 1349–c. 1520: Preparation for Agricultural Revolution*, Dugdale Soc. Occasional Paper XXVII (Oxford, 1981), pp. 14–15; M. Mate, 'Agrarian Economy after the Black Death: The Manors of Canterbury Cathedral Priory, 1348–91', *EcHR*, 2nd ser., 37 (1984), p. 347; Saul, *Scenes*, p. 121.

from its early fourteenth-century peak, and yields were sometimes lower. On many of Canterbury Cathedral Priory's manors the pigmen were being made redundant by the 1380s as a direct result of rising costs.[42] Rising labour costs also implied higher transport and management costs. Large, scattered estates were particularly vulnerable to the erosion of landlords' profits because of the increased costs of administering them and handling their produce. To some extent landlords could safeguard their position by leasing their demesnes. Sometimes demesnes were let intact, or at least in large units, so that they remained units of exceptional size dependent on hired labour, and survived as such to modern times.[43] When demesnes were wholly or partially fragmented, however, the land in the hands of smaller tenants increased.[44] In these cases household labour was substituted, at least in part, for that of hired labourers.

These changes altered the managerial system introduced between 1180 and 1220. Short leases had become more acceptable than they were around 1200, having lost the social stigma they had had in the twelfth century. Even the greatest nobleman might on occasion lease property for a life or term of years.[45] Administrative competence in recording leases and overseeing the collection of regular dues had improved since the twelfth century, so there was less danger of rights being overlooked or lost.[46] The abandonment of direct demesne agriculture began gradually before the Black Death, and became common from the 1350s. By the 1430s very few manors on large estates were still managed directly.[47] Manorial accounts no longer recorded details of demesne

---

[42] Mate, 'Labour', p. 61.

[43] N. S. B. Gras and E. C. Gras, *The Economic and Social History of an English Village (Crawley, Hampshire), A.D. 909–1928* (Cambridge, Mass., 1930), pp. 82–3; Newton, *Manor of Writtle*, pp. 68–77.

[44] E.g. Davenport, *Economic Development*, p. 57; C. Howell, *Land, Family and Inheritance in Transition: Kibworth Harcourt, 1280–1700* (Cambridge, 1983), p. 19; A. Jones, 'Bedfordshire: Fifteenth Century', in Harvey, ed., *Peasant Land Market*, pp. 199, 206; Raftis, *Estates*, pp. 281–2.

[45] *John of Gaunt's Register, 1379–83*, ed. E. C. Lodge and R. Somerville, Camden Soc., 3rd ser., 2 vols., LVI, LVII (London, 1937), II, no. 904, pp. 284–5.

[46] Clanchy, *From Memory to Written Record*, pp. 79–82; Harvey, *Westminster Abbey*, pp. 152–3.

[47] A. R. H. Baker, 'Changes in the Later Middle Ages', in H. C. Darby, ed., *A New Historical Geography of England* (Cambridge, 1973), pp. 203–4; Du Boulay, *Lordship of Canterbury*, pp. 220–1; Dyer, *Lords and Peasants*, pp. 82, 118–19, 147–8; J. N. Hare, 'The Demesne Lessees of Fifteenth Century Wiltshire', *AHR*, 39 (1981), pp. 1–2; Harvey, *Westminster Abbey*, pp. 148–51; Holmes, *Estates*, p. 92; Jones, 'Bedfordshire', pp. 181–2; Lomas, 'Priory of Durham', pp. 341–5; Raftis, *Estates*, pp. 259–66; C. Rawcliffe, *The Staffords, Earls of Stafford and Dukes of Buckingham, 1394–1521* (Cambridge, 1978), p. 53; Searle, *Lordship and Community*, pp. 324–7; Smith, *Canterbury Cathedral Priory*, p. 192.

agriculture but only rents of various kinds. So John Smyth of Nibley in his *Lives of the Berkeleys*, when he came to Thomas IV who died in 1417, bade farewell to husbandry as a topic he could write about with the comment that 'for the plough, none gaineth thereby but he that layeth his eye or hand daily upon it'.[48]

The new pattern of estate organisation is shown in Figure 3, which represents three principal manors and a submanor. Usually demesnes were leased without the attached hereditary tenancies, so that landlords continued to collect rents and to hold manorial courts through their servants.[49] Only one knight's estate is shown. The others that appeared in Figures 1 and 2 may be supposed by now to have split up, and to be barely distinguishable from free peasant tenures.

As a result of these organisational changes the proportion of landlords' incomes constituted by rents was enlarged and the proportion represented by profits declined. It was not unknown for demesne leases to include rents in kind, but this was exceptional, and became still more unusual in the course of the fifteenth century.[50] Even at Canterbury Cathedral Priory, where food farms continued to be required from individual manors to the end of our period, the system ran into difficulties in the 1430s and 1440s so that the prior had to purchase more grain than he was receiving from his manors. By the end of the century the grain received at the priory was less than a half what it had been in the 1420s.[51]

The value of demesnes altered variously on different estates and the period 1330–1500 is long enough to have been one of very mixed experience. It was rarely one of sustained decline. In favourable circumstances the leasing of demesnes stabilised the lord's income without affecting it adversely, as on the estates of the bishopric of Worcester.[52] After demesnes had been leased, many lords aimed to achieve stable rents from reliable tenants, rather than to bargain for the highest sum to be obtained at any given moment. Long leases, too, made rents static for long periods. For both these reasons demesne rents often responded to market trends imperfectly, tardily or not at all.[53]

Perfect stability was not, however, to be expected as a general rule

---

[48] *Berkeley Manuscripts*, ed. Maclean, II, pp. 5–7.
[49] Harvey, *Manorial Records*, pp. 7, 36.
[50] Du Boulay, *Lordship of Canterbury*, p. 230; Harvey, *Westminster Abbey*, pp. 156–7.
[51] Smith, *Canterbury Cathedral Priory*, p. 201.
[52] Dyer, *Lords and Peasants*, pp. 145–6.
[53] E.g., Bean, *Estates*, pp. 19, 20, 30; Davenport, *Economic Development*, appendix XI, pp. lxxv–vi; B. F. Harvey, 'The Leasing of the Abbot of Westminster's Demesnes in the Later Middle Ages', *EcHR*, 2nd ser., 22 (1969), p. 23–4; Newton, *Manor of Writtle*, pp. 70–4.

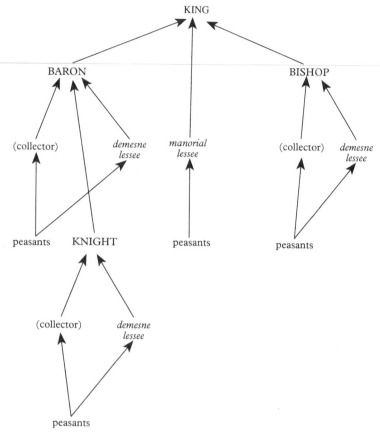

Figure 3   Types of land tenure, *c.* 1420–1500

Capitals indicate a feudal tenure, italics a lease, brackets an employed officer and lower case letters a peasant tenure. The arrows indicate who receive rent and services from whom. Peasants paid money rents to their lord's collector and any surviving labour services to the demesne lessee.

over the whole period from 1330 to 1500. These years were generally less favourable to demesne agriculture then the years 1180–1330, so that the income from demesne assets commonly declined.[54] Already by the time of the Black Death the most prosperous age of direct demesne

---

[54] E.g. Dyer, *Warwickshire Farming*, p. 21; Hilton, *Economic Development*, pp. 86–7; Jones, 'Bedfordshire', pp. 182–3.

farming was over on many estates.[55] The Black Death itself caused widespread disruption and loss of income for a few years.[56] Lords often recovered surprisingly well from this disaster between the mid-1350s and about 1380,[57] though for a variety of reasons the profitability of many estates remained lower than before.[58] The period between about 1380 and 1430 was one of renewed difficulties, when lords found it harder to get tenants on the old terms. Income from demesne lands often fell. In the mid-fifteenth century land in north-central Essex could be leased for only half the rent per acre it had fetched before the Black Death, and land values were similarly depressed throughout the county.[59] The fifteenth century after the 1420s was a period of greater stability in much of England, though there was a severe depression in the north after the crisis of 1438–40[60] and another in eastern England in the early 1460s[61]. There is more evidence for rising demesne rents in the final decades of the fifteenth century, but such increases were still exceptional.[62]

Though 'scarcity of money' became a recurrent problem from the later fourteenth century, money rents from peasant tenures replaced rents in labour and kind. From the 1390s, and in some places earlier than that, landlords lost the power to exact traditional labour dues.[63] In the early fourteenth century they had sold works to suit their own convenience, but had often demanded that labour services should be performed. The choice had been theirs. Now that it was in their interests to

---

[55] Dyer, *Lords and Peasants*, pp. 78–83; Raftis, *Estates*, p. 217; Smith, *Canterbury Cathedral Priory*, pp. 143–4.

[56] Bailey, *Marginal Economy?*, pp. 222–4; Britnell, 'Agricultural Technology', pp. 61–2; Coleman, *Downham-in-the-Isle*, p. 18; Harvey, *Medieval Oxfordshire Village*, pp. 136–7; Levett, *Studies*, pp. 292–4; *VCH Cambs.*, IV, pp. 91, 98, 142–3, 153, 244, and V, p. 92.

[57] Bailey, *Marginal Economy?*, pp. 225–34; Bolton, *Medieval English Economy*, pp. 211–12; A. R. Bridbury, 'The Black Death', *EcHR*, 2nd ser., 26 (1973), pp. 580–1, 587–8; K. G. Feiling, 'An Essex Manor in the Fourteenth Century', *EHR*, 26 (1911), p. 335; Holmes, *Estates*, pp. 90–3, 114–15; Levett, *Studies*, pp. 252–5; Page, *Estates*, pp. 126–8.

[58] R. H. Britnell, 'Feudal Reaction after the Black Death in the Palatinate of Durham', *PP*, 128 (1990), pp. 43–7; Dyer, *Lords and Peasants*, pp. 118–23; Harvey, *Medieval Oxfordshire Village*, pp. 138–9; Howell, *Land, Family and Inheritance*, pp. 43–4; Mate, 'Agrarian Economy', pp. 341–52.

[59] Britnell, *Growth and Decline*, pp. 152–7; Dyer, *Lords and Peasants*, pp. 167–70; Harvey, *Westminster Abbey*, pp. 268–9; Holmes, *Estates*, pp. 115–20; Page, *Estates*, pp. 152–3.

[60] A. J. Pollard, 'The North-Eastern Economy and the Agrarian Crisis of 1438–40', *NH*, 35 (1989), pp. 93–105.

[61] Britnell, *Growth and Decline*, pp. 188, 202; Britnell, 'Pastons', pp. 137–42.

[62] *The Duchy of Lancaster's Estates in Derbyshire, 1485–1540*, ed. I. S. W. Blanchard, Derb. Archl. Soc. Rec. Ser., III (1971), pp. 8, 64–5; *Grey of Ruthin Valor*, ed. Jack, pp. 26, 29–35; 'Three Carrow Accounts', ed. Redstone, pp. 30, 50; Bean, *Estates*, pp. 43–9; Dyer, *Lords and Peasants*, pp. 167–71; Pollard, *North-Eastern England*, p. 59.

[63] Evidence for the various regions of England is summarised by the contributors to *AHEW*, III, pp. 593–4, 604, 620, 629–30, 639, 667–9, 708.

take the labour services, because of the higher cost of employing day labourers to do the work, they lost the power to choose. Sometimes lords were obliged to transform customary tenure to leasehold in order to find tenants.[64] In other instances they had to negotiate a commutation of labour services to an agreed annual money payment.[65] Even where it was not formally commuted, week work was invariably sold by the mid-fifteenth century, and often long before.[66] The only labour services to survive were some of the seasonal ones, like ploughing or harvesting boons. Unlike week work, these often had communal rituals and festivities attached to them.[67]

Why did tenants prefer to pay in coin? One consideration was growing aversion to servile status. Week work, in particular, was a defining attribute of villainage. Another consideration – probably the crucial one – was the greater availability of cash from sources other than sales of produce. Because of labour scarcity tenants could earn good money by agricultural labour or some domestic industrial activity. Even middle-ranking tenants frequently supplemented their income with wage-earning.[68] Tenants could pay a money rent with less labour than their customary services required.

Commutation made only a minor contribution to landlords' money incomes. Long before 1330, we have seen, most rents were already paid in money. Heavy labour services were chiefly characteristic of large estates. Not only did they represent only a small proportion of feudal rent, but already by 1330 they were often acquitted with money payments. Where labour services had been used rather than sold their commutation made it necessary to employ workers at piece rates, so that increases in a lord's money income was offset by higher labour costs. Changes in the total value of services, often after commutation had taken place, were of greater significance for landlords' incomes than commutation itself.

Many different circumstances affected the level of peasant rents. Enclosed land enhanced its annual value relative to open-field land. At Sherington (Bucks.) enclosed demesne rose from $8\frac{1}{2}$d to $9\frac{1}{2}$d an acre

---

[64] Davenport, *Economic Development*, p. 58; F. W. Maitland, 'The History of a Cambridgeshire Manor', *EHR*, 9 (1894), p. 428; Poos, *Rural Society*, pp. 48–50; *VCH Cambs.*, V, p. 10, and VI, p. 268.

[65] Dewindt, *Land and People*, pp. 143–5; Maitland, 'History of a Cambridgeshire Manor', pp. 433–4; Massingberd, 'Social and Economic History', p. 319; *VCH Cambs*, V, pp. 92, 102.

[66] Britnell, 'Feudal Reaction', pp. 44–5; Newton, *Manor of Writtle*, p. 74; *VCH Cambs.*, IV, p. 104.

[67] E.g. Maitland, 'History of a Cambridgeshire Manor', pp. 433–4; Moss, 'Economic Development', p. 109; *VCH Essex*, V, pp. 216, 282.

[68] Dyer, 'Small Landowner', pp. 13–14.

between 1408 and 1439 while open-field customary land fell from 5d to
2½d.[69] Some rents increased during the periods of the late Middle Ages
as a result of local circumstances. In Dedham (Essex) some rose in the
1430s and 1440s because the village shared the prosperity of Colchester's
cloth industry, and a similar upward movement occurred at the same
time in the clothmaking villages of Wiltshire.[70] The duchy of Cornwall
manors of Climsland, Liskeard, Calstock, Rillaton and Helstone in
Triggshire experienced a sustained increase in rents through most of the
period between the 1360s and the 1440s as a result of the growth of local
tin mining and clothmaking. The rents on these manors were higher in
the 1480s than in 1330.[71] Some rents and entry fines in various parts of
the country increased in the last quarter of the fifteenth century as a
result of local economic revival.[72]

Nevertheless, tenants' rents were more commonly static or falling
than rising. Large numbers of long-established money rents, particularly freehold rents, remained uncontested and unchanged through the
fourteenth and fifteenth centuries. They do not make interesting history,
and tend to be overlooked.[73] Many other rents, particularly customary
rents, had to be reduced. Often such reductions were negotiated
tenement by tenement so that there is no set pattern to them, but their
total effect could be considerable. An account of Snape (N.R. Yorks.)
from 1457–8 records thirty-two reduced rents, amounting up to £23 7s
5½d out of the total unadjusted rent of £74 10s 2½d. By such modifica-
tions to individual rents the average rent per acre of land declined.[74]
Landlords reluctant to moderate their rents were likely to lose income
from having tenements lying vacant.[75] In some manors the amount of
land which was technically demesne – that is, at the lord's disposal –
increased as a result of the accumulation of unwanted tenements in the
lord's hands.[76] At Feering (Essex) in 1403 a half virgate was described
as 'lately leased for 14s then for 8s but nothing this year for want of a

[69] Chibnall, *Sherington*, p. 153.
[70] Britnell, *Growth and Decline*, pp. 251–2; Hare, 'Wiltshire Risings', pp. 18–19.
[71] Hatcher, *Rural Economy and Society*, pp. 129–32, 151–4, 167–72, 262–4.
[72] E.g. Bailey, *Marginal Economy?* pp. 279–80; Britnell, *Growth and Decline*, p. 253; Dyer, *Lords and Peasants*, p. 288; Jones, 'Bedfordshire', p. 220.
[73] R. H. Britnell, 'Tenant Farming and Tenant Farmers: Eastern England', in *AHEW*, III, p. 618.
[74] N.R. Yorks. RO, ZAL, 1/2/1; Bailey, *Marginal Economy?*, pp. 268–9; Davenport, *Economic Development*, p. 78; W. G. Hoskins, *The Midland Peasant: The Economic and Social History of a Leicestershire Village* (London, 1957), p. 84.
[75] C. Dyer, 'A Redistribution of Incomes in Fifteenth-Century England?', in Hilton, ed., *Peasants, Knights and Heretics*, p. 203.
[76] H. E. Hallam, 'The Agrarian Economy of South Lincolnshire in the Mid-Fifteenth Century', *Nottingham Med. Stud.*, 11 (1967), p. 88; *VCH Cambs.*, V. p. 206.

lessee, and it is sown with oats on the lord's behalf'.[77] Accounts often contain an entry headed 'decay of rent' in which are listed those properties from which no rent has been paid or whose rent has been reduced. Such entries had occasionally been needed in the thirteenth and fourteenth centuries, but they became more normal in the fifteenth century, and often constitute a major feature of an account.[78] Accumulations of arrears, some of which were never paid off, tell another side of the story. They resulted from tenants' inability or refusal to pay. Even rents which were eventually paid could often not be collected without persistence over many years.[79] From the mid-fourteenth century, too, landlords became less able to exact entry fines and other customary dues than in the past.[80] Where rentals appear to be unchanging over long periods, reality was often more sombre from a landlord's point of view.

The final component of the cash flow out of the countryside was that going to purchase goods and services from towns. The evidence here cannot be reliably assessed. Towns, as we have seen, often fared better than the countryside in the late Middle ages. To the extent that this was the effect of export demand, or, in the case of Westminster, to an exceptional concentration of expenditure by families in the upper income brackets, it had little to do with rural demand. The decline in rural population and of arable farming suggests that demand for some urban goods and services was smaller than it had been. On the other hand, improvements in rural standards of housing and dress probably stimulated some urban crafts. Perhaps a higher proportion of rural income was spent on urban products and services than in the past. We may speculate that a larger share of rural incomes in this period was spent on symmetrical exchanges, which directly benefited the spenders, rather than on payments to kings and landlords. Yet this does not answer any questions about total rural expenditure on goods and services. It may have contracted. Towns that depended for their livelihood on the supply of goods and services to neighbouring communities – and this means the majority of provincial towns – were already smaller in the late fourteenth century than they had been in 1330. Oxford in the age of Wyclif, for example, had declined from its

[77] PRO, S.C.6/841/10r.
[78] E.g. *Grey of Ruthin Valor*, ed. Jack; *Ministers' Accounts of the Warwickshire Estates of the Duke of Clarence, 1479–80*, ed. R. H. Hilton, Dugdale Soc., XXI (Stratford-upon-Avon, 1952).
[79] Bailey, *Marginal Economy?*, pp. 269–76; R. R. Davies, 'Baronial Accounts, Income and Arrears in the Later Middle Ages', *EcHR*, 2nd ser., 21 (1968), pp. 219–29; Dyer, 'Redistribution', pp. 197–200; Pollard, 'Estate Management', pp. 563–5.
[80] Dewindt, *Land and People*, pp. 145–6; R. Faith, 'Berkshire: Fourteenth and Fifteenth Centuries', in Harvey, ed., *Peasant Land Market*, pp. 114–18; Raftis, *Estates*, pp. 260–1.

thirteenth-century prosperity and had become more dependent upon its university as a resource.[81] Stagnation usually became more marked in the fifteenth century. The decline in urban rents in the late Middle Ages, particularly from the 1420s, is even better attested than that of rural properties, chiefly because they were contractual.[82] Maybe these urban economic problems were in part the result of a decline in local spending, even if some urban trades benefited in the process.

If we examine the evidence for the reverse flow of currency back into country areas, the evidence is poor. These aspects of trade are examined here for the sake of completing the analysis rather than for any clear evidence they can offer about the changing volume of trade.

Mercantile activity in the countryside remained great enough to support many regions of poor land in their former specialised use, and some local trades expanded to meet new opportunities, particularly in the later fourteenth century. Such, for example, is the trade in rabbits from the East Anglian Breckland, a trade which reached its medieval peak in the late fourteenth century.[83] Some mining activities expanded during parts of the late Middle Ages, opening up new commercial opportunities to landlords who owned accessible mineral deposits. The mining of tin in Cornwall declined from a peak of over 1m lb a year in the 1330s and 1340s to less than a quarter of that figure immediately after the Black Death, but it had regained its former level by the later 1380s. There was a long period of lower output between the 1430s and the 1480s – with recorded levels falling to below 600,000 lb in the depression of the early 1460s – but output arose again to over 1m lb again by 1494.[84] The mining of lead and iron also had phases of growth; output of both metals is estimated to have grown by at least 50 per cent during the fifteenth century.[85] Bolton Priory's rising income from lead mining at Appletreewick was the one bright spot in an otherwise disappointing period.[86] In the north-east coal mining increased from the 1470s.[87] Many parts of the country benefited from high wool

[81] K. B. McFarlane, *Wycliffe and English Non-Conformity* (London, 1952), pp. 32–3.
[82] N. W. Alcock, 'The Catesbys in Coventry: A Medieval Estate and its Archive', *MH*, 15 (1990), pp. 14–16; Bartlett, 'Expansion and Decline', p. 30; Bonney, *Lordship*, pp. 114–15, 123–31; A. F. Butcher, 'Rent, Population and Economic Change in Late-Medieval Newcastle', *NH*, 14 (1978), pp. 67–74; Butcher, 'Rent and the Urban Economy', pp. 18–43; Keene, *Cheapside*, pp. 19–20; Keene, *Survey*, I, pp. 237–48; Rees Jones, 'Property', pp. 263–70.
[83] M. Bailey, 'The Rabbit and the Medieval East Anglian Economy', *AHR*, 36 (1988), pp. 10–11.
[84] Hatcher, *English Tin Production*, pp. 156–60.
[85] Blanchard, 'Labour Productivity' p. 24.   [86] Kershaw, *Bolton Priory*, p. 182.
[87] Pollard, *North-Eastern England*, pp. 74–7.

exports and a growing cloth industry in the decades immediately after the Black Death. The surge in cloth exports from the 1470s again encouraged sheep farming.[88] The regional specialisations that had emerged before 1330 demonstrably remained a primary feature of English internal trade thereafter, but we cannot discuss their aggregate fortunes with any confidence. There is more evidence for growth in the periods 1360–90 and 1470–1500 than in the intervening decades, when the level of trade was probably below its late fourteenth-century level.

In some towns whose population recovered or increased after the Black Death demand for grain increased during the later fourteenth and early fifteenth centuries. Brewing and grain-milling in Colchester increased between 1385–9 and 1405–9.[89] Urban demand for meat and dairy produce is likely to have been higher in this period than before the Black Death, since for most social groups average consumption was rising.[90] There is more evidence of the importance of cattle raising and dairy farming around 1400 than in earlier times. London's demand was important both for the city's immediate environs and for graziers in parts of the midlands. From the 1420s, however, an urban stimulus to agriculture is less in evidence. Even cattle farmers had fewer grounds for complacency between the 1430s and 1480s than earlier.[91] The evidence for the decay of markets indicates that urban retail trade in many kinds of agricultural produce contracted, and it was probably lower in 1500 than it had been in the early decades of the fifteenth century.

III

The personal involvement of magnates in the supervision of their affairs depended in part, as in the past, on what other things they had to do. When bishops and members of the nobility were encumbered with service of the crown at Westminster or, up to 1450, in France, their affairs had to be entrusted to their wives and their councils. The choice of administrative officers was an important one, especially for a non-

---

[88] Carus-Wilson and Coleman, *England's Export Trade*, pp. 122, 138–9.

[89] Britnell, *Growth and Decline*, pp. 88–91.

[90] C. Dyer, 'Changes in Diet in the Late Middle Ages: The Case of Harvest Workers', *AHR*, 36 (1988), pp. 24–37; C. Dyer, 'English Diet in the Later Middle Ages', in Aston and others, eds., *Social Relations and Ideas*, pp. 213–14.

[91] *Duchy of Lancaster's Estates*, ed. Blanchard, pp. 1–13; Bailey, *Marginal Economy?*, pp. 257–8, 294–5; Dyer, *Warwickshire Farming*, pp. 9–12, 18–20; M. Mate, 'Pastoral Farming in South-East England in the Fifteenth Century', *EcHR*, 2nd ser., 40 (1987), pp. 527–32; Moss, 'Economic Development', pp. 109–10; Pollard, *North-Eastern England*, pp. 36–7, 59–65; Tupling, *Economic History*, pp. 31–3; A. Watkins, 'Cattle Grazing in the Forest of Arden in the Later Middle Ages', *AHR*, 37 (1989), pp. 12–20.

resident bishop or nobleman. Administrators of large estates had to be alert, even when all the manorial demesnes in their charge were leased to tenants. They had many rents to negotiate, since mills, fisheries, markets and mines were often leased separately from the principal manors of the estate. In periods of economic difficulty finding suitable tenants took up a lot of time. Even when rents did not need to be negotiated, the terms of payment needed revision whenever tenants fell into arrears. Auditors had to assess what allowances lessees were justified in requesting. Their duties required them to appreciate the prevailing circumstances of trade, and they were often obliged to attend to current local problems.[92] Lords and their councils, if they were effective in their supervision of their estates, tried to ensure that the terms of leases were being fully observed, and that properties were not being allowed to deteriorate.[93]

Larger landlords kept some direct responsibility for marketing produce. They often retained a direct interest in sheep farming, and continued to be responsible for the marketing of their wool. Though some of them reduced or abandoned their pastoral activities in the middle of the century there was a widespread revival of interest in the last few decades.[94] We still have notes that Sir Roger Townshend made on his sheep and arable husbandry.[95] Some landlords, notably in Norfolk where surplus barley and malt were major sources of prosperity, received rents in kind and negotiated their sale. The Paston family's livelihood depended heavily on the sale of barley they received in rents, and in periods of depression they bore the tiresome consequences of sluggish markets and low prices.[96]

However, the widespread abandonment of direct demesne husbandry inevitably meant that landlords and their councils were less involved in the monitoring of commercial decisions than they had been in the thirteenth and early fourteenth centuries. The leaseholder's obligation to pay a fixed rent for the demesne lands under his control removed from him any need to account in detail to the landlord for his receipts and expenses. The work of estate auditors was to that extent less concerned with commercial strategies.[97] Even the negotiation of rents became less frequent in the course of time. By the mid-fifteenth century leases for life, or for terms of thirty years or more, were not uncommon, and

[92] Harvey, *Manorial Records*, pp. 36–7; Rawcliffe, *Staffords*, p. 150.
[93] Du Boulay, *Lordship of Canterbury*, pp. 227–9; Page, *Estates*, p. 149; Rawcliffe, *Staffords*, p. 153–4.
[94] Bailey, *Marginal Economy?*, pp. 290–4; Dobson, *Durham Priory*, p. 277; Dyer, *Lords and Peasants*, pp. 150–1, 210; Hare, 'Demesne Lessees', p. 2; Harvey, *Westminster Abbey*, pp. 150–1; Pollard, *North-Eastern England*, pp. 35–6.
[95] Richmond, *John Hopton*, p. 97.   [96] Britnell, 'Pastons', pp. 134, 137–9.
[97] Harvey, *Manorial Records*, pp. 35–7.

some were much longer, though such long terms were by no means the rule and estate policies differed quite widely in this respect.[98]

There were no sharp differences between the commercial orientation of the great estates and those of minor landlords. Even the gentry commonly leased out their demesnes.[99] The gentry, too, employed estate officers for routine administrative duties.[100] However, minor landlords continued to practise direct management longer than their social superiors, and were more likely to take demesne lands back into their own hands from time to time. A small and compact estate could be very profitable in the hands of an energetic landlord like John Brome of Lapworth and Baddesley Clinton (Warws.), whose main source of income was beef cattle.[101] Even when their demesnes were leased out, small landowners were often personally involved in the finer details of estate management. Members of the Paston family are recorded in their letters to have held manor courts, interviewed potential tenants and negotiated sales of agricultural produce.[102]

Some minor landlords leased the demesnes of larger estates. Those entrepreneurially inclined would take up land that could be worked well with their existing properties. Such was William Harewell, who complemented existing estates at Shottery and Wootton Wawen (Warws.) by leasing the demesne at Stratford-upon-Avon between 1464 and 1500.[103] The Darknalls, who leased the demesne at Otford (Kent) from the archbishop of Canterbury, had property in the vicinity.[104] Many lessees of gentleman or yeoman status worked the land commercially, paid the running costs and took the profits.[105] The attractions of leasing additional property depended on the detailed circumstances of the contract, and varied according to time and place. On the estates of the bishopric of Worcester gentry were of slight importance as demesne lessees early in the fifteenth century but became more prominent

---

[98] Davenport, *Economic Development*, p. 57 and appendix VII, pp. xix–xxix; Dyer, *Lords and Peasants*, pp. 210–11; Harvey, *Westminister Abbey*, pp. 154–5; Raftis, *Estates*, p. 291; Smith, *Canterbury Cathedral Priory*, p. 200. For short-lease policies see Dobson, *Durham Priory*, p. 283; R. A. Lomas, 'Developments in Land Tenure on the Prior of Durham's Estate in the Later Middle Ages', *NH*, 13 (1977), pp. 37–40; Lomas, 'South-East Durham', pp. 311–13.

[99] Dyer, *Warwickshire Farming*, pp. 16–17; S. M. Wright, *The Derbyshire Gentry in the Fifteenth Century*, Derb. Rec. Soc., VIII (Chesterfield, 1983), p. 14.

[100] Richmond, *John Hopton*, pp. 96–7; Saul, *Scenes*, pp. 98–104; Wright, *Derbyshire Gentry*, pp. 14–16.

[101] Dyer, 'Small Landowner', pp. 5–8; Richmond, *John Hopton*, pp. 84–5; Saul, *Scenes*, p. 110.

[102] Britnell, 'Pastons', pp. 135–44.   [103] Dyer, *Lords and Peasants*, p. 215.

[104] Du Boulay, *Lordship of Canterbury*, p. 221.

[105] Hare, 'Demesne Lessees', pp. 8–9; Pollard, *North-Eastern England*, pp. 63–4.

towards its close when the bishops became more inclined to give patronage in this form.[106] In Derbyshire, away from any major marketing centre, there are few examples before the sixteenth century.[107]

Merchants increased their stake in the land by direct purchases in the fifteenth century, particularly in the London area and the home counties.[108] Sometimes they, too, leased demesnes as commercial ventures.[109] There are good examples of rural mercantile enterprise to be found, particularly in the London region. John Gedney, the draper, acquired four manors in Tottenham (Mdx.) and developed the village during the 1430s as a centre for pasture farming and rural industry. He greatly increased the profitability of his properties.[110] However, not all mercantile estate management was so assertive. Merchants were more likely than any other category of lessee to be acquiring leases in order to be able to sublet, just as they purchased estates for the same purpose. Their impact on agriculture is in these circumstances difficult to distinguish from that of other rentiers. There are no good grounds for singling out mercantile property developers for their distinctive talents as entrepreneurs.

Meanwhile the leasing of demesnes expanded greatly the scope of entrepreneurial aspirations amongst small farmers. Previous service as a reeve or rent collector was a sound preparation for a villager to take responsibility for the demesne in this way. In Wiltshire, for example, demesnes were usually leased intact to a single tenant, and here a wealthy class of lessees, often of peasant origins, retained control over particular demesnes for several generations. Some families leased more than one demesne.[111] A different pattern of tenant responsibility is found in some parts of the country, notably in the north, where it was common for landlords to make over their demesnes to whole village communities. The bishop of Durham's demesnes had been split up in part in this way even before the Black Death. After 1349 it was common for whole villages to be collectively responsible for the management of demesne lands on the estates both of the bishop and of the Durham Priory.[112] In the parish church at Sutton (Lincs.) in 1367, 1,000 acres of

[106] Du Boulay, *Lordship of Canterbury*, p. 232; Dyer, *Lords and Peasants*, p. 211; Lomas, 'Priory of Durham', p. 347.

[107] Wright, *Derbyshire Gentry*, p. 16.

[108] Britnell, *Growth and Decline*, pp. 209–10; Jones, 'Bedfordshire', pp. 189–90, 234–5; McIntosh, *Autonomy and Community*, pp. 125–6, 221–3; Moss, 'Economic Development', pp. 108–9.

[109] Dobson, *Durham Priory*, p. 282; Dyer, *Lords and Peasants*, p. 211; Hare, 'Demesne Lessees', pp. 9–11; Harvey, *Westminster Abbey*, p. 152.

[110] Moss, 'Economic Development', pp. 112–13.

[111] Hare, 'Demesne Lessees', pp. 4–12; Harvey, 'Leasing', pp. 20–1.

[112] Britnell, 'Feudal Reaction', pp. 44–6; Lomas, 'Developments', pp. 36–7.

demesne, together with the manorial fisheries, were leased to the whole homage for an annual rent of £162 4s 6d, a sum that was reduced to £128 13s 6d in 1422. The arrangement was maintained at this lower level of rent until at least 1485.[113]

Demesne lands leased in parcels added an important new component to the village land market.[114] They contributed to the ease with which a few tenants were able to accumulate large agglomerations of property.[115] Even when a large proportion of the demesne was left intact parts of it were often leased off in smaller units. For example, at Donnington Castle (Leics.) in 1421 there were about 269 acres of demesne in the hands of two lessees, 109 acres was leased to various tenants in eighteen lots and a further 23 acres were unlet for want of tenants willing to have them.[116] A similar development was encouraged by the fall in land values, which enabled enterprising tenants to accumulate large holdings. Particularly from about 1390 many holdings which had previously supported a single family were amalgamated into larger complexes.[117] Both this, and the smaller average size of families, imply that an increased proportion of peasant output was available to be marketed. In eastern England, though not on all estates, it became common for accumulations of property to combine free and unfree land.[118] By acquiring free land, some villain families established themselves as yeomen or even gentlemen. The Grene family of Ingold-mells (Lincs.) were copyholders who became gentry in the century before 1477.[119] The Candelers of Yoxford (Suff.) and the Pastons of Paston (Norf.) are other examples.[120]

The greater availability of land did not lead to the disappearance of smallholding. In Essex and East Anglia, in particular, there was a substantial cottager class. Even allowing for the fact that tenants might hold land from more than one manor, many held fewer than ten acres

---

[113] Massingberd, 'Social and Economic History', p. 317.
[114] Dewindt, *Land and People*, pp. 60. 108; Howell, *Land, Family and Inheritance*, p. 19; A. Jones, 'Land and People at Leighton Buzzard in the Later Fifteenth Century', *EcHR*, 2nd ser., 25 (1972), pp. 23–4.
[115] Jones, 'Bedfordshire', pp. 199, 207.
[116] Hilton, *Economic Development*, pp. 157–8.
[117] Campbell, 'Population Pressure', p. 125; Davenport, *Economic Development*, pp. 81–7; Dewindt. *Land and People*, pp. 110–15; Dyer, *Warwickshire Farming*, pp. 7–8; Hare, 'Demesne Lessees', pp. 14–15; Harvey, *Westminster Abbey*, pp. 288–90; Hilton, *Economic Development*, pp. 100–5; Page, *Estates*, pp. 123, 152–3.
[118] R. H. Tawney, *The Agrarian Problem in the Sixteenth Century* (London, 1912), pp. 23–4. Cf. Harvey, *Westminster Abbey*, pp. 285–6.
[119] Massingberd, 'Social and Economic History', p. 319.
[120] *Sibton Abbey Estates*, ed. Denney, p. 21; C. Richmond, *The Paston Family in the Fifteenth Century: The First Phase* (Cambridge, 1990), pp. 13–22.

and could not be considered commercial farmers.[121] Large peasant farms were a minority. More significant than their absolute number, however, was the proportion of the land drawn under their control. At Castle Camps (Cambs.) in 1450 only six out of the thirty-six tenants had more than 30 acres, but between them they held about 265 acres, which was 44 per cent of the tenant land.[122]

Not only did wealthier peasants accumulate arable land. They also assumed greater importance than before in pasture farming. The sheep flocks in the hands of ordinary villagers became larger in the later fourteenth century. The numbers of sheep reported by manor court juries for trespassing increased. The number of large flocks recorded in peasant wills of the fifteenth century is further supporting evidence.[123] The beef cattle trade became a distinctive specialisation in the regions accessible to urban markets, as in the Forest of Arden (Warws.) where former peasant families like the Deys of Drakenage and the Baillys of Middleton created profitable cattle farms. The graziers from this part of the world sold their beasts to butchers as far away as London, as well as to those nearer home.[124]

For all these reasons we may be confident that there was a significant change in the locus of commercial decision-taking in late medieval society. Fewer decisions were taken by large landlords and their agents, and more were taken by comparatively small producers. This transition was important for the contrast between medieval and early modern society, and can for that reason be interpreted as a stage in the transition from feudalism to capitalism. Whether it was a necessary stage is not a question that can be tackled here. The view that it was necessary, or that is was in itself a development in capitalism, seems to depend upon a definition of capitalism that excludes landlord enterprise.[125]

Peasant farming did not use labour services, but it was more dependent than landlord enterprise on household labour. It was not distinctively captitalist in terms of the social relations between property owners and workers that it entailed. In any case, even before the 1390s labour

[121] Britnell, 'Tenant Farming', pp. 614–17; C. M. Hoare, *The History of an East Anglian Soke* (Bedford, 1918), pp. 207–12; Jones, 'Bedfordshire', p. 197; Poos, *Rural Society*, pp. 18–19.
[122] *VCH Cambs.*, V, p. 42.
[123] Britnell, *Growth and Decline*, p. 146; Dyer, *Lords and Peasants*, p. 328–9; Dyer, *Warwickshire Farming*, p. 30; Jones, 'Bedfordshire', pp. 180–1; Lloyd, *Movement of Wool Prices*, p. 28.
[124] Dyer, *Warwickshire Farming*, p. 20; Watkins, 'Cattle Grazing', pp. 18–19.
[125] C. Dyer, 'Were There any Capitalists in Fifteenth-Century England?', in J. Kermode, ed., *Enterprise and Individuals in Fifteenth-Century England* (Stroud, 1991), pp. 16–19.

services accounted for only a minor part of the total labour requirement of manorial demesnes. Peasant husbandry required less than seigniorial husbandry by way of planning, calculation and record-keeping and to that extent its management was less formally rational than demesne agriculture. It is difficult to say in what sense ambitious peasant husbandry of the fifteenth century was governed more by the pursuit of profit than ambitious seigniorial husbandry of the thirteenth and fourteenth.

Not all peasant farming was governed by entrepreneurial ambition. To judge from some evidence from mining communities, the prevailing work ethic in village societies aimed at satisfying a particular set of requirements rather than at high profitability. Conservatism of this sort was conspicuous in regions where arable remained the most profitable form of husbandry and where there were consequently fewer inducements for farmers to reorganise or reinvest.[126] Even the accumulation of land and livestock by the more prominent few might be a matter of status rather than of commercial calculation. Fifteenth-century peasants regarded their sheep as a store of value rather than a source of profit, and were willing to produce wool without regard to the profitability of their activities.[127] Andreas Franciscius thought that the extent of sheep farming was a measure of the laziness and torpor of English farmers.[128] Another Italian visitor thought that English farmers neglected their opportunities to export grain to surrounding countries.[129]

On the other hand, the experience of the fifteenth century meant that opportunities for entrepreneurship were more widespread and less constrained by large families, high taxes or seigniorial exactions than in the past. Rural enterprise was less confined to the managers of manorial demesnes, and the structure of rural society showed a greater tolerance of contractual relationships. Minor landlords and wealthier peasants exploited the market opportunities available to them, and are likely to have accounted for an even larger proportion of marketed produce than they had been in 1500. Peasants worked more efficiently for themselves than they would ever have done for an employer or a lord.[130] They were less extravagant with the inessentials of life. They often invested in their land to provide enclosures suitable for protecting their flocks and herds.

---

[126] Blanchard, 'Labour Productivity', pp. 8–9; Dyer, *Warwickshire Farming*, pp. 32–4.
[127] Lloyd, *Movement of Wool Prices*, p. 28.
[128] *English Historical Documents, V: 1485–1558*, ed. Williams, p. 191.
[129] *Relation*, ed. Sneyd, p. 10.
[130] Campbell, 'Agricultural Progress', p. 39; Dyer, *Lords and Peasants*, p. 322; Dyer, *Warwickshire Farming*, pp. 22–5.

They could use their land more flexibly, and were thereby able to work more effectively and respond better to commercial opportunity.[131]

In conclusion, then, the implications of rural change in this period for the history of commercialisation will vary according to how commercialisation is defined. On the one hand the volume of currency in circulation was smaller, the total volume of trade was reduced and rural trading enterprises were less elaborate or formally rational than in the early fourteenth century. On the other hand, the new organisation of agriculture probably means that a higher proportion of what was produced was marketed than in the past. The old dual structure of demesne land and tenant land had been broken down to permit a wider range of types of agrarian enterprise, and some of these were in the hands of vigorous individualists.

---

[131] John Fortescue, *De Laudibus Legum Anglie*, ed. S. B. Chrimes (Cambridge, 1949), pp. 68–9; Davenport, *Economic Development*, pp. 80–1; Dyer, *Lords and Peasants*, pp. 333–8; Dyer, *Warwickshire Farming*, pp. 25–8; Lloyd, *Movement of Wool Prices*, p. 28.

9   Lordship

I

Though economic constraints affected the resources of which kings and noblemen could dispose, the commercial problems of the fourteenth and fifteenth centuries did not undermine the traditional exercise of power. Seigniorial authority was not closely dependent on particular levels of income. The institutions of lordship that had grown up in the age of commercial expansion matured in the following period. Economic problems caused change to slow down rather than to develop in new directions. This conclusion is borne out by the ways in which the nobility and the crown responded to the economic problems of the age.

Not all landlords experienced falling incomes, as we have seen. Nor, where they did know economic adversity, were the causes all the same. There were direct links between financial hardship and the contraction of local economies. This is particularly in evidence in northern England, where both Percy and Neville families suffered from the severe agrarian crisis of 1438–40 and subsequently became contestants for power. The Percies prepared for violent action in 1453 when they heard that their ancient manor of Wressle (E.R. Yorks.), forfeited in 1405 and still unrecovered, was about to be settled on Sir Thomas Neville.[1] Some lords lost income from estates in Wales and the Welsh Marches, where problems of economic stagnation were compounded by a legacy of conflict and disorder after Glyn Dŵr's Rebellion. These Marcher lords were obliged, in effect, to withdraw from the close supervision of their interests, though they were able to safeguard some seigniorial income by taking cash in lump sums in lieu of the profits of jurisdiction.[2] Some difficulties arose from political involvement. Richard, duke of York,

[1] A. J. Pollard, *The Wars of the Roses* (London, 1988), pp. 54–5; Pollard, 'North-Eastern Economy', pp. 104–5; Pollard, *North-Eastern England*, pp. 255–7.
[2] *Marcher Lordships*, ed. Pugh, pp. 36–43; R. A. Griffiths, *King and Country: England and Wales in the Fifteenth Century* (London, 1991), pp. 61–6; Rawcliffe, *Staffords*, pp. 113–14, 154–5; G. Williams, *Recovery, Reorientation and Reformation: Wales, c. 1415–1642* (Oxford, 1987), pp. 14–24, 39–42.

could claim to have lost money in the service of the crown.[3] Other problems were of more private origin. Richard III's usurpation was partly motivated by the insecurity of his title to former Neville properties in the north.[4] Given the variety of problems and experiences, economic change cannot provide any general clue to the development of lordship, though financial concerns were frequently relevant to the attitude and conduct of particular individuals.

Some outlay on patronage was necessary for the exercise of lordship, though its extent was not directly related to differences of income between individuals. Affinities varied according to the geographical and political circumstances of different lords. The size of military followings ranged particularly widely. Some large retinues of knights are recorded amongst the higher nobility. Already before 1330 Thomas of Lancaster had demonstrated their relevance to a high political profile.[5] The exceptionally large retinue of John of Gaunt included perhaps eighty-four knights and eighty-five squires at the end of 1386, and even more at the time of his death in 1399.[6] Northern noblemen needed military support adequate to their obligations on the Scottish border. When the third earl of Northumberland died in 1461 at least a third of his gross revenues were disbursed in this way. The Nevilles of Middleham retained on a comparable scale.[7] Across the whole nobility, however, heavy expenditure on retainers was unusual. Richard, duke of York, apparently spent less than 10 per cent of his income on his retinue.[8] In spite of his powerful connections, and perverse ambitions, George, duke of Clarence, had only a handful of indentured retainers in peacetime.[9]

In normal circumstances, as in the past, aristocratic affinities were chiefly recruited to serve the administration of estates and to manage local affairs. Abandonment of direct demesne management during the later fourteenth century inevitably carried implications for estate management. Every major landlord had the assistance of a council, with his estate officers as an inner circle, whose importance lay not so much in its collective wisdom, since councils did not often meet, as in the advice

[3] P. A. Johnson, *Duke Richard of York, 1411–1460* (Oxford, 1988), pp. 54–64.
[4] M. A. Hicks, *Richard III as Duke of Gloucester: A Study in Character*, University of York, Borthwick Paper LXX (York, 1986), pp. 25–30.
[5] J. R. Maddicott, *Thomas of Lancaster, 1307–1322: A Study in the Reign of Edward II* (Oxford, 1970), pp. 43–5, 65–6.
[6] Bean, *From Lord to Patron*, pp. 245–50.
[7] Bean, *Estates*, p. 91; Pollard, *North-Eastern England*, pp. 125–9.
[8] Bean, *From Lord to Patron*, pp. 166–7, 170–4.
[9] M. A. Hicks, *False, Fleeting, Perjur'd Clarence: George, Duke of Clarence 1449–78* (Gloucester, 1980), p. 183.

individual members could give if asked.[10] Even smaller landlords normally had councils of some sort.[11] After the leasing of manorial demesnes, estate management narrowed to monitoring relationships between lords and tenants. Such problems could be time-consuming. They often involved points of law, and so required outside expertise. In addition, some officials were sinecurists, retained for their status rather than for any particular skill.[12] For these reasons the number of officers on large estates was not greatly affected by the changes in estate administration.

The formation of royal and aristocratic retinues created complex social mixtures of men from different geographical and social backgrounds. Prospects of good employment drew migrants over unprecedentedly long distances to the service of royal and aristocratic masters. From the late thirteenth century men of the Welsh Marches and the north were competing effectively with those from the south-eastern counties of England.[13] Relations between such careerists and their employers were often of a professional, and to that extent commercial, character. Lords sought followers partly for utilitarian goals, such as the securing of legal advice or the competent administration of landed estates.[14] Feed lawyers usually received only between £1 and £2 a year as a retainer from any single client in the fifteenth century.[15] If they had any ability they received fees from so many sources that they were not heavily dependent on a single patron.

Relationships between lords and their men were nevertheless often based on long-standing loyalties. Much depended upon local political stability, but everywhere there were men who relied upon particular connections for their livelihood and status.[16] Many retainers were from a magnate's own countryside. Of the ninety men retained by William, Lord Hastings, between 1461 and 1483 at least fifty-four were closely

---

[10] C. Given-Wilson, *The English Nobility in the Later Middle Ages: The Fourteenth-Century Political Community* (London, 1987), pp. 98–103; Rawcliffe, *Staffords*, p. 144.

[11] *The Hylle Cartulary*, ed. R. W. Dunning, Som. Rec. Soc., LXVIII (1968), p. xxiii; Britnell, 'Pastons', p. 135; Richmond, *John Hopton*, pp. 151–5; Saul, *Knights and Esquires*, p. 85; Saul, *Scenes*, p. 99.

[12] Given-Wilson, *English Nobility*, p. 100; McFarlane, *Nobility*, pp. 216–17.

[13] M. J. Bennett, 'Careerism in Late Medieval England', in J. Rosenthal and C. Richmond, eds., *People, Politics and Community in the Later Middle Ages* (Gloucester, 1987), pp. 23–5.

[14] C. Carpenter, 'The Beauchamp Affinity: A Study of Bastard Feudalism at Work', *EHR*, 95 (1980), pp. 516, 519.

[15] E. W. Ives, *The Common Lawyers of Pre-Reformation England. Thomas Kebell: A Case Study* (Cambridge, 1983), p. 288.

[16] Bean, *From Lord to Patron*, pp. 187–8; Carpenter, 'Beauchamp Affinity', p. 518; J. W. Kirby, 'A Fifteenth-Century Family, the Plumptons of Plumpton, and their Lawyers, 1461–1515', *NH*, 25 (1989), p. 110.

associated with Derbyshire and the honour of Tutbury, and seventeen other were from adjacent counties.[17] In some cases a retaining fee was only a small part of a more far-reaching commitment. In the 1480s Sir Robert Plumpton was feed by the fourth earl of Northumberland for military service on the Scottish border, but he also held office from the earl as steward of Spofforth (W.R. Yorks.), and after 1487 as bailiff of Knaresborough and constable of Knaresborough Castle (W.R. Yorks.)[18] Many retainers were bound to their lords by old family connections. As in the past, bonds between man and man were expected to strengthen the individual security of each, and such security could not be obtained from exclusively ephemeral expectations. Often the long-term interests of families were involved in their alliances. Within the bonds of lordship, protection of titles to land was important for both parties. Both lords and their men needed dependable witnesses to transactions. Uses created upon lay estates required a landlord to have confidence in the loyalty of groups of trustees, some of whom at least would be formally retained.[19] Even lawyers became attached to their clients by loyalty and interest. Having developed his legal career in the service of the Hastings family during the 1470s, Thomas Kebell remained closely associated with them for at least twenty years, despite the downfall and execution of Lord William in 1483.[20] The aristocratic patronage of the late Middle Ages was not the decadent and destabilising consequence of the commercialisation of English society.

Relationships between lords and their men were structured according to an aristocratic code of values. Formal retaining was only a minor facet of this complex order. Many relations between magnates and their men were based on traditional or widely recognised expectations concerning good lordship. The absence of a contract of retinue for life did not imply that the bond between a lord and his followers was temporary or fragile. Lordship was integral to the structure of local society. It shaped alliances between the families of local gentry, amongst whom respect for social rank combined easily with conventions of neighbourliness and kinship.[21] Men waited on their more powerful neighbours for many

---

[17] I. Rowney, 'Resources and Retaining in Yorkist England: William, Lord Hastings and the Honour of Tutbury', in A. J. Pollard, ed., *Property and Politics: Essays in Later Medieval English History* (Gloucester, 1984), pp. 144–5.

[18] Pollard, *North-Eastern England*, p. 127.

[19] Carpenter, 'Beauchamp Affinity', pp. 521–2.

[20] Ives, *Common Lawyers*, pp. 93–7.

[21] M. J. Bennett, *Community, Class and Careerism: Cheshire and Lancashire Society in the Age of Sir Gawain and the Green Knight* (Cambridge, 1983), pp. 22–40; M. Cherry, 'The Courtenay Earls of Devon: The Formation and Disintegration of a Late Medieval Aristocratic Affinity', *SH*, 1 (1979), pp. 76–80; A. J. Pollard, 'The Northern Retainers

reasons – love, fear, entertainment, protection, hope of future advance-
ment – quite apart from any negotiated reciprocal benefit. Lords were
used to their rank carrying with it publicly recognised responsibilities in
local government. They expected their authority to be recognised by a
wide range of people, especially in regions where they were powerful,
and were used to being addressed in terms which modern taste rejects as
sycophantic.[22]

In towns, as we have seen, the problems of commercialisation had
bred a corporatist ideology stressing the need for public controls.
Economic individualism was not a recognised ideal. The regulatory
practices questioned by Adam Smith were being built up on earlier
foundations. Similarly, in the country at large, the established institutions of authority at the disposal of nobility and gentry had been
entrenched since the thirteenth century, and even the associated forms
of local corruption were not new. Though feudal institutions decayed
even further than they had already done, older structures of patronage,
and the habits of mind that went with them, remained a normal feature
of relations between greater and lesser men. The importance of contractual relationships in everyday life did not change people's basic hier-
archic assumptions about the world in which they lived.

This argument can be extended to the power of central government.
Undoubtedly the economic problems of the crown made it harder to
govern England in the fifteenth century. We have already considered
one way in which the king's income was dependent upon economic
trends. Before 1330 the range of royal taxes had expanded as England's
economy had become more commercialised. After 1330 the types of tax
raised did not change much, apart from ephemeral experiments, and the
normal level of income from taxation was lower, as we have seen.
Revenue suffered from falling exports of wool, which reduced royal
income from customs, and from the general problems facing all landowners, which affected the rents that could be obtained from the royal
demesne. Total royal income fell from about £140,000 a year on average
in Richard II's reign to about £64,000 a year in the 1460s. Although this
was partly the result of Lancastrian mismanagement of the royal
demesne it was also in part the result of economic factors quite outside
any king's control.[23]

of Richard Nevill, Earl of Salisbury', *NH*, 11 (1975), pp. 62–4; A. J. Pollard, 'The
Richmondshire Community of Gentry during the Wars of the Roses', in C. Ross,
ed., *Patronage, Pedigree and Power in Later Medieval England* (Gloucester, 1979), pp.
47–52.

[22] Pollard, *North-Eastern England*, pp. 121–2.

[23] J. H. Ramsay, *Genesis of Lancaster, 1307–1399*, 2 vols. (Oxford, 1913), II, p. 381; C.
Ross, *Edward IV* (London, 1974), pp. 371–3.

Yet economic and social change between 1330 and 1500 cannot account for all the fluctuations in royal authority and had no permanent debilitating effect. The reign of Henry V, which stands out as a period of confident monarchy and national assertiveness, was a period of economic depression. Only Henry's political skills, and his easy success against the divided French, can account for the willingness of parliaments to pay for so much warfare.[24] Just as Henry V's strength did not depend on England's economic recovery, so economic decline did not predetermine his son's weakness. Henry VI was notoriously unable to control patronage and expenditure, and his perceived financial incompetence did him more political harm than the less easily visible economic trends.[25] The slow reconstruction of royal income after the nadir of the 1450s and 1460s was not primarily dependent on economic revival, though it owed something to rising cloth exports from the 1470s. The improved finances of the Yorkist and Tudor kings were more a matter of newly acquired property, better estate administration and careful budgeting. By the end of Henry VII's reign annual royal income was again comfortably over £100,000, but this cannot be ascribed to any general recovery of prices, rents or the volume of trade.[26]

Feudal institutions continued to weaken chiefly because kings modified their seigniorial rights to maintain better relations with their leading subjects and for reasons of military expediency. Jointures and uses were allowed to undermine the rights of feudal superiors at the moment when tenants died. The crown, as we have seen, lost substantial sources of income from wardships. In this period, too, the monarchy abandoned feudal obligations as a prime component in the recruitment of armies. In 1327, at the opening of his long reign, Edward III summoned a general feudal levy for war in Scotland, but he cannot have been pleased with the result. He never summoned another one.[27] Instead he chose a predominantly contractual method of raising troops. The armies he levied for warfare in France depended upon indentures drawn up with military commanders. This system was first used for raising a whole army for Edward III's campaign against France in 1337.[28] Only one more feudal

[24] G. L. Harriss, 'The Management of Parliament', in *idem*, ed., *Henry V: The Practice of Kingship* (Oxford, 1985), pp. 145–9.

[25] Griffiths, *Reign of King Henry VI*, pp. 310–20, 376–8.

[26] S. B. Chrimes, *Henry VII* (London, 1972), pp. 124–34, 196, 205–8, 217; Lander, *Government and Community*, pp. 83–5; Ross, *Edward IV*, pp. 371–87; B. P. Wolffe, *The Crown Lands, 1461–1536* (London, 1970), pp. 54–65.

[27] N. B. Lewis, 'The Summons of the English Feudal Levy, 5 April 1327', in T. A. Sandquist and M. R. Powicke, eds., *Essays in Medieval History Presented to Bertie Wilkinson* (Toronto, 1969), pp. 236, 248.

[28] Ormrod, *Reign of Edward III*, pp. 103–4.

levy was ever attempted, and that was a desperate expedient adopted by Richard II to oppose Scottish raiding in the north in 1385.[29]

Other changes in the way kings exercised their power similarly continued what had gone before. Edward I had consulted his subjects about direct taxation and new legislation as a matter of political art. Under his son and grandson expectations of how parliament should be used, though never encoded in any constitutional law, became firmer, and the king's room for discretion narrowed.[30] The day-to-day working of late medieval government, from the thirteenth century onwards, depended upon regular co-operation from the nobility and commons of the realm. In this respect the king's power was circumscribed by the power of aristocratic retinues.[31] The king's finances rested upon a more formal foundation of negotiation than it had done in the past, and a wider range of interests had to be considered. The implications of these changes were still being worked out during the fourteenth century. For example, parliamentary control over grants of customs on wool was established only after 1348.[32] The importance of law as a check on royal arbitrariness, and the expectation that the king would rule through consultation rather than through personal whim, were both emphasised in political crises of the fourteenth century, as in the list of charges against Richard II compiled to serve Bolingbroke's turn in 1399.[33]

Yet though royal government became more restrained by legal and political expectations during the fourteenth century, the scope of its activity suffered no diminution. In the twelfth century kingship had been almost entirely a matter of royal rights. As a result of later developments, especially the growth of substantive and procedural law, royal duties had become increasingly numerous. Their inadequate performance invited widespread criticism, and could nourish political opposition. Those who set themselves up against kings and their retinues, like Henry Bolingbroke in 1399, Richard, duke of York, in 1459 and Richard, earl of Warwick, in 1469, did so to control them or to replace them, not as potential separatists.

In fact neither the decay of feudal institutions, nor the greater

[29] N. B. Lewis, 'The Last Medieval Summons of the English Feudal Levy, 13 June 1385', *EHR*, 73 (1958), p. 1; J. J. N. Palmer, 'The Last Summons of the Feudal Army in England', *EHR*, 83 (1968), pp. 771–5.

[30] E. B. Fryde and E. Miller, *Historical Studies of the English Parliament*, 2 vols. (Cambridge, 1970), pp. 10–22; Prestwich, *Edward I*, pp. 464–8.

[31] Coss, 'Bastard Feudalism Revised', pp. 55, 61–2.

[32] G. L. Harriss, *King, Parliament and Public Finance in Medieval England to 1369* (Oxford, 1975), pp. 429–32.

[33] C. Barron, 'The Tyranny of Richard II', *BIHR*, 41 (1968), pp. 1–18; A. Tuck, *Richard II and the English Nobility* (London, 1973), pp. 203–4.

prominence of nobility and gentry in local government, nor the development of legal and representative institutions, undermined the central
importance of monarchy in English government. The standing of the
crown had never depended upon feudal ties of obligation. The king's
subjects were no less bound to obey because of the waning of his feudal
rights. Royal income had never depended principally upon feudal dues,
and the military resources of the crown were far broader than those of
knight service. Kings had never been able to govern the shires without
the mediation of local interests. Throughout the late Middle Ages the
king could command, if he chose, the largest affinity of all, and the
structures of royal patronage, jurisdiction and taxation remained a
matter of moment for the local balance of power. The way kings
distributed their favours directly affected the cohesion of local groupings.[34] It was through neglect of this principle that Henry VI lost the
capacity to control his kingdom.[35]

In the long term, despite recurrent competition for power between
kings and their disaffected relations, the crown in fact achieved an
unprecedented measure of control over the nobility, while the institutions of law and central government contributed to the tighter classification of the king's subjects in terms of social rank. Thirteenth-century
barons had been defined by reference to their feudal relationship to the
crown as tenants of baronies. During the fourteenth century, by contrast, the peerage came to be defined as the smaller, more exclusive
group of families whose head was personally summoned to parliament.
The phrase 'peers of the land' is first on record in this parliamentary
sense in a letter sent in 1317 by Thomas, earl of Lancaster. By the
fifteenth century the nobility was narrowed to sixty or seventy families,
and though its members frequently failed to leave heirs the number of
peers could be made up by the king. Even the weakest king controlled
the entrance to this charmed circle.[36] The peerage also became a more
formally stratified group. By the end of the period there were five
different grades – earls, dukes (invented in 1337), marquisses (invented
in 1385), baronies by patent (invented in 1387) and viscounts (invented
in 1440). Below the ranks of the nobility the lesser landlords became
more self-consciously stratified in the fourteenth century, so that by
1400 it was necessary to distinguish between knights, esquires and

[34] Cherry, 'Courtenay Earls', pp. 90–4, 97.
[35] S. J. Payling, *Political Society in Lancastrian England: The Greater Gentry of Nottinghamshire* (Oxford, 1991), pp. 152–6.
[36] R. Butt, *A History of Parliament: The Middle Ages* (London, 1989), pp. 207–8; Given-
Wilson, *English Nobility*, pp. 55–8; McFarlane, *Nobility*, pp. 124–5, 268–9; S. L.
Waugh, *England in the Reign of Edward III* (Cambridge, 1991), pp. 119–21.

gentlemen. Below the gentry, in turn, there were distinctions to be made between yeomen and husbandmen.[37] The commercialised society of the later Middle Ages passed on this uncompromisingly hierarchical ideal to the even more commercialised early modern period. Throughout the fourteenth and fifteenth centuries the finicky determination of status and authority in England was significantly closer to the world of Henry VIII than to that of Henry II.

II

Collision between the interests of noble retinues and the interests of the community is a recurrent theme of late medieval history. Forms of patronage and principles of law which had grown up together in the twelfth and thirteenth centuries were not wholly compatible with each other. Historians did not have to discover this; it was a commonplace of the age. Royal statutes attest it, since the perversion of justice by the hirelings of the nobility was a matter of frequent parliamentary concern.[38] The theme was elaborated in sermons, poems and plays. The shepherd whose speech opens the Second Shepherds' Play from the Wakefield cycle equates liveried men with the gentry, and blames their high-handedness and oppression for the poverty of the countryside.[39] The maintenance of retinues by the great was not the only problem; the power of money was another. Justice, it was said, was bought and sold, so that poor men had no hope of redress. Some complained naively that litigation cost money. Others alleged, not without reason, that men of law were venal, and that victory often went to the longest purse.[40]

These threnodies for Justice had their foundation in fact. Yet the problem of the English legal system had little to do with the commercialisation of society. The availability of money was no more the root of all evil in 1450 than in 1150. The recurrent problem was one of effective authority. Even in periods of strong government medieval kings lacked the machinery to maintain law and order by force. It was politic for Henry V to conciliate well-born criminals rather than to attempt to punish them.[41] Commissions of oyer and terminer appointed by the crown could be used as the weapons with which well-connected

---

[37] Dyer, *Standards of Living*, pp. 13–21; Given-Wilson, *English Nobility*, pp. 69–70; McFarlane, *Nobility*, pp. 122–5, 273.

[38] J. G. Bellamy, *Bastard Feudalism and the Law* (London, 1989), pp. 80–90.

[39] The Second Shepherds' Play, lines 10–45: *The Wakefield Mystery Plays*, ed. M. Rose (London, 1961), pp. 178–9; Scattergood, *Politics and Poetry*, pp. 316–18.

[40] Scattergood, *Politics and Poetry*, pp. 322–3.

[41] E. Powell, *Kingship, Law and Society: Criminal Justice in the Reign of Henry V* (Oxford, 1989), pp. 192–4, 229–32.

local factions outflanked their enemies.[42] Much of the blame for the maladministration of justice attached directly to the self-interest of the nobility and gentry upon whose unpaid services royal jurisdiction had come to depend. Justices of the peace acquired additional responsibilities in the later fourteenth century, partly because of the decision to assign them responsibility for enforcing new labour legislation after the Black Death.[43] The exercise of patronage within county society undermined the dispassionate administration of justice. Open attempts to overawe local courts by force were comparatively unusual, but influence was often deployed behind the scenes. Successful litigation depended upon having the sheriff's ear, and this meant having the right patron.[44]

The authority of the law was particularly vulnerable in times of exceptional political conflict like the 1450s,[45] and in areas of weak royal government like the Welsh and Scottish Marches.[46] In those circumstances litigation was accompanied or circumvented by violent self-help, often between families competing for local influence. One of the most politically disruptive features of the 1450s was the simultaneous outbreak of feuds between powerful families in different parts of England. In Devon open antagonism between the earl of Devon and Lord William Bonville began in 1451, though bad relations went back over ten years. In the north the Percies and the Nevilles came to blows in 1453. Then in Derbyshire the following year there was armed conflict between two gentry families, the Longfords and the Blounts, who involved many of their friends.[47] Once noblemen resorted to violent retribution without the sanction of the courts well-bred men became unprincipled thugs. One of the nastiest murders of the 1450s was committed in the interests of the earl of Devon and organised by his son.[48]

Admittedly, critics of the legal system had no true perspective on the past.[49] Praise of ancient virtues was in mythic terms, as when the 'law of Winchester' was idealised in 1381.[50] The development of the king's

---

[42] S. J. Payling, 'Law and Arbitration in Nottinghamshire, 1399–1461', in Rosenthal and Richmond, eds., *People, Politics and Community*, pp. 143–6.

[43] Harding, *Law Courts*, pp. 94–8.

[44] Carpenter, 'Beauchamp Affinity', p. 524; McFarlane, *Nobility*, pp. 115–19.

[45] McFarlane, *Nobility*, p. 118.

[46] R. L. Storey, 'The North of England', in S. B. Chrimes, C. D. Ross and R. A. Griffiths, eds., *Fifteenth Century England, 1399–1509: Studies in Politics and Society* (Manchester, 1972), pp. 131–2; R. A. Griffiths, 'Wales and the Marches', in *ibid.*, pp. 150–5.

[47] Pollard, *North-Eastern England*, pp. 255–7; R. L. Storey, *The End of the House of Lancaster*, 2nd edn (Gloucester, 1986), pp. 87–92, 151–5.

[48] Storey, *End of the House of Lancaster*, pp. 167–9.

[49] McFarlane, *Nobility*, pp. 114–15.

[50] A. Harding, 'The Revolt against the Justices', in R. H. Hilton and T. H. Aston, eds., *The English Rising of 1381* (Cambridge, 1984), pp. 165–7.

courts in the thirteenth century, and the multiplication of laws and procedures, had never eliminated inefficiency, arbitrariness and lawlessness.[51] There were some types of violence which were even more common before 1330 than in later periods, such as disputes over parks and pastures, and there had been marked variations in the level of petty crime, partly because of variations in the level of taxation, the state of employment and the price of food.[52] Voluble concern for law and order in the mid-fifteenth century does not imply the existence of some earlier golden age. Nevertheless, there can be no doubt that by the 1450s the procedures of the English legal system needed reform. The structure of the courts had become excessively rigid, so that inefficiencies, delays, complexities and opportunities for corruption had multiplied.[53]

For these reasons, respect for the law often took forms that bypassed the normal courts. Arbitration was a time-honoured device to avoid violence or to circumvent the delays, expenses and uncertainties of litigation.[54] In financial matters arbitration was a natural accompaniment to the auditing of accounts, and as such could be a wholly private matter.[55] Often, however, litigation was opened in the courts in the expectation that arbitration would follow.[56] In urban disputes, with or without the intervention of the courts, arbitration was a normal procedure for resolving complex problems of mercantile obligation and debt, or for those requiring expert assessment of losses and damages.[57] In county society quarrels were terminated by the intervention of friends, local lawyers, JPs or clergy.[58] Help in resolving intractable disagreements was one of the forms of good lordship that magnates, with the legal expertise they could command from their councillors, extended to those within their influence.[59] The same councillors, and particularly

---

[51] J. B. Given, *Society and Homicide in Thirteenth-Century England* (Stanford, 1977), pp. 33–40; Prestwich, *Edward I*, pp. 280–8.

[52] R. H. Britnell, 'The Fields and Pastures of Colchester, 1280–1350', *Essex Arch. and Hist.*, 19 (1988), pp. 162–4; B. A. Hanawalt, *Crime and Conflict in English Communities, 1300–1348* (Cambridge, Mass., 1979), pp. 229–60.

[53] Ives, *Common Lawyers*, p. 194.

[54] J. G. Bellamy, *Crime and Public Order in England in the Later Middle Ages* (London, 1973), pp. 117–19; Given, *Society and Homicide*, pp. 201–6; E. Powell, 'Arbitration and the Law in England in the Late Middle Ages', *TRHS*, 5th ser., 33 (1983), pp. 52–6.

[55] Britnell, *Growth and Decline*, p. 106.   [56] Powell, 'Arbitration', pp. 57–62.

[57] *Ibid.*, p. 53; C. Rawcliffe, ' "That Kindliness Should be Cherished More, and Discord Driven Out": The Settlement of Commercial Disputes by Arbitration in Later Medieval England', in Kermode, ed., *Enterprise and Individuals*, pp. 99–117.

[58] Bennett, *Community*, p. 33; Pollard, *North-Eastern England*, pp. 116–18; Pollard, 'Richmondshire Community', pp. 50–1; Wright, *Derbyshire Gentry*, p. 123.

[59] R. Horrox, *Richard III: A Study of Service* (Cambridge, 1989), p. 66; M. Jones, 'Richard III and the Stanleys', in R. Horrox, ed., *Richard III and the North* (Hull, 1986), p. 29; Pollard, *North-Eastern England*, pp. 118–19; Powell, 'Arbitration', p. 66.

the lawyers amongst them, mediated in disputes between magnates themselves.[60]

Reform of the legal system remained a proper object of policy. Though there were no developments equivalent in their speed or their scope to those of the later twelfth century, and though there were many set-backs, the late Middle Ages was a period of legal reconstruction. New courts were developed to complement the existing ones, the most important being chancery, whose origins went back to the late fourteenth century. Chancery jurisdiction arose from the practice by which the king referred to his chancellor the petitions of supplicants who could not obtain justice in existing courts. Many of these cases concerned commercial loans that could not be adequately handled by other means. Another important set of chancery cases arose from complicated uses created upon landed property. Chancery also handled cases arising from arbitration awards that had failed through the bad faith of one of the parties. The growth of chancery jurisdiction did not eliminate the judicial responsibilities of the king's council, particularly in matters relating to law and order, administration, economic regulation and heresy. Conciliar jurisdiction, which was exercised in the Star Chamber within Westminster Palace, was another development of the late Middle Ages. In Henry VII's reign this court was mostly occupied with civil suits set in motion by private petitions. Both these new developments asserted the king's primary responsibility for administering justice, and both were responses to public demand in the form of petitions for redress.[61]

Despite continuing imperfections, English law had its enthusiasts, notably Sir John Fortescue, who lauded it from exile with the Lancastrians in France between 1468 and 1471.[62] The ideal to which people remained loyal was a central body of law built up in the king's courts, sanctioned by time and by royal authority. Legal knowledge became more widespread as the sons of landed families prepared for the management of their property and the execution of their public duties. In the fifteenth century the inns of court provided instruction for gentlemen who had no intention of becoming professional lawyers.[63] In this way legal learning penetrated the political community to an unprecedented degree.

[60] Given-Wilson, *English Nobility*, p. 102; Rawcliffe, *Staffords*, pp. 156–7.
[61] J. A. Guy, *The Cardinal's Court: The Impact of Thomas Wolsey in Star Chamber* (Hassocks, 1977), pp. 6–21; Ives, *Common Lawyers*, pp. 194–9; Powell, 'Arbitration', pp. 64–5.
[62] Fortescue, *De Laudibus Legum Anglie*, ed. Chrimes, pp. lxxxvi–lxxxviii.
[63] H. S. Bennett, *The Pastons and their England* (Cambridge, 1922), pp. 103, 105; Ives, *Common Lawyers*, pp. 38–9; Richmond, *John Hopton*, pp. 135–6, 187, 245.

The problems were quite unlike those of the twelfth century. In those days magnates had exploited the law's imprecision. In the fifteenth century they set out to exploit the law's excessively complicated technicalities. Caxton in 1474 speculated that there were more pleaders, attorneys and men of law in England than elsewhere in Christendom.[64] Their careers depended upon their services being valued by others. In fact the practice of feeing lawyers became more general in this period. Magnates employed many lawyers as councillors, and it became normal for borough councils to retain a lawyer.[65] The frequent employment of lawyers as feoffees in the creation of uses implies that landlords were confident of their probity.[66] To some extent, as we have seen, lawyers were employed to circumvent the use of the courts. Yet this period of English history was one of considerable litigiousness.[67] In view of the alternatives, this was not an unhealthy state of affairs.

Despite outcries against false judges, standards rose in some respects. Professional ethics may have improved. After 1390 the retaining of judges in the central courts seems to have been rare, the bribery of judges became less of a problem.[68] Legal training was enhanced by the educational provisions of the inns of court.[69] The first textbook of common law, Sir Thomas Littleton's *New Tenures*, long remained a standard authority on land law.[70] Within the profession intellectual effort was devoted to collecting judgements and commenting on their significance. The precision of mind which such exercises fostered permitted lawyers to adapt existing law to new problems.[71] Men paid for lawyers because they supposed the law could help them. Professionalism had its less attractive side. Judges undoubtedly used their knowledge and power for personal advantage. An unpleasing example of this from the end of our period was Sir Richard Empson's attempt to deprive Sir Robert Plumpton of manors he had inherited in the midlands and Yorkshire.[72] In this respect we should not expect too much. Lawyers

---

[64] N. L. Ramsay, 'What was the Legal Profession?', in Hicks, ed., *Profit, Piety and the Professions*, pp. 62–3.

[65] Cherry, 'Courtenay Earls', pp. 82–4; Du Boulay, *Lordship of Canterbury*, p. 276; Given-Wilson, *English Nobility*, pp. 101–2; Ives, *Common Lawyers*, pp. 131–40; Rawcliffe, *Staffords*, pp. 146–7.

[66] Ramsay, 'What was the Legal Profession?', p. 65.

[67] Wright, *Derbyshire Gentry*, p. 120.

[68] Powell, *Kingship, Law and Society*, p. 114.

[69] Ives, *Common Lawyers*, pp. 36–59; Ramsay, 'What was the Legal Profession?', pp. 63–5.

[70] E. W. Ives, 'The Common Lawyers', in C. H. Clough, ed., *Profession, Vocation and Culture in Later Medieval England* (Liverpool, 1982), pp. 196–7.

[71] Ives, 'Common Lawyers', pp. 193–7; Ives, *Common Lawyers*, pp. 263–81.

[72] *Plumpton Correspondence*, ed. Stapleton, pp. cii–cx; Kirby, 'Fifteenth-Century Family', pp. 116–19.

were subject to many temptations, and they sometimes took their morals from those of their noble clients.[73]

III

Until the early fourteenth century, as we have seen, land hunger made it possible for landlords to retain traditions of serfdom which went back before recorded history. By contrast, the late Middle Ages is a phase of more revolutionary social change. Declining demand for land, coupled with a substantial rise in wage rates, created unprecedented opportunities for rural freedom because it enabled countrymen of all levels of wealth to make real choices about what they wanted to do.

The policies of central government weighed heavily on the countryside in the generation after the Black Death. Legislation was introduced to limit the damage to landlords' interests, demonstrating how far the ruling classes were from valuing market forces as a system by which to allocate scarce resources. The Ordinance of Labourers (1349) and the Statute of Labourers (1351) were chiefly concerned with the terms on which employers could hire workers. The Statute of 1351 aimed not only to fix wage rates but to restrict the mobility of both free and unfree wage-earners. During the 1350s some wage increases were held back as a result of this legislation, and the consequent misallocations of labour throughout the economy were presumably a handicap to economic recovery.[74] The law empowered local officials to enforce contracts of employment, and in some cases the unemployed were perhaps drafted into work.[75]

The enforcement of manorial custom was, as ever, a matter for seigniorial courts. Lords did not lightly surrender their authority over serfs. After the Black Death many asserted their seigniorial rights in order to maintain their incomes. Court fines were stepped up.[76] Lords attempted to thwart the operation of market forces by restricting or overruling the free choice of tenants. The bishop of Durham used customary procedures, which had perhaps once worked in favour of village communities, to assign unwanted lands to tenants thought able to

---

[73] Ives, *Common Lawyers*, pp. 309–18; Richmond, *Paston Family*, pp. 34–40.

[74] Bolton, *Medieval English Economy*, p. 213; D. L. Farmer, 'Prices and Wages, 1350–1500', in *AHEW*, III, p. 490; Mate, 'Labour', p. 60; B. H. Putnam, *The Enforcement of the Statute of Labourers during the First Decade after the Black Death, 1349–59* (New York, 1908), p. 221.

[75] L. R. Poos, 'The Social Context of Statute of Labourers Enforcement', *Law and Hist. R.*, 1 (1983), pp. 32–7.

[76] C. Dyer, 'The Social and Economic Background to the Rural Revolt of 1381', in Hilton and Aston, eds, *English Rising*, pp. 28–9.

work them. If no individual could be found to take on vacant properties, their rents were made the collective responsibility of other tenants.[77] Even where labour services had been discontinued after the Black Death they were often reimposed in the course of economic recovery.[78]

Yet attempts to obstruct market forces had only limited success even in the generation after the Black Death. Wages rose, particularly after 1361.[79] And despite landlords' best endeavours, a lot of land could not be tenanted on the old terms.[80] The harsh expedients employed by estate officers to maintain custom were themselves breaches of custom in tenants' eyes. One consequence of the oppressive policies which landlords pursued in these years was the widespread questioning of seigniorial authority. This in turn encouraged a mood of non-cooperation.[81]

Some form of radical ideology was important for the acceleration of social change from the later fourteenth century, and features of that ideology are dimly to be seen in the revolt of 1381. The revolt was triggered by resistance to exceptionally heavy and ham-fisted taxation – the poll tax granted by parliament in 1380 and collected in the following year – but amongst its circumstantial causes was antagonism to seigniorial authority in the countryside and to burghal privileges in the towns. At Mile End on 14 June Wat Tyler included among the aims of the rebels the abolition of villainage and all non-contractual work.[82] The intensity of this desire in the eastern counties was demonstrated in the widespread burning of records in which details of customary land tenures were recorded.[83] For obvious reasons, the ideological reaction against serfdom did not favour a free market in land. The rebels wanted land to be rented at 4d an acre regardless of quality or location, so that one form of tenurial rigidity would be replaced by another more favourable to sitting tenants. Radicalism was underpinned by heterodox beliefs that the government identified with the Lollard critique of the

[77] Britnell, 'Feudal Reaction', pp. 30–6; R. H. Hilton, *The Decline of Serfdom in Medieval England* (London, 1969), pp. 38–43.

[78] Hilton, *Decline of Serfdom*, pp. 40–1; Mate, 'Labour', pp. 62–3.

[79] Farmer, 'Prices and Wages, 1350–1500', p. 486.

[80] Bailey, *Marginal Economy?*, pp. 226–7; Britnell, 'Feudal Reaction', pp. 42–7; Davenport, *Economic Development*, pp. 70–1; Harvey, *Medieval Oxfordshire Village*, pp. 136–40.

[81] Dyer, 'Social and Economic Background', pp. 36–42; Z. Razi, 'The Struggles between the Abbots of Halesowen and their Tenants in the Thirteenth and Fourteenth Centuries', in Aston and others, eds., *Social Relations and Ideas*, pp. 164–5.

[82] *The Anonimalle Chronicle, 1333 to 1381*, ed. V. H. Galbraith (Manchester, 1970), pp. 144–5.

[83] Dyer, 'Social and Economic Background', pp. 11–12, 35; McIntosh, *Autonomy and Community*, pp. 83–4.

church.[84] The strength of this connection was exaggerated by the political and ecclesiastical establishments. On the other hand, the social values which came to the surface in 1381 continued to affect people's actions after the former hierarchy of authority was restored.

Ideological discrediting of custom was not enough to bring about social change. One reason for the decay of serfdom in fifteenth-century England was simply that families died out. In a period of high death rates and low rates of reproduction the chances of a tenant dying without a known heir were higher than they had been when households were larger. However, serfdom declined more rapidly than demographic causes alone would have brought about, because surviving families were consciously opting for less servile terms of tenure. Often the death of a tenant ended a villain family's occupancy of a tenement not because there was no heir but because the heir did not want to inherit and had put himself out of reach.[85] Much depended upon the stance of different lords. Those who adapted to harder times had a better chance of keeping their tenants at modified levels of rent. Those who stood out for high rents risked having tenements unoccupied or provoking conflict with sitting tenants.[86] Competition between landlords for tenants made it easier for the latter to resist the *status quo*.

Often defiance took the form of flight from bondage. Not all migration was for this reason. Many of the villains who migrated from Ramsey Abbey manors moved to other manors of the monastic estate, and so remained subject to the abbot's authority.[87] Free tenants too, like the Randalls, Swans and Herricks of Wigston Magna, left their hereditary lands in favour of better livelihoods elsewhere.[88] Nevertheless the hereditary stigma of serfdom aggravated the discontent felt by many villains.[89] On many estates the out-migration of tenants was noticeable from the 1350s, and it was a universal problem for landlords by the 1390s.[90] By the first quarter of the fifteenth century there were everywhere empty dwellings for which lords found it difficult to find tenants on the old terms.[91] As always, they were powerless to recover

[84] M. Aston, 'Lollardy and Sedition, 1381–1431', in Hilton, ed., *Peasants, Knights and Heretics*, pp. 273–9.

[85] Dyer, *Lords and Peasants*, p. 271.

[86] E.g. C. Dyer, 'Population and Agriculture on a Warwickshire Manor in the Later Middle Ages', *University of Birmingham Hist. J.*, 2 (1968), pp. 116–18, 122–3.

[87] Raftis, *Tenure and Mobility*, pp. 170–2.   [88] Hoskins, *Midland Peasant*, p. 87.

[89] M. Bailey, 'Blowing up Bubbles: Some New Demographic Evidence for the Fifteenth Century', *J. of Med. Hist.*, 15 (1989), p. 350; Hilton, *Decline of Serfdom*, pp. 50–1.

[90] Britnell, 'Feudal Reaction', pp. 37, 40–1; Page, *Estates*, p. 149; Raftis, *Estates*, pp. 282–4; Raftis, *Tenure and Mobility*, p. 153; Razi, *Life, Marriage and Death*, p. 119.

[91] Britnell, *Growth and Decline*, pp. 142–3; Davenport, *Economic Development*, p. 104–5; Hoskins, *Midland Peasant*, p. 85; Page, *Estates*, p. 426.

those who had fled.[92] A surprising number of countrymen moved to urban employment, expecting a better life as artisans or traders than they could hope for as small farmers.[93] In most cases, though, families took land on other estates, often in places where they had family connections.[94]

The rate of migration from English villages had been high before the depopulation of the fourteenth century. There may have been some temporary increase after 1349, but there is no good evidence of a permanent increase.[95] The context of migration, and the social characteristics of migrants, had nevertheless changed. In the thirteenth century migrants had been the landless in search of a livelihood. In the fifteenth century they were often the wealthier and well-established families, confident that they could abandon their land and find as good or better elsewhere.[96] When the king's tenants at Banstead (Surr.) were oppressed by a high-handed lessee, sometime about 1416, they complained that 'John Taillour, Richard Colcok and John Clerc, which that were most sufficient and old tenants of the foresaid lordship, are avoided and gone out of the foresaid lordship for ever more, and many more been in purpose to avoid.'[97]

Flight was not the only form of resistance. Even before 1349 tenants had on occasion refused to co-operate with their lords and sabotaged traditional procedures.[98] Such opposition became more effective once the hold of tradition started to crumble. In 1432 the abbot of Binham was obliged to draw up a formal indenture with his tenants at Binham (Norf.) as a result of troubles they had caused him the previous year; amongst other things, entry fines on villain land were reduced from 4s to 2s an acre.[99] In 1452, when the abbess of Syon was in dispute with her customary tenants in Cheltenham (Glos.) over the amount they owed in lieu of labour services, the disagreement was put to arbitration before a neighbouring landlord, Ralph Boteler, Lord of Sudeley. He granted the

[92] Britnell, 'Feudal Reaction', p. 40; Page, *Estates*, pp. 151–2.

[93] Britnell, *Growth and Decline*, p. 149; Davenport, *Economic Development*, p. 97; Dyer, *Lords and Peasants*, p. 271; Hoskins, *Midland Peasant*, p. 87; Howell, *Land, Family and Inheritance*, pp. 45–7; Page, *Estates*, p. 150; Raftis, *Tenure and Mobility*, pp. 169, 177–8.

[94] Razi, *Life, Marriage and Death*, pp. 120–1.

[95] L. R. Poos, 'Population Turnover in Medieval Essex: The Evidence of Some Early Fourteenth-Century Tithing Lists', in L. Bonfield, R. Smith and K. Wrightson, eds., *The World We Have Gained* (Oxford, 1986), pp. 10–22; Razi, *Life, Marriage and Death*, pp. 30–1, 117–20.

[96] Davenport, *Economic Development*, pp. 88–97; Homans, *English Villagers*, p. 135.

[97] *A Book of London English, 1384–1425*, ed. R. W. Chambers and M. Daunt (Oxford, 1931), p. 227.

[98] Hilton, *Class Conflict*, pp. 108–13, 122–38; Razi, 'Struggles', pp. 154–64.

[99] E. B. Burstall, 'A Monastic Agreement of the Fourteenth Century', *Norf. Arch.*, 31 (1957), pp. 211–18.

tenants what they demanded – a reduction from £10 0s 7¼ to £6 13s 4d.[100] The early and mid-fifteenth century was perhaps the period when tenants stood most to gain by digging in their heels. Tenants resisted strongly simply because they thought they had the upper hand. By the end of the century demand for land was increasing in some places, so that tenants found escape more problematic.[101] But that can hardly account for the widespread evidence for tenant resistance in the long period of depressed rents and empty holdings, between the 1390s and the 1460s.[102]

From the 1380s, and often earlier, tenant flight and resistance made it impossible for landlords to maintain traditional patterns of authority. Not only were many rents falling but the incidents of tenant dependence, particularly those associated with serfdom, were reduced. Labour services were abandoned. In some places, as on the large estates of the bishopric and priory of Durham, this followed shortly after the Black Death.[103] Simultaneously landlords' relations with their subordinates came to be governed by contract to an unprecedented extent. The manorial lease replaced the looser obligation of the manorial servant, and many of the lessees of demesne land were customary tenants.[104] Simultaneously lords were making specific contracts with tenants to hold customary lands by lease, usually on non-customary terms.[105] At Southwick (co. Dur.) in 1340 there were two freehold tenements, ten bondlands, two tenements of six acres and a cottage. In 1495, by contrast, there were two freeholds and four leasehold tenures.[106] On some manors leases to villains were recorded in the rolls of the manor courts, and each lessee was given a slip of parchment with a copy of the relevant court roll entry. Such land was described as being leased 'by copy'. This device was used for leasing both demesne lands and former villain lands.[107] Leases were usually treated as hereditary tenures.[108] Lords wanted to keep tenants rather than lose them.

[100] Hart, *History of Cheltenham*, pp. 41–2; Hilton, *English Peasantry*, pp. 67–9.
[101] Dyer, *Lords and Peasants*, p. 277.
[102] Britnell, 'Pastons', pp. 140–1; Dyer, *Lords and Peasants*, pp. 275–82; Dyer, 'Redistribution', pp. 203–15; Howell, *Land, Family and Inheritance*, pp. 50–1.
[103] Lomas, 'Priory of Durham', pp. 345–6; Britnell, 'Feudal Reaction', pp. 44–5.
[104] Davenport, *Economic Development*, pp. 53, 74; Dyer, *Lords and Peasants*, pp. 212–14; Faith, 'Berkshire', pp. 165–6; Page, *Estates*, pp. 129–30, 154; Hare, 'Demesne Lessees', pp. 4–6.
[105] Davenport, *Economic Development*, p. 58; Dewindt, *Land and People*, p. 134; Dyer, *Lords and Peasants*, pp. 120, 292–3; Harvey, *Westminster Abbey*, pp. 246–56; Page, *Estates*, p. 129.
[106] Lomas, 'Developments', p. 42.
[107] BL, Harleian MS 144, fos. 6r–9v, 14r–16r; PRO, S.C.6/942/19, S.C.12/10/66.
[108] Davenport, *Economic Development*, p. 57; Dyer, *Lords and Peasants*, pp. 293–4; Harvey, *Westminster Abbey*, pp. 276–7; Searle, *Lordship and Community*, pp. 330, 368.

Even those serfs who survived as customary tenants held their lands on terms different from those of the past. The need to keep a written record of new contracts, in circumstances where long memory was no longer a guide to current terms of tenure, was the main reason for the development of hereditary copyhold, which developed in parallel with copyhold leases.[109] Copies of court roll registrations were also supplied for family settlements of villain land made with the lord's agreement. In 1384 Joan Derby produced her copy in the manor court of New Hall in Boreham (Essex) to prove that she had held two villain tenements jointly with her late husband, and so had a life interest in them.[110] On some manors the issuing of copies to customary tenants became the normal procedure.[111] This practice carried even further the modification of customary relationships by record-keeping.

On some manors it became more difficult to distinguish between demesne land, villain land and free land.[112] Demesne lands split up between tenants were absorbed into hereditary tenures and lost their separate identity.[113] Servile lands came into the hands of free men.[114] However, the place of contractual tenures in the overall structure of peasant society remained much greater than it had been in the thirteenth century, and it was often only a matter of antiquarian research on the lord's part to discover which tenures were no longer held by hereditary tenure.

Looked at in long-term perspective, some tenant gains of the fifteenth century were Pyrrhic victories. Customary tenants with acknowledged hereditary rights remained in a strong position, and some went on to become capitalist farmers. The time was to come, however, when land values rose again, and at that point it went against tenants if the shield of custom had broken. Contractual tenures were advantageous to tenants only so long as their bargaining position was strong. In the sixteenth century those who held by leases were vulnerable to land holders who wanted to reconstruct their estates. Where entry fines had fallen by force of circumstance, not by recognised agreement, lords could revive the standard policy of their thirteenth-century predecessors – raising the entry fines payable by hereditary copyholders to compensate

[109] Harvey, *Westminster Abbey*, pp. 284–5.
[110] PRO, S.C.2/171/27, m. 10r.
[111] Dyer, *Lords and Peasants*, p. 294; Faith, 'Berkshire', pp. 130, 137–8; E. B. and N. Fryde, 'Peasant Rebellion and Peasant Discontents', in *AHEW*, III, pp. 816–17; Jones, 'Bedfordshire', pp. 192–3, 203, 233; Maitland, 'History of a Cambridgeshire Manor', p. 438; Raftis, *Tenure and Mobility*, p. 200.
[112] Faith, 'Berkshire', p. 149; Searle, *Lordship and Community*, p. 335.
[113] Jones, 'Bedfordshire', pp. 206–7; Lomas, 'Priory of Durham', p. 347.
[114] Davenport, *Economic Development*, p. 88; Rawcliffe, *Staffords*, p. 53.

for fixed customary rents. In the sixteenth century it paid landlords once more to study their manorial rights, because they were again in a strong economic position to enforce them.[115]

The reduction of personal serfdom was nevertheless a permanent change. The extent to which serfdom disappeared varied from estate to estate. Even in East Anglia land was still often recorded as 'native' in the late fifteenth century.[116] Transfer of customary land was still controlled by manorial courts, and lords continued to exact entry fines, even if they were low by past standards.[117] Many families were still regarded as 'native' in 1500, and serfdom only disappeared in the course of the Tudor and early Stuart period.[118] Yet the number of such families was everywhere reduced. On some manors of the bishopric of Worcester serfs are last heard of in the 1380s, and by 1530 there were only about thirty families of serfs on the whole estate. Serfdom had virtually disappeared north of the Trent by 1485.[119]

The collapse of serfdom was the most important thing that happened between 1330 and 1500. It cannot be attributed either to ongoing commercialisation or to advances in legal theory and practice. Nor did it owe much to earlier changes in the character of serfdom. Had population been driven down by epidemic disease between 1180 and 1330 serfdom could hardly have survived. On the other hand, given that population grew in the twelfth and thirteenth centuries, the possibilities for liberty were objectively greater in the later fifteenth century than they had been, at much the same level of population, in the late twelfth. This was because the quantity and productive capacity of resources other than labour had increased. In detail, too, many features of fifteenth-century tenure, in particular the increased use of contractual forms for small parcels of land, were possible only because of the advances in manorial record-keeping made between 1180 and 1330. By 1500 estate officers relied less on memory than they had done in 1000.

---

[115] C. G. A. Clay, *Economic Expansion and Social Change: England, 1500–1700*, 2 vols. (Cambridge, 1984), I, pp. 87–91; Tawney, *Agrarian Problem*, pp. 287–310.

[116] E.g. BL, Add. MSS 23949 (Hollesley, Suff.), 6275 (Langhale, Norf.), Stowe MS 934 (Mettingham College estates, Suff.); *Sibton Abbey Estates*, ed. Denney, pp. 77–109.

[117] E.g. *Tudor Economic Documents*, ed. R. H. Tawney and E. Power, 3 vols. (London, 1924), I, pp. 1–4.

[118] Davenport, *Economic Development*, pp. 96–7; Gras, *Economic and Social History*, p. 94; C. M. Hoare, 'The Last of the Bondmen in a Norfolk Manor', *Norf. Arch.*, 19 (1917), pp. 9–32.

[119] Dyer, *Lords and Peasants*, p. 270; D. MacCulloch, 'Bondmen under the Tudors', in C. Cross, D. Loades and J. J. Scarisbrick, eds., *Law and Government under the Tudors* (Cambridge, 1988), p. 95.

IV

Villagers who moved into towns in the fourteenth and fifteenth centuries did so for the sake of better economic opportunities. They did not need to migrate into town to escape from serfdom, since residence under another lord on another manor would have served this purpose just as well. There was no particular freedom to be gained from moving to a town unless the move was accompanied by formal admission to the body of urban free men, and this step was pointlessly expensive except for the commercial advantages it would bring. Urban societies resolutely retained the division between free men and others. In 1387 the mayor and aldermen of London ordained that in time to come no villain should be allowed to apprentice himself or become a free man of the city. This shows how closely the idea of freedom in an urban sense could be equated with freedom in the rural sense by those who wanted to create barriers of privilege.[120]

Jealousy of the privileges of urban free men was a secondary issue in the revolt of 1381. Some groups of rebels played on the analogy between the rural distinction between free men and serfs and the urban distinction between burgesses and non-burgesses. The rebels had demanded freedom of trade in English cities, boroughs, market towns and elsewhere.[121] The leaders of the revolt from village society were characteristically the wealthier householders rather than the poor. They were more likely, therefore, to be alert to urban rules of trade.[122] Fishermen and rural craftsmen were similarly concerned to remove urban restrictions. The demand for liberty of trade corresponded to the interests of the lower ranks in urban communities, and might receive backing from employers who were concerned about the effects of high food prices on wage rates. It was consequently a divisive issue among townsfolk. One of the charges against John Northampton, the populist mayor of London in 1382–3, was that he had changed the rules of trade to allow outside victuallers to retail their goods freely in the city.[123]

Unlike the countryside, where free tenants were not adversely affected by improvements in the status of the unfree, in towns there was a direct conflict of interests. Burgesses mostly favoured more restrictiveness

---

[120] *Munimenta Gildhallae Londoniensis: Liber Albus, Liber Custumarum et Liber Horn*, ed. H. T. Riley, RS, 3 vols. in 4 parts (London, 1859–62), I, p. 452.
[121] Thomas Walsingham, *Historia Anglicana*, ed. H. T. Riley, RS, 2 vols. (London, 1863–4), II, p. 21.
[122] Dyer, 'Social and Economic Background', pp. 14–19.
[123] *The Peasants' Rising and the Lollards: A Collection of Unpublished Documents*, ed. E. Powell and G. M. Trevelyan (London, 1899), p. 28.

rather than less in order to keep trade in fewer hands. A further consideration, more important in some towns than others, was that non-burgesses could be expected to pay regular fines into the town's coffers for limited licences to trade. In these circumstances the establishment won hands down. The insurgents at Dunstable in the summer of 1381 exacted from the prior the right to exclude rural butchers and fish-mongers from the town.[124] It is difficult to point to any significant gains in freedom of trade during the late Middle Ages, and in some towns new restrictions were imposed. In larger towns non-burgesses remained numerous, and often a majority of the population.[125]

Urban government remained directly responsible to the king or to some other landlord for the exercise of jurisdiction and the management of particular sources of income, like rents, tolls and court fines. Since these sources of income were often in decline the responsibility for them could be a source of embarrassment unless some new agreement could be reached with the recipient. Such problems sometimes went back before the Black Death, as in Winchester.[126] Many towns, too, were expected to send members to parliament. This could be a severe burden, and often required forbearance on the part of a badly remunerated MP.[127] Urban office was often onerous because of the financial risks it incurred. At its worst these various hazards discouraged men from taking up office, though except in York the evidence for this is mostly from the very end of our period.[128] Even where there were worthy citizens willing to serve it was often necessary to compensate them with added dignities for the position in which they found themselves.

In these circumstances urban authorities became characteristically more hierocratic than they had been in the past. Those elected to office were given greater status in the form of urban liveries. They were also given greater security of tenure of office. Rules for the election of town officers were altered to protect the standing of existing officers. This seems to be the main reason for the increasingly oligarchic nature of town government in the late Middle Ages – oligarchic in the sense that

[124] 'Annales de Dunstaplia', in *Annales Monastici*, ed. Luard, III, pp. 417–18.
[125] 'The 1377 Poll Tax Return for the City of York', ed. J. I. Leggett, *Yorks. Archl. J.*, 43 (1971), pp. 129–30; Britnell, 'Bailiffs and Burgesses', p. 104; Veale, 'Craftsmen', p. 136.
[126] E.g. Hill, *Medieval Lincoln*, p. 270; Keene, *Survey*, I, pp. 94–8; D. M. Palliser, *Tudor York* (Oxford, 1979), pp. 203–4, 207, 215–16.
[127] M. McKisack, *The Parliamentary Representation of the English Boroughs during the Middle Ages* (Oxford, 1932), pp. 82–99.
[128] Britnell, *Growth and Decline*, pp. 229–30; Palliser, *Tudor York*, pp. 204–5; D. M. Palliser, 'Urban Decay Revisited', in J. A. F. Thomson, ed., *Towns and Townspeople in the Fifteenth Century* (Gloucester, 1988), pp. 5–6; S. H. Rigby, 'Urban Decline in the Later Middle Ages: The Reliability of the Non-Statistical Evidence', *Urban Hist. Yearbook, 1984*, p. 56.

office-holders were more immune from external challenges than they had been in the past.[129]

Economic change, too, encouraged the emergence of more marked inequalities of power in towns. Even at the end of the fifteenth century craftsmen were usually independent of an employer. The gild rules of the period relate to artisans who were publicly regulated rather than privately controlled. Yet in the later fifteenth century some textile manufacturing developed in a more capitalist direction. The more fortunate or more enterprising clothmakers, calling themselves clothiers, employed craftsmen as dependent workmen. Thomas Spring of Lavenham, who died in 1486, left £66 13s 4d to his spinners, fullers and weavers to be distributed at the discretion of his executors.[130] This development was not wholly dependent upon commercial expansion. In the countryside the enterprise of wealthier peasants was originally a feature of economic depression, and the same may be true of incipient capitalist organisation in industry.[131]

V

During the period 1180–1330 the most conspicuous opportunities for greater freedom had come to men of the landowning class and the wealthier ranks of townsmen. These people had been able to weaken older restrictions on their powers of self-determination, while in agriculture the bonds that tied tenants to their lords had remained mostly in place. The period 1330–1500 was very different. There was little change in the structure of aristocratic patronage or the career possibilities that it offered. Both in town and countryside hierarchies of rank became more formal. The articulation of rank within the peerage had parallels lower down the social scale, where distinctions were being made between knights, esquires, gentlemen, yeomen, husbandmen and labourers.[132] In the towns the families of aldermen became a rank apart. Below them there were distinctions between burgesses who could vote or could not vote, as well as the older distinction between burgesses and non-burgesses. In village society, by contrast, the opportunities of freedom for ordinary villagers were broadening. The old status distinction between free and unfree was becoming less meaningful, often disappearing altogether.

[129] S. H. Rigby, 'Urban "Oligarchy" in Late Medieval England', in Thomson, ed., *Towns and Townspeople*, pp. 74–81.

[130] Carus-Wilson, 'Evidences', pp. 196–205; Dymond and Betterton, *Lavenham*, p. 68; Thornton, *History of Clare*, pp. 155–6, 179–82.

[131] Britnell, *Growth and Decline*, pp. 183–6.

[132] Dyer, *Standards of Living*, pp. 13–26.

The implications of these changes for social welfare were oddly mixed. On the one hand English society in this period created new social barriers and new degrees of snobbery which remained into the modern period, particularly amongst wealthier income groups. On the other hand the withering away of serfdom, accompanied as it was by improvements in the economic welfare of the poorer classes in society, was social progress by both liberal and Marxist criteria.

Conclusions

Commercial development in the Middle Ages can be assessed according to a number of criteria, not all of which are equivalent. Interpreted in accordance with the weaker definition of commercialisation – a simple increase in commercial activity[1] – there can be no doubt that the economy was more commercialised in 1300 than it was in 1000, though the level of transactions attained at that time was not sustained over the following two hundred years.[2] The decades either side of 1300 were outstanding for the volume of commerce and the quantity of money in circulation. Urban populations were larger then than at any other period of the Middle Ages, and the number of formal markets and fairs was at its height. Even by the stronger definition of commercialisation – an increase in commercial activity outstripping population growth – there are several indications that the economy was more commercialised in 1300 than in 1000. At the latter date a larger proportion of the population was urban, the volume of currency *per capita* was larger, and a larger proportion of total output was produced for sale. It seems likely, too, that there had been a significant increase in regional specialisation.[3]

By the stronger definition, though not by the weaker, commercialisation continued during the later Middle Ages. The urban proportion of the population probably did not increase significantly, but the currency in circulation *per capita* was larger in 1500 than in 1300.[4] There is even more evidence of regional specialisation in the fifteenth century than in the thirteenth, particularly in agriculture, where there were numerous dynamic local developments in livestock farming.[5]

---

[1] For the 'stronger' and 'weaker' definitions of commercialisation, see above, pp. xi.
[2] For a local study of late medieval contraction, see M. Mate, 'The Rise and Fall of Markets in Southeast England', *Canadian J. of Hist.*, 31 (1996), pp. 59–85.
[3] Britnell, 'Commercialisation and Economic Development', pp. 9–19.
[4] Above, pp. 184–5.
[5] Above, pp. 196, 198–9, 201; B. M. S. Campbell and M. Overton, 'A New Perspective on Medieval and Modern Agriculture: Six Centuries of Norfolk Farming, c. 1250–c. 1850', *PP*, 141 (1993), pp. 38–105.

To draw this contrast between stronger and weaker definitions of commercialisation is not a way of evading a major issue in medieval historiography. On the contrary, it is an example of the well known proposition that if measured quantities are defined in different ways the conclusions to be drawn from them may also be different. Some debate about the course of economic change in the fourteenth and fifteenth centuries has arisen simply because such distinctions have not been observed.

Table 6 *Estimates of the size of the English economy, 1086–1470*

	1086	1300	1470
1 Population	2.25m.	6m.	2.3m.
2 National income	£0.4m.	£4.66m.	£3.5m.
3 National income *per capita*	£0.18	£0.78	£1.52
4 Relative price level	1	4	4
5 National income at 1300 prices	£1.6m.	£4.66m.	£3.5m.
6 National income *per capita* at 1300 prices	£0.72	£0.78	£1.52
7 Money in circulation	£37,500	£900,000	£900,000
8 Money in circulation *per capita*	£0.02	£0.15	£0.39

Sources: N. J. Mayhew, 'Modelling Medieval Monetisation', in Britnell and Campbell, eds., *Commercialising Economy*, p. 72; *idem*, 'Population, Money Supply and the Velocity of Circulation in England, 1300–1700', *EcHR*, 48 (1995), p. 244.

These various conclusions may be illustrated by means of Dr Mayhew's estimates of economic activity in England (Table 6). These figures necessarily incorporate many more guesses than equivalent estimates of national income for modern periods.[6] The proposed levels of national income in 1086, 1300 and 1470 depend upon estimates of population for those years that are notoriously the subject of debate. These figures are nevertheless of interest for the arguments of this book, since they illustrate the likely implications of some of the arguments it advances. The estimates propose an increase in national income by almost three times between 1086 and 1300, even when the figures are adjusted to allow for a

---

[6] Table 6 does not included Dr Mayhew's lower estimates for 1086, which are based on alternative interpretations of the Domesday evidence: Mayhew, 'Modelling Medieval Monetisation', p. 72.

fourfold increase in prices (lines 4 and 5). They also propose a steep increase in the quantity of money in circulation, both absolutely and relative to population size (lines 7 and 8). They are therefore fully in accordance with the view that the economy was becoming more commercialised in both the weaker and the stronger sense, though there is no significant increase in what the average income *per capita* would buy (line 6).

After 1300 the estimates show the level of national income contracting, which implies a decline in the number of commercial transactions (line 5). The estimated money stock in 1470 is the same as that in 1300 (line 7), though, as observed earlier in commenting on Table 3, the figure of £900,000 is uncharacteristically high for the fifteenth century, and throughout the period 1320–1470 the currency in circulation had been below the level it had reached around 1300.[7] Meanwhile, Table 6 registers some increase in both real income and money stock *per capita* between 1300 and 1470 (lines 6 and 8), and this supports the suggestion that commercialisation in the stronger sense of the term had continued through this period.

Commercialisation had encouraged and permitted increases in productivity, though not through the discovery of new commercial principles so much as the development of traditional activities. The search for a livelihood in hard times could lead to innovation in many ways. In the course of these five centuries, and particularly during the thirteenth century, the number of market-dependent occupations increased.[8] Specialisation in crafts using old methods could itself be a source of productivity growth if it saved time and materials, though it remained common for people to engage in more than one kind of work. Meanwhile, many important new developments, far from being the results of harsh necessity, were the response of wealthy individuals to new commercial opportunities. The structuring of the formal apparatus of trade – the founding of new boroughs and the establishment of markets and fairs – was almost all the product of landlord enterprise, and depended upon very particular aristocratic traditions of estate management.[9] New commercial techniques, most notably in the organisation of overseas trade and the sanctioning of credit relationships, were pioneered by urban merchants and lawyers. New commercial and industrial practices were transmitted within different groups from generation to generation, and constituted an accumulating resource of practical

---

[7]   Above, p. 179.
[8]   Above, pp. 79–81, 104, 115, 126, Miller and Hatcher, *Medieval England: Towns, Commerce and Crafts*, pp. 128–34.
[9]   Above, pp. 23–4, 81–2; R. H. Britnell, 'Boroughs, Markets and Trade in Northern England, 1000–1216', in R. H. Britnell and J. Hatcher, eds., *Progress and Problems in Medieval England: Essays in Honour of Edward Miller* (Cambridge, 1996), pp. 50–1, 57, 61–2.

knowledge. Such institutional developments, with the associated changes in habitual behaviour and development of practical skills, help to explain why the English economy of the fifteenth century was so different from that of the eleventh, despite a prolonged period in which rising standards of living were precluded by population growth.[10]

One of the areas of change in everyday practices that must force itself on the attention of any historian is the development of the use of literacy for administrative purposes. Commercialisation was positively associated with the development of record-keeping and official routine, implying less reliance on memory and more dependence upon the written word. The history of economic development has this theme in common with the history of government and law. By the end of the thirteenth century many peasants held documents relating to their land, and men who could write were to be found even in small villages.[11] The written word came to be used for the transmission of instructions to local officers, and so permitted greater precision in the administration of property. But there were other areas in which literacy was important. Records made it possible to define more accurately the boundaries of power between different individuals and groups, notable in the form of title deeds and charters of urban liberties. Related developments were the multiplication of negotiated restrictions upon arbitrary authority, and the growing status of law as a symbol of order in society. The legal changes in question were not confined to the development of the common law from Henry II's reign, and the limitation of arbitrary feudal lordship associated with Magna Carta, but extended to the codification of customary law as well.[12] Pragmatic literacy also enabled administrations to store information and so expanded their effective memory of available resources (as in the case of estate surveys) and current operations (as in the case of accounts and court records of all kinds).[13] It thereby facilitated the development of contractual forms of taxation and rent that depended less than those of the past on the memories of old men. Such records, furthermore, permitted tighter checks upon subordinate officials in an attempt to make peculation and fraud more difficult. These developments account for some of the main differences in the exercise of power between the eleventh and fifteenth centuries.

A good deal of current debate concerns the explanatory force of population change in the pre-industrial period. The arguments proposed in this book accept that population change may be treated as a partly autonomous

[10] Above, pp. 166–8.
[11] Above, pp. 80–1, 132, 139; *Carte Nativorum*, ed. Brooke and Postan, pp. xxviii–lxv.
[12] Above, pp. 134–40, 142–4; J. S. Beckerman, 'Procedural Innovation and Institutional Change in Medieval English Manorial Courts', *Law and Hist. R.*, 10 (1992), pp. 197–252.

variable, particularly in discussion of epidemic disease, and that demographic change had an important influence upon standards of living and social relations between 1000 and 1500. This does not imply that the social consequences of changing population can be explained without reference to the characteristics of the population in question.[14] Social change in the later fourteenth century can be understood only with the premise that the English economy had attained such a degree of commercialisation, and the institutions for the exchange of labour and land were so well developed, that the relative power of employers and employees or landlords and tenants was directly affected by changes in supply and demand. The sharp upward movement of wages after the Black Death, in defiance of repeated bursts of legislation to prevent it, demonstrates that England's market economy was more robust than the constitutional forces of king, lords and commons.[15] Since the bargaining power of tenants and employees had been greatly enhanced by demographic change, most of the victories they achieved required no violent confrontation.[16] Nor does an acceptance of the causal importance of changing population imply that demographic change was the main determinant of standards of living; because of the accumulation of cultural resources of practical advantage in everyday life, change in medieval standards of living were not, in fact, determined simply by the ratio of population to land.[17]

As these comments imply, bargaining and conflict between lords and tenants, and between employers and employees, became of increasing importance for the distribution of incomes, even if rents and wages changed only slowly. Commercialisation was no threat to kings and lords, even if it encouraged them to exercise their authority in different ways.[18] In the twelfth and thirteenth centuries the growth of commerce opened up new potential for the growth of the income of the crown at the expense of its subjects, permitting kings to wage wars through the creation of new forms of taxation.[19] Lords, too, benefited from higher land values; the idea that their interests were challenged by the growth of trade is plainly false, since noblemen and leading churchmen were among the most self-con-

---

[13] Above, pp. 116–17, 142–4.
[14] Britnell, 'Commerce and Capitalism', pp. 370–1; Rigby, *English Society*, pp. 141–3.
[15] J. Hatcher, 'England in the Aftermath of the Black Death', *PP*, 144 (1994), pp. 3–35.
[16] Above, pp. 219–20; M. Bailey, 'Rural Society', in R. Horrox, ed., *Fifteenth-Century Attitudes: Perceptions of Society in Late Medieval England* (Cambridge, 1994), pp. 154–9.
[17] Above, pp. 80, 103–4, 119, 127, 166–8.
[18] Above, pp. 128–36.
[19] Above, p. 105; J. L. Bolton, 'Inflation, Economics and Politics in Thirteenth-Century England', in Coss and Lloyd, *Thirteenth Century England*, IV, pp. 8–14.

scious promoters and leading beneficiaries of this growth.[20] Meanwhile in the countryside the development of a land market amongst the peasantry had the effect of multiplying the number of smallholdings and creating wider income differentials within village society.[21] There was also polarisation within towns between the incomes of urban landlords and international merchants, at the top, and the numerous landless immigrants from the countryside who came to towns in the desperate search for employment or alms.[22]

Between the eleventh and the thirteenth centuries the distribution of income must have become more unequal. However, these tendencies were not maintained through the fourteenth and fifteenth centuries, when the bargaining power of tenants and wage-earners increased at the expense of landlords and employers, for reasons that have already been noted. The evidence implies that medieval commercialisation, at least in the stronger sense, had no uniform implications for the distribution of income. The differences of experience in the earlier and later parts of the period 1000–1500 are not observable from Table 6, which shows only change in the average income *per capita* at different times.

The transformation from feudalism to capitalism is not a topic that can easily be accommodated in a study that closes in 1500, when the English economy retained many pre-capitalist features.[23] However, the conclusions to be drawn relating to the commercialisation of the economy during the Middle Ages have close relevance to Marx's historical observations on the development of capitalism. The principal contrasts between feudalism and capitalism to be found in his analysis are listed in Table 7. Judged by these criteria there can be no doubt that the commercialisation of the economy between 1000 and 1500 should be regarded as part of the transition between feudalism and capitalism. However, the argument in favour of this proposition is stronger for the eleventh, twelfth and thirteenth centuries than for the fourteenth and fifteenth, especially since a rising standard of living is not included amongst Marx's criteria for capitalism. Towns had a greater impact upon agriculture in the earlier period, when they were growing, than later on.[24] The key elements in the local marketing structure of late medieval trade were already in place by the third quar-

---

[20] Above, pp. 22–4, 43–7, 81–2, 108–12.
[21] Above, pp. 103–4, 145–7.
[22] Above, pp. 85, 104, 149–50; Miller and Hatcher, *Medieval England: Towns, Commerce and Crafts*, pp. 330–42.
[23] R. H. Hilton, 'A Crisis of Feudalism', in Aston and Philpin, eds., *The Brenner Debate*, pp. 136–7.
[24] Above, pp. 85–8, 156–60. For evidence against interpreting the taxation records of 1334 and 1524 to imply that the proportion of the national wealth in towns had increased, see S. H. Rigby, *Medieval Grimsby: Growth and Decline* (Hull, 1993), pp. 141–4.

ter of the thirteenth century.[25] Increasing orientation towards the market is more easily demonstrable for the period 1100–1300, when the number of markets and fairs for the sale of agrarian produce was growing, than for the years 1300–1500, when it was contracting.[26] The growth of larger units of production is more characteristic of the thirteenth century, when demesne farming was expanding, than of the fourteenth and fifteenth, when demesnes were often being split up into smaller units.[27] Dependence on wage labour was a more marked feature of thirteenth-century agriculture, when units of production were larger and labour was becoming cheaper, than of the shrunken demesnes and peasant farms of the fifteenth century.[28] There is little reason to suppose that the shift of the entrepreneurial focus of the later Middle Ages towards smaller units did anything to increase the overall propensity to innovate or invest, even though there was some diversion of investment into new directions, notably livestock farming.[29] Only in respect of the last two criteria for distinguishing feudalism and capitalism was there any significant movement in the direction of capitalism during the later Middle Ages. After the Black Death, rents and wages became more generally contractual,[30] and at least in the cloth industry towards the very end of the fifteenth century there are signs of increasing dependence on merchant clothiers in some parts of the country.[31] This latter development, however, cannot have affected more than a few thousand people by 1500. Within the terms of Marx's own ideas, the emphasis that has long been placed upon the late Middle Ages as a period of transition from feudalism to capitalism lacks adequate foundations, and seriously misrepresents the magnitude of earlier change.[32]

To what extent did commercialisation strengthen or weaken social cohesion? Economic specialisation made families more dependent upon

---

[25] Above, p. 82; Britnell, 'Proliferation', pp. 218–19; J. Masschaele, 'Market Rights in Thirteenth-Century England, *EHR*, 107 (1992), pp. 78–89; *idem*, 'The Multiplicity of Medieval Markets Reconsidered', *J. Hist. Geog.* 20 (1994), pp. 255–71.

[26] Above, pp. 81–5, 88–9, 156–61. For differences between demesnes, see Campbell, 'Measuring the Commercialisation', pp. 139–47; D. Postles, 'Some Differences between Manorial Demesnes in Medieval Oxfordshire', *Oxoniensia*, 58 (1993), pp. 219–32.

[27] Above, pp. 115–19, 187–9. The demesnes of St Paul's cathedral were expanding in the twelfth century: R. Faith, 'Demesne Resources and Labour Rent on the Manors of St Paul's Cathedral, 1066–1222', *EcHR*, 47 (1994), pp. 657–78.

[28] Above, pp. 104–5, 187–8, 201; D. L. Farmer, 'The *Famuli* in the Later Middle Ages', in Britnell and Hatcher, eds., *Progress and Problems*, pp. 210–11, 236.

[29] Above, pp. 123, 201–3.

[30] Above, pp. 188, 192, 197–200, 221.

[31] Above, p. 226.

[32] Britnell, 'Commerce and Capitalism', pp. 359–69.

the activities of others. To that extent commerce encouraged a higher degree of spontaneous interaction between individuals. The expansion and multiplication of towns is an unambiguous indicator of this growth of interdependence between households. Commercial interrelationships encouraged the development of informal transactions, many of which must escape the historical record, but they also made people more dependent upon the functioning of public institutions – notably money, the law, markets and fairs. Even in village life the greater use of money is associated with some striking forms of public communal activity.[33] Com-

Table 7 *Contrasts between feudalism and capitalism*

Feudalism	Capitalism
1 The agricultural economy governed what happened in the urban economy.	The urban economy governs what happens in the rural economy.
2 Production was predominantly for the use of the producer's family or of someone to whom he owed renders in kind.	Production is predominantly for exchange, and the ultimate destination of products is unknown to the producer.
3 Agrarian production was predominantly conducted in small units.	Agrarian production is conducted in larger units as a result of the accumulation of land in fewer hands.
4 Agrarian production was predominantly dependent on the labour of tenant occupiers, though they owed some labour rent to their landlords.	Agrarian production is predominantly dependent upon wage labour, following the elimination of peasant producers and labour rents.
5 Those responsible for production had a low propensity to innovate and accumulate.	Those responsible for production have a high propensity to innovate and accumulate.
6 Economic dependence was not a contractual relationship.	Economic dependence is a contractual relationship.
7 Industrial activity was organised by independent craftsmen who employed day labourers if necessary.	Both craftsmen and other industrial workers depend upon a class of entrepreneurs who co-ordinate the different manufacturing operations.

Source: R. H. Britnell, 'Commerce and Capitalism in Late Medieval England: Problems of Description and Theory', *J. Hist. Sociology*, 6 (1993), pp. 360–1, where references are given.

---

[33] C. Dyer, 'The English Medieval Village Community and its Decline', *J. British Stud.*, 33 (1994), pp. 407–29; *idem*, 'Taxation and Communities in Late Medieval England', in Britnell and Hatcher, eds., *Progress and Problems*, pp. 177–90.

mercialisation brought with it an elaboration of private and public codes of social conduct, some of great complexity, into which people were educated to differing degrees from childhood.

At the same time, in a world with such great inequalities of wealth and power as that of medieval England, almost all forms of increasing economic complementarity were ambiguous in their implications. The period from 1000 to 1500 witnessed a great elaboration of distinctions of social rank.[34] Not all the multiplying divisions can be related to gradations of wealth or to expressions of economic interest, but it was not unusual for particular groups to restrict entry specifically for commercial advantage. The growth of towns, for example, was associated both with the reservation particular trading rights to merchant gilds and with the elaboration of trading rules by which burgesses disadvantaged traders from other places.[35] Outsiders who wanted to share in the privileges of the townsmen had formally to take out membership of the gild or borough community,[36] or pay regular fines to the community.[37] In fourteenth-century Wells it was an offence against the community to give assistance to an outsider in a lawsuit against a fellow townsman, whatever the rights or wrongs of the case.[38]

The creation of new forms of social closure was not confined to large social groups.[39] Within towns, increasing specialisation of employment, though it made families more interdependent, also created a multiplicity of status distinctions between different occupations. It brought into existence a new class of merchants,[40] whose members came to exercise considerable political and economic power simply because of their accumulated wealth.[41] In addition, the fact that knowledge was accumulating within particular crafts gave specialised groups the desire and the opportunity to exclude newcomers, particularly when trading conditions were poor. So craft gilds, where they existed, were not simply sodalities, or agencies of local government, but existed also to defend the status of occupational groups and to control the number of men employed in them.[42] In some cases commercial development gave both livelihood and definition to

[34] Above, pp. 211–12; Rigby, *English Society*, pp. 190–1, 195–8.
[35] Above, pp. 27–8.
[36] J. Masschaele, 'Urban Trade in Medieval England: The Evidence of Foreign Gild Membership Lists', in Coss and Lloyd, eds., *Thirteenth Century England*, V, pp. 115–28.
[37] Kowaleski, *Local Markets*, pp. 194–5.
[38] D. G. Shaw, *The Creation of a Community: The City of Wells in the Middle Ages* (Oxford, 1993), p. 185.
[39] For a succinct explanation of the concept of social closure, see Rigby, *English Society*, pp. 9–12. The usefulness of the concept is demonstrated throughout that book.
[40] Miller and Hatcher, *Medieval England: Towns, Commerce and Crafts*, pp. 225–54.
[41] Kowaleski, *Local Markets*, pp. 95–119.
[42] Swanson, *Medieval Artisans*, pp. 111–18.

groups whose activities were despised by the rest of society. This was the case with felons who preyed on the money economy,[43] and with prostitutes who inevitably congregated in towns.[44] But the English Jews are the best example of an urban pariah group: they made a major contribution to trade and money-lending in England before popular and royal anti-Semitism joined forces against them in the later thirteenth century.[45]

The multiplication of lines of cleavage encouraged the elaboration of formal social regulations, both at national and local levels, from the thirteenth century. These regulations, and the accompanying police work and litigation, illustrate well the way in which literacy contributed to the political resolution of the emergent problems of a trading economy. In towns the multiplication of statutes and by-laws often rested on the assumption that co-operation in the common interest could be achieved only by intrusive regulation.[46] Even the setting of prices in the public markets for grain and fish became subject to tight regulation by appointed officials rather than being left to haggling between individual traders.[47] Coercion was exercised in the belief that too much spontaneous interaction between individuals was a dangerous thing. Though many of these forms of intervention were clumsy or ineffective, they nevertheless amounted to a considerable extension of the role of government in everyday life.

At this point the study of commercialisation becomes enmeshed with other branches of history. Indeed, the purpose of chapters 3, 6 and 9 has been to explore some of the wider implications of economic development. Commercial development could take place only through existing legal and political apparatus, but in turn it created new possibilities for the restructuring of such institutions and so helps to account for the way in which they were transformed over the centuries. Few aspects of government can be understood in long-term perspective without some awareness of the commercialisation of English society. On the other hand, the changing role of money and commerce is unintelligible without recurrent reference to kings and lords, whose demand frequently determined patterns of exchange, and whose interest shaped many of the institutions of trade.

---

[43] Above, p. 81.
[44] M. Carlin, *Medieval Southwark* (London and Rio Grande, 1996), pp. 209–29; P. J. P. Goldberg, *Women, Work, and Life Cycle in a Medieval Economy: Women in York and Yorkshire, c. 1300–1520* (Oxford, 1992), pp. 149–55; Rosser, *Medieval Westminster*, pp. 143–4.
[45] R. C. Stacey, 'Jewish Lending and the Medieval English Economy', in Britnell and Campbell, *Commercialising Economy*, pp. 78–101; Rigby, *English Society*, pp. 284–302.
[46] Above, pp. 173–8.
[47] R. H. Britnell, 'Price-Setting in English Borough Markets, 1349-1500', *Canadian J. of Hist.*, 31 (1996), pp. 2–15.

Bibliography

PRINTED PRIMARY SOURCES

The Account-Book of Beaulieu Abbey, ed. S. F. Hockey, Camden Soc., 4th ser., XVI (London, 1975)

Accounts and Surveys of the Wiltshire Lands of Adam de Stratton, ed. M. W. Farr, Wilts. Archl. and Nat. Hist. Soc. Recs. Branch, XIV (Devizes, 1959)

Anglo-Saxon Charters, ed. A. J. Robertson, 2nd edn (Cambridge, 1956)

Annales Monastici, ed. H. R. Luard, RS, 5 vols. (London, 1864–9)

The Anonimalle Chronicle, 1333 to 1381, ed. V. H. Galbraith (Manchester, 1970)

The Beauchamp Cartulary Charters 1100–1268, ed. E. Mason, Pipe Roll Soc., LXXXI (London, 1980)

Bedfordshire Coroners' Rolls, ed. R. F. Hunnisett, Beds. Histl. Rec. Soc., XLI (Streatley, 1961)

The Berkeley Manuscripts, ed. J. Maclean, 3 vols. (Gloucester, 1883–5)

Bishop Hatfield's Survey, ed. W. Greenwell, Surtees Soc., XXXII (Durham, 1857)

Boldon Buke, ed. W. Greenwell, Surtees Soc., XXV (Durham, 1852)

A Book of London English, 1384–1425, ed. R. W. Chambers and M. Daunt (Oxford, 1931)

Bracton De Legibus et Consuetudinibus Anglie, ed. G. E. Woodbine, 4 vols. (New Haven, 1915–42)

British Borough Charters, 1042–1216, ed. A. Ballard (Cambridge, 1913)

British Borough Charters, 1216–1307, ed. A. Ballard and J. Tait (Cambridge, 1923)

Britton, ed. F. M. Nichols, 2 vols. (Oxford, 1865)

'The Burton Abbey Twelfth-Century Surveys', ed. C. G. O. Bridgeman, *Collections for a History of Staffordshire*, William Salt Archl. Soc., vol. for 1916 (1918) pp. 209–300

Calendar of Charter Rolls, HMSO, 6 vols. (London, 1903–27)

Calendar of Close Rolls, HMSO, 46 vols. (London, 1892–1963)

Calendar Letter-Books Preserved among the Archives of the Corporation of the City of London, 1275–1498, ed. R. R. Sharpe, 11 vols. (London, 1899–1912)

Calendar of Patent Rolls, HMSO, 54 vols. (London, 1891–1916)

Calendar of Pleas and Memoranda Rolls Preserved among the Archives of the Corporation of the City of London, A.D 1323–64, ed. A. H. Thomas (Cambridge, 1926)

Cartae, Antiquae, ed. L. Landon and J. C. Davies, Pipe Roll Soc., 2 vols., new ser., XVII, XXXIII (London, 1939, 1960)

Carte Nativorum: A Peterborough Abbey Cartulary of the Fourteenth Century, ed. C. N. L. Brooke and M. M. Postan, Northants. Rec. Soc., XX (Northampton, 1960)

Cartularium Monasterii de Rameseia, ed. W. H. Hart and P. A. Lyons, RS, 3 vols. (London, 1884–93)

Cartularium Prioratus de Colne, ed. J. L. Fisher, Essex Archl. Soc. (Colchester, 1946)

The Cartulary of Cirencester Abbey, Gloucestershire, ed. C. D. Ross and M. Devine, 3 vols. (Oxford, 1964–77)

The Cartulary of Haughmond Abbey, ed. U. Rees (Cardiff, 1985)

The Cartulary of the Knights of St. John of Jerusalem in England, Secunda Camera: Essex, ed. M. Gervers, BARSEH, new ser., VI (London, 1982)

The Cartulary of Worcester Cathedral Priory (Register 1), ed. R. R. Darlington, Pipe Roll Soc., LXXVI (London, 1968)

Charters and Custumals of the Abbey of Holy Trinity Caen, ed. M. Chibnall, BARSEH, new ser., V (London, 1982)

The Charters of Endowment, Inventories and Account Rolls of the Priory of Finchale, ed. J. Raine, Surtees Soc., II (Durham, 1837)

Charters of the Honour of Mowbray, 1107–1191, ed. D. E. Greenway, BARSEH, new ser., I (Oxford, 1972)

The Chronicle of Battle Abbey, ed. and trans. E. Searle, OMT (Oxford, 1980)

Chronicles of the Reigns of Stephen. Henry II and Richard I, ed. R. Howlett, RS, 4 vols. (London, 1884–9)

Chronicon Abbatiae Ramesiensis, ed. W. D. Macray, RS (London, 1886)

Chronicon Monasterii de Abingdon (A.D. 201–1189), ed. J. Stevenson, RS, 2 vols. (London, 1858)

Chronicon Petroburgense, ed. T. Stapleton, Camden Soc., 1st ser., XLVII (London, 1849)

Close Rolls of the Reign of Henry III, HMSO, 14 vols. (London, 1902-38)

Court Roll of Chalgrave Manor, 1278–1313, ed. M. K. Dale, Beds. Histl. Rec. Soc., XXVIII (Streatley, 1950)

Court Rolls of The Abbey of Ramsey and of the Honor of Clare, ed. W. O. Ault (New Haven, 1928)

Court Rolls of the Manor of Wakefield (1274–1331), ed. W. P. Baildon, J. Lister and J. W. Walker, Yorks. Archl. Soc. Rec. Ser., 5 vols., XXIX, XXXVI, LVII, LXXVIII, CIX (1901–45)

Court Rolls of the Wiltshire Manors of Adam de Stratton, ed. R. B. Pugh, Wilts. Rec. Soc., XXIV (Devizes, 1970)

The Coventry Leet Book, ed. M. D. Harris, EETS, 4 vols., CXXXIV, CXXXV, CXXXVIII, CXLVI (London, 1907–13)

Dialogi Laurentii Dunelmensis Monachi ac Prioris, ed. J. Raine, Surtees Soc., LXX Durham, 1880)

Dialogus de Scaccario, ed. and trans. C. Johnson (London, 1950)

Domesday Book, ed. A. Farley, RC, 2 vols. (London, 1783)

The Domesday of St Paul's of the Year MCCXXII. ed W. H. Hale, Camden Soc., 1st ser., LXIX (London, 1858)

The Duchy of Lancaster's Estates in Derbyshire, 1485–1540, ed. I. S. W. Blanchard, Derb. Archl. Soc. Rec. Ser., III (1971)

Dunwich Bailiffs' Minute Book, 1404–1430, ed. M. Bailey, Suff. Rec Soc., XXXIV (Woodbridge, 1992)

Durham Cathedral Priory Rentals, I: Bursars Rentals, ed. R. A. Lomas and A. J. Piper, Surtees Soc. (Durham, 1989)

Earldom of Gloucester Charters to A.D 1217, ed. R. B. Patterson (Oxford, 1973)

Early Charters of the Cathedral Church of St. Paul, London, ed. M. Gibbs, Camden Soc., 3rd ser., LVIII (London, 1939)

The Early Charters of Essex: The Norman Period, ed. C. Hart, Leicester Department of Local History, Occasional Papers, XI (Leicester, 1957)

The Early Records of Medieval Coventry, ed. P. R. Coss, BARSEH, new ser., IX (London, 1986)

Early Yorkshire Charters, ed. W. Farrer and C. T. Clay, Yorks. Archl. Soc. Rec. Ser., extra series, 12 vols. (Edinburgh, 1913–65)

English Historical Documents, III: 1189–1327, ed. H. Rothwell (London, 1975)

English Historical Documents, V: 1485–1558, ed. C. H. Williams (London, 1971)

Facsimiles of Early Charters from Northamptonshire Collections, ed. F. M. Stenton, Northants. Rec. Soc., IV (Northampton, 1930)

Feet of Fines for Essex, ed. R. E. G. Kirk and others, Essex Archl. Soc., 4 vols. (Colchester, 1899–1964)

Feodarium Prioratus Dunelmensis, ed. W. Greenwell, Surtees Soc., LVIII (Durham, 1872)

Fortescue, John, *The Governance of England*, ed. C. Plummer (Oxford, 1885)
    De Laudibus Legum Anglie, ed. S. B. Chrimes (Cambridge, 1949)

Die Gesetze der Angelsachsen, ed. F. Liebermann, 3 vols. (Halle, 1903–16)

Gesta Stephani, ed. and trans. K. R. Potter and R. H. C. Davis, 2nd edn, OMT (Oxford, 1976)

The Grey of Ruthin Valor of 1467–8, ed. R. I. Jack (Sydney, 1965)

Historia et Cartularium Monasterii Sancti Petri Gloucestriae, ed. W. H. Hart, RS, 3 vols. (London, 1863–7)

The Hylle Cartulary, ed. R. W. Dunning, Som. Rec. Soc., LXVIII (1968)

John of Gaunt's Register, 1379–83, ed. E. C. Lodge and R. Somerville, Camden Soc., 3rd ser., 2 vols., LVI, LVII (London, 1937)

John of Glastonbury, *Cronica*, ed. J. P. Carley, BAR, XLVII, 2 vols. (Oxford, 1978)

The Kalendar of Abbot Samson of Bury St. Edmunds and Related Documents, ed. R. H. C. Davis, Camden Soc., 3rd ser., LXXXIV) London, 1954)

The Laws of the Kings of England from Edmund to Henry I, ed. A. J. Robertson (Cambridge, 1926)

The Lay of Havelock the Dane, ed. W. W. Skeat and K. Sisam, 2nd edn (Oxford, 1915)

Leet Jurisdiction in the City of Norwich during the XIIIth and XIVth Centuries, ed. W. Hudson, Selden Soc., V (London, 1892)

Leges Henrici Primi, ed. and trans. L. J. Downer (Oxford, 1972)

Liber Henrici de Soliaco Abbatis Glastoniensis, ed. J. E. Jackson, Roxburghe Club (London, 1882)

Liber Quotidianus Contrarotulatoris Garderobae Anno Regni Regis Edwardi Primi

Vicesimo Octavo, ed. J. Topham (London, 1787)

Libri Censualis Vocati Domesday Book Additamenta, ed. H. Ellis, RC (London, 1816)

Luffield Priory Charters, ed. G. R. Elvey, Bucks. and Northants. Rec. Socs., 2 vols. (1968–75)

The Making of King's Lynn: A Documentary Survey, ed. D. M. Owen, BARSEH, new ser., IX (London, 1984)

Manorial Records of Cuxham, Oxfordshire, circa 1200–1359, ed. P. D. A. Harvey, HMC, JP23 (London, 1976)

The Marcher Lordships of South Wales, 1415–1536: Select Documents, ed. T. B. Pugh (Cardiff, 1963)

Medieval Framlingham: Select Documents, 1270–1524, ed. J. Ridgard, Suff. Recs. Soc., XXVII (Woodbridge, 1985)

Ministers' Accounts of The Earldom of Cornwall, 1296–1297, ed. L. M. Midgley, Camden Soc., 3rd ser., 2 vols., LXVI, LXVIII (London, 1942, 1945)

Ministers' Accounts of the Warwickshire Estates of the Duke of Clarence, 1479–80, ed. R. H. Hilton, Dugdale Soc., XXI (Stratford-upon-Avon, 1952)

Munimenta Gildhallae Londoniensis: Liber Albus, Liber Custumarum et Liber Horn, ed. H. T. Riley, RS, 3 vols. in 4 parts (London, 1859–62)

The Northumberland Lay Subsidy Roll of 1296, ed. C. M. Fraser, Soc. of Antiquaries of Newcastle upon Tyne, Rec. Ser., I (Newcastle upon Tyne, 1968)

Paris, Matthew, *Chronica Majora*, ed. H. R. Luard, RS, 7 vols. (London, 1872-83)

Paston Letters and Papers of the Fifteenth Century, ed. N. Davis, 2 vols. out of 3 (Oxford, 1971–6)

'Patrington: A Fifteenth-Century Manorial Account', ed. A. Alexander, F. Casperson, M. Habberjam, M. Hall and M. Pickles, *Yorks. Archl. J.*, 42 (1990), pp. 141–52.

The Peasants' Rising and the Lollards: A Collection of Unpublished Documents, ed. E. Powell and G. M. Trevelyan (London, 1899)

Percy Bailiff's Rolls of the Fifteenth Century, ed. J. C. Hodgson, Surtees Soc., CXXXIV (Durham, 1921)

The Percy Chartulary, ed. M. T. Martin, Surtees Soc., CXVII (Durham, 1911)

The Peterborough Chronicle, 1070–1154, ed. C. Clark, 2nd edn (Oxford, 1970)

The Pipe Roll of the Bishopric of Winchester, 1208–9, ed. H. Hall (London, 1903)

Pipe Rolls: *The Great Rolls of the Pipe*, 5 Henry II to 5 Henry III, various editors, Pipe Roll Soc., 58 vols. (London, 1884–1990)

Plumpton Correspondence, ed. T. Stapleton, Camden Soc., 1st ser., IV (London, 1839)

'The 1377 Poll Tax Return for The City of York', ed. J. I. Leggett, *Yorks. Archl. J.*, 43 (1971), pp. 128–46

Records of Anthony Bek, Bishop and Patriarch, 1283–1311, ed. C. M. Fraser, Surtees Soc., CLXII (Durham, 1953)

Records of the Borough of Nottingham, ed. W. H. Stevenson, 5 vols. (London, 1882–1900)

The Records of the City of Norwich, ed. W. Hudson and J. C. Tingey, 2 vols. (Norwich and London, 1906–10)

Records of The Templars in England in the Twelfth Century: The Inquest of 1185 and Illustrative Charters and Documents, ed. B. A. Lees, BARSEH, 1st ser., IX (Oxford, 1935)

Records of the Wardrobe and Household, 1285–1286, ed. B. F. Byerly and C. R. Byerly (London, 1977)

The Red Book of the Exchequer, ed. H. Hall, RS, 3 vols. (London, 1896)

Regesta Regum Anglo-Normannorum, ed. H. W. C. Davis, C. Johnson, H. A. Cronne and R. H. C. Davis, 4 vols. (Oxford, 1913–69)

Regesta Regum Scottorum, ed. G. W. S. Barrow and B. Webster, 3 vols. (Edinburgh, 1960–82)

Registrum Malmesburiense, ed. J. S. Brewer and C. T. Martin, RS, 2 vols. London, 1879–80)

A Relation of the Island of England about the Year 1500, ed. C. A. Sneyd, Camden Soc., 1st ser., XXXVII (London, 1847)

Roger of Howden, *Chronica*, ed. W. Stubbs, RS, 4 vols. (London, 1868-71)

The Roll and Writ File of the Berkshire Eyre of 1248, ed. M. T. Clanchy, Selden Soc., XC (London, 1973)

The Rolls of Highworth Hundred, 1275–1287, ed. B. Farr, Wilts. Rec. Soc., 2 vols., XXI, XXII (Devizes, 1966–8)

Rotuli Hundredorum, ed. W. Illingworth, RC, 2 vols. (London, 1812–18)

Rotuli Litterarum Clausarum, ed. T. D. Hardy, RC, 2 vols. (London, 1833–4)

Select Cases concerning the Law Merchant, ed. C. Gross and H. Hall, Selden Soc., 3 vols., XXIII, XLVI, XLIX (London, 1908–32)

Select Charters and Other Illustrations of English Constitutional History, ed. W. Stubbs, 9th edn, revised H. W. C. Davis (Oxford, 1921)

Select Documents of the English Lands of Ihe Abbey of Bec, ed. M. Chibnall, Camden Soc., 3rd ser., LXXIII (London, 1951)

Select Pleas in Manorial and Other Seignorial Courts, ed. F. W. Maitland, Selden Soc., II (London, 1889)

Sibton Abbey Cartularies and Charters, ed. P. Brown, Suff. Recs. Soc., Suff. Charters, VII–X (Woodbridge, 1985–8)

The Sibton Abbey Estates: Select Documents 1325–1509, ed. A. H. Denney, Suff. Recs. Soc., II (Ipswich, 1960)

Simeon of Durham, *Opera Omnia*, ed. T. Arnold, RS, 2 vols. (London, 1882, 1885)

Sir Christopher Hatton's Book of Seals, ed. L. C. Loyd and D. M. Stenton, Northants. Rec. Soc., XV (Oxford, 1950)

'A Stanley Account Roll. 1460', ed. R. Sharpe France, *Trans. of the Historic Soc. of Lancs. and Ches.*, 113 (1961), pp. 203–9

Statutes of the Realm (1101–1713), ed. A. Luders, T. E. Tomlins, J. France, W. E. Taunton and J. Raithby, RC, 11 vols. (London, 1808–28)

Stoke by Clare Cartulary, ed. C. Harper-Bill and R. Mortimer, 3 vols., Suff. Recs. Soc., Suff. Charters, IV–VI (Woodbridge, 1982–4)

The Stonor Letters and Papers, 1290–1483, ed. C. L. Kingsford, Camden Soc., 3rd ser., 2 vols., XXIX, XXX (London, 1919)

Stow, John, *A Survey of London*, ed. C. L. Kingsford, 2 vols. (Oxford, 1908)

A Terrier of Fleet Lincolnshire, ed. N. Neilson, BARSEH, 1st ser., IV (London, 1920)

'Three Carrow Account Rolls', ed. L. J. Redstone, *Norf. Arch.*, 29 (1946), pp. 41–88

'A Transcript of "The Red Book" of the Bishopric of Hereford (*c*1290)', ed. A. T. Bannister, in *The Camden Miscellany, XV*, Camden Soc., 3rd ser., XLI (London, 1929)

Tudor Economic Documents, ed. R. H. Tawney and E. Power, 3 vols. (London, 1924)

Two 'Compoti' of the Lancashire and Cheshire Manors of Henry de Lacy, Earl of Lincoln, ed. P. A. Lyons, Chetham Soc., CXII (Manchester, 1884)

Two of the Saxon Chronicles Parallel, ed. C. Plummer and J. Earle, 2 vols. (Oxford, 1892)

The Vision of William concerning Piers the Plowman, ed. W. W. Skeat, 2 vols. (Oxford, 1886)

The Wakefield Mystery Plays, ed. M. Rose (London, 1961)

Walsingham, Thomas, *Historia Anglicana*, ed. H. T. Riley, RS, 2 vols. (London, 1863–4)

Walter of Henley and Other Treatises on Estate Management and Accounting, ed. D. Oschinsky (Oxford, 1971)

Wellingborough Manorial Accounts, A.D. 1258–1323, ed. F. M. Page, Northampton-shire Rec. Soc., VIII (Northampton, 1936)

William of Malmesbury, *De Gestis Regum Anglorum*, ed. W. Stubbs, RS, 2 vols. (London, 1887–9)

   Historia Novella, ed. and trans. K. R. Potter, OMT (Oxford, 1955)

'Wiltshire Geld Rolls', ed. R. R. Darlington, *VCH Wilts.*, II, pp. 169–221.

The Works of Geoffrey Chaucer, ed. F. N. Robinson, 2nd edn (Oxford, 1957)

York Civic Ordinances, 1301, ed. M. C. Prestwich, Borthwick Paper XLIX (York, 1976)

York House Books, 1461–1490, ed. L. C. Attreed, 2 vols. (Stroud, 1991)

The York Plays, ed. R. Beadle (London, 1982)

SECONDARY SOURCES

Alcock, N. W., 'The Catesbys in Coventry: A Medieval Estate and its Archive', *MH*, 15 (1990), pp. 1–36

Astill, G. G., 'Economic Change in Later Medieval England: An Archaeological Review', in Aston and others, *Social Relations and Ideas*, pp. 217–47

   'The Towns of Berkshire', in J. Haslam, ed., *Anglo-Saxon Towns in Southern England* (Chichester, 1984), pp. 53–86

   'Towns and Town Hierarchies in Saxon England', *Oxford J. of Arch.*, 10 (1991), pp. 95–117

Aston, M., 'Lollardy and Sedition, 1381–1431', in Hilton, ed., *Peasants, Knights and Heretics*, pp. 273–318

Aston, T. H., 'The Origins of the Manor in England' with 'A Postscript', in Aston and others, eds., *Social Relations and Ideas*, pp. 1–43

   ed., *Landlords, Peasants and Politics in Medieval England* (Cambridge, 1987)

Aston, T. H., Coss, P. R., Dyer, C., and Thirsk, J., eds., *Social Relations and Ideas:*

Essays in Honour of R. H. Hilton (Cambridge, 1983)

Aston, T. H., and Philpin, C. H. E., eds., *The Brenner Debate: Agrarian Class Structure and Economic Development in Pre-Industrial Europe* (Cambridge, 1985)

Ault, W. O., *Private Jurisdiction in England* (New Haven, 1923)

Bailey, M., 'Blowing up Bubbles: Some New Demographic Evidence for the Fifteenth Century', *J. of Med. Hist.*, 15 (1989), pp. 347–58

'The Concept of the Margin in the Medieval Economy', *EcHR*, 2nd ser., 42 (1989), pp. 1–17

A Marginal Economy? East Anglian Breckland in the Later Middle Ages (Cambridge, 1989)

'The Rabbit and the Medieval East Anglian Economy', *AHR*, 36 (1988), pp. 1–20

'Rural Society', in R. Horrox, ed., *Fifteenth-Century Attitudes: Perceptions of Society in Late Medieval England* (Cambridge, 1994), pp. 150–68

Baker, A. R. H., 'Changes in the Later Middle Ages', in H. C. Darby, ed., *A New Historical Geography of England* (Cambridge, 1973), pp. 186–247

Baring, F. H., 'The Making of the New Forest', *EHR*, 16 (1901), pp. 427–38

Barlow, F., *Edward the Confessor* (London, 1970)

Thomas Becket (London, 1986)

William Rufus (London, 1983)

Barron, C., 'The Tyranny of Richard II', *BIHR*, 41 (1968), pp. 1–18

Bartlett, J. N., 'The Expansion and Decline of York in the Later Middle Ages', *EcHR*, 2nd ser., 12 (1959–60), pp. 17–33

Bean, J. M. W., *The Decline of English Feudalism, 1215–1540* (Manchester, 1968)

The Estates of the Percy Family, 1416–1537 (Oxford, 1958)

From Lord to Patron: Lordship in Late Medieval England (Manchester, 1989)

Becker, M. J., *Rochester Bridge, 1387–1856: A History of its Early Years* (London, 1930)

Beckerman, J. S., 'Procedural Innovation and Institutional Change in Medieval English Manorial Courts'., *Law and Hist. R.*, 10 (1992), pp. 197–252

Bellamy, J. G., *Bastard Feudalism and the Law* (London, 1989)

Crime and Public Order in England in the Later Middle Ages (London, 1973)

Bennett, H. S., *Life on the English Manor: A Study of Peasant Conditions, 1150–1400* (Cambridge, 1937)

The Pastons and their England (Cambridge, 1922)

Bennett, J. M., *Women in the Medieval English Countryside: Gender and Household in Brigstock before the Plague* (Oxford, 1987)

Bennett, M. J., 'Careerism in Late Medieval England', in Rosenthal and Richmond, eds., *People, Politics and Community*, pp. 19–39

Community, Class and Careerism: Cheshire and Lancashire Society in the Age of Sir Gawain and the Green Knight (Cambridge, 1983)

Beresford, M., *The Lost Villages of England* (London, 1954)

New Towns of the Middle Ages: Town Plantation in England, Wales and Gascony (London, 1967)

Beresford, M., and Finberg, H. P. R., *English Medieval Boroughs: A Handlist* (Newton Abbot, 1973)

Beveridge, W., 'Wages in the Winchester Manors', *EcHR*, 7 (1936), pp. 22–43.
'Westminster Wages in the Manorial Era', *EcHR*, 2nd ser., 8 (1955), pp. 18–35
Biddick, K., 'Missing Links: Taxable Wealth, Markets, and Stratification among Medieval English Peasants', *J. of Interdisciplinary Hist.*, 18 (1987), pp. 277–98
The Other Economy: Pastoral Husbandry on a Medieval Estate (Berkeley and Los Angeles, 1989)
Biddle, M., 'Towns', in Wilson, ed., *Archaeology of Anglo-Saxon England*, pp. 99–150
Birrell, J. R., 'Peasant Craftsmen in the Medieval Forest', *AHR*, 17 (1969), pp. 91–107
Bishop, T. A. M., 'Monastic Granges in Yorkshire', *EHR*, 51 (1936), pp. 193–214
'The Rotation of Crops at Westerham, 1297–1350', *EcHR*, 9 (1938–9), pp. 38–44
Blake, J. B., 'The Medieval Coal Trade of the North-East: Some Fourteenth-Century Evidence', *NH*, 2 (1967), pp. 1–26
Blanchard, I. S. W., 'Labour Productivity and Work Psychology in the English Mining Industry, 1400–1600', *EcHR*, 2nd ser., 31 (1978), pp. 1–24
'Lothian and Beyond: The Economy of the "English Empire" of David I', in Britnell and Hatcher, eds., *Progress and Problems*, pp. 23–45.
Bloch, M., *Feudal Society*, trans. L. A. Manyon (London, 1961)
Bolton, J. L., 'Inflation, Economics and Politics in Thirteenth-Century England', in Coss and Lloyd, *Thirteenth Century England*, IV, pp. 1–14
The Medieval English Economy, 1150–1500 (London, 1980)
Bonney, M., *Lordship and the Urban Community: Durham and its Overlords, 1250–1540* (Cambridge, 1990)
Bradshaw, F., 'Social and Economic History', *VCH co. Dur.*, II, pp. 175–274
Brandon, P. F., 'Demesne Arable Farming in Coastal Sussex during the Later Middle Ages', *AHR*, 19 (1971), pp. 113–34
'Farming Techniques: South-Eastern England', in *AHEW*, II, pp. 312-25
Brenner, R., 'Agrarian Class Structure and Economic Development in Pre-Industrial Europe', in Aston and Philpin, eds., *The Brenner Debate*, pp. 10–63
Bridbury, A. R., 'The Black Death', *EcHR*, 2nd ser., 26 (1973), pp. 577–92
'Dr. Rigby's Comment: A Reply', *EcHR*, 2nd ser., 39 (1986), pp. 417–22
'Domesday Book: A Reinterpretation', *EHR*, 105 (1990), pp. 283–309
Economic Growth: England in the Later Middle Ages (London, 1962)
England and the Salt Trade in the Later Middle Ages (Oxford, 1955)
Medieval English Clothmaking: An Economic Survey (London, 1982)
Britnell, R. H., 'Abingdon: A Lost Buckinghamshire Hamlet', *Recs. of Bucks.*, 22 (1980), pp. 48–52
'*Advantagium Mercatoris*: A Custom in Medieval English Trade', *Nottingham Med. Stud.*, 24 (1980), pp. 37–50
'Agriculture in a Region of Ancient Enclosure, 1185–1500', *Nottingham Med. Stud.*, 27 (1983), pp. 37–55
'Agricultural Technology and the Margin of Cultivation in the Fourteenth Century', *EcHR*, 2nd ser., 30 (1977), pp. 53–66
'Bailiffs and Burgesses in Colchester, 1400–1525', *Essex Arch. and Hist.*, 21 (1990), pp. 103–9

'Boroughs, Markets and Trade in Northern England, 1000–1216', in Britnell and Hatcher, eds., *Progress and Problems*, pp. 46–67

'Burghal Characteristics of Market Towns in Medieval England', *Dur. Univ. J.*, new ser., 42 (1981), pp. 147–51

'Commerce and Capitalism in Late Medieval England: Problems of Description and Theory', *J. Histl. Sociology*, 6 (1993), pp. 359–76

'Commercialisation and Economic Development in England, 1000–1300', in Britnell and Campbell, *Commercialising Society*, pp. 7–26

'English Markets and Royal Administration before 1200', *EcHR*, 2nd ser., 31 (1978), pp. 183–96

'Essex Markets before 1350', *Essex Arch. and Hist.*, XIII (1981), pp. 15–21

'Farming Practice and Techniques: Eastern England', in *AHEW*, III, pp. 194–210

'Feudal Reaction after the Black Death in the Palatinate of Durham', *PP*, 128 (1990), pp. 28–47

'The Fields and Pastures of Colchester, 1280–1350', *Essex Arch. and Hist.*, 19 (1988), pp. 159–65

'*Forstall*, Forestalling and the Statute of Forestallers', *EHR*, 102 (1987), pp. 89–102

Growth and Decline in Colchester, 1300–1525 (Cambridge, 1986)

'King John's Early Grants of Markets and Fairs', *EHR*, 94 (1979), pp. 90–6

'The Making of Witham', *Hist. Stud.*, 1 (1968), pp. 13–21

'Minor Landlords and Medieval Agrarian Capitalism', in Aston, ed., *Landlords, Peasants and Politics*, pp. 227–46

'The Origins of Stony Stratford', *Recs. of Bucks.*, 20 (1977), pp. 451–3

'The Pastons and their Norfolk', *AHR*, 36 (1988), pp. 132–44

'Price-Setting in English Borough Markets, 1349–1500', *Canadian J. of Hist.* 31 (1996), pp. 2–15

'Production for the Market on a Small Fourteenth-Century Estate', *EcHR*, 2nd ser., 19 (1966), pp. 380–7

'The Proliferation of Markets in England, 1200–1349', *EcHR*, 2nd ser., 34 (1981), pp. 209–21

'Sedentary Long-Distance Trade and the English Merchant Class in Thirteenth-Century England', in Coss and Lloyd, eds., *Thirteenth-Century England*, V, pp. 129–39

'Tenant Farming and Tenant Farmers: Eastern England', in *AHEW*, III, pp. 611–24

'The Towns of England and Northern Italy in the Early Fourteenth Century', *EcHR*, 2nd ser., 44 (1991), pp. 21–35

Britnell, R. H., and Campbell, B. M. S., eds., *A Commercialising Economy: England 1086 to c. 1300* (Manchester, 1995)

Britnell, R. H., and Hatcher, J., eds., *Progress and Problems in Medieval England: Essays in Honour of Edward Miller* (Cambridge, 1996)

Brooke, C., *London, 800–1216: The Shaping of a City* (London, 1975)

Brooke, G. C., *English Coins from the Seventh Century to the Present Day*, 3rd edn (London, 1950)

Brown, H. P., and Hopkins, S. V., *A Perspective of Wages and Prices* (London, 1981)

Brown, R. A., *The Normans and the Norman Conquest*, 2nd edn (Woodbridge, 1985)

'The Status of Norman Knights', in J. Gillingham and J. C. Holt, eds., *War and Government in the Middle Ages* (Woodbridge, 1984), pp. 18–32

Burstall, E. B., 'A Monastic Agreement of the Fourteenth Century', *Norf. Arch.*, 31 (1957), pp. 211–18

Butcher, A. F., 'Rent and the Urban Economy: Oxford and Canterbury in the Later Middle Ages ', *SH*, 1 (1979), pp. 11–43

'Rent, Population and Economic Change in Late-Medieval Newcastle', *NH* 14 (1978), pp. 67–77

Butt, R., *A History of Parliament: The Middle Ages* (London, 1989)

Cam, H. M., 'The City of Cambridge', *VCH Cambs.*, III, p. 1–149

The Hundred and the Hundred Rolls: An Outline of Local Government in Medieval England (London, 1930)

Liberties and Communities in Medieval England: Collected Studies in Local Administration and Topography (Cambridge, 1933)

Campbell, B. M. S., 'Agricultural Progress in Medieval England: Some Evidence from Eastern Norfolk', *EcHR*, 2nd ser., 36 (1983), pp. 26–46

'The Diffusion of Vetches in Medieval England', *EcHR*, 2nd ser., 41 (1988), pp. 193–208

'Ecology Versus Economics in Late Thirteenth- and Early Fourteenth-Century English Agriculture', in D. Sweeney, ed., *Agriculture in the Middle Ages: Technology, Practice, and Representation* (Philadelphia, 1995), pp. 76–108

'Land, Labour, Livestock and Productivity Trends in English Seignorial Agriculture, 1208–1450', in B. M. S. Campbell and M. Overton, eds., *Land, Labour and Livestock: Historical Studies in European Agricultural Productivity* (Manchester, 1991)

'Measuring the Commercialisation of Seigneurial Agriculture c. 1300', in Britnell and Campbell, eds., *Commercialising Economy*, pp. 132–93

'The Population of Early Tudor England: A Re-Evaluation of the 1522 Muster Returns and 1524 and 1525 Lay Subsidies', *J. of Histl. Geog.*, 7 (1981), pp. 145–54

'Population Pressure, Inheritance and the Land Market in a Fourteenth-Century Peasant Community', in Smith, ed., *Land, Kinship and Life-Cycle*, pp. 87–134

'Towards an Agricultural Geography of Medieval England', *AHR*, 36 (1988), pp. 87–98

ed., *Before the Black Death: Studies in the 'Crisis' of the Early Fourteenth Century* (Manchester, 1991)

Campbell, B. M. S., Galloway, J. A., Keene, D., and Murphy, M., *A Medieval Capital and its Grain Supply: Agrarian Production and Distribution in the London Region c. 1300*, Histl. Geog. Research Ser., 30 (London, 1993)

Campbell, B. M. S., and Overton, M., 'A New Perspective on Medieval and Modern

Agriculture: Six Centuries of Norfolk Farming, c. 1250–c. 1850', *PP*, 141 (1993), pp. 38–105

Campbell, B. M. S., and Power, J. P., 'Mapping the Agricultural Geography of Medieval England', *J. of Histl. Geog.*, 15 (1989), pp. 24–39

Campbell, J., 'Was it Infancy in England? Some Questions of Comparison', in M. Jones and M. Vale, eds., *England and her Neighbours, 1066–1453: Essays in Honour of Pierre Chaplais* (London, 1989), pp. 1–17

Carlin, M., *Medieval Southwark* (London and Rio Grande, 1996)

Carpenter, C., 'The Beauchamp Affinity: A Study of Bastard Feudalism at Work', *EHR*, 95 (1980), pp. 514–32

Carus-Wilson, E. M., 'Evidences of Industrial Growth on Some Fifteenth Century Manors', *EcHR*, 2nd ser., 12 (1959), pp. 190–205

  The Expansion of Exeter at the Close of the Middle Ages (Exeter, 1963)

  'The First Half-Century of the Borough of Stratford-upon-Avon', *EcHR*, 2nd ser., 18 (1965), pp. 46–63

  Medieval Merchant Venturers, 2nd edn (London, 1967)

  'The Oversea Trade of Late Medieval Coventry', in *Economies et sociétés au Moyen Age: Mélanges offerts à Edouard Perroy* (Paris, 1973), pp. 371–81

Carus-Wilson, E. M., and Coleman, O., *England's Export Trade, 1275–1547* (Oxford, 1963)

Cate, J. L., 'The English Mission of Eustace de Flay (1200–1)', in *Etudes d'histoire dédiées à la mémoire de Henri Pirenne par ses anciens élèves* (Brussels, 1937), pp. 67–89

Challis, C. E., 'Currency and the Economy in Mid-Tudor England', *EcHR*, 2nd ser., 25 (1972), pp. 313–22

Cherry, M., 'The Courtenay Earls of Devon: The Formation and Disintegration of a Late Medieval Aristocratic Affinity', *SH*, 1 (1979), pp. 71–97

Chibnall, A. C., *Beyond Sherington* (Chichester, 1979)

  Sherington: Fiefs and Fields of a Buckinghamshire Village (Cambridge, 1965)

Chibnall, M., *Anglo-Norman England, 1066–1166* (Oxford, 1986)

Chrimes, S. B., *English Constitutional Ideas in the Fifteenth Century* (Cambridge, 1936)

  Henry VII (London, 1972)

Chrimes, S. B., Ross, C. D., and Griffiths, R. A., eds., *Fifteenth Century England, 1399–1509: Studies in Politics and Society* (Manchester, 1972)

Clanchy, M. T., *From Memory to Written Record: England 1066–1307* (London, 1979)

Clapham, J. H., 'A Thirteenth-Century Market Town: Linton, Cambs.', *Cambridge Hist. J.*, 4 (1933), pp. 194–202

Clay, C. G. A., *Economic Expansion and Social Change: England, 1500–1700*, 2 vols. (Cambridge, 1984)

Coates, B., 'The Origin and Distribution of Markets and Fairs in Medieval Derbyshire', *Derb. Archl. J.*, 85 (1965), pp. 92–111

Cobban, A. B., *The King's Hall within the University of Cambridge in the Later Middle Ages* (Cambridge, 1969)

Coleman, M. C., *Downham-in-the-Isle: A Study of an Ecclesiastical Manor in the Thirteenth and Fourteenth Centuries* (Woodbridge, 1984)

Cornwall, J. C. K., 'English Population in the Early Sixteenth Century', *EcHR*, 2nd ser., 23 (1970), pp. 32–44

Wealth and Society in Early Sixteenth Century England (London, 1988)

Coss, P. R., 'Bastard Feudalism Revised', *PP*, 125 (1989), pp. 27–64

'Knighthood and the Early Thirteenth-Century County Court', in Coss and Lloyd, eds., *Thirteenth Century England*, II, pp. 45–57

Lordship, Knighthood and Locality: A Study in English Society, c.1180–c.1280 (Cambridge, 1991)

'Sir Geoffrey de Langley and the Crisis of the Knightly Class in Thirteenth-Century England', in Aston, ed., *Landlords, Peasants and Politics*, pp. 166–202

Coss, P. R., and Lloyd, S. D., eds., *Thirteenth Century England*, 5 vols. (Woodbridge, 1986–91)

Craig, J., *The Mint: A History of the London Mint from A.D. 287 to 1948* (Cambridge, 1953)

Crouch, D., *The Beaumont Twins: The Roots and Branches of Power in the Twelfth Century* (Cambridge, 1986)

William Marshal: Court, Career and Chivalry in the Angevin Empire, 1147–1219 (London, 1990)

Dale, M. K., 'The City of Leicester: Social and Economic History', *VCH Leics.*, IV, pp. 31–54

Darby, H. C., *Domesday England* (Cambridge, 1977)

The Medieval Fenland (Cambridge, 1940)

Davenport, F. G., *The Economic Development of a Norfolk Manor, 1086–1565* (Cambridge, 1906)

Davies, R. R., 'Baronial Accounts, Incomes and Arrears in the Later Middle Ages', *EcHR*, 2nd ser., 21 (1968), pp. 211–29

Davis, N., 'The Proximate Etymology of "Market"', *The Modern Language R.*, 47 (1952), pp. 152–5

Davis, R. H. C., *King Stephen, 1135–1154* (London, 1967)

Day, J., *The Medieval Market Economy* (Oxford, 1987)

Denholm-Young, N., *Richard of Cornwall* (Oxford, 1947)

Seignorial Administration in England (Oxford, 1937)

DeWindt, E. B., *Land and People in Holywell-cum-Needingworth: Structures of Tenure and Patterns of Social Organization in an East Midlands Village, 1252–1457*, PIMSST, XXII (Toronto, 1971)

Dobson, R. B., *Durham Priory, 1400–1450* (Cambridge, 1973)

'Urban Decline in Late Medieval England', *TRHS*, 27 (1977), pp. 1–22

Donkin, R. A., 'Settlement and Depopulation on Cistercian Estates during the 12th and 13th Centuries, especially in Yorkshire', *BIHR*, 33 (1960), pp. 141–65

Douglas, D. C., *William the Conqueror: The Norman Impact upon England* (London, 1964)

Du Boulay, F. R. H., *The Lordship of Canterbury: An Essay on Medieval Society*

(London, 1966)

Duby, G., *The Early Growth of the European Economy: Warriors and Peasants from the Seventh to the Twelfth Century*, trans. H. B. Clarke (London, 1974)

Dyer, A., *Decline and Growth in English Towns, 1400–1640* (London, 1991)

Dyer, C., 'Changes in Diet in the Late Middle Ages: The Case of Harvest Workers', *AHR*, 36 (1988), pp. 21–37

'The Consumer and the Market in the Later Middle Ages', *EcHR*, 2nd ser., 42 (1989), pp. 305–27

'English Diet in the Later Middle Ages', in Aston and others, eds., *Social Relations and Ideas*, pp. 191–216

'The English Medieval Village Community and its Decline', *J. British Stud.*, 33 (1994), pp. 407–29

'The Hidden Trade of the Middle Ages: Evidence from the West Midlands of England', in *Everyday Life in Medieval England* (London and Rio Grande, 1994), pp. 283–303

Lords and Peasants in a Changing Society: The Estates of the Bishopric of Worcester, 680–1540 (Cambridge, 1980)

'Population and Agriculture on a Warwickshire Manor in the Later Middle Ages', *University of Birmingham Hist. J.*, 2 (1968), pp. 113–27

'A Redistribution of Incomes in Fifteenth-Century England?', in Hilton, ed., *Peasants, Knights and Heretics*, pp. 192-215

'A Small Landowner in the Fifteenth Century', *MH*, 1, part 3 (1972), pp. 1–14

'The Social and Economic Background to the Rural Revolt of 1381', in Hilton and Aston, eds., *English Rising*, pp. 9–42

Standards of Living in the Later Middle Ages: Social Change in England, c. 1200–1520 (Cambridge, 1989)

'Taxation and Communities in Late Medieval England', in Britnell and Hatcher, eds., *Progress and Problems*, pp. 168–90

Warwickshire Farming, 1349-c.1520: Preparations for Agricultural Revolution, Dugdale Soc. Occasional Paper XXVI I (Oxford, 1981)

'Were There any Capitalists in Fifteenth-Century England?', in Kermode, ed., *Enterprise and Individuals*, pp. 1–24

Dymond, D., and Betterton, A., *Lavenham: 700 Years of Textile Making* (Woodbridge, 1982)

Eales, R., 'Henry III and the End of the Norman Earldom of Chester', in Coss and Lloyd, eds., *Thirteenth Century England*, I, pp. 100–13

Ekwall, E., *The Place Names of Lancashire* (Manchester, 1922)

Ellis, J. R., 'Chopwell: A Problematical Durham Place-Name', *Nomina*, 12 (1988–9), pp. 65–76

Endemann, T., *Markturkunde und Markt in Frankreich und Burgund vom 9 bis 11 Jahrhundert* (Konstanz and Stuttgart, 1964)

Everitt, A., 'The Marketing of Agricultural Produce', in *AHEW*, IV, pp. 466–592

Faith, R., 'Berkshire: Fourteenth and Fifteenth Centuries', in Harvey, ed., *Peasant Land Market*, pp. 107–77

'Demesne Resources and Labour Rent on the Manors of St Paul's Cathedral,

1066–1222', *EcHR*, 47 (1994), pp. 657–78

D. L. Farmer, 'The *Famuli* in the Later Middle Ages', in Britnell and Hatcher, eds., *Progress and Problems*, pp. 207–36

'Some Grain Price Movements in Thirteenth-Century England', *EcHR*, 2nd ser., 10 (1957–8), pp. 207–20

'Grain Yields on Westminster Abbey Manors, 1271–1410', *Canadian J. of Hist.*, 18 (1983), pp. 331–47

'Grain Yields on the Winchester Manors in the Later Middle Ages', *EcHR*, 2nd ser., 30 (1977), pp. 555–66

'Marketing the Produce of the Countryside, 1200–1500', in *AHEW*, III, pp. 324–430

'Prices and Wages [1000–1355]', in *AHEW*, II, pp. 716–817

'Prices and Wages, 1350–1500', in *AHEW*, III, pp. 431–525

'Two Wiltshire Manors and their Markets', *AHR*, 37 (1989), pp. 1–11

'Woodland and Pasture Sales on the Winchester Manors in the Thirteenth Century: Disposing of a Surplus or Producing for the Market?', in Britnell and Campell, eds., *Commercialising Economy*, pp. 102–31

Feiling, K. G., 'An Essex Manor in the Fourteenth Century', *EHR*, 26 (1911), pp. 333–8

Finberg, H. P. R., 'An Early Reference to the Welsh Cattle Trade', in *AHR*, II (1954), pp. 12–14

Tavistock Abbey: A Study in the Social and Economic History of Devon (Cambridge, 1951)

Finn, R. W., *Domesday Studies: The Liber Exoniensis* (London, 1964)

Fowler, P. J., 'Agriculture and Rural Settlement', in Wilson, ed., *Archaeology of Anglo-Saxon England*, pp. 23–48

Fox, H. S. A., 'The Alleged Transformation from Two-Field to Three-Field Systems in Medieval England', *EcHR*, 2nd ser., 39 (1986), pp. 526–48

Fraser, C. M., *A History of Anthony Bek, Bishop of Durham, 1283–1311* (Oxford, 1957)

'Medieval Trading Restrictions in the North East', *Archaeologia Aeliana*, 4th ser., 39 (1961), pp. 135–50

Fryde, E. B., 'The Deposits of Hugh Despenser the Younger with Italian Bankers', *EcHR*, 2nd ser., 3 (1951), pp. 344–62

'Italian Maritime Trade with Medieval England (c.1270–c.1530)', *Recueils de la Société Jean Bodin*, 32 (1974), pp. 291–337

Fryde, E. B., and N., 'Peasant Rebellion and Peasant Discontents', in *AHEW*, III, pp. 744–819

Fryde, E. B., and Miller, E., *Historical Studies of the English Parliament*, 2 vols. (Cambridge, 1970)

Galbraith, V. H., *Domesday Book: Its Place in Administrative History* (Oxford, 1974)

The Latin Charters of the Anglo-Saxon Period (Oxford, 1955)

Gelling, M., ed., *The Place-Names of Berkshire*, EPNS, 3 vols., XLIX–LI (London, 1973–6)

Gillett, E., and MacMahon, K. A., *A History of Hull* (Hull, 1980)

Gillingham, J., 'Chronicles and Coins as Evidence for Levels of Taxation in Late Tenth- and Early Eleventh-Century England', *EHR*, 105 (1990), pp. 939–50

'"The Most Precious Jewel in the English Crown": Levels of Danegeld and Heregeld in the Early Eleventh Century', *EHR*, 104 (1989), pp. 373–84

Given, J. B., *Society and Homicide in Thirteenth-Century England* (Stanford, 1977)

Given-Wilson, C., *The English Nobility in the Late Middle Ages: The Fourteenth-Century Political Community* (London, 1987)

Godden, M. R., 'Money, Power and Morality in Late Anglo-Saxon England', *Anglo-Saxon England*, 19 (1990), pp. 41–65

Goldberg, P. J. P., 'Mortality and Economic Change in the Diocese of York, 1390–1514', *NH*, 24 (1988), pp. 38–55

Women, Work, and Life Cycle in a Medieval Economy: Women in York and Yorkshire, c. 1300–1520 (Oxford, 1992)

'Women's Work, Women's Role in the Late Medieval North', in Hicks, ed., *Profit, Piety and the Professions*, pp. 34–50

Gover, J. E. B., Mawer, A., and Stenton, F. M., *The Place-Names of Surrey*, EPNS, XI (Cambridge, 1934)

Graham, R., *English Ecclesiastical Studies* (London, 1929)

Gras, N. S. B., *The Evolution of the English Corn Market from the Twelfth to the Eighteenth Century* (Cambridge, Mass., 1915)

Gras, N. S. B., and Gras, E. C., *The Economic and Social History of an English Village (Crawley, Hampshire), A.D. 909–1928* (Cambridge, Mass., 1930)

Green, A. S., *Town Life in the Fifteenth Century*, 2 vols. (London, 1894)

Green, J. A., *The Government of England under Henry I* (Cambridge, 1986)

'The Last Century of Danegeld', *EHR*, 96 (1981), pp. 241–58

Grierson, P., 'Sterling', in R. H. M. Dolley, ed., *Anglo-Saxon Coins: Studies Presented to F. M. Stenton on the Occasion of his Seventieth Birthday* (London, 1961), pp. 266–83

Grieve, H., *The Sleepers and the Shadows. Chelmsford: A Town, its People and its Past, I: The Medieval and Tudor Story*, Essex RO Publication c (Chelmsford, 1988)

Griffiths, R. A., *King and Country: England and Wales in the Fifteenth Century* (London, 1991)

The Reign of King Henry VI: The Exercise of Royal Authority, 1422–1461 (London, 1981)

'Wales and the Marches', in Chrimes, Ross and Griffiths, eds., *Fifteenth Century England*, pp. 145–72

Gross, C., *The Gild Merchant: A Contribution to British Municipal History*, 2 vols. (Oxford, 1890)

Guy, J. A., *The Cardinal's Court: The Impact of Thomas Wolsey in Star Chamber* (Hassocks, 1977)

Hadwin, J. F., 'Evidence on the Possession of "Treasure" from the Lay Subsidy Rolls', in Mayhew, ed., *Edwardian Monetary Affairs*, pp. 147–65

Hallam, H. E., 'The Agrarian Economy of South Lincolnshire in the Mid-Fifteenth Century', *Nottingham Med. Stud.*, 11 (1967), pp. 86–95

Settlement and Society: A Study of the Early Agrarian History of South Lincolnshire

(Cambridge, 1965)
ed., *The Agararian History of England and Wales, II: 1042–1350* (Cambridge, 1988)
Hanawalt, B. A., *Crime and Conflict in English Communities, 1300–1348* (Cambridge, Mass., 1979)
Hanham, A., *The Celys and their World: An English Merchant Family of the Fifteenth Century* (Cambridge, 1985)
Harding, A., *The Law Courts of Medieval England* (London, 1973)
'The Revolt against the Justices', in Hilton and Aston, eds., *English Rising*, pp. 165–93
Hare, J. N., 'The Demesne Lessees of Fifteenth Century Wiltshire', *AHR*, 29 (1981), pp. 1–15
'The Wiltshire Risings of 1450: Political and Economic Discontent in Mid-Fifteenth Century England', *SH*, 4 (1982), pp. 13–31
Harley, J. B., 'Population Trends and Agricultural Developments from the Warwickshire Hundred Rolls of 1279', *EcHR*, 2nd ser., 11 (1958), pp. 8–18
Harmer, F. E., '*Chipping and Market*: A Lexicographical Investigation', in C. Fox and B. Dickens, eds., *The Early Cultures of North-West Europe* (Cambridge, 1950), pp. 335–60
Harriss, G. L., *King, Parliament and Public Finance in Medieval England to 1369* (Oxford, 1975)
'The Management of Parliament', in *idem*, ed., *Henry V: The Practice of Kingship* (Oxford, 1985), pp. 137–58
Hart, G., *A History of Cheltenham* (Leicester, 1965)
Harvey, B. F.. 'Introduction: The "Crisis" of the Early Fourteenth Century', in Campbell, ed., *Before the Black Death*, pp. 1–24
'The Leasing of the Abbot of Westminster's Demesnes in the Later Middle Ages', *EcHR*, 2nd ser., 22 (1969), pp. 17–27
Westminster Abbey and its Estates in the Middle Ages (Oxford, 1977)
Harvey, P. D. A., 'The English Inflation of 1180–1220', in Hilton, ed., *Peasants, Knights and Heretics*, pp. 57–84
'The English Trade in Wool and Cloth, 1150–1250: Some Problems and Suggestions', in Istituto Internazionale di Storia Economica 'F. Datini', *Produzione, commercio e consumo dei panni di lana* (Florence, 1976), pp. 369–75
'Introduction', in *idem*, ed., *Peasant Land Market*, pp. 1–28
Manorial Records, British Records Association: Archives and the User, V (London, 1984)
A Medieval Oxfordshire Village: Cuxham, 1240 to 1400 (Oxford, 1965)
'Non-Agrarian Activities in the Rural Communities of Late-Medieval England', in Istituto Internazionale di Storia Economica 'F. Datini', Settimana di Studio XIV (forthcoming)
'Non-Agrarian Activities in Twelfth-Century English Estate Surveys', in D. Williams, ed., *England in the Twelfth Century* (Woodbridge, 1990), pp. 101–11
'The Pipe Rolls and the Adoption of Demesne Farming in England', *EcHR*, 2nd ser., 27 (1974), pp. 345–59
ed., *The Peasant Land Market in Medieval England* (Oxford, 1984)

Harvey, S. P. J., 'Domesday England', in *AHEW*, II, pp. 45–136

'The Extent and Profitability of Demesne Agriculture in England in the Later Eleventh Century', in Aston and others, eds., *Social Relations and Ideas*, pp. 45–72

'The Knight and the Knight's Fee in England', in Hilton, ed., *Peasants, Knights and Heretics*, pp. 133–73

'Taxation and the Ploughland in Domesday Book', in P. Sawyer, ed., *Domesday Book: A Reassessment* (London, 1985), pp. 86–103

Hatcher, J., 'England in the Aftermath of the Black Death', *PP*, 144, (1994), pp. 3–35

'The Great Slump of the Mid Fifteenth Century', in Britnell and Hatcher, eds., *Progress and Problems*, pp. 237–72

'English Serfdom and Villeinage: Towards a Reassessment', in Aston, eds., *Landlords, Peasants and Politics*, pp. 247–83

English Tin Production and Trade before 1500 (Oxford, 1973)

Plague, Population and the English Economy, 1348–1530 (London, 1977)

Rural Economy and Society in the Duchy of Cornwall, 1300–1500 (Cambridge, 1970)

Herbert, N. M., 'Gloucester's Livelihood in the Middle Ages', in N. M. Herbert, R. A. Griffiths, S. Reynolds and P. Clark, *The 1483 Gloucester Charter in History* (Gloucester, 1983), pp. 16–28

Hibbert, A. B., 'The Economic Policies of Towns', in M. M. Postan, E. E. Rich and E. Miller, eds., *The Cambridge Economic History of Europe, III: Economic Organization and Policies in the Middle Ages* (Cambridge, 1963), pp. 157–229

Hicks, M. A., *False, Fleeting, Perjur'd Clarence: George, Duke of Clarence 1449–78* (Gloucester, 1980)

Richard III as Duke of Gloucester: A Study in Character, University of York Borthwick Paper LXX (York, 1986)

ed., *Profit, Piety and the Professions in Later Medieval England* (Gloucester, 1990)

Hill, D., *An Atlas of Anglo-Saxon England* (Oxford, 1981)

Hill, F., *Medieval Lincoln* (Cambridge, 1965)

Hilton, R. H., *Class Conflict and the Crisis of Feudalism: Essays in Medieval Social History* (London, 1985)

'A Crisis of Feudalism', in Aston and Philpin, eds., *The Brenner Debate*, pp. 119–37

The Decline of Serfdom in Medieval England (London, 1969)

The Economic Development of Some Leicestershire Estates in the Fourteenth and Fifteenth Centuries (Oxford, 1947)

The English Peasantry in the Later Middle Ages (Oxford, 1975)

'Freedom and Villeinage in England', in *idem*, ed., *Peasants, Knights and Heretics*, pp. 174–91

'Medieval Agrarian History', *VCH Leics.*, II, pp. 145–98

'Medieval Market Towns and Simple Commodity Production', *PP*, 109 (1985), pp. 3–23

A Medieval Society: The West Midlands at the End of the Thirteenth Century, 2nd edn (Cambridge, 1983)

ed., *Peasants, Knights and Heretics: Studies in Medieval English Social History*

(Cambridge, 1976)

Hilton, R. H., and Aston, T. H., eds., *The English Rising of 1381* (Cambridge, 1984)

Hoare, C. M., *The History of an East Anglian Soke* (Bedford, 1918)

'The Last of the Bondmen in a Norfolk Manor', *Norf. Arch.*, 19 (1917), pp. 9–32

Holdsworth, W. S., *A History of English Law*, II, 3rd edn (London, 1923)

Hollister, C. W., *The Military Organization of Norman England* (Oxford, 1965)

Holmes, G. A., *The Estates of the Higher Nobility in Fourteenth-Century England* (Cambridge, 1957)

Holt, J. C., 'Feudal Society and the Family in Early Medieval England', 3 parts, *TRHS*, 5th ser., 32 (1982), pp. 193–212; 33 (1983), pp. 193–220; 34 (1984), pp. 1–25

Magna Carta (Cambridge, 1965)

The Northerners: A Study in the Reign of King John (Oxford, 1961)

'Politics and Property in Early Medieval England', in Aston, ed., *Landlords, Peasants and Politics*, pp. 65—114

'A Rejoinder', in Aston, ed., *Landlords, Peasants and Politics*, pp. 132–40

Holt, R., *The Early History of The Town of Birmingham*, Dugdale Soc., Occasional Paper XXX (Oxford, 1985)

'Gloucester in the Century after the Black Death', in R. Holt and G. Rosser, eds., *The Medieval Town: A Reader in English Urban History, 1200–1540* (London, 1990), pp. 141–59

Homans, G. C., *English Villagers of the Thirteenth Century* (New York, 1960)

Horrox, R., *Richard III: A Study of Service* (Cambridge, 1989)

Hoskins, W. G., *The Midland Peasant: The Economic and Social History of a Leicestershire Village* (London, 1957)

Howell, C., *Land, Family and Inheritance in Transition: Kibworth Harcourt, 1280–1700* (Cambridge, 1983)

Hyams, P. R., *King, Lords, and Peasants in Medieval England: The Common Law of Villeinage in the Twelfth and Thirteenth Centuries* (Oxford, 1980)

'The Origins of a Peasant Land Market in England', *EcHR*, 2nd ser., 23 (1970), pp. 18–31

Ives, E. W., 'The Common Lawyers', in C. H. Clough, ed., *Profession, Vocation and Culture in Later Medieval England* (Liverpool, 1982), pp. 181–217

The Common Lawyers of Pre-Reformation England. Thomas Kebell: A Case Study (Cambridge, 1983)

Jacob, E. F., *The Fifteenth Century, 1399–1485* (Oxford, 1961)

James, M. E., *Society, Politics and Culture: Studies in Early Modern England* (Cambridge, 1986)

James, M. K., *Studies in the Medieval Wine Trade* (Oxford, 1971)

Johnson, C., 'Domesday Survey', *VCH Norf.*, II, pp. 1–211

Johnson, J. H., 'The King's Wardrobe and Household', in J. F. Willard, W. A. Morris, J. R. Strayer and W. H. Dunham, eds., *The English Government at Work, 1327–1336*, The Mediaeval Academy of America, 3 vols., XXXVII, XLVIII, LVI (Cambridge, Mass., 1940–50), I, pp. 206–49

Johnson, P. A., *Duke Richard of York, 1411–1460* (Oxford, 1988)

Jolliffe, J. E. A., *Angevin Kingship*, 2nd edn (London, 1963)

'Northumbrian Institutions', *EHR*, 161 (1926), pp. 1–42

Jones, A., 'Bedfordshire: Fifteenth Century', in Harvey, ed., *Peasant Land Market*, pp. 178–251

'Land and People at Leighton Buzzard in the Later Fifteenth Century', *EcHR*, 2nd ser., 25 (1972), pp. 18–27

Jones, M., 'Richard III and the Stanleys', in R. Horrox, ed., *Richard III and the North* (Hull, 1986), pp. 27–50

Kapelle, W. E., *The Norman Conquest of the North: The Region and its Transformation, 1000–1135* (London, 1979)

Keen, M. H., *England in the Later Middle Ages* (London, 1973)

The Outlaws of Medieval Legend (London, 1961)

Keene, D., *Cheapside before the Great Fire*, Economic and Social Research Council (London, 1985)

'Medieval London and its Region', *London J.*, 14 (1989), pp. 99–111

'A New Study of London before the Great Fire', *Urban Hist. Yearbook, 1984*, pp. 11–21

Survey of Medieval Winchester, 2 vols. (Oxford, 1985)

Kermode, J., ed., *Enterprise and Individuals in Fifteenth-Century England* (Stroud, 1991)

Kershaw, I., *Bolton Priory: The Economy of a Northern Monastery, 1286–1325* (Oxford, 1973)

'The Great Famine and Agrarian Crisis in England, 1315–1322' in Hilton, ed., *Peasants, Knights and Heretics*, pp. 85–132

King, E. 'The Anarchy of Stephen's Reign', *TRHS*, 5th ser., 34 (1984), pp. 133–53

Peterborough Abbey, 1086–1310: A Study in the Land Market (Cambridge, 1973)

'The Tenurial Crisis of the Early Twelfth Century', in Aston, ed., *Landlords, Peasants and Politics*, pp. 115–22

'The Town of Peterborough in the Early Middle Ages', *Northants. Past and Present*, 6 (1980), pp. 187–95

Kirby, J. W., 'A Fifteenth-Century Family, the Plumptons of Plumpton, and their Lawyers, 1461–1515', *NH*, 25 (1989), pp. 106–19

Knowles, D., *The Monastic Order in England: A History of its Development from the Times of Saint Dunstan to the Fourth Lateran Council, 943–1216* (Cambridge, 1950)

The Religious Orders in England, 3 vols. (Cambridge, 1948–61)

Kondo, A., 'The Rise of Market Economy in Rural Wiltshire, 1086–1461', *Stud. in Market Hist.*, 5 (1988), pp. 35–53

Kosminsky, E. A., *Studies in the Agrarian History of England*, trans. R. Kisch (Oxford, 1956)

Kowaleski, M., 'The Commercial Dominance of a Medieval Provincial Oligarchy: Exeter in the Late Fourteenth Century', *Med. Stud.*, 46 (1984), pp. 355–84

'Local Markets and Merchants in Late Fourteenth-Century Exeter', unpublished PhD thesis, Toronto, 1982

Local Markets and Regional Trade in Medieval Exeter (Cambridge, 1995)

'Town and Country in Late Medieval England: The Hide and Leather Trade',
   in P. J. Corfield and D. Keene, eds., *Work in Towns, 850–1850* (Leicester,
   1990), pp. 57–73
'Women's Work in a Market Town: Exeter in the Late Fourteenth Century', in
   B. A. Hanawalt, ed., *Women and Work in Pre-Industrial Europe* (Bloomington,
   1986), pp. 145–64
Kula, W., *Measures and Men*, trans. R. Szreter (New Jersey, 1986)
Labarge, M. W., *A Baronial Household of the Thirteenth Century* (London, 1965)
Lander, J. R., *Government and Community: England, 1450–1509* (London, 1980)
Langdon, J., *Horses, Oxen and Technological Innovation: The Use of Draught Animals
   in English Farming from 1066 to 1500* (Cambridge, 1986)
Lapsley, G. T., 'Boldon Book', *VCH Dur.*, I, pp. 259–341
Lawson, M. K., 'The Collection of Danegeld and Heregeld in the Reigns of
   Aethelred II and Cnut', *EHR*, 99 (1984), pp. 721–38
'Danegeld and Heregeld Once More', *EHR*, 105 (1990), pp. 951–61
'"Those Stories Look True": Levels of Taxation in the Reigns of Aethelred II
   and Cnut', *EHR*, 104 (1989), pp. 385–406
Lennard, R., *Rural England, 1086–1135: A Study of Social and Agrarian Conditions*,
   2nd edn (Oxford, 1966)
Levett, A. E., *Studies in Manorial History* (Oxford, 1938)
Lewis, N. B., 'The Last Medieval Summons of the English Feudal Levy, 13 June
   1385', *EHR*, 73 (1958), pp. 1–26
'The Summons of the English Feudal Levy, 5 April 1327', in T. A. Sandquist
   and M. R. Powicke, eds., *Essays in Medieval History Presented to Bertie
   Wilkinson* (Toronto, 1969), pp. 236–49
Liebermann, F., *Über die Leges Anglorum saeculo XIII ineunte Londoniis collectae*
   (Halle, 1894)
Lipson, E., *The Economic History of England, I: The Middle Ages*, 12th edn (London,
   1959)
Lloyd, S. D., 'Crusader Knights and the Land Market in the Thirteenth Century',
   in Coss and Lloyd, eds., *Thirteenth Century England*, II, pp. 119–36
Lloyd, T. H., *Alien Merchants in England in the High Middle Ages* (Brighton, 1982)
The English Wool Trade in the Middle Ages (Cambridge, 1977)
The Movement of Wool Prices in Medieval England, *EcHR* supplement VI (Cam-
   bridge, 1973)
'Ploughing Services on the Demesnes of the Bishop of Worcester in the Late
   Thirteenth Century', *University of Birmingham Hist. J.*, 8 (1962), pp. 189–96
Lobel, M. D., *The Borough of Bury St. Edmund's: A Study in the Government and
   Development of a Monastic Town* (Oxford, 1935)
Lockyer, R., *Henry VII*, 2nd edn (London, 1983)
Lomas, R. A., 'The Black Death in County Durham', *J. of Med. Hist.*, 15 (1989),
   pp. 127–40
'Developments in Land Tenure on the Prior of Durham's Estate in the Later
   Middle Ages', *NH*, 13 (1977), pp. 27–43
'The Priory of Durham and its Demesnes in the Fourteenth and Fifteenth

Centuries', *EcHR*, 2nd ser., 31 (1978), pp. 339–53

Lomas, T., 'South-East Durham: Late Fourteenth and Fifteenth Centuries', in Harvey, ed., *Peasant Land Market*, pp. 252-327

Loyn, H. R., *Anglo-Saxon England and the Norman Conquest* (London, 1962)

MacCulloch, D., 'Bondmen under the Tudors', in C. Cross, D. Loades and J. J. Scarisbrick, eds., *Law and Government under the Tudors* (Cambridge, 1988), pp. 91–109

McDonnell, J., 'Upland Pennine Hamlets', *NH*, 26 (1990), pp. 20–39

McDonnell, K., *Medieval London Suburbs* (Chichester, 1978)

McFarlane, K. B., *The Nobility of Later Medieval England* (Oxford, 1973)

Wycliffe and English Non-Conformity (London, 1952)

McIntosh, M. K., *Autonomy and Community: The Royal Manor of Havering, 1200–1500* (Cambridge, 1986)

McKisack, M., *The Parliamentary Representation of the English Boroughs during the Middle Ages* (Oxford, 1932)

Maddicott, J. R., 'Edward I and the Lessons of Baronial Reform: Local Government, 1258–80', in Coss and Lloyd, eds., *Thirteenth Century England*, I, pp. 1–30

'The English Peasantry and the Demands of the Crown, 1294–1341', in Aston, ed., *Landlords, Peasants and Politics*, pp. 285–359

Law and Lordship: Royal Justices as Retainers in Thirteenth- and Fourteenth-Century England, *PP* supplement IV (Oxford, 1978)

Thomas of Lancaster, 1307–1322: A Study in the Reign of Edward II (Oxford, 1970)

Maitland, F. W., *Domesday Book and Beyond: Three Essays in the Early History of England* (Cambridge, 1897)

The Forms of Action at Common Law (Cambridge, 1936)

'The History of a Cambridgeshire Manor', *EHR*, 9 (1894), pp. 417–39

Selected Historical Essays, ed. H. M. Cam (Cambridge, 1957)

Martin, J. E., *Feudalism to Capitalism: Peasant and Landlord in English Agrarian Development*, 2nd edn (London, 1986)

Massachaele, J., 'Market Rights in Thirteenth-Century England', *EHR*, 107 (1992), pp. 78–89

'The Multiplicity of Medieval Markets Reconsidered', *J. Histl. Geog.*, 20 (1994), pp. 255–71.

'Urban Trade in Medieval England: The Evidence of Foreign Gild Membership Lists', in Coss and Lloyd, eds., *Thirteenth Century England*, V, pp. 115–28

Massingberd, W. O., 'Social and Economic History', *VCH Lincs.*, II, pp. 293–379

Mate, M., 'Agrarian Economy after the Black Death: The Manors of Canterbury Cathedral Priory, 1348-91', *EcHR*, 2nd ser., 37 (1984), pp. 341–54

'High Prices in Early Fourteenth-Century England: Causes and Consequences', *EcHR*, 2nd ser., 28 (1975), pp. 1–16

'Labour and Labour Services on the Estates of Canterbury Cathedral Priory in the Fourteenth Century', *SH*, 7 (1985), pp. 55–67

'Medieval Agrarian Practices: The Determining Factors?', *AHR*, 33 (1985), pp. 22-31

'The Occupation of the Land: Kent and Sussex', in *AHEW*, III, pp. 119–36

'Pastoral Farming in South-East England in the Fifteenth Century', *EcHR*, 2nd ser., 40 (1987), pp. 523–36

'Profit and Productivity on the Estates of Isabella de Forz (1260–92)', *EcHR*, 2nd ser., 33 (1980), pp. 326–34

'The Rise and Fall of Markets in Southeast England', *Canadian J. of Hist.*, 31 (1996), pp. 59–85

May, P., 'Newmarket 500 Years Ago', *Proc. of the Suff. Inst. of Arch.*, 33 (1975), pp. 253–74

Mayhew, N. J., 'Modelling Medieval Monetisation', in Britnell and Campbell, eds., *Commercialising Economy*, pp. 55–77

'Money and Prices in England from Henry II to Edward III', *AHR*, 35 (1987), pp. 121–32

'Numismatic Evidence and Falling Prices in the Fourteenth Century', *EcHR*, 2nd ser., 27 (1974), pp. 1–15

'Population, Money Supply and the Velocity of Circulation in England, 1300–1700', *EcHR*, 48 (1995), pp. 238–57

ed., *Edwardian Monetary Affairs (1279–1344)*, BAR, XXXVI (Oxford, 1977)

Metcalf, D. M., 'A Survey of Numismatic Research into the Pennies of the First Three Edwards (1279–1344) and their Continental Imitations', in Mayhew, ed., *Edwardian Monetary Affairs*, pp. 1–31

Miller, E., *The Abbey and Bishopric of Ely: The Social History of an Ecclesiastical Estate from the Tenth Century to the Early Fourteenth Century* (Cambridge, 1951)

'England in the Twelfth and Thirteenth Centuries: An Economic Contrast?', *EcHR*, 2nd ser., 24 (1971), pp. 1–14

'The English Economy in the Thirteenth Century: Implications of Recent Research', *PP*, 28 (1964), pp. 21–40

'Farming in Northern England during the Eleventh and Twelfth Centuries', *NH*, 11 (1976), pp. 1–16

'Farming of Manors and Direct Management', *EcHR*, 2nd ser., 26 (1973), pp. 138–40

'Medieval York', in *VCH Yorks.: The City of York*, pp. 25–116

'New Settlement: Northern England', in *AHEW*, II, pp. 245–59

'Rulers of Thirteenth Century Towns: The Cases of York and Newcastle upon Tyne', in Coss and Lloyd, eds., *Thirteenth Century England*, I, pp. 128–41

'Social Structure: Northern England', in *AHEW*, II, pp. 685–98

War in the North (Hull, 1960)

ed., *The Agrarian History of England and Wales, III: 1348–1500* (Cambridge, 1991)

Miller, E., and Hatcher, J., *Medieval England: Rural Society and Economic Change, 1086–1348* (London, 1978)

Medieval England: Towns, Commerce and Crafts, 1086–1348 (London, 1995)

Mitchell, S. K., *Taxation in Medieval England* (New Haven, 1951)

Moore, E. W., *The Fairs of Medieval England: An Introductory Study*, PIMSST, LXXII (Toronto, 1985)

Morant, P., *The History and Antiquities of the County of Essex*, 2 vols. (London, 1768)

Morgan, M., *The English Lands of the Abbey of Bec* (Oxford, 1946)

Morris, W. A., *The Frankpledge System* (New York, 1910)

Moss, D., 'The Economic Development of a Middlesex Village', *AHR*, 28 (1980), pp. 104–14

Munro, J. H., *Wool, Cloth and Gold: The Struggle for Bullion in Anglo-Burgundian Trade, 1340–1478* (Toronto, 1972)

Newton, K. C., *The Manor of Writtle* (Chichester, 1970)

Thaxted in the Fourteenth Century (Chelmsford, 1960)

Nightingale, P., 'Monetary Contraction and Mercantile Credit in Later Medieval England', *EcHR*, 2nd ser., 43 (1990), pp. 560–75

Ogle, O., 'The Oxford Market', in M. Burrows, ed., *Collectanea II*, Oxford Hist. Soc., XVI (Oxford, 1890), pp. 1–135

Ormrod, W. M., 'The Crown and the English Economy, 1290–1348', in Campbell, ed., *Before the Black Death*, pp. 149–83

The Reign of Edward III: Crown and Political Society in England 1327–1377 (New Haven, 1990)

Page, F. M., 'Bidentes Hoylandie (A Medieval Sheep Farm)', *Economic Hist.*, 1 (1926–9), pp. 603–13

The Estates of Crowland Abbey: A Study in Manorial Organization (Cambridge, 1934)

Palliser, D. M., *Tudor York* (Oxford, 1979)

'Urban Decay Revisited', in Thomson, ed., *Towns and Townspeople*, pp. 1–21

Palliser, D. M., and Pinnock, A. C., 'The Markets of Medieval Staffordshire', *North Staffs. J. of Field Stud.*, 11 (1971), pp. 49–63

Palmer, J. J. N., 'The Last Summons of the Feudal Army in England', *EHR*, 83 (1968), pp. 771–5

Palmer, N. J., and Mayhew, N. J., 'Medieval Coins and Jettons from Oxford Excavations', in Mayhew, ed., *Edwardian Monetary Affairs*, pp. 81–95

Palmer, R. C., *The Whilton Dispute, 1264–1380: A Social-Legal Study of Dispute Settlement in Medieval England* (Princeton, 1984)

Payling, S. J.., 'Law and Arbitration in Nottinghamshire, 1399–1461', in Rosenthal and Richmond, eds., *People, Politics and Community*, pp. 140–60

Political Society in Lancastrian England: The Greater Gentry of Nottinghamshire (Oxford, 1991)

Penn, S., 'Female Wage-Earners in Late Fourteenth-Century England', *AHR*, 35 (1987), pp. 1–14

Penn, S. A. C., 'Social and Economic Aspects of Fourteenth-Century Bristol', PhD thesis, Birmingham, 1989

Penn, S. A. C., and Dyer, C., 'Wages and Earnings in Late Medieval England: Evidence from the Enforcement of the Labour Laws', *EcHR*, 2nd ser., 43 (1990), pp. 356–76

Persson, K. G., *Pre-Industrial Economic Growth: Social Organization and Technical Progress in Europe* (Oxford, 1988)

Phythian-Adams, C., 'Ceremony and the Citizen: The Communal Year at Coventry, 1450–1550', in P. Clark and P. Slack, eds., *Crisis and Order in English Towns, 1500–1700* (London, 1972), pp. 57–85

Desolation of a City: Coventry and the Urban Crisis of the Late Middle Ages (Cambridge, 1979)

Platt, C., *Medieval England: A Social History and Archaeology from the Conquest to A.D. 1600* (London, 1978)

Medieval Southampton: The Port and Trading Community, A.D. 1000–1600 (London, 1973)

Platts, G., *Land and People in Medieval Lincolnshire*, Hist. of Lincs., IV (Lincoln, 1985)

Plucknett, T. F. T., *Legislation of Edward I* (Oxford, 1949)

Pollard, A. J., 'Estate Management in the Later Middle Ages: The Talbots and Whitchurch, 1383–1525', *EcHR*, 2nd ser., 25 (1972), pp. 553–66

'The North-Eastern Economy and the Agrarian Crisis of 1438–40', *NH*, 25 (1989), pp. 88–105

North-Eastern England during the Wars of the Roses: Lay Society, War and Politics, 1450–1500 (Oxford, 1990)

'The Northern Retainers of Richard Nevill, Earl of Salisbury', *NH*, 11 (1975), pp. 52-69

'The Richmondshire Community of Gentry during the Wars of the Roses', in C. Ross, ed., *Patronage, Pedigree and Power in Later Medieval England* (Gloucester, 1979), pp. 37–59

The Wars of the Roses (London, 1988)

Pollock, F., and Maitland, F. W., *The History of English Law before the Time of Edward I*, 2nd edn, 2 vols. (Cambridge, 1898)

Poole, A. L., *From Domesday Book to Magna Carta, 1087–1216*, 2nd edn (Oxford, 1954)

Poos, L. R., 'Population Turnover in Medieval Essex: The Evidence of Some Early Fourteenth-Century Tithing Lists', in L. Bonfield, R. Smith and K. Wrightson, eds., *The World We Have Gained* (Oxford, 1986), pp. 1–22

'The Rural Population of Essex in the Later Middle Ages', *EcHR*, 2nd ser., 38 (1985), pp. 515–30

A Rural Society after the Black Death: Essex, 1350–1525 (Cambridge, 1991)

'The Social Context of Statute of Labourers Enforcement', *Law and Hist. R.*, 1 (1983), pp. 27–52

Postan, M. M., *Essays on Medieval Agriculture and General Problems of the Medieval Economy* (Cambridge, 1973)

The Famulus: The Estate Labourer in the XIIth and XIIIth Centuries, EcHR supplement II (Cambridge, 1954)

'Medieval Agrarian Society in its Prime: England', in *idem*, ed., *The Cambridge Economic History of Europe, I: The Agrarian Life of the Middle Ages*, 2nd edn (Cambridge, 1966), pp. 548-632

Medieval Trade and Finance (Cambridge, 1973)

Postan, M. M., and Titow, J. Z., 'Heriots and Prices on Winchester Manors', *EcHR*, 2nd ser., 11 (1959), pp. 383–411

Postles, D., 'Some Differences between Manorial Demesnes in Medieval Oxfordshire', *Oxoniensia*, 58 (1993), pp. 219–32

'Markets for Rural Produce in Oxfordshire, 1086–1350', *MH* 12 (1987), pp. 14–26

'The Perception of Profit before the Leasing of Demesnes', *AHR*, 34 (1986), pp. 12-28

'Securing the Gift in Oxfordshire Charters in the Twelfth and Early Thirteenth Centuries', *Archives*, 84 (1990), pp. 183–91

Powell, E., 'Arbitration and the Law in England in the Late Middle Ages', *TRHS*, 5th ser., 33 (1983), pp. 49–67

Kingship, Law and Society: Criminal Justice in the Reign of Henry V (Oxford 1989)

Power, E., *Medieval People* (London, 1924)

The Wool Trade in English Medieval History (Oxford, 1941)

'The Wool Trade in the Fifteenth Century', in Power and Postan, eds., *Studies*, pp. 39–90

Power, E., and Postan, M. M., eds., *Studies in English Trade in the Fifteenth Century* (London, 1933)

Prestwich, M. C., 'The Crown and the Currency: The Circulation of Money in Late Thirteenth- and Early Fourteenth-Century England', *Numismatic Chronicle*, 141 (1982), pp. 51–65

'Currency and the Economy of Early Fourteenth Century England', in Mayhew, ed., *Edwardian Monetary Affairs*, pp. 45–58

Edward I (London, 1988)

The Three Edwards: War and State in England, 1272–1377 (London, 1980)

War, Politics and Finance under Edward I (London, 1972)

Putnam, B. H., *The Enforcement of the Statute of Labourers during The First Decade after the Black Death, 1349–59* (New York, 1908)

Raban, S., *The Estates of Thorney and Crowland: A Study in Medieval Monastic Land Tenure*, University of Cambridge, Department of Land Economy Occasional Paper VII (Cambridge, 1977)

Raftis, J. A., *The Estates of Ramsey Abbey: A Study in Economic Growth and Organization*, PIMSST, III (Toronto, 1957)

Tenure and Mobility: Studies in the Social History of the Medieval English Village, PIMSST, VIII (Toronto, 1964)

Warboys: Two Hundred Years in the Life of an English Medieval Village, PIMSST, XXIX (Toronto, 1974)

Ramsay, J. H., *Genesis of Lancaster, 1307–1399*, 2 vols. (Oxford, 1913)

Ramsay, N. L., 'What was the Legal Profession?', in Hicks, ed., *Profit, Piety and the Professions*, pp. 62-71

Ravensdale, J. R., *Liable to Floods: Village Landscape on the Edge of the Fens, A.D. 450–1850* (Cambridge, 1974)

'Population Changes and the Transfer of Customary Land on a Cambridgeshire Manor in the Fourteenth Century', in Smith, ed., *Land, Kinship and Life-Cycle*, pp. 197–225

Rawcliffe, C., *The Staffords, Earls of Stafford and Dukes of Buckingham, 1394–1521* (Cambridge, 1978)

'"That Kindliness Should be Cherished More, and Discord Driven Out": The

Settlement of Commercial Disputes by Arbitration in Later Medieval England', in Kermode, ed., *Enterprise and Individuals*, pp. 99–117

Razi, Z., *Life, Marriage and Death in a Medieval Parish: Economy, Society and Demography in Halesowen, 1270–1400* (Cambridge, 1980)

'The Struggles between the Abbots of Halesowen and their Tenants in the Thirteenth and Fourteenth Centuries', in Aston and others, eds., *Social Relations and Ideas*, pp. 151–67

Reaney, P. H., ed., *The Place-Names of Cambridgeshire and the Isle of Ely*, EPNS, XIX (Cambridge, 1943)

Reed, C. G., and Anderson, T. L., 'An Economic Explanation of English Agricultural Organization in the Twelfth and Thirteenth Centuries', *EcHR*, 2nd ser., 26 (1973), pp. 134–7

Reed, M., 'Markets and Fairs in Medieval Buckinghamshire', *Recs. of Bucks.*, 20 (1975–8), pp. 563–85

Rees, W., *South Wales and the March, 1284–1415: A Social and Agrarian Study* (Oxford, 1924)

Rees Jones, S. R., 'Property, Tenure and Rents: Some Aspects of the Topography and Economy of Medieval York', PhD thesis, York, 1987

Reynolds, S., *An Introduction to the History of English Medieval Towns* (Oxford, 1977)

'Towns in Domesday Book', in J. C. Holt, ed., *Domesday Studies* (Woodbridge, 1987), pp. 295–309

Richardson, H. G., and Sayles, G. O., *The Governance of Medieval England from the Conquest to Magna Carta* (Edinburgh, 1963)

Law and Legislation from Aethelberht to Magna Carta (Edinburgh, 1966)

Richmond, C., *John Hopton: A Fifteenth Century Suffolk Gentleman* (Cambridge, 1981)

The Paston Family in the Fifteenth Century: The First Phase (Cambridge, 1990)

Rigby, S. H., *English Society in the Later Middle Ages: Class, Status and Gender* (London, 1995)

'Late Medieval Urban Prosperity: The Evidence of the Lay Subsidies', *EcHR*, 2nd ser., 39 (1986), pp. 411–16

Medieval Grimsby: Growth and Decline (Hull, 1993)

'"Sore Decay" and "Fair Dwellings": Boston and Urban Decline in the Later Middle Ages', *MH* 10 (1985), pp. 47–61

'Urban Decline in the Later Middle Ages: The Reliability of the Non-Statistical Evidence', *Urban History Yearbook, 1984*, pp. 45–60

'Urban "Oligarchy" in Late Medieval England', in Thomson, ed., *Towns and Townspeople*, pp. 62–86

Rigold, S. E., 'Small Change in the Light of Medieval Site-Funds', in Mayhew, ed., *Edwardian Monetary Affairs*, pp. 59–80

Robo, E., *Mediaeval Farnham: Everyday Life in an Episcopal Manor*, 2nd edn (Farnham, 1939)

Roffe, D., 'Domesday Book and Northern Society: A Reassessment', *EHR*, 105 (1990), pp. 310–36

Rosenthal, J., and Richmond, C., eds., *People, Politics and Community in the Later*

Middle Ages (Gloucester, 1987)

Ross, A. S., 'The Assize of Bread', *EcHR*, 2nd ser., 9 (1956–7), pp. 332–42

Ross, C., *Edward IV* (London, 1974)

Rosser, G., *Medieval Westminster, 1200–1540* (Oxford, 1989)

Rowney, I., 'Resources and Retaining in Yorkist England: William, Lord Hastings and the Honour of Tutbury', in A. J. Pollard, ed., *Property and Politics: Essays in Later Medieval English History* (Gloucester, 1984), pp. 139–55

Rubin, M., *Charity and Community in Medieval Cambridge* (Cambridge, 1987)

Corpus Christi: The Eucharist in Late Medieval Culture (Cambridge, 1991)

Salzman, L. F., *English Trade in the Middle Ages* (Oxford, 1931)

'The Legal Status of Markets', *Cambridge Histl. J.*, 2 (1928), pp. 205–12

Sanders, I. J., *English Baronies: A Study of their Origin and Descent, 1086–1327* (Oxford, 1960)

Saul, N., 'The Despensers and the Downfall of Edward II', *EHR*, 99 (1984), pp. 1–33

Knights and Esquires: The Gloucestershire Gentry in the Fourteenth Century (Oxford, 1981)

Scenes from Provincial Life: Knightly Families in Sussex, 1280–1400 (Oxford, 1986)

Sawyer, P. H., 'Early Fairs and Markets in England and Scandinavia', in B. L. Anderson and A. J. H. Latham, eds., *The Market in History* (London, 1986), pp. 59–77

'Fairs and Markets in Early Medieval England', in N. Skyum-Nielsen and N. Lund, eds., *Danish Medieval History: New Currents* (Copenhagen, 1981), pp. 153–68

From Roman Britain to Norman England (London, 1978)

'The Wealth of England in the Eleventh Century', *TRHS*, 5th ser., 15 (1965), pp. 145–64

Scammell, J., 'Freedom and Marriage in Medieval England', *EcHR*, 2nd ser., 27 (1974), pp. 523–37

Scattergood, V. J., *Politics and Poetry in the Fifteenth Century* (London, 1971)

Searle, E., *Lordship and Community: Battle Abbey and its Banlieu, 1066–1538*, PIMSST, XXVI (Toronto, 1974)

Shaw, D. G., *The Creation of a Community: The City of Wells in the Middle Ages* (Oxford, 1993)

Sherborne, J. W., *The Port of Bristol in the Middle Ages* (Bristol, 1965)

Smith, A. H., *The Place-Names of Gloucestershire*, EPNS, 4 vols., XXXVIII–XLI (Cambridge, 1964–5)

Smith, R. A. L., *Canterbury Cathedral Priory: A Study in Monastic Administration* (Cambridge, 1943)

Smith, R. M., 'Demographic Developments in Rural England, 1300–48: A Survey', in Campbell, ed., *Before the Black Death*, pp. 25–77

'Human Resources', in G. Astill and A. Grant, eds., *The Countryside of Medieval England* (Oxford, 1988), pp. 188–212

'Some Thoughts on "Hereditary" and "Proprietary" Rights in Land under Customary Law in Thirteenth and Early Fourteenth Century England', *Law and*

Hist. R., 1 (1983), pp. 95–128

ed., *Land, Kinship and Life-Cycle* (Cambridge, 1984)

Spufford, P., *Money and its Use in Medieval Europe* (Cambridge, 1988)

Stacey, R. C., 'Jewish Lending and the Medieval English Economy', in Britnell and Campbell, *Commercialising Economy*, pp. 78–101

Politics, Policy and Finance under Henry III, 1216–1245 (Oxford, 1987)

Stafford, P. A., 'The "Farm of One Night" and the Organization of King Edward's Estates in Domesday', *EcHR*, 2nd ser., 33 (1980), pp. 491–502

Stenton, D. M., *English Justice between the Norman Conquest and the Great Charter, 1066–1215* (London, 1965)

English Society in the Early Middle Ages (1066–1307), 4th edn (Harmondsworth, 1965)

Stenton, F. M., *Anglo-Saxon England*, 2nd edn (Oxford, 1947)

The First Century of English Feudalism, 1066–1166, 2nd edn (Oxford, 1961)

The Free Peasantry of the Northern Danelaw, 2nd edn (Oxford, 1969)

Preparatory to Anglo-Saxon England, ed. D. M. Stenton (Oxford, 1970)

Stone, E., 'Profit-and-Loss Accountancy at Norwich Cathedral Priory', *TRHS*, 5th ser., 12 (1962), pp. 25–48

Storey, R. L., *The End of the House of Lancaster*, 2nd edn (Gloucester, 1986)

'The North of England', in Chrimes, Ross and Griffiths, eds., *Fifteenth Century England*, pp. 129–44

Summerson, H., 'The Place of Carlisle in the Commerce of Northern England in the Thirteenth Century', in Coss and Lloyd, eds., *Thirteenth Century England*, I, pp. 142–9

Sutherland, D. W., *Quo Warranto Proceedings in the Reign of Edward I, 1278–1294* (Oxford, 1963)

Swanson, H., *Medieval Artisans: An Urban Class in Late Medieval England* (Oxford, 1989)

Swinlden, H., *The History and Antiquities of Great Yarmouth* (Norwich, 1772)

Tait, J., *The Medieval English Borough: Studies on its Origins and Constutitional History* (Manchester 1936)

Medieval Manchester and the Beginnings of Lancashire (Manchester, 1904)

Tawney, R. H., *The Agrarian Problem in the Sixteenth Century* (London, 1912)

Taylor, C., *Village and Farmstead: A History of Rural Settlement in England* (London, 1983)

Thirsk, J., ed., *The Agrarian History of England and Wales, IV: 1500–1640* (Cambridge, 1987)

Thomson, J. A. F., ed., *Towns and Townspeople in the Fifteenth Century* (Gloucester, 1988)

Thornton, G. A., *A History of Clare, Suffolk* (Cambridge, 1930)

Thrupp, S. L., 'The Grocers of London: A Study of Distributive Trade', in Power and Postan, eds., *Studies*, pp. 247–92

The Merchant Class of Medieval London (Chicago, 1948)

Titow, J. Z., *English Rural Society, 1200–1350* (London, 1969)

'Evidence of Weather in the Account Rolls of the Bishopric of Winchester,

1209–1350', *EcHR*, 2nd ser., 12 (1960), pp. 360–407

Winchester Yields: A Study in Medieval Agricultural Productivity (Cambridge, 1972)

Treharne, R. F., *The Baronial Plan of Reform, 1258–1263* (Manchester 1932)

Tuck, A., *Richard II and the English Nobility* (London, 1973)

Tupling, G. H., 'An Alphabetical List of Markets and Fairs of Lancashire Recorded before the Year 1701' , *Trans. of the Lancs. and Ches. Antiquarian Soc.*, 51 (1936), pp. 86–110

The Economic History of Rossendale, Chetham Soc., new ser., LXXXVI (Manchester, 1927)

Turner, R. V., 'Exercise of King's Will in Inheritance of Baronies: The Example of King John and William Briwerre', *Albion*, 22 (1990), pp. 383–401

Unwin, T., 'Rural Marketing in Medieval Nottinghamshire', *J. of Histl. Geography*, 7 (1981), pp. 231–51

Urry, *W.*, *Canterbury under the Angevin Kings* (London, 1967)

Van Caenegem, R. C., *Royal Writs in England from the Conquest to Glavill: Studies in the Early History of the Common Law*, Selden Soc., LXXVII (London, 1959)

Van Uytven, R., 'Cloth in Medieval Literature of Western Europe', in N. B. Harte and K. G. Ponting, eds., *Cloth and Clothing in Medieval Europe* (London, 1983), pp. 151–83

Veale, E., M., 'Craftsmen and the Economy of London in the Fourteenth Century', in A. E. J. Hollaender and W. Kellaway, eds., *Studies in London History Presented to Philip Edmund Jones* (London, 1969), pp. 133–51

The Victoria History of the Counties of England (London, 1900–in progress)

Vinogradoff, P., *English Society in the Eleventh Century* (Oxford, 1908)

Villainage in England (Oxford, 1892)

Waites, B., *Moorland and Vale-Land Farming in North-East Yorkshire: The Monastic Contribution to the Thirteenth and Fourteenth Centuries*, Borthwick Paper XXXII (York, 1967)

Wallenberg, J. K., *The Place-Names of Kent* (Uppsala, 1934)

Walmsley, J. F. R., 'The "Censarii" of Burton Abbey and the Domesday Population', *North Staff. J. of Field Stud.*, 8 (1968), pp. 73–80

Warren, W. L., *The Governance of Norman and Angevin England, 1086–1272* (London, 1987)

Henry II (London, 1973)

King John (Harmondsworth, 1966)

Watkins, A., 'Cattle Grazing in the Forest of Arden in the Later Middle Ages'. *AHR*, 37 (1989), pp. 12–25

Waugh, S. L., *England in the Reign of Edward III* (Cambridge, 1991)

'The Fiscal Uses of Royal Wardships in the Reign of Edward I', in Coss and Lloyd, eds., *Thirteenth Century England*, I, pp. 53–60

'Tenure to Contract: Lordship and Clientage in Thirteenth-Century England', *EHR*, 41 (1986), pp. 811–39

'Women's Inheritance and the Growth of Bureaucratic Monarchy in Twelfth- and Thirteenth-Century England', *Nottingham Med. Stud.*, 34 (1990), pp. 71–92

White, S. D., 'Succession of Fiefs in Early Medieval England', in Aston, ed., *Land-*

lords, Peasants and Politics, pp. 123–32

Wightman, W. E., *The Lacy Family in England and Normandy, 1066–1194* (Oxford, 1966)

Willard, J. F., *Parliamentary Taxes on Personal Property, 1290 to 1334: A Study in Medieval English Financial Administration* (Cambridge, Mass., 1934)

Williams, A., 'Cockles among the Wheat: Danes and English in the West Midlands in the First Half of the Eleventh Century', *MH*, 11 (1986), pp. 1–22

Williams, G., *Recovery, Reorientation and Reformation: Wales, c. 1415–1642* (Oxford, 1987)

Williams, G. A., *Medieval London: From Commune to Capital*, 2nd edn (London, 1970)

Williamson, J., 'Norfolk: Thirteenth Century', in Harvey, ed., *Peasant Land Market*, pp. 31–105

Wilson, D. M., ed., *The Archeology of Anglo-Saxon England* (Cambridge, 1976)

Winchester, A. J. L., *Landscape and Society in Medieval Cumbria* (Edinburgh, 1987)

Wolffe, B. P., *The Crown Lands, 1461–1536* (London, 1970)

   The Royal Demesne in English History: The Crown Estate in the Governance of the Realm from the Conquest to 1509 (London, 1971)

Wright, S. M., *The Derbyshire Gentry in the Fifteenth Century*, Derb. Rec. Soc., VIII (Chesterfield, 1983)

Index